Territories of Faith

LEUVEN UNIVERSITY PRESS

TERRITORIES OF FAITH

**RELIGION,
URBAN PLANNING
AND DEMOGRAPHIC CHANGE
IN POST-WAR EUROPE**

SVEN STERKEN
EVA WEYNS EDS

This book appears in the peer-reviewed series
KADOC Studies on Religion, Culture & Society

EDITORIAL BOARD

Timothy Brittain-Catlin, University of Cambridge
James Chappel, Duke University
Kim Christiaens, KADOC - KU Leuven
Wilhelm Damberg, Ruhr-Universität Bochum
Jean-Dominique Durand, Université Lyon
James C. Kennedy, Universiteit Utrecht
Rupert Klieber, Universität Wien
Mathijs Lamberigts, KU Leuven
Peter Jan Margry, Meertens Instituut / Universiteit van Amsterdam
Francisca Metzger, Pädagogische Hochschule Luzern
Madalena Meyer-Resende, Universidade Nova de Lisboa
Anne Morelli, Université Libre de Bruxelles
Silvia Mostaccio, Université catholique de Louvain
Patrick Pasture, KU Leuven
Isabelle Saint-Martin, EPHE Sorbonne I Paris
Joachim Schmiedl, Philosophisch-Theologische Hochschule Vallendar
J.T. (Thijl) Sunier, VU Amsterdam
Steven Van Hecke, KU Leuven

Cover: The Saint-Marc church in Uccle (Belgium) (1970), by André Milis.
[Uccle, Parisch Archives of Saint-Marc] (See il. 5.9)

© 2022 Leuven University Press/Presses universitaires de Louvain/Universitaire Pers Leuven,
Minderbroedersstraat 4, B-3000 Leuven (Belgium)

All rights reserved. Except in those cases expressly determined by law, no part of this publication may be multiplied, saved in an automated data file or made public in any way whatsoever without the express prior written consent of the publishers.

ISBN 978 94 6270 309 4
eISBN 978 94 6166 423 5
D/2022/1869/11
https://doi.org/10.11116/9789461664235
NUR: 648

GPRC
Guaranteed
Peer Reviewed
Content
www.gprc.be

CONTENTS

Preface　7

Introduction　9
Faith and its Territories
Sven Sterken and Eva Weyns

Negotiation

1. Planning for Faith in Wythenshawe, Manchester　37
Angela Connelly

2. Lyons's Post-War Churches　63
Two Contexts, Two Churches, One Architect: Pierre Genton
Judi Loach and Mélanie Meynier-Philip

3. Constructing Country, Community and City　95
Alvar Aalto's Lakeuden Risti, 1951-1966
Sofia Anja Singler

4. Faith in a Divided City　123
Church Building in Berlin and the 1957 Interbau Exhibition
Marina Wesner

Expertise

5. Rethinking the Urban Parish　157
François Houtart, the Centre de Recherches Socio-Religieuses
and the 1958 Pastoral Plan for Brussels
Eva Weyns and Sven Sterken

6. Catholic Parishes in the Lisbon Master Plan of 1959   191
The Legacy of the SNIP and the MRAR
João Alves da Cunha and João Luís Marques

7. "A Silent Revolution"   221
Jacinto Rodríguez Osuna, Luis Cubillo de Arteaga and the 1965
Plan Pastoral for Madrid
Jesús García Herrero

Authority

8. A Laboratory of Pastoral Modernity   251
Church Building in Milan under Cardinal Montini and Enrico Mattei
from 1955 to 1963
*Umberto Bordoni, Maria Antonietta Crippa, Davide Fusari and
Ferdinando Zanzottera*

9. Reconstructing the Diocese of Barcelona   281
Parish Reform and Church Building under Monsignor Modrego
Casaus from 1943 to 1967
Alba Arboix-Alió and Sven Sterken

10. Mass Housing and the Catholic Hierarchy in Dublin, 1930s–1970s   305
The Case of Ballymun Estate
Ellen Rowley

11. Epilogue   339
A Divine Dwelling Crisis? Notes for a Paradigm of Emptiness
Kees Doevendans

Authors	353
Index of persons	356
Index of organisations	361
Colophon	363

PREFACE

As is often the case with edited volumes, this book has been long in the making. It started with the international seminar "Territories of Faith: Religion, Demographic Change and Urban Planning in Europe, 1945-1975" on 2-3 July 2017, which was organised by our research group, Architectural Cultures of the Recent Past, at the Faculty of Architecture of KU Leuven, in cooperation with KADOC, the Documentation and Research Centre on Religion, Culture and Society at KU Leuven. The seminar brought together a number of scholars who responded to an international call we had launched to find out who else was pursuing investigations similar to our research project, "Catholic Territories in a Suburban Landscape: Religion and Urbanisation in Belgium, 1945-1975". This project, generously funded by KU Leuven's Research Council (project IF 14030), addressed the intersection between pastoral provision and urban planning — a relatively new research field that seems to be attracting primarily younger researchers. With the seminar, it was precisely our aim to give this fresh research a dedicated forum and see whether we could work together towards a more enduring and ambitious output.

In the optimism of those two beautiful, early summer days, we committed ourselves to producing a book based on the various papers that had been presented and thoroughly discussed at the seminar. That was easier said than done, however: the processes of fine-tuning the scope of each paper in relation to the overarching theme; the selection of cases to be discussed; the choice of illustration material to be included; the copy-editing of the texts (most of which were written by non-native speakers); and last but not least, the peer reviewing of the final manuscript have taken over four years to complete. It has been an "adventure" in the literal sense of the word (a "be-coming"), illustrating that even in a unified Europe, and despite academia being an international environment, a myriad of cultural differences come into play when trying to systematise the way ideas, facts and data are to be put into words. We are therefore very proud to say that all the authors remained aboard and wish to thank them explicitly for their patience and perseverance. So thank you Angela, Judi, Mélanie, Sofia, João, João, Jesus, Umberto, Maria Antonietta, Davide, Ferdinando, Alba and Ellen. Along the way, two additional authors, Marina Wesner and Kees Doevendans, have joined us, and we are grateful to them for having accepted our invitation and being so cooperative with our often short deadlines.

The wonderful exchange of ideas, discussion of cases and conversations about methodological issues we had at the original seminar was due to a large extent to the generosity and expertise of the members of the international scientific committee we brought together for the occasion. We are extremely grateful to Ricardo Agarez (University of Evora), Olivier Chatelan (Université Jean Moulin - Lyon 3), Jan De Maeyer (KU Leuven), Rajesh Heynickx (KU Leuven), Peter Heyrman (KU Leuven), Andrea Longhi (Turin Polytechnic) and Robert Proctor (University of Bath) for not only their active participation in the seminar, but also having reviewed this book's papers at a later stage in the editing process. Robert deserves a special mention for his nuanced but clear advice at certain stages of the project, while the input of Jan and Peter has been vital for Eva's doctoral research project, which lies at the centre of this book.

We are further very much indebted to Nina Woodson for the copy-editing of the manuscript; hers was not an easy task, for the majority of the essays have been written by authors that are non-native speakers, the editors themselves included. Yet she committed to it with the velocity, nuance and patience that is the hallmark of a true professional. Along the same lines, Luc Vints, our contact at KADOC, should be mentioned; throughout the process, he has continued to encourage the project in his typically calm, but firm, manner. Lastly, we want to express our deep gratitude towards the anonymous peer reviewers and the editorial board of the KADOC Studies Series and Leuven University Press for giving us the chance to share this research with the wider scholarly community. The Faculty of Architecture of KU Leuven helped make this possible through generously supporting the language editing.

A final word of thanks goes to our partners and families for their enduring patience and their support in the pursuit of our academic ambitions.

Sven Sterken, Eva Weyns
Mechelen, October 2021

INTRODUCTION
FAITH AND ITS TERRITORIES

SVEN STERKEN AND EVA WEYNS

"Parish Planning and Church Construction Techniques for Churches" at the 1958 World's Fair in Brussels

From 8 to 10 May 1958, over one hundred specialists from across Europe gathered at a colloquium entitled "Parish Planning and Construction Techniques for Churches", held in the Vatican Pavilion at the World's Fair in Brussels.[1] Its central theme was well summarised by the title of the

1 The 1958 World Fair was a pivotal moment in the recent history of Belgium for it engendered an important wave of cultural modernity. Religious art and architecture, in particular, became important sites of renewal and experimentation, as can be derived from the modernist aspect of the Vatican Pavilion itself. Designed by a consortium of architects headed by Roger Bastin (1913-1986), it officially sanctioned the use of modern forms for religious buildings. As part of the Fair's cultural programme, the emerging art critic and Jesuit Geert Bekaert (1928-2016) curated the *Ars Sacra* exhibition in the St Peter's church in Leuven, the central statement of which was that religious art ought to become secularised if it wanted to have artistic pretentions. Bekaert was also instrumental in promoting the architectural work of his friend architect Paul Felix (1913-1981), whose use of exposed concrete and brick in the Clarisse Convent in Ostend (inaugurated in 1958) introduced brutalism in Belgium. Bekaert also actively supported the career of his young protégé Marc Dessauvage (1931-1984), who won that year's Pro Arte Christiana's Christmas Prize with a design for a parish church reduced to its very essence of a shelter for the community of the faithful. In the Francophone part of the country, Canon André Lanotte (1914-2010) did pioneering work, inviting for example Bastin to rearrange the interior of the chapel of the abbey church in Maredsous, and curating an exhibition on modern religious art in 1958 in the very same space. Still that same year, the young and progressive Benedictine monk Frédéric Debuyst (1922-2017) was appointed as editor of the Benedictine periodical *Art d'Eglise*, which he transformed in an important forum for liturgical and architectural renewal.

proceedings: "The Church in the City". Despite its affirmative character, this title should, in fact, be read in the context of a fuller question, namely, "How can the Catholic Church be present in the ever-expanding urban realm?" Indeed, towards the end of the 1950s, there was much reason to believe that the traditional parish church no longer constituted the people's self-evident spatial and social compass. The exponential growth of urban agglomerations had resulted in overburdened parishes, a shortage of priests and a rapid decline in church attendance — thus seemingly confirming the received historiographical narrative of the inevitably secularising effect of urbanisation.[2] Building more churches seemed the logical solution and — just like in the nineteenth century — became the primary instrument in Christianising the urban masses, hence the massive church-building campaigns launched in the course of the 1950s across Europe.

However, as this book argues, this ecclesiastical provision differed fundamentally from earlier times, in terms of not only stylistic modernity, liturgical concept and typological innovation, but also sheer numbers. The scale and rapidity of construction in the period under study here is truly impressive: for example, no fewer than 1250 churches were built in the southern part of Rheinland-Westphalen (the area around Cologne, Aachen and Bonn); almost 500 in Flanders (the northern part of Belgium) and around 200 in the Nord-Pas-de-Calais in the north of France.[3] The immense effort required to compensate for either war damage or urban expansion made church building the affair of entire dioceses rather than local communities, which in turn stimulated the development of specific expertise with regards to planning, fund-raising and building construction. The development, circulation and application of this specific know-how, as well as its impact on clerical policies, has been largely overlooked to date, for most scholarship on post-war religious architecture deals with aspects of style, liturgy or construction technique, or focuses on a particular architect or region.[4] This book fills this lacuna by approaching church building as a multidisciplinary field at the crossroads of pastoral theology, religious sociology and urban planning.

Since the 1958 colloquium precisely addressed this new condition, it is worth briefly summarising the viewpoints of its four main speakers as an introduction to this volume. Not only were they highly regarded experts in their

2   Various historiographical positions concerning this idea are discussed in Hugh McLeod's excellent introduction to *European Religion in the Age of Great Cities*, 1-42.
3   Hoffmann and Gregori, *Moderne Kirchen im Rheinland*; Heyrman, "Vergeten patrimonium? Register van twintigste-eeuwse kerken in Vlaanderen"; Frémaux, *Eglises du Nord et du Pas-de-Calais. De la commande à la patrimonialisation*.
4   Exceptions are Chatelan, "Expertise urbaine dans le monde catholique francophone au XXe siècle"; Chatelan, *L'église et la ville*; Price, *Temples for a Modern God: Religious Architecture in Postwar America*; McFarland, "Building the Promised Land: The Church of Scotland's Church Extension Movement, 1944-1961"; Sterken, "A House for God or a Home for his People?"

fields, their divergent profiles also illustrate the variety of ideas and opinions that came into play in tackling the issue. First, Jacques de Chalendar (1920-2015), a high-ranking civil servant from France with a background in law and urban planning, summarised the prevailing understanding of the latter discipline at the time.[5] Based on facts and figures about society, it was, in his view, a crucial constituent of a much wider "positive reformist action" focused on the well-being of man by providing a living environment fostering his material, social and spiritual welfare. Such humanist aspirations were also central for Jean Labbens (1921-2005), a prominent sociologist from Lyons, who discussed the place of religion in the context of mass society.[6] As he stated, when individuals were guided primarily by their own motives and no longer by common cultural values and ideals, religion could not thrive. The resurgence of a "group" identity amongst urban dwellers was therefore key to remediating the downfall in religious observance. As he stated, this would require expertise from sociology and urban planning, for a purely pastoral approach based on simply multiplying churches and parishes would no longer do.

This latter aspect constituted the central preoccupation of the next speaker, as well, the French cleric Paul Winninger (1920-2016). Summarising the principal ideas developed in his popular book, *Construire des Eglises* (1957), he stated that it was not the phenomenon of urbanisation per se that led to a decrease in religious zeal, but rather the inadequacy of the pastoral infrastructure: parishes were systematically too large and the number and distribution of parish churches totally insufficient.[7] Winninger even went so far as to state that the overpopulated parishes were "agents of de-Christianisation" — thus pointing to the Church hierarchy's incapacity for dealing with the problem. For him, the remedy was simple: "Open more churches, occupy the terrain, immediately group together the remaining faithful that will be lost if we wait another ten or twenty years."[8] Whereas Winninger deliberately stayed within the confines of canon law (which he taught at Strasbourg), the last speaker, the Belgian Canon François Houtart (1925-2017), took things a step further. Trained both in sociology and urban planning, he openly questioned the territorial basis of the traditional parish: codified in a pre-industrial context, it was no longer a meaningful social and pastoral unit in a mobile and diverse urban society.[9] Rather, urban mission was to be considered on the scale of the agglomeration, just like the provision of healthcare, education and recreation

5   De Chalendar, "Tendances de l'urbanisme moderne".
6   Labbens, "L'homme des villes, l'urbanisme et la religion". The ideas presented at the colloquium were developed at length in the book he published the following year, *L'Eglise et les centres urbains*.
7   Winninger, "Les conséquences religieuses d'une politique inadéquate de la construction des églises"; Winninger, *Construire des Eglises*.
8   Winninger, "Les conséquences religieuses", 508.
9   Houtart, "L'aménagement religieux des territoires urbains".

was increasingly planned at the metropolitan level. Thus, instead of creating ever more single parishes, each attempting (but ultimately, failing) to cater to all the needs of their inhabitants (catechetic instruction, primary education, leisure, etc.), overarching structures needed to be created that would allow the local parish priests to focus fully on their core task, namely urban mission. The title of Houtart's essay, "The Religious Planning of the Urban Territories", was thus well-meditated: keeping up with the newly urbanised territories required strategic pastoral planning.

Although dominated by speakers from the francophone world and focusing on the Catholic parish, the colloquium touched upon a universal question, namely, how organised religion could maintain its presence in an increasingly urbanised, individualistic and mobile society. Whereas in earlier times, an almost self-evident unity had existed between faith, territory and community, the question now became how this triad could be meaningfully translated in a rapidly modernising world. To this effect, this introduction briefly sketches the historical context and conceptual background against which this discussion took place, before outlining how the various chapters in this volume present various permutations and configurations of these core concepts.

Faith, Territory and Community in Post-war Europe

It is an understatement to say that the religious landscape of Western Europe underwent major changes after the Second World War. Indeed, whereas the war may have heralded a restoration and renewal of the Christian churches, by the end of the 1960s, these occupied an increasingly peripheral place in people's lives and the collective consciousness.[10] Immediately after the war, Christianity still profoundly influenced the lives of millions across Europe; its dictates regulated life patterns down to the most intimate details. In a few cases, one particular denomination enjoyed a quasi-monopoly, such as Catholicism in Belgium, Ireland, Italy and France, but in most countries, various branches of Christianity competed or co-existed with one another, such as in the Netherlands, Germany and England. The relationship between religious and civic authorities also varied widely across the continent. Although in theory, church and state were separated constitutionally almost everywhere, religious and civic authorities cooperated on various levels, ranging from the provision of subsidies for church building to adapting zoning regulations for their construction. Religion also played a major part in politics through either the personal beliefs of politicians or confessional political parties. Christian Democracy, for example, became the single most important political force up through the 1970s, while confessional organised welfare and cultural activi-

---

10 Pasture and Kenis, *The Transformation of Christian Churches in Western Europe*, 7.

ties expanded enormously: in Germany, for example, the Catholic welfare organisation Caritas became the biggest non-governmental employer in Europe, with nearly 500,000 people on its payroll, its Protestant counterpart, the Diakonie, following closely behind.[11] In Belgium, the Catholic Church remained the main provider of primary and secondary education even after the so-called School Struggle of 1958, a failed attempt by the liberal and socialist parties to dismantle its towering impact on the youth. The Netherlands offered perhaps the most extreme example of "pillarisation", a term referring to closed political and cultural communities based on a set of shared values, practices and ideals: apart from the Liberals and Socialists, Protestants and Catholics also competed with one another for influence, editing their own newspapers and setting up their own unions, sports clubs and so forth.[12] The permeation of the public sphere by symbols, rituals and processions was commonplace everywhere, but became perhaps most apparent in Dublin, where the visiting New Zealand Archbishop P. T. B. McKeefrey once observed how its streets were "impregnated with faith".[13] At the centre of this *civilisation paroissiale* stood the local priest or pastor, whose authority in moral and private matters was undisputed.[14] He watched with a firm eye over his flock, which in most cases constituted a homogenous religious, social and cultural group with a clear geographical delineation.

Nevertheless, cracks started to appear under the surface of this seemingly organic unity of territory, community and faith. Apart from increasing spending power, the emancipation of women and the introduction of leisure time, one phenomenon in particular challenged this ecosystem: the spectacular urbanisation of Western Europe, for spectacular it was indeed: whereas around 1900, an estimated fourteen per cent of the population lived in cities, by 1950 this number had risen to over thirty per cent.[15] Resulting primarily from a massive migration from the countryside to the cities, there was both a geographical and a demographic aspect to this massive urbanisation: not only did the cities become much more spread out through low-density suburbanisation, their social composition changed drastically through the massive influx of (mostly) unskilled workers. "Mobility" became the new keyword, in both geographical terms (commuting) and social terms (people engaging simultaneously or successively in various sociocultural milieus).[16]

11   Damberg and Pasture, "Restoration and Erosion of Pillarised Catholicism in Western Europe", 69.
12   See on this aspect Pasture and Kenis, *The Transformation of Christian Churches*; Damberg and Pasture, "Restoration and Erosion of Pillarised Catholicism in Western Europe"; Janssen, "Religiously Inspired Urbanism".
13   McKeefrey, as quoted in Rowley, "The Architect, the Planner and the Bishop".
14   On the notion of *civilisation paroissiale*, see Damberg and Pasture, "Restoration and Erosion of Pillarised Catholicism in Western Europe", 58.
15   Oswalt, ed., *Atlas of Shrinking Cities*, 2: "Urbanization", n.p.
16   Labbens, *L'Eglise et les centres urbains*.

In fact, most Christian denominations had struggled to keep up with the waves of urbanisation that manifested themselves in the wake of the industrial revolution of the nineteenth century, whereby the official policy of the churches had often been one of denial.[17] Not until 1909, did the priest, pastoral theologian and university professor Heinrich Swoboda (1856-1926) address the pastoral situation in European capitals such as Paris, London, Berlin and his native Vienna in an objective, quantified way, in his monumental study *Grossstadt und Seelsorge*.[18] The Austrian capital embodied the challenges the Church was facing like no other; in the working-class Favoriten area, for example, a single church served a population of 102,000.[19] The sociocultural variety of the population was also truly impressive; no less than seven per cent of the capital's populace was registered as Czech, for example. For Swoboda, it was clear: in order to enable personal contact between the clergy and the faithful — a prerequisite for a successful urban pastorate, in his eyes — the number of inhabitants per parish needed to be reduced to about 6,000 and many more churches needed to be built. Typically, however, after the Viennese archbishop proposed a redesign of the parish boundaries in 1898, he faced fierce opposition from his local clergy, for most priests prided themselves on the size of their parish, and ceding part of it to a neighbouring or new community was considered a failure akin to giving in to a future competitor.

Swoboda's diagnosis of the late-nineteenth-century metropolis as the locus of material and spiritual poverty installed (or reinforced?) a typical anti-urban narrative amongst Catholic writers, that gained even more momentum with the publication of *Le Christ dans la banlieue* (1927) by Pierre Lhande (1877-1957), who sketched a dramatic portrait of the Parisian suburbs as a "spiritual desert".[20] More an emotional appeal than a reflection on urban religion, it led to a massive church-building programme nevertheless, baptised "Les Chantiers du Cardinal" (the Cardinal's Construction Sites). This did little to alleviate the problem, however. As Fathers Henry Godin (1906-1944) and Yves Daniel (1909-1986) stated in their bestselling *La France, Pays de Mission?* (1943), reviving faith amongst the urban masses required not only building more churches, but first and foremost building real, active communities of faith (lay and otherwise).[21] The Anglican priest Edward Wickham (1911-1994) came to a similar conclusion in his classic *Church and People in an Industrial City* (1957).[22] Having studied the religious practices of working class people in

17 McLeod, *European Religion in the Age of Great Cities*; Poulat, "La découverte de la ville par le catholicisme français contemporain"; Houtart, *Les paroisses de Bruxelles: 1803-1951*.
18 Swoboda, *Grossstadt und Seelsorge*.
19 Weissensteiner, "Grossstadtseelsorge in Wien. Zur Pfarrentwicklung von der Josephinischen Pfarreguleirung bis in das 20. Jahrhundert", 119.
20 Lhande, *Le Christ dans la banlieue*.
21 Godin and Daniel, *La France, Pays de Mission?*
22 Wickham, *Church and People in an Industrial City*.

0.1 Cardinal Lercaro's *carosello* touring the periphery of Bologna on 26 June 1955: a cross was planted and blessed at each place where a new parish church was to be erected.
[Courtesy of the Archivio Nuove Chiese, Dies Domini Study Centre, Bologna. Originally published in Manenti, ed., *Il Cardinale Lercaro e la Città Contemporanea*, 20]

Sheffield, he stated that the Church had failed to anticipate the processes of industrialisation and urbanisation due to its tendency to hold on to rural pastoral strategies and vocabularies.

The publications mentioned above had a tremendous impact, for they made clear that the church provinces at home had now become missionary territory. As this book illustrates, this notion unleashed an impressive number of initiatives amongst diocesan leaders, lower clergy, politicians, architects and artists alike, and engendered an almost unlimited public support for massive church-building campaigns. Realising that the future relevance of the Church was, to a large extent, in their hands, both religious leaders and ordinary faithful were propelled by a belief that at long last, Christianity would not only prevail in the newly urbanised territories, but possibly also become renewed. In this book, "faith" therefore refers to not only a set of shared religious beliefs, but also the shared notion of "hope" that underpinned these building campaigns — a conviction that was excellently summarised by Labbens: "If Christians know how to be present in this great movement, it will become possible to bring about a new and prodigious expansion of Christianity and a civilisation marked with the seal of Christ."[23] The pompous tone of this statement reflects the heroism of the task at hand, which was perhaps best embodied by the flamboyant Cardinal Giacomo Lercaro (1891-1976) of Bologna, who, on a single day in June 1955, consecrated no fewer than eleven newly acquired building sites during a widely publicised pilgrimage by car around

23 Labbens, *L'Eglise et les centres urbains*, 15.

the city's periphery.[24] The significance of this ritual went beyond the spiritual or propagandist: besides their role as new sources of Christian life, these new churches also served as centres of social integration, offering a familiar reference point with opportunities for companionship, education and recreation in the often barren new urban environments.

The fact that, in the mind of all these actors, church construction, parish formation and community building became intrinsically linked is not a coincidence. Indeed, by mid-century, the notion of community had become ubiquitous amongst theologians, sociologists, planners and political leaders alike. Their increasingly pessimistic view of the effects of urbanisation on social bonds traces back to the Chicago school sociologist Louis Wirth (1897-1952), who, in his seminal essay "Urbanism as a Way of Life" (1935), stated that the impersonality of metropolitan life resulted from the hollowing out of communal ties traditionally fostered by the family, the village or the neighbourhood. Wirth thus set the tone for a discourse on "community" as a panacea for the perceived moral degeneration of humankind.[25] Accordingly, after the Second World War, the received idea was that the once natural, organic bonds between people needed to be re-established, so promoting, and even enforcing, their reconstruction naturally seemed a good cause. In Western Europe, in particular, a general consensus existed that affirmative action was required to "humanise" the urban realm, preferably according to Christian principles.[26]

The almost obsessive focus on community in the post-war period may explain the dominance of sociological concepts in the discourses on pastoral and urban planning, and constitutes a particular example of what Lutz Raphael has coined the "scientisation of the social".[27] This concept encompasses the transformation of social data into public categories, professional routines and behavioural patterns by means of often pseudoscientific visualisations and categorisations. Raphael's claim that this phenomenon is vital for an understanding of Western societies in the last 150 years (by reason of its impact on common beliefs and convictions) has been corroborated by various scholars who have examined the impact of concepts and actors from the sociological field on religious leaders and urban planners.

The impact of "pastoral sociologists" (often lay experts or self-taught clerics) on episcopal decision making in Germany and the Netherlands, for example, has been investigated by Benjamin Ziemann and Chris Dols, respec-

---

24 Lercaro, "La paroisse, moyen d'intégration religieuse et sociale. L'expérience de la périphérie de Bologna"; Manenti, ed., *Il Cardinale Lercaro e la Città Contemporanea*.
25 Couperus and Kraal, "In Search of the Social", 988.
26 Bérubé and Chatelan, "'Humaniser' la ville".
27 Raphael, "Die Verwissenschaftlichung des Sozialen als methodische und konzeptionelle Herausforderung für eine Sozialgeschichte des 20. Jahrhunderts".

tively.[28] As they state, by analysing and quantifying the socio-religious consequences of migration, urbanisation and mass communication, these experts provided a much-needed correction to the existing theological knowledge regimes and "opened the windows of the Church" (Dols's expression) — a role that was also explicitly encouraged by the Second Vatican Council:

> The forms of the apostolate should be duly adapted to the needs of the times, taking into account the human condition, not merely spiritual and moral, but also social, demographic and economic. This can be done effectively with the help of social and religious research conducted by institutes of pastoral sociology, the establishment of which is strongly recommended.[29]

This statement is remarkable, for initially, the Church had developed a rather hostile attitude vis-à-vis the emerging field of sociology, which it confused with positivism and its understanding of religion as a merely social fact that could be scientifically measured and understood.[30] However, out of a concern to rethink the social bonds that were being rapidly disrupted by the major transformations of the era, within Christian-Democratic circles, a certain sympathy originated towards the pioneering sociologist studies of, for example, Frédéric Le Play (1806-1882). As it was understood, his approach could provide information capable of helping the Church in its pastoral reflections by giving it a better knowledge of the field, and provide a basis for adopting the more rational administration and planning methods which were at that time beginning to be applied in other sectors. This was a daunting task, for the large surveys conducted in France, for example, by Gabriel Le Bras (1891-1970) and Fernand Boulard (1898-1977) revealed in the first place how *little* was known about the faithful in terms of sex, age, education etc.[31] Yet, as Voyé and Billiet note, sociology received a positive evaluation only insofar that it left the monopoly of interpretating these data and developing a corresponding strategy to the Church.[32] The sociology of religion, in particular, saw itself thus relegated to the a-critical, service role of socio*graphy* (i.e. *describing* social phenomena rather than explaining them), carried out in many cases by clergy with only little training. The expansion of the sociological activity concerning religion around mid-century had thus not only to do with an increased demand in statistical data, but also with diverging and competing views as to the epistemological basis and the disciplinary boundaries of this emerging

28 Dols, *Fact Factory*, 18-19; Dols and Paul, "Introduction: Pastoral Sociology in Western Europe, 1940-1970"; Ziemann, "The Practical Sociologist".
29 Quoted in Froehle, "Catholic Pastoral Sociology in the United States since Vatican II: Making a Path by Walking", 87; Dols, *Fact Factory*, 108.
30 Voyé and Billiet, *Sociology and Religions*, 9.
31 Paquot, "Théologie chrétienne et urbanisation", 8-9.
32 Voyé and Billiet, *Sociology and Religions*, 10.

field amongst clerics and academics, approaching it as religious sociology and sociology of religion respectively.[33]

As this book illustrates, a wide variety of research centres in religious sociology arose across Europe in the post-war era, supporting the pastoral policies of all major Christian denominations and often directly influencing diocesan or congregational strategies.[34] The blueprint for this type of consultancy bodies came from the Dutch Katholiek Sociaal-Kerkelijk Instituut (KASKI), which determined future pastoral requirements on the basis of demographic extrapolations and assessments of local planning policies.[35] In Brussels, the Centre de Recherches Socio-Religieuses de Bruxelles (Centre for Socio-Religious Studies, Brussels) was established by Canon Houtart in 1956, while in France, the Centre Regional d'Etudes Socio-religieuses de Lille also quickly became a reference in its genre, along with the Institut de Sociologie in Lyons, directed by Labbens.[36] Outside Europe, as well, religious sociology was on the rise; in the United States, for example, the Center for Applied Research in the Apostolate (CARA) arose under Cardinal Richard Cushing in 1964, whose mission was to "provide the reliable scientific and technical information we require for proper and thoughtful decisions in the very complicated areas of our ministry."[37]

Apart from fostering deeper insights into how to approach people's religious behaviour, sociology was also fundamental in shaping the discipline of urban planning in the early twentieth century. In particular, social scientists of all sorts fostered a profound entanglement between the notions of "neighbourhood" and "community", which became embodied by the notion of the "neighbourhood unit" — arguably the most ubiquitous concept in urban plan-

33 As the Belgian sociologist of religion Karel Dobbelaere explains, in the course of this shift, "The profession and not the churches became the reference of a new generation of sociologists. Religion rather than the churches became the focus of study, which restored our discipline to mainstream sociology.". See his overview of this dichotomy from a historical and international perspective, in Dobbelaere, "From Religious Sociology to Sociology of Religion: Towards Globalisation?". For a more general overview beyond Christianity, see Voyé and Billiet, *Sociology and Religions*. On religious sociology in relation to the urban in the Francophone world, see Paquot, "Théologie chrétienne et urbanisation"; Dumons, "Villes et Christianisme dans la France contemporaine. Historiographie et débats"; Chalon, "Implantation de la Sociologue Religieuse en Belgique". For a general overview of the relation between sociology and theology in the Anglophone world (Britain in particular), see Brewer, "Sociology and Theology Reconsidered: Religious Sociology and the Sociology of Religion in Britain".
34 Dols and Paul, "Pastoral Sociology in Western Europe", 102.
35 Dols, *Fact Factory*, 33-111; Holl and Crépin, "La recherche appliquée: le cas du KASKI aux Pays-Bas".
36 On Houtart, see the essay by Weyns and Sterken in this book; on the Centre Regional d'Etudes Socio-religieuses de Lille, see Duriez, "Sociologie et pastorale. Les trente anneés du centre regional d'études socio-religieuses de Lille". On the Institut de Sociologie in Lyons, see Chatelan, *L'Eglise et la ville*, 52-63.
37 Froehle, "Catholic Pastoral Sociology in the United States", 88

ning theory in the first half of the twentieth century.[38] Derived from late-nineteenth-century ideas of the garden suburb, as developed by Raymond Unwin (1863-1940) and Patrick Geddes (1854-1932), it was first formalised by Clarence Perry (1872-1944) in the 1929 Regional Plan of New York as an adequate spatial framework for the spontaneous sociability of what sociologists call "primary groups" (family, childhood friends, etc.). The underlying assumption that physical proximity equalled social bonding was spatially translated into small-scale, geographically well-defined and functionally autonomous areas, equipped with all the necessary amenities (schools, shops, etc.) within walking distance of one another and the housing. As Kenny Cupers has convincingly argued, the idea that social life could thus be plotted in space, and reciprocally, that physical space could shape the social life within it, was of course very attractive and explains the theory's almost universal application in postwar planning schemes, for on both extremities of the spectrum, modernist or traditionalist, the question of how to plan, or at least stimulate spontaneous neighbourhood grouping or natural community formation, was a central concern.[39] Although the term as such was rarely used in the discourse of the Congrès Internationaux d'Architecture Moderne (CIAM), the most important think tank and lobby group for the modernist cause in architecture and urbanism, the concepts of community and civic identity were of central concern throughout its history.

During a talk in 1944, Josep Lluis Sert (1902-1983), the organisation's later president, stated for example that to counterbalance the rather technocratic turn urban planning was taking, the human scale needed to be reintroduced.[40] To this effect, human contacts had to be increased in number, and this could only be accomplished by breaking up the cities and their suburbs into smaller, well-defined and well-planned neighbourhood units. Their size was to be such that they could be easily crossed by a pedestrian, the yardstick of the 'human scale'. Thus, Sert stated,

> Such an organic structure as the modern city should facilitate community life and social contacts without in any way curtailing individual activities, as long as these do not constitute obstacles to the collective aspiration of the population as a whole (...). Respect for the human factor demands economy in human energy, which results in greater moral and physical efficiency.[41]

38 Cupers, "Mapping and Making Community in the Postwar European City". See also Brody, "How ideas work: Memes and institutional material in the first 100 years of the neighborhood unit"; Lawhon, "The Neighborhood Unit: Physical Design or Physical Determinism?".
39 Cupers, "Mapping and Making Community in the Postwar European City".
40 Kuchenbuch, "In Search of the 'Human Scale': Delimiting the Social in German and Swedish Urban Planning in the 1930s and 1940s".
41 Sert, quoted in Kuchenbuch, "In Search of the 'Human Scale'", 1051.

Sert's talk has to be seen in the light of a revisionist tendency within the CIAM, which increasingly refrained from the purely functionalist stance as laid out in Le Corbusier's Athens Charter (1943). This became especially clear at the 8th CIAM congress in Hoddesdon (1951), the central theme of which was the "Heart of the city", or the question how civic and communal values could become spatially expressed and enhanced, with a view to humanising the city.[42]

On the other side of the spectrum, the traditionalist French urban planner Gaston Bardet (1907-1989) expressed very similar concerns. Vehemently opposing the functionalist CIAM approach, Bardet saw urban planning not as a technical discipline but as a social science based on precise knowledge about the interaction between man and his environment.[43] As he stated, the social fabric of the city existed in fact as a federation of interdependent communities: the planner's task was to uncover this social structure before intervening in the built fabric.[44] Bardet claimed that there were at least three successive types of social groupings, the most fundamental one being the so-called *échelon paroissial*: totalling 500 to 1,500 families, it constituted the fundamental building block of the city, for it possessed a certain autonomy in spiritual and administrative matters, its name serving as "a reminder of the community role played by the parish many centuries ago".[45]

In many cases, the neighbourhood unit's "technical rationality" (Cupers's term) went hand in hand with an explicitly spiritual approach to community, for it was seen by both civic and religious leaders as the ideal vehicle for counterbalancing the decaying social fabric and the perceived loss of civic identity and spiritual life in the urban agglomerations. This was the case, for example, in the Netherlands, where the authors of the 1946 reconstruction plan for Rotterdam (entitled *De Stad der Toekomst, de Toekomst der Stad* (The City of the Future, the Future of the City)), apart from aspiring to the optimal functional organisation of the city, explicitly conceived of their work as a response to the spiritual uprooting of war.[46] To this effect, the family was reinstituted as the cornerstone of future urban society and the churches cast as "educators of community spirit".[47] In the pillarised context of post-war Netherlands, social engineering and re-Christianising efforts thus went hand in hand, a fact that was spatially expressed by modelling the standard layout of new areas on an idealised version of the Catholic parish — the latter's attraction being such that the Nederlandse Hervormde Kerk (one of the branches of the Dutch Protestant Church) subsequently decided to remodel its administrative structure on a similar territorial basis: every new neighbourhood now

42 Mumford, *The CIAM Discourse on Urbanism, 1928-1960*, 201-215.
43 Sterken and Weyns, "Urban Planning and Christian Revival".
44 Bardet, "Social Topography: An Analytico-Synthetic Understanding of the Urban Texture".
45 Bardet, *Pierre sur pierre*, 249.
46 Cupers, "Mapping and Making Community in the Postwar European City", 1012.
47 Melchers, "De parochie als stedenbouwkundig concept".

constituted a congregation of its own, with its own proper church and pastor.[48] By contrast, for Dutch Catholics, the concept of the neighbourhood unit felt natural. Indeed, when in 1948, at a seminar entitled "Parish and Neighbourhood Formation", the well-known Catholic architect Marinus Granpré Molière (1883-1972) claimed that the neighbourhood unit was in fact not at all new, he was referring to the fact that its central principle, namely, the equation of physical proximity with social bonding, constituted the foundation of the Catholic parish. Not without pride, he then concluded, "The idea of the parish now only has to become realised in the civic realm."[49]

As we have seen, a decade later, the speakers at the 1958 colloquium on parish planning in Brussels also understood that contemporary thinking on urban planning, and the neighbourhood unit in particular, offered opportunities for rethinking the parish and renewing the approach to the urban pastorate. For Labbens, this seemed a key solution in remediating the downfall in religious observance in the urban agglomeration, for it aimed at reviving a "group" identity amongst its inhabitants – which, as we have seen, he considered as a prime condition for religious life. Houtart, in turn, had already expressed his expectations well before. In a paper from 1955, he had asked, "Do we have to abandon the parish in the modern city?", and gone on to suggest that the neighbourhood unit could come to the parish's rescue, since, as he stated, "(...) from the religious standpoint, it is the parish that corresponds best to this local unit."[50] In his view, the parish thus appeared to be the natural "spiritual" counterpart to the "worldly" neighbourhood unit, which therefore held the promise of a new integration of faith, community and territory.

A Conversation across Disciplines, Boundaries and Denominations

As this book illustrates, the question about the place of the Church in the postwar urban realm led to an intense conversation across disciplines, territorial boundaries and denominations and became formalised in very divergent ways throughout Europe. It involved experts in sociology, urban planning and pastoral theology who together formed a closely knit, technocratic elite at the edge between the clerical and academic milieus. Although sociologists of religion often struggled to be taken seriously by their academic colleagues, while also meeting resistance from bishops uncomfortable about giving away so much terrain to social scientists, the impact of this interdisciplinary exper-

---

48 Doevendans, "De ontgoddelijkte stad".
49 Granpré Molière in *Katholiek Bouwblad*, 22 (1947), 261.
50 Houtart, "Faut-il abandonner la paroisse dans la ville moderne?", 612.

tise was nonetheless highly significant, to the point that it sometimes became unclear who was in fact steering the course of the dioceses.[51]

Throughout the time frame discussed in this book, actors, ideas and concepts travelled across the continent, forming different constellations at an impressive array of international conferences. In 1955, for example, Cardinal Lercaro managed to gather an exquisite range of international guests in Bologna (amongst whom, Le Corbusier) to debate on the topic of the church in the city.[52] By the 1960s, there were major conferences about church building being held every year in all corners of the continent. For example, in 1963 in Barcelona, a session on parish sociology and urbanism was held, with talks by Aldo Milani (Cardinal Giovanni Battista Montini's right-hand man in Milan), Father Jean Capellades (editor of *L'Art Sacré*) and Paul Winninger.[53] Interestingly, their work was picked up by not only fellow clerics, but also professional planners. In 1964, for example, at the National Week of Sacred Art in Léon, the well-known architect and planner Rodolfo García Pablos (1913-2001) presented a paper in which he referenced almost all the protagonists of the day, namely Bardet, Houtart, Milani and the Dutch KASKI.[54] The most important conference in this series was perhaps the one organised by the French Comité National de Construction d'Eglises at UNESCO in Paris in 1965, which gathered together representatives from the nation's clerical, political and financial elite. In their speeches, both Paul Delouvrier (1914-1995), the father of the *villes nouvelles* around Paris, and the former Minister of Reconstruction Eugène Claudius-Petit (1907-1989) solemnly committed themselves to addressing the lack of pastoral infrastructure in the new towns across France.[55]

Although the focus of this book is principally on the Catholic Church, it also highlights a third feature of the church–city debate, namely, the fact that it pertained to all Christian denominations. For example, in the Netherlands, the establishment of the KASKI (focused on Catholic matters) incited the two major branches of the Dutch Protestant Church to found their own research centres.[56] In Berlin, at Interbau 57, the Evangelische Kirchenbautagung (Protestant Church's Building Conference) took place under the title "Church Ar-

---

51   Dols, *Fact Factory*, 14-15; Debié and Vérot, *Urbanisme et Art Sacré*, 184-185.
52   Centro di studio e informazione per l'architettura sacra di Bologna, *Dieci anni di architettura sacra in Italia, 1945-1955*.
53   *Conversaciones de arquitectura religiosa*. The congress is briefly discussed in the contribution by Arboix Alió and Sterken in this book.
54   García Pablos, "Necesidad de establecer ordenaciones parroquiales integradas en los Planeamientos Urbanísticos".
55   *L'Implantation des lieux de culte dans l'aménagement du territoire*.
56   The Sociologisch Instituut van de Nederlandse Hervormde Kerk (SINHK) lasted from 1945 to 1965; the Gereformeerd Sociologisch Instituut in Amsterdam was more short-lived (1954-1966). On the rivalry between the three institutes, see Zeegers, "Sociale research als politiek instrument".

chitecture in the City of the Future".[57] And in Birmingham, the Institute for the Study of Worship and Religious Architecture published a number of pastoral recommendations for the Anglican church in Telford New Town. Most striking, perhaps, was its suggestion that since the housing stock in the new areas was expected to last no more than forty to sixty years, the church should not invest in buildings that would outlive their pastoral relevance.[58] Interestingly, the church that was eventually built there in the mid-1970s was the first in England specifically conceived as an interdenominational one, with one hall for Anglicans and Methodists, who (uniquely) worshipped together here, and another hall for the Catholics.[59]

A final feature of the crossovers between pastoral and urban planning discussed in this book has to do with the institutionalisation and centralisation of expertise at the diocesan level. As Winninger stated in *Construire des Eglises*, the initiative for church building was no longer to be left to the local clergy, but to be professionalised by entrusting it to diocesan urban planning agencies which would monitor demographic evolutions, negotiate loans with banks and raise public support through advertising and fund-raising. Apart from the examples discussed in this book, other pioneering examples of such bodies include the Ufficio diocesano nuove chiese di periferia (Diocesan Office for the New Churches in the Suburbs) in Bologna (which was well-known thanks to Cardinal Lercaro's international outreach); Domus Dei in the Belgian Archbishopric ("a model of its genre", according to Winninger); the Bonifatiusverein (which financed churches in the Catholic diaspora in Germany); the Bauamt of the Viennese Archbishopric (which, under Bishop Franz Jáchym played no small part in the Austrian Kirchenbauboom); and, finally, the National Church Extension Committee of the Scottish Kirk (which promoted the construction of no fewer than thirty-six new churches in the decade right after the war, thus outperforming its Catholic counterpart).[60]

---

57 See the contribution on the Hansaviertel by Wesner in this book.
58 Bridges, *Socio-religious institutes, lay academies, pastoral care and church building in Holland, the Rhineland, Belgium and Northern France*, 48.
59 Communication to the authors by Judi Loach, architectural historian and former resident of Telford (8 November 2020). Until 1968, Telford was called Dawley New Town.
60 On the Ufficio diocesano in Bologna, see Manenti, *Il Cardinale Lercaro*; on Domus Dei, see Sterken, "A House for God or a Home for his People"; on Vienna, see Bäumler and Zeese, eds., *Wiener Kirchenbau nach 1945*; for Scotland, see McFarland, "Building the Promised Land".

Negotiation, Expertise and Authority

The various essays in this book address how the Christian churches dealt with the rapid (sub)urbanisation of Europe in the period after the Second World War and how they relied on architecture and planning in their endeavour to imbue the once-evident unity of religion, territory and society with contemporary meaning. This led to complex, often lengthy, conversations between local congregations, diocesan and political authorities, sociologists, urban planners and designers. The various essays in this book offer particular instances of such dialogues on the basis of one or more case studies, mostly within the contours of a specific diocese, and broadly fall into three categories, depending on the nature of the conversation: based on negotiation, driven by exchange or dominated by one authoritative actor.

The first group of essays focuses on the negotiations between various actors (a local congregation, diocesan authorities, expert bodies, representatives of various Christian denominations, etc.) about the siting, design or financing of church buildings. The emphasis here is on how specific actors or bodies managed to find an equilibrium in their sharing of the same territory, with or without arbitration by a third party. What is often striking in these cases is the degree of pragmatism and the often unconcealed non-religious agency. In her chapter, "Planning for Faith in Wythenshawe, Manchester", Angela Connelly reveals, for example, how local authorities actively supported ecclesiastical provision in the public housing estates — albeit not for religious reasons, but rather for the beneficial effects on the population. However, in order to avoid any perceived favouritism for particular denominations, the responsibility for site allocations was handed over to the Churches Main Committee, a cross-denominational intermediary body. Through a discursive analysis of the negotiations over the location and construction of these buildings, Connelly demonstrates the ecumenical cooperation that occurred across the major Christian denominations in England regarding planning, a distinguishing feature of the case in comparison to other European countries.

By contrast, in the case of the Office Diocésain des Paroisses Nouvelles (OPDN) in Lyons, discussed by Judi Loach and Mélanie Meynier-Philip in their chapter, "Lyons's Post-War Churches — Two Contexts, Two Churches, One Architect: Pierre Genton", the diocese left most of the responsibility for the construction of new churches to the local communities — thus allowing local actors to come into play. This is illustrated by comparing two OPDN churches designed by the same architect in two strikingly contrasting contexts — a greenfield site in the new town of La Duchère and an infill site within the industrial district of Villeurbanne. The discussion of agency is also central to Sofia Singler's essay, "Constructing Country, Community and City: Alvar Aalto's Lakeuden Risti (1951-1966)", in which she shows how a wide range of factors and broad group of agents — in addition to architects and Church officials — shaped one of the finest examples of post-war ecclesiastical architecture in Finland. Disentangling the manifold influences in the project, Singler illuminates how complex interrelationships between international, national and local spheres of influence affected the church's design and construction and suggests that ecclesiastical commissions provided Aalto with a fruitful realm within which to develop his modernism. The final contribution in this section deals with the legendary 1957 Interbau building exhibition in Berlin. In "Faith in a Divided City: Church Building in Berlin and the Interbau Exhibition of 1957", Marina Wesner discusses the specific challenges brought about for the Catholic and Protestant churches in Berlin by the building of the Wall. As a case study, she zooms in on two new churches built as part of the modernist Hansaviertel, the centrepiece of the Interbau exhibit. By comparing the various forms of agency that steered the commission, design and construction of the Protestant Kaiser-Friedrich-Gedächtniskirche and the Catholic St.-Ansgar-Kirche, the contribution not only reconstructs their intended meaning, but also assesses how they were perceived in later historiography.

The second group of case studies looks into the particular forms of expertise and its exchange that developed within the great many diocesan bodies that were created at the time. As the essays in this section show, innovative pastoral concepts circulated internationally but often encountered obstacles and conservative attitudes. In their chapter, "Rethinking the Urban Parish: François Houtart, the Centre de Recherches Socio-Religieuses and the 1958 Pastoral Plan for Brussels", Eva Weyns and Sven Sterken discuss the Centre de Recherches Socio-Religieuses (CRSR) and the ideas developed by its founder, Canon Houtart. The latter increasingly criticised the Catholic Church's concept of the singular, territorially defined parish, proposing that pastoral care be organised on the scale of the agglomeration instead. To that end, the CRSR developed a dedicated planning method for urban parishes based on a strikingly hierarchical, quantitative approach. By comparing the CRSR's 1958 pastoral recommendations for the Brussels region with the foundation process of three new parishes, Weyns and Sterken point to the discrepancies between this theoretical framework and the reality on the ground, with a view to assessing its operational value. A similar reformist drive is also central to João Alves da Cunha and João Luís Marques' contribution, "Catholic Parishes in the Lisbon Master Plan of 1959: The Legacy of the SNIP and the MRAR". It discusses how the Patriarchate of Lisbon embarked on an ambitious parish reform in accordance with the newly developed urban master plan for the capital and did so with the help of two interwoven organisations, namely the MRAR (Religious Art Renewal Movement, 1953-1969) and the SNIP (Secretariat for New Churches of the Patriarchate, 1961-2014). As the chapter shows on the basis of two specific cases (Sagrado Coraçao de Jesus by Nuno Pereira and Nuno Portas and Nossa Senhora da Conceição by Pedro Vieira de Almeida), the SNIP, in particular, became an important forum for exchange and developing ideas — culminating in the development of a prototype for a "chapel hall" that served as a basis for no fewer than thirty buildings. A similar attempt to rationalise and modernise church building is discussed by Jesús García Herrero in his contribution, "'A Silent Revolution': Jacinto Rodríguez Osuna, Luis Cubillo de Arteaga and the 1965 *Plan Pastoral* for Madrid". It highlights how in Madrid, too, parish reform, sociological research and typological renewal went hand in hand. To support the ambitious reform of the Madrid diocese, a small but energetic Technical Office for Religious Sociology was established, whose "Instructions for the Construction of Parish Centres" became the blueprint for future church building during the next decade. In order to assess the operational value of this document, the chapter focuses on a series of churches built by Cubillo de Arteaga which, as García Herrero argues, embody a shift from the church as a *domus Dei* towards the church as a *domus ecclesiae* — a change not without significance at a time of severe socio-political tension in Spain.

In the third and last set of conversations, the key word is authority, for these essays focus on powerful individuals (both lay and clerical) who strongly advocated for the place of religion in contemporary society. The figure of the Milanese Cardinal Montini (the future Pope Paul VI) immediately comes to mind here, for he ruled his diocese with an iron hand — yet with the firm support of the city's industrial establishment. Indeed, as Umberto Bordoni, Maria Antonietta Crippa, Davide Fusari and Ferdinando Zanzottera show in their chapter, "A Laboratory of Pastoral Modernity: Church Building in Milan under Cardinal Montini and Enrico Mattei from 1955 to 1963", he appointed Enrico Mattei, one of Italy's chief captains of industry and an emblematic figure of the Catholic establishment, as head of a citizens committee whose mission consisted of developing strategies for the planning, financing and execution of parish centres. On the basis of one particular case study (Santa Barbara in Metanopoli), the contribution examines how Mattei set about achieving these goals and how we are to consider the legacy of Montini's ambitious vision today. While the cultural climate in Milan was favourable to innovation, one might not perhaps expect this in Barcelona under Franco's dictatorship. Yet, as Alba Arboix Alió and Sven Sterken show in their chapter, "Reconstructing the Diocese of Barcelona: Parish Reform and Church Building under Monsignor Modrego Casaus from 1943 to 1967", a very large part of the city's parish churches were built after the Spanish Civil War, often designed by modernist architects. This suggests that, despite the general conservative climate in Spain at that time, there was an opportunity for typological and liturgical renewal. With a view to unravelling this alleged contradiction, Modrego's take on modernising his diocese is discussed and illustrated with two flagship developments that arose under his tenure: the El Congrés neighbourhood and the modernist estate of Montbau. The last chapter in this section, "Mass Housing and the Catholic Hierarchy in Dublin, 1930s-1970s: The Case of Ballymun Estate", by Ellen Rowley, also focuses on public housing. It establishes how Ireland was a Catholic corporatist state from the late 1930s but underwent a significant shift in economic policy starting in 1958, ultimately modernising many social processes, which coincided with the extensive reform occurring within the Catholic Church, the Second Vatican Council in particular. Examining mass housing development in Ireland's largest archbishopric during the late 1960s, Rowley maps the influence of the Catholic Church on Irish architecture and planning processes. Because of its high-rise, prefabricated nature, Ballymun is posited as an Irish heterotopia, at once "other" and indigenous, where the declining influence of the theocracy was made manifest. Or was it?

As Kees Doevendans points out in his epilogue by referring to the Netherlands, the context in which the projects discussed here arose has evolved beyond recognition. Many concepts and ideas discussed in this book have indeed taken on an entirely different meaning today. For example, the phenomenon of secularisation, then narrowly interpreted in absolute, statistical terms as "de-Christianisation", is itself now considered (and relativised) as a historical concept. The same holds true for the neighbourhood unit: planners and politicians have long given up on the technocratic belief in the unilateral impact of physical space on people's behaviour. Accepting that the building blocks of the "old" paradigm — the nuclear family, parish or district and nation — have been lost, Doevendans asks how a new spatial paradigm for the material culture of the church can be outlined, for the question today is no longer where, or how, to build churches, but what their meaning can be for the next generations.

"Do we still have to build churches?"

As the essays discussed above make clear, there was no shortage of visions and expertise in the fields of architectural design, urban planning, sociology of religion and pastoral theology in relation to the intricate question of how and where to provide the sprawling urban agglomerations with religious infrastructure. Indeed, congregations, dioceses, government bodies and private patrons took a wide variety of initiatives with a view to securing a religious presence in the rapidly evolving (sub)urban landscape of the post-war world. The essays also map the multiple exchanges between these actors across Europe, and reveal how the shared concern about organising faith in the post-war urban condition led to very divergent visions on funding, planning and building places of worship. Finally, the various contributions make clear how the operational quality of new planning concepts (both in the material and spiritual realm) unavoidably became tinted by the social, cultural and political dimensions of the local context.

Yet, however impressive and fascinating, the essays also bring to light the limitations and shortcomings of the church building boom of the postwar period. They reveal, for example, the largely idiosyncratic nature of the conversations sketched above, for most of the 'experts' the work of which is discussed here, belonged to, or were affiliated to the Church. This explains why the fundamental question, namely the place of the Church in contemporary (urban) society (both as an institution and as a building) was rarely addressed. Inversely, most church leaders remained locked within their presumption that urbanisation was the instrument of secularization; despite realising the futility of combating the phenomenon itself, they indeed put more energy in attempting to neutralise its effects than in developing a theological vision on the contemporary city. They did not, for example, incorporate the theological reflections about the city as developed by, amongst others, Harvey Cox and Joseph Comblin.[61] As the essays in this book show, in most cases, diocesan leaders simply didn't busy themselves with theoretical reflexions, giving priority to pragmatic and economic considerations instead. Perhaps, Cox's suggestions were simply too radical to assume for them, for he paradoxically stated that the secular city was the only true city of God — a provocative standpoint with far-reaching consequences, for it accepted displacement and anonymity as essential characteristics of an urban society, implicitly admitting that the idea of a single religious community might be at odds with the times.

It is perhaps precisely for reason of this lack of genuine conceptual exchange and fundamental reflection, that most dioceses failed to develop a sustainable strategy towards the maintaining of a religious presence in their rapidly urbanising peripheral areas. Indeed, only towards the end of the 1960s – at least within the Catholic Church – did the fundamental principle of the territorial organisation of pastoral care become questioned, as it appeared that an increasingly secularising society was also a mobile one, resulting in the multiplication of one's places of reference. This phenomenon challenged the specific quality of the parish as a stable, socially homogenous territorial unit, and undermined the idea that a religious presence in the city necessarily required dedicated buildings in the form of churches. Moreover, on a theological level, the opposition between the sacred aspect of the church and the "profane" character of its environment grew to be seen as artificial and counterproductive. For example, in reaction to the Council's message that a living church ought to be made of people rather than bricks, in the large housing

---

[61] Cox, *The Secular City. A Celebration of its Liberties and an Invitation to its Discipline*; Comblin, *Théologie de la ville*; Paquot, "Théologie chrétienne et urbanisation"; Chatelan, "Les capitales, un objet de réflexion dans le monde catholique français et belge des années 1950-1960?".

estates around Paris, progressive priests started to hold services in domestic spaces or existing rooms amidst other social and cultural organisations, while in Lyons, the ecumenical centre 'Mains ouvertes' was installed in the vast shopping centre at the new Part-Dieu train station.[62] In clear reference to Christianity's origins as a clandestine movement under the Roman Empire, these priests sought a different form of religious presence, namely, one where the sacred became embedded in the daily routines of the faithful. This represented an important shift: rather than a triumphant organisation governing over a given territory, they conceived of their church as a social body in a constant state of becoming. In France, the radical consequences of this new pastoral current came dramatically to the fore in a report prepared by the Comité national de construction d'églises in 1970 that was provocatively subtitled "Do we still have to build churches?"[63] One of the report's conclusions was that, at least from a pastoral point of view, the strategy of uniformly distributing churches across the territory (as defended by Winninger, for example) had failed: many of the new churches were too big for regular Sunday services and too small for the high moments of the liturgical year, such as the Easter celebration; moreover, there were simply too many of them. In the La Duchère housing estate in Lyons, for example, no fewer than four churches had been built between 1964 and 1973, each catering to approximately five thousand parishioners in accordance with the then-accepted optimum. However, already by 1980, the church in the Château district was sold off and converted into a centre for small children.[64] Apart from their redundance, this case also revealed the heavy debts incurred to realise these churches and their burden on the young (and generally not wealthy) parishes. Worst of all, church attendance did not really seem to rise in these areas (resulting in even less revenue), a phenomenon that also had to do with the fact that many faithful found it difficult to recognise these austere, economical churches as "signs of God" in the already heavily standardised new urban realm. For the authors of the aforementioned report, it was clear: the prevailing pastoral strategy, based on an equal distribution of churches and parishes over the new suburban territories, had failed for through its focus on physical proximity and the small scale, it replicated in fact the traditional village church in a metropolitan context, instead of offering a modern and genuinely urban alternative.

    Nonetheless, these church building campaigns have left a profound mark on the built environment of the after-war period, and have shaped the everyday experience of a great many people. Today, the question as to the future of

---

62 Debié and Vérot, *Urbanisme et Art Sacré*, 223-234; Chatelan, "Quelle visibilité chrétienne dans la ville contemporaine?".

63 Baboulène, Brion and Delalande, *Faut-il encore construire des églises?*; Debié and Vérot, *Urbanisme et art sacré*, 184-190.

64 Debié and Vérot, *Urbanisme et art sacré*, 187; see also the contribution by Loach and Meynier-Philip in this book.

these buildings has become inevitable. As it is difficult for us now to fully appreciate the notions of identity, collectivity and spirituality embodied by these buildings (for they have acquired a totally different meaning today), an assessment of their heritage values requires a careful study of the context within which these buildings came about. By offering a broad view of the practice of religion and its material expression in the rapidly evolving urban environment of the post-war era in Europe, this book offers valuable clues for such a study and contributes to a more balanced interpretation of this built heritage, that is severely under thread everywhere. Studying the typological renewal of church building as the outcome of particular configurations between religion, urban planning and demographic change in the post-war world, this book constitutes a critical contribution to the historiography of both religion and urban planning in post-war Europe. It takes scholarship on post-war church building a step further and allows for comparison with, for example, the American and Australian situations.[65] Finally, by analysing how organised religion manages and marks its presence within a given area, this book also offers valuable insights in how such claims are negotiated and materialised, for the question of how religions can practice, together, in the same territory remains a critical question even today.

---

65 With regard to the United States, see Buggeln, *The Suburban Church: Modernism and Community in Postwar America*; Price, *Temples for a Modern God: Religious Architecture in Postwar America*; Osborne, "Managing and Quantifying Grace? Reverend Robert G. Howes, the Archdiocese of Baltimore, and the Origins of 'Pastoral Planning'". For Australia, see Hilliard, "The religious culture of Australian cities in the 1950s"; Daunt and Goad, eds., "Constructing Faith".

BIBLIOGRAPHY

Bardet, Gaston. *Pierre sur pierre*. Paris: Editions LCB, 1945.

Bardet, Gaston. "Social Topography: An Analytico-Synthetic Understanding of the Urban Texture". *The Town Planning Review*, 22 (1951), 3, 237-260.

Bäumler, Ann Kathrin and Zeese, Andreas, eds. *Wiener Kirchenbau nach 1945*. Vienna: Technische Universität, 2007.

Bérubé, Harold and Chatelan, Olivier. "'Humaniser' la ville". Theme issue of *Histoire urbaine*, no 48, April 2017.

Brewer John D. "Sociology and Theology Reconsidered: Religious Sociology and the Sociology of Religion in Britain". *History of the Human Sciences*, 20 (2007), 2, 7-28.

Bridges, Peter. *Socio-religious institutes, lay academies, pastoral care and church building in Holland, the Rhineland, Belgium and Northern France*. Birmingham: Institute for the Study of Worship and Religious Architecture, n.d.

Brody, Jason. "How ideas work: Memes and institutional material in the first 100 years of the neighborhood unit". *Journal of Urbanism*, 9 (2016), 4, 329-352.

Buggeln, G. *The Suburban Church: Modernism and Community in Postwar America*. Minneapolis: University of Minnesota Press, 2015.

Centro di studio e informazione per l'architettura sacra di Bologna. *Dieci anni di architettura sacra in Italia, 1945-1955*. Bologna: Ufficio Tecnico Organizzativo Arcivescovile, 1956.

Chalon, P. "Implantation de la Sociologue Religieuse en Belgique". *Social Compass*, 6 (1959), 155-164.

Chatelan, Olivier. "Expertise urbaine dans le monde catholique francophone au XXe siècle". Theme issue of *Chrétiens et Sociétés*, no 21, 2015.

Chatelan, Olivier. *L'Eglise et la ville. Le Diocèse de Lyon à l'épreuve de l'urbanisation (1954-1975)*. Paris: L'Harmattan, 2012.

Chatelan, Olivier. "Les capitales, un objet de réflexion dans le monde catholique français et belge des années 1950-1960?" *Archives de sciences sociales des religions*, 59 (2014) 165, 105-118.

Chatelan, Olivier. "Quelle visibilité chrétienne dans la ville contemporaine?" *Territoire en mouvement* (2012), retrieved from <http://journals.openedition.org/tem/1542> (3 May 2019).

Comblin, Joseph. *Théologie de la ville*. Paris: Éditions universitaires, 1968.

Conversaciones de arquitectura religiosa. Barcelona: Patronato Municipal de la Vivienda, 1965.

Couperus, S. and Kraal, H. "In Search of the Social: Neighborhood and Community in Urban Planning in Europe and Beyond, 1920-1960". *Journal of Urban History*, 42 (2016), 6, 987-991.

Cox, Harvey. *The Secular City. A Celebration of its Liberties and an Invitation to its Discipline*. New York: The Macmillan Company, 1966.

Cupers, Kenny. "Mapping and Making Community in the Postwar European City". *Journal of Urban History*, 42 (2016), 6, 1009-1028.

Damberg, Wilhelm and Pasture, Patrick. "Restoration and Erosion of Pillarised Catholicism in Western Europe". In: Leo Kenis, Jaak Billiet and Patrick Pasture, eds. *The Transformation of the Christian Churches in Western Europe 1945-2000*. Leuven: Leuven University Press, 2010, 55-76.

Daunt, Lisa and Goad, Philp, eds. "Constructing Faith". Theme issue of *Architecture Australia*, May-June 2019, 55-112.

Debié, Franck and Vérot, Pierre. *Urbanisme et Art Sacré. Une aventure du XXe siècle*. Paris: Critérion, 1991.

de Chalendar, Jacques. "Tendances de l'urbanisme moderne". *La Revue Nouvelle*, 14 (1958), 12, 481-492.

Dobbelaere, Karel. "From Religious Sociology to Sociology of Religion: Towards Globalisation?" *Journal for the Scientific Study of Religion*, 39 (2000), 4, 433-447.

Doevendans, Kees. "De ontgoddelijkte stad: stedenbouw en secularisatie". In: Anne Schram, Bernard Colenbrander, Kees Doevendans en Bruno De Meulder. *Stadsperspectieven: Europese tradities in de stedenbouw*. Nijmegen: Vantilt, 2015, 212-227.

Dols, Chris. *Fact Factory. Sociological Expertise and Episcopal Decision Making in the Netherlands*. Nijmegen: Valkhof, 2015.

Dols, Chris and Paul, Herman. "Introduction: Pastoral Sociology in Western Europe, 1940-1970". *Journal of Religion in Europe*, 9 (2016), 99-105.

Dumons, Bruno. "Villes et Christianisme dans la France contemporaine. Historiographie et débats". *Histoire urbaine*, 2 (2015) 13, 155-166.

Duriez, Bruno. "Sociologie et pastorale. Les trente anneés du centre regional d'études socio-religieuses de Lille". *Revue du Nord*, 33 (2016), 207-222.

Frémaux, Céline. *Eglises du Nord et du Pas-de-Calais. De la commande à la patrimonialisation*. Rennes: Presses universitaires de Rennes, 2011.

Froehle, Bryan T. "Catholic Pastoral Sociology in the United States since Vatican II: Making a Path by Walking". *U.S. Catholic Historian*, 25 (2007), 4, 85-116.

García Pablos, Rodolfo. "Necesidad de establecer ordenaciones parroquiales integradas en los Planeamientos Urbanísticos". In: *Ponencias y Communicaciones de la 2e Semana Nacional de Arte Sacro*. Leon, 1964, 115-122.

Godin, Henry and Daniel, Yves. *La France, Pays de Mission?* Lyon: Les Editions de l'Abeille, 1943.

Heyrman, Peter. "Vergeten patrimonium? Register van twintigste-eeuwse kerken in Vlaanderen". *KADOC Nieuwsbrief*, 2009/1, 3-7.

Hilliard, David. "The religious culture of Australian cities in the 1950s". *Hispania Sacra*, 42 (1990), 86, 469-481.

Hoffmann, Godehard and Gregori, Jürgen. *Moderne Kirchen im Rheinland*. Worms: Wernersche Verlagsgesellschaft, 2014.

Holl, Adolf and Crépin, Hyacinthe. "La recherche appliquée: le cas du KASKI aux Pays-Bas". *Social Compass*, 18 (1971), 621-637.

Houtart, François. "Faut-il abandonner la paroisse dans la ville moderne?" *Nouvelle revue théologique*, 77 (1955), 6, 602-613.

Houtart, François. "L'aménagement religieux des territoires urbains". *La Revue Nouvelle*, 14 (1958), 12, 517-527.

Houtart, François. *Les paroisses de Bruxelles: 1803-1951*. Leuven: Institut de recherches économiques et sociales, 1953.

L'Implantation des lieux de culte dans l'aménagement du territoire. Paris: Cerf, 1966.

Janssen, J. "Religiously Inspired urbanism: Catholicism and the Planning of the Southern Dutch Provincial Cities Eindhoven and Roermond, c 1900 to 1960. *Urban History* 43 (2016) 1, 135-156.

Kuchenbuch, David. "In Search of the 'Human Scale": Delimiting the Social in German and Swedish Urban Planning in the 1930s and 1940s". *Journal of Urban History*, 42 (2016), 6, 1044-1064.

Labbens, Jean. *L'Eglise et les centres urbains*. Paris: Spes, 1959.

Labbens, Jean. "L'homme des villes, l'urbanisme et la religion". *La Revue Nouvelle*, 14 (1958), 12, 492-498.

Langlois, Claude. "Le Catholicisme à la rencontre de la ville. Entre après-guerre et Concile". *Les Annales de la Recherche Urbaine*, 96 (2004), 7-23.

Lawhon, Larry Lloyd. "The Neighborhood Unit: Physical Design or Physical Determinism?". *Journal of Planning History*, 8 (2009), 2, 111-132.

Lercaro, Giacomo. "La paroisse, moyen d'intégration religieuse et sociale. L'expérience de la périphérie de Bologna". *Social Compass*, 3 (1960), 3, 195-208.

Lhande, Pierre. *Le Christ dans la banlieue*. Paris: Plon, 1927.

Manenti, Claudia, ed. *Il Cardinale Lercaro e la Città Contemporanea*. Bologna: Editrici Compositori, 2010.

McFarland, E.W. "Building the Promised Land: The Church of Scotland's Church Extension Movement, 1944-1961". *Twentieth Century British History*, 23 (2012), 2, 190-220.

McLeod, Hugh. *European Religion in the Age of Great Cities, 1830-1930*. London-New York: Routledge, 1995.

Melchers, Marisa. "De parochie als stedenbouwkundig concept. De ligging van naoorlogse kerken in Venlo-Blerick". In: Antoine Jacobs, ed. *Kerken bouwen langs Maas en Rijn na 1945*. Leuven: Leuven University Press, 2019, 97-114.

Mumford, Eric. *The CIAM Discourse on Urbanism, 1928-1960*. Cambridge: MIT Press, 2002.

Osborne, Catherine R. "Managing and Quantifying Grace? Reverend Robert G. Howes, the Archdiocese of Baltimore, and the Origins of 'Pastoral Planning'". *American Catholic Studies*, 125 (2014), 1, 1-23.

Oswalt, Philipp, ed. *Atlas of Shrinking Cities*. Ostfildern: Hatje Cantz, 2006.

Paquot, T. "Théologie chrétienne et urbanisation", *Les Annales de la Recherche Urbaine*, 96 (2004), 6-16.

Pasture, Patrick and Kenis, Leo. "The Transformation of Christian Churches in Western Europe – An Introduction". In: Leo Kenis, Jaak Billiet and Patrick Pasture, eds. *The Transformation of the Christian Churches in Western Europe 1945-2000*. Leuven: Leuven University Press, 2010.

Poulat, Emile. "La découverte de la ville par le catholicisme français contemporain". *Annales*, 15 (1960), 6, 1168-1179.

Price, J.M. *Temples for a Modern God: Religious Architecture in Postwar America*. New York: Oxford University Press, 2013.

Raphael, L. "Die Verwissenschaftlichung des Sozialen als methodische und konzeptionelle Herausforderung für eine Sozialgeschichte des 20. Jahrhunderts". *Geschichte und Gesellschaft*, 22 (1996), 2, 165-193.

Rowley, Ellen. "The Architect, the Planner and the Bishop: the shapers of ordinary Dublin 1940-1970. *Footprint*, 9 (2015), 2, 69-88.

Sterken, Sven. "A House for God or a Home for his People? The Domus Dei Church Building Action in the Belgian Archbishopric". *Architectural History*, 56 (2013), 387-425.

Sterken, Sven and Weyns, Eva. "Urban Planning and Christian Revival. The Institut supérieur d'urbanisme appliqué in Brussels under Gaston Bardet (1947-1973)". In: *Re-humanizing Architecture: New Forms of Community, 1950-1970*. Berlin-Basel: Birkhäuser-De Gruyter, 2016, 89-100.

Swoboda, Heinrich. *Grossstadt und Seelsorge*. Regensburg: Pustet Verlag, 1909.

Voyé, Liliane and Billiet, Jaak. *Sociology and Religions. An Ambiguous Relationship*. Leuven: Leuven University Press, 1999.

Weissensteiner, Johann. "Grossstadtseelsorge in Wien. Zur Pfarrentwicklung von der Josephinischen Pfarreguleirung bis in das 20. Jahrhundert". In: Kaspar Elm and Hans-Dietrich Loock, eds. *Seelsorge und Diakonie in Berlin*. Berlin-New York: De Gruyter, 1990, 95-128.

Wickham, Edward. *Church and People in an Industrial City*. London: Lutterworth Press, 1957.

Winninger, Paul. "Les conséquences religieuses d'une politique inadéquate de la construction des églises". *La Revue Nouvelle*, 14 (1958), 12, 498-516.

Winninger, Paul. *Construire des Eglises. Les Dimensions des paroisses et les contradictions de l'apostolat dans les villes*. Paris: Cerf, 1957.

Zeegers, G.H.L. "Sociale research als politiek instrument". *Social Compass*, 3 (1956) 4, 145-154.

Ziemann, B. "The Practical Sociologist: Role and Performance of Pastoral Sociologists in the West-German Catholic Church, 1945-1970". *Journal of Religion in Europe*, 9 (2016), 133-156.

NEGOTIATION

1
PLANNING FOR FAITH IN WYTHENSHAWE, MANCHESTER

ANGELA CONNELLY

In the midst of our joy, we are deeply grateful to His Lordship the Bishop for allowing us to build such a noble and majestic church that so proudly dominates the whole estate. We are grateful to the inspiration of Mr Adrian Gilbert Scott that has so admirably suited the church to its site and purpose.[1]

In a brochure to accompany the opening ceremony for Saint Anthony's (1960), a Roman Catholic church in the City of Manchester's garden suburb of Wythenshawe, the writers extended their gratitude to those people they deemed most relevant: the bishop and the architect. On focussing only on these two, they overlooked both a variety of actors working at different scales who may have had a less direct impact on the shaping of the church's final siting, form and programme and the impact of a novel set of planning strategies that took effect in post-1945 England. Indeed, the planning context is all too often overlooked in narratives around twentieth-century religious history and architecture. The passing of the 1946 New Towns Act and the 1947 Town and Country Planning Act gave England a comprehensive planning system that included powers to compulsory purchase of sites required for redevelopment. This meant that religious organisations became involved with local planning authorities in a more formalised way than before. Moreover, the widespread clearance of inner city slum housing presented a major problem to England's religious organisations, with many nineteenth-century churches

---

1   Woodchurch, DSA. "The New St Anthony's Church, Woodhouse Park, Manchester". Souvenir of Solemn Opening, 3 November 1960 (Manchester: J.E. Mulligan & Co. Ltd, 1960), 9.

left bereft of their former congregations. Religious organisations needed to follow the people to proposed new housing estates and, consequently, construct new buildings and form new congregations. The extent to which religious organisations were engaged in or consulted on the development of such strategies is under-researched. An analysis of the negotiations that took place between municipal and church authorities reveals much about the social and cultural position of religion in the post-1945 period; a period when, arguably, secularisation was taking hold and religion was perceived to be losing significance.[2]

The relationship between post-1945 planners and the Roman Catholic Church in England points to the pragmatic discussions held regarding land acquisition and site exchanges and the desire for religious groups to provide "landmark buildings".[3] This suggests that church buildings held importance for post-1945 planners and were seen as an integral part of the new housing estates. Beyond the provision of church buildings, academic neighbourhood scale surveys hint at the social value of religious organisations in providing space and activities for developing communities on the new estates — whether for religious or secular purposes.[4] Similarly, research on the Church of England's architectural response to being placed in interwar suburbs demonstrates how their church buildings sought to respond to their context and contribute to community development.[5] Churches were perceived to be essential parts of communities, and their buildings often provided a focal point for groups. Nevertheless, a detailed study of suburban estates in southern England reveals the fears of church leaders about the encroachment of secular use, particularly because their own premises were often sidelined on secondary streets.[6] The interface of sacred and secular — which can be examined through an analysis of the religious built environment — remains an interesting line of enquiry to pursue.

The post-1945 period of English religious history provides a distinctive context because of the growing collaboration amongst the major Christian denominations in a range of matters, such as community development. Despite this, architectural and planning historians tend to focus on individual denominations and, consequently, overlook this wider faith experience, which came as a result of intense negotiations. The impact of liturgical renewal also leads

[2] The secularisation thesis, which posits that the shift to modern, urban societies rooted in science would lead to religion dwindling, is widely contested. A critical overview of the debates can be found in Nash, "Reconnecting Religion with Social and Cultural History".
[3] Proctor, *Building the Modern Church*, 278.
[4] Ravetz, *Council Housing and Culture*; Walford, *The Growth of 'New London'*; Clapson, *Working-Class Suburb*.
[5] Dwyer et al., "Faith and Suburbia".
[6] Walford, *The Growth of "New London" in Suburban Middlesex*.

many historians to focus on the buildings rather than the processes leading up to their creation, which occur at a variety of spatial scales. Given that the Church of England was, and still is, regarded as the established state church, questions arise around the nature of the collaborative Christian networks and their impact on the final sites and forms of church buildings.[7] Moreover, how did the churches relate to the secular planning authorities, and what impact did this have on their strategies for rebuilding? By widening the analytical focus, the multiple actors and sources of knowledge around religious buildings come into view.

This chapter therefore focusses on the post-1945 English context by examining the negotiations and debates around the placement of churches in new estates. Both the planning authorities and the churches themselves worked at multiple scales and, consequently, the chapter outlines the debates at national, municipal and neighbourhood levels. The national-level negotiations of the Churches Main Committee — a collaborative body set up to negotiate with the UK Government — set the scene for a consideration of how their fears played out, or not, in the city of Manchester. The chapter then discusses Manchester's flagship, experimental housing development at Wythenshawe and the building of Saint Anthony's in one neighbourhood sector. The main argument is that the churches worked closely with policymakers and local planners at various levels in order to balance competing interests. Religious analyses of the situation dovetailed with those of the planners, albeit in a socially deterministic way; church buildings were perceived as crucial in fostering social ties and good citizenship habits in developing communities, which belied their collective significance to the people the churches were intended to serve. The analysis therefore fills gaps in our understanding around inter-denominational cooperation, the negotiations at different spatial scales and the influence of various actors involved in church design at a local level.[8] Before delving into the primary data, it is essential to provide a contextual understanding of the legal status of Christian denominations in England and the sources of funding they could draw upon.

---

7   The global ecumenical movement which sought to bring various Christian organisations into unity had an influence in England. It has been argued that the twentieth century saw the passing of "Protestant England" to "Christian England". See Green, *The Passing of Protestant England*. That said, the ecumenical movement may have encouraged closer collaboration between the churches in England, but it resulted in very little direct displays of unity, with the exception of the United Reformed Church in 1972, which brought together the Congregational Church and the Presbyterian Church of England. See Guest, Olson and Wolffe, "Christianity: The loss of monopoly", and Orchard, "The formation of the United Reformed Church".

8   In line with science and technology studies, the term "actors" here refers to both human and non-human agents (which can take the form of materials, strategies, technologies and so on). See Latour, *Reassembling the Social*.

Toleration and Pluralism: Relationships between Church and State

In England, the Church of England (also referred to as the "Anglicans") became the established church when it broke away from Roman Catholicism in the early sixteenth century. Once governed by Parliament, with the reigning monarch as its head, the Church of England today is largely self-governing, with powers to create new parishes, for example; such measures must, in turn, be approved by Parliament, but they are rarely, if ever, amended. The Church of England therefore has a particularly close relationship to the governing body of the United Kingdom. A number of other Christian denominations also co-exist and, consequently, England has long been known as a place of religious tolerance.[9] In 1828, the practice of Roman Catholicism was permitted again after having been illegal for around three centuries. Subsequently, large-scale immigration, particularly from Ireland, ensured that Roman Catholic church attendance grew until the 1970s. Additionally, there are a number of "dissenting" or "non-conformist" faiths, such as Congregationalists, Methodists and Quakers, who broke away from the Church of England over the seventeenth and eighteenth centuries. The popularity of the non-conformist denominations peaked in the late-nineteenth century, when they enjoyed a share of around one-quarter of all churchgoers. The relationship between the state and the Church of England may seem arcane to contemporary English citizens, but it has been asserted that "the state is as confessional as ever: it is just that sacral values have been in practice secularised".[10] Questions may be raised, however, about the privileges that were afforded to the Church of England through its relationship with the state and the consequent implications this had for other religious denominations.

Funding for new churches, across all denominations, came from a variety of sources. This was particularly problematic for the Church of England due to its inflexible, centralised structure. However, in 1954, Parliament passed the Housing Areas (Church Buildings) Measure enabling the Church of England Commissioners to make interest-free loans or grants to erect new church buildings or acquire sites where it could be demonstrated that a substantial new population had come into being since 1936.[11] Such centrally allocated funds were matched by those raised within the diocese and locally amongst parishioners. For example, the Bishop of Manchester, William Greer, raised 259,000 pounds from businesspeople and other professions in order to supplement "The Bishop's New Appeal". The Appeal was designed to raise funds

---

9   Broad overviews of the relationships between the different Christian organisations in England can be found in Hastings, *A History of English Christianity*, and Brown, *The Death of Christian Britain*.
10 Norman, "Notes on Church and State", 9.
11 Chandler, *The Church of England in the Twentieth Century*, 96-104.

for building new churches in the Manchester Diocese and, as a result, fourteen new churches were constructed.[12] Many denominations launched their own funds for rebuilding: the Methodist Church, for example, raised 250,000 pounds nationally with contributions from interested Methodists.[13] In the Roman Catholic Church, loans could be taken out to finance buildings, and many local parishioners donated time, money and other resources to ensure that the buildings were free of debt.[14] Further funding sources in the post-1945 period, such as war damage compensation payments, emerged from the national policy debates to which we now turn.

Devolving Decision Making at National Level

Negotiations between the various religious organisations and the state, along with newly developing planning arrangements, had the potential to undermine the privileged position of the churches, particularly the Church of England, in identifying and purchasing prime sites. Across all of the religious organisations, the problem of population migration and rebuilding in the new housing areas posed a challenge.[15] However, the same religious organisations also thought that they had a moral and spiritual duty to not only physically build in the new areas, but also offer guidance with regard to the new planning arrangements. When Sir Montague Barlow (1868-1951) was commissioned by the Church of England's Church Assembly to lead a report into *The Church and the Planning of Britain* in 1944, he pointed out that new housing units in interwar estates "have been spread like a red belt round so many of our cities and towns" without the necessary amenities.[16] Their cause had been hampered by the speculative developments where:

> [private] builders were covering whole areas of the land to the last yard so that when churches and schools were found to be needed, the cost was prohibitive, and the wrong sites had to be chosen, and often inadequate ones as well.[17]

---

12   Dobb, *Like a Mighty Tortoise*, 200-202. The Bishop's New Appeal fell short of the targeted amount. Thus, new churches were required to pay back twenty-five per cent of the capital cost, with further sums for churches that sat over two hundred fifty people, over a twenty-year interest free period.
13   Manchester, The Methodist Church Property Office, "Minutes of a Meeting of the Committees on Plan and Design", Minutes of the Department of Chapel Affairs, 13 October 1942.
14   Proctor, *Building the Modern Church*, 268-269.
15   Chandler, *The Church of England in the Twentieth Century*, 96. For the Methodists, see Perkins, *So Appointed*, 111.
16   Church Assembly, *The Church and the Planning of Britain*, 4.
17   Ibid., 22.

The report was written against the backdrop of fears over ribbon development, as popularly characterised in the architect Clough Williams-Ellis' (1883-1978) *England and the Octopus* published in 1928, which demonstrates the way in which the churches absorbed wider secular insights into their thinking on urban development.[18] As we shall see later, this analysis dovetailed with local planning recommendations concerning community life in newly developed neighbourhoods.

The Church of England's concerns went beyond the mere provision of church buildings: it sought to influence the development of "communities". A detailed section in the report on its moral duty in helping to create community life argued that:

> The responsibility has fallen on us of giving physical expression to our real beliefs on man and society in the homes and towns which we build. What we build will inevitably help to make or mar the social and personal lives of many generations to come.[19]

However, the inflexibility that hampered the Church of England's expansion in cities during the industrial revolution remained, and it was again slow to respond to population shifts post-1945.[20] A Church of England commission was set up to look specifically into post-1945 church building and was comprised of senior figures from the Church Assembly, as well as their trusted interwar architects.[21] Their report, published in 1946, discouraged temporary buildings, building in stages or having any relaxation in building standards imposed by the Church Commissioners:

---

18   Williams-Ellis, *England and the Octopus*.
19   Church Assembly, *The Church and the Planning of Britain*, 21.
20   The Church of England was particularly strong in rural English villages and towns, which were often built around a church or cathedral. As cities expanded rapidly in the nineteenth century, the Church of England struggled to keep up with population movements. This was partly due to the legal requirements that surrounded the creation of a new parish. The nonconformist churches were able to capitalise on the stasis and expanded in cities and towns where the Church of England was weak. See Gregory and Chamberlain, "National and Local Perspectives on the Church of England".
21   The architects were William Henry Ansell as vice chair, Romilly B. Craze, Edward Maufe, Nugent Francis Cachemaille-Day and Bernard Miller. Maufe, for example, was the first principal architect in the United Kingdom from 1943 and was noted for his churches, cathedrals and war memorials, including Guildford Cathedral (1936-1961), which he won the competition for in 1932. Craze exclusively worked on church design and became well-known for his work on the renewal of war-damaged churches. Cachemaille-Day was, even in the interwar period, regarded as the most innovative church designer in England and had two notable examples in Manchester: Saint Nicholas, Burnage (1930-1932), and Saint Michael and All Angels, Northern Moor (1936-1937).

> The general public expects qualities in its Church buildings, as in its civic buildings, in advance of those it is often compelled to accept in its own domestic life. This same high standard should be applied to all fittings and articles of furniture, so that the completed structure, ready for worship, should present one homogenous body of excellence.[22]

As well as such internal discussions, the major religious denominations began to formally discuss planning matters with one another in what was a sign of growing inter-denominational collaboration during the twentieth century.[23] In 1941, the Anglican Bishop of London, Geoffrey Fisher (1887-1972), established the Churches Main Committee as an "ecumenical body" that included clerical and lay representation from the major Christian denominations, and later Jewish organisations, with a high proportion of architects, surveyors and lawyers represented.[24] The Committee's first major task was to negotiate the terms of compensation for war-damaged places of worship.

Religious buildings received special consideration under the terms of the 1941 War Damage Act. The chancellor responsible for this, Sir Kingsley Wood (1891-1943), was the son of a Methodist minister and himself a Methodist. He gave an audience to two leading members of the Methodist Church during which they advanced their case for "sympathetic interest and understanding".[25] Compensation for damaged buildings was paid at their 1939 asset value, as recommended by the Uthwatt Report (1942), a document drafted by the Expert Committee on Compensation and Betterment chaired by Justice Augustus Uthwatt (1879-1949).[26] This was not straightforward in the case of church buildings, however, because of their recognised social worth. Over several meetings each month, and in close communication with the government, the Churches Main Committee worked out a specific form of payment for church buildings. There were three significant elements: all denominations were to be accorded equal treatment; assessed payments were to be portable, so that churches did not have to be rebuilt on the same site, whereby proposed redevelopment options would be indicated in local authority plans; and new premises were to be plain.[27] While disregarding the market value of churches, the guiding principle was:

---

22 Post-war Church Building: Report to the Ecclesiastical Commissioners by an Advisory Panel (London: The Press and Publications Board of the Church Assembly, 1946), 6.
23 Green, *The Passing of Protestant England*, 54-55.
24 Perkins, *So Appointed*, 112-113. This body continues as the Churches Legal Advisory Service (CLAS), conveying to the government the views of the churches on legislation and matters such as heritage grants, planning and building regulations. See <http://www.churchesleg-islation.org.uk> (accessed 24 June 2018).
25 Perkins, *So Appointed*, 111.
26 Uthwatt, *Final Report*.
27 The Department for Chapel Affairs, *Serving the Church*, 83-85.

the sort of building in type and size which might reasonably be erected on the site of the damaged building by the denomination if it were paying the bill from their own fund and were neither financially embarrassed nor unduly rich.[28]

As a body comprising all the major faiths, the Churches Main Committee soon took on a wider role. The government accepted the views of the committee "on matters of policy without having to face the complication of dealing with each separate denomination".[29] Consequently, a series of delegations from the Churches Main Committee were sent to the Ministry of Town and Country Planning to negotiate the terms of the draft Town and Country Planning Bill. Here, there were two primary concerns. The first was the proposal for a one hundred per cent development charge to be imposed on all developments, with the intention of ensuring that land values remained a public good and not for private exploitation.[30] However the religious organisations, particularly the Church of England, regarded themselves as charitable organisations working for the public good and felt they should be exempt from the charge.[31] Second, the churches sought assurances on the acquisition of sites in new housing areas and the expectation that those sites be obtained on freehold.

The freehold issue was particularly contentious. The 1947 Town and Country Planning Act gave local authorities the right to compulsory purchase of areas of land for redevelopment. Once that land came into public ownership, local authorities were advised that it should only be:

disposed of by way of lease only and not by way of sale, and the authority should have the power to impose such covenants in the lease as planning requirements make desirable.[32]

The Minister for Town and Country Planning, Lewis Silkin (1889-1972), met with the Bishop of London, Reverend W. J. Anderson (1926-2006), representing the Roman Catholic Church, Reverend E. Benson Perkins (1881-1974) of the Methodist Church and members of the Church of England's Church Commis-

---

28 "War-Damaged Churches: Basis of Payment Accepted by the Commission", *The Manchester Guardian*, 16 May 1944, 3; Department for Chapel Affairs, *Serving the Church*, 83.
29 Perkins, *So Appointed*, 113.
30 The one hundred per cent development charge was a contentious piece of policy introduced in the 1947 Town and Country Planning Act that was intended as a "tax on betterment". It was designed to ensure that land would change hands at the existing price, so that developers did not profit out of rising land values associated with post-1945 planning proposals. See Corkindale, "Land Development in the United Kingdom", 2061.
31 The Church of England had particular interests here because it also owned land and acted as developers; however, it argued that its development was in the interests of the public. See Chandler, *The Church of England in the Twentieth Century*, 97.
32 Uthwatt, *Final Report*, 158.

sioners to discuss their views on the draft bill. The Church of England pointed out that, legally, they were unable to consecrate a church unless it was freehold, yet the proposed planning act instructed local authorities that land should be given over as leasehold, not freehold. The Roman Catholics held similar concerns, albeit consecrated Catholic churches were, it was conceded, only recognised under Roman canon law and could thus be disregarded by the state. The Methodists, unconstrained by the issue of consecration, nevertheless pointed to the vast sums they had raised for new church buildings through public subscription; surely they "could not expect the public to contribute such large sums if the churches were to pass out of their control after so short a period as 99 years".[33]

Silkin "was not unsympathetic to the needs of the churches" but was nevertheless "tied by the Act", which said that only in "exceptional circumstances" could a minister give consent to the sale of land by a local planning authority on freehold or to a lease of longer than ninety-nine years.[34] Exceptional circumstances were interpreted by Silkin to be "where full use could not be made of the land except by way of freehold".[35] Clearly, under the terms of ecclesiastical law, this applied to the Church of England; however, Silkin could not see how leaseholds would prevent other denominations from making full use of the land. Silkin was concerned not to expose the ministry to accusations from other parties that provided a public benefit. He observed that:

> Such claims as they [religious organisations] had made could equally apply to cinemas or public houses. They too wanted security of tenure and served the needs of the community.[36]

In this case, the minister was keen to treat both sacred and secular organisations in the same way. However, later that year, he conceded that religious organisations could be considered to be subject to "exceptional circumstances" and that this should apply to all of them, not just the Church of England. Nevertheless, the exceptional circumstances would only cover places of worship and not ancillary buildings such as clerical housing or Sunday schools. All of this was on the condition that if the nonconformist organisations were given a freehold and they ceased to use the site as a place of worship, the freehold should immediately become available for re-purchase by the local authority.[37] Clearly, there were some reservations over the longevity of nonconformist buildings.

33 London, CERO, ECE/SEC/LEGN/4/2. Notes on the Deputation from the Churches Committee Received by the Minister of Town and Country Planning on 17 May 1946.
34 Ibid.
35 Ibid.
36 Ibid.
37 London, CERO, ECE/SEC/LEGN/4/2. Letter from Lewis Silkin to the Lord Bishop of London, 16 October 1946.

Other deputations and letters from the Churches Main Committee to the Ministry for Town and Country Planning sought assurances over the allocation of sites in any newly planned housing area. As far as the ministry was concerned, local authority plans indicated broad zoning of uses and did not designate specific building uses. Therefore, Silkin argued that:

> It is expected that the Churches Main Committee or other organisation would have consulted the local planning authority beforehand to ensure inclusion. In addition, there will be a sketch plan which (...) will be available for inspection.[38]

The Churches Main Committee was keen to avoid infighting between denominations and thought it better that deliberation occur at a local level through interdenominational "area" committees, to the extent that "it is the view of the Churches Committee that where an Area Committee do not already exist steps should be taken to establish them".[39] Therefore, whilst strategic direction was provided at the national level, it was at the more local level that awkward decisions would have to be taken, and preferably not by local authority planners, but by the churches themselves in a collaborative fashion.

By 1946 the Churches Main Committee was strongly urging its members to set up local interdenominational committees in order to negotiate with local planning authorities.[40] Questionnaires were sent by the Churches Main Committee to its local interdenominational committees for them to indicate the extent of their building programmes within the next five years, and it was thought that "it would clearly be an advantage to the Churches that their needs should be included in the review and any allocations of materials and labour that may be found possible".[41] The only injunction was that inclusion should imply a definite and genuine intention to undertake building when permitted, with regard to disposable funds and the availability of sites.[42]

So, at the national level, the Churches Main Committee had regular access to civil servants and politicians, who were reluctant to offer too many concessions and preferred to leave the thorny decisions to the local authorities. The churches managed to band together to show that many of their interests were in common, but again, it was at the local level that major decisions were made. The next section thus turns to how such national-level debates played out in practice at the municipality level through a case study of Manchester. That city had a strong area interdenominational committee that engaged

---

38 London, NA, HLG-71-1486. Letter from the Ministry of Town and Country Planning to G. E. Holder, the Churches Main Committee, 22 December 1947.
39 Ibid.
40 Ibid.
41 Manchester, MALS, Churches Main Committee, M196/10/4/4/1. Circular, 5 March 1947.
42 Ibid.

closely with local authority planners, who, arguably, perceived a strong role for church buildings in developing community spirit in the early formulations of the city's post-1945 redevelopment plans, particularly on the Wythenshawe estate.

Spiritual and Architectural Focal Points

Wythenshawe lies approximately six miles south of Manchester city centre and was conceived during the interwar period to relieve the city of its cramped conditions. Originally located in the neighbouring local authority of Cheshire, Wythenshawe was incorporated into the City of Manchester in 1930. Around 5,500 acres of land was acquired in order to house 100,000 people in 25,000 new houses, with Manchester Corporation retaining control of the land and property.[43] The renowned town planner and architect Barry Parker (1867-1947) was contracted to draw up an overall plan for the estate, which was to include a substantial amount of agricultural green belt, open spaces and housing at a density of twelve to the acre. Influenced by the Arts and Crafts movement, Parker's vision incorporated the then fashionable Radburn road layouts with simple and plain housing. The two main features governing the plan were the introduction of a "parkway" for through traffic and the notion of neighbourhood units as self-contained areas for 5,000 to 10,000 people — two ideas imported from American town planning.[44] By 1934, just over 4,500 houses had been constructed in two neighbourhood units.[45]

Prior to the Second World War, church building had occurred in Wythenshawe as soon as the first "pioneer" residents moved in. Indeed, the Congregationalists constructed a small church on what would become Brownley Road before the houses and roads had yet been built.[46] Other churches were of particularly high quality, and their placement, close to the housing rather than the shops, seems to be in line with picturesque ideals. Nugent Francis Cachemaille-Day's (1896-1976) Saint Michael and All Angels (1937), located in the northern neighbourhood now known as Northern Moor, was an early example of the fan-shaped seating arrangement which became favoured post-Vatican II after experimentations with centralised altars.

The Second World War delayed the further development of Wythenshawe, but efforts were revived in the simultaneous publications of the 1945 City of Manchester Plan and the Manchester and District Regional Planning

43 Simon and Simon, "Wythenshawe", 6.
44 Miller, *English Garden Cities*, 80.
45 Simon and Simon, "Wythenshawe", 46.
46 "Wythenshawe's New Church: The Congregationalists", *The Manchester Guardian*, 14 November 1936.

Proposals.[47] Together, these two documents dealt with the problems of housing renewal and standards, as well as the adoption of the neighbourhood unit as a planning principal.[48] The 1945 City of Manchester Plan was based on accumulated evidence, such as surveys of buildings and quantitative analyses of the population, but was also underpinned by the "spirit of idealism" germane to its main author: the city surveyor Rowland Nicholas (life dates unknown).[49] Generously illustrated, the plan could be regarded as a "seductive" document that heralded a brighter future; it was a blueprint for how things *might* be.[50] In common with many major conurbations at the time, a primary objective was to move the population to new settlements outside of the core city to ease density issues.[51]

An entire chapter of the 1945 City of Manchester Plan was devoted to a two-tiered arrangement of neighbourhoods and district centres to provide a social life for the domestic arrangements. The narrative demonstrates an admiration of the spirit of communality displayed through the Second World War, and the Plan showed a keenness to avoid reverting to the perceived pre-1945 trajectory of individualism. The answer lay in providing enough spaces for leisure and cultural activities within the urban layout. Neighbourhood units — for roughly 10,000 people — were considered to be akin to a "modernised, urbanised version of the traditional village".[52] Indeed, the renewed focus on the neighbourhood unit concept was integral to Wythenshawe's post-1945 development, in order to rectify the perceived inadequacies of the sections of the estate that were completed before 1939. The City of Manchester Plan pointed to Wythenshawe's "anaemic social atmosphere — a lack of a robust community life — attributable in part to its newness, but more particularly to the absence

---

47 Nicholas, *City of Manchester Plan*; Nicholas, *Manchester and District Regional Planning Proposals*. The central government did not accept the plan until 1961.
48 Williams, "Manchester: City Profile", 207.
49 Ibid., p.v.
50 Perkins and Dodge, "Mapping the Imagined Future", 248. The images were collated over a long period of time and, whilst Wythenshawe was laid out to the designs of Barry Parker, the City of Manchester Plan drew on visual materials drawn by various individuals in the city's Architect's Office.
51 Kitchen, "The Future of Development Plans", 337.
52 By 1944, the neighbourhood unit principle had become UK government policy and had been anticipated in Wythenshawe with subsequent modifications. Arguably, the adoption of the neighbourhood unit in the post-1945 period differed from a pre-1945 conception with its origins in the work of Clarence Perry in New York in the late 1920s. After 1945, there was an identifiable move away from mainly aesthetic and infrastructural considerations to a belief that the neighbourhood unit could, in a spatially deterministic fashion, drive sociability and community spirit. See Greenhalgh, "Consuming Communities", 161. See also Johnson, "The Origin of the Neighbourhood Unit".

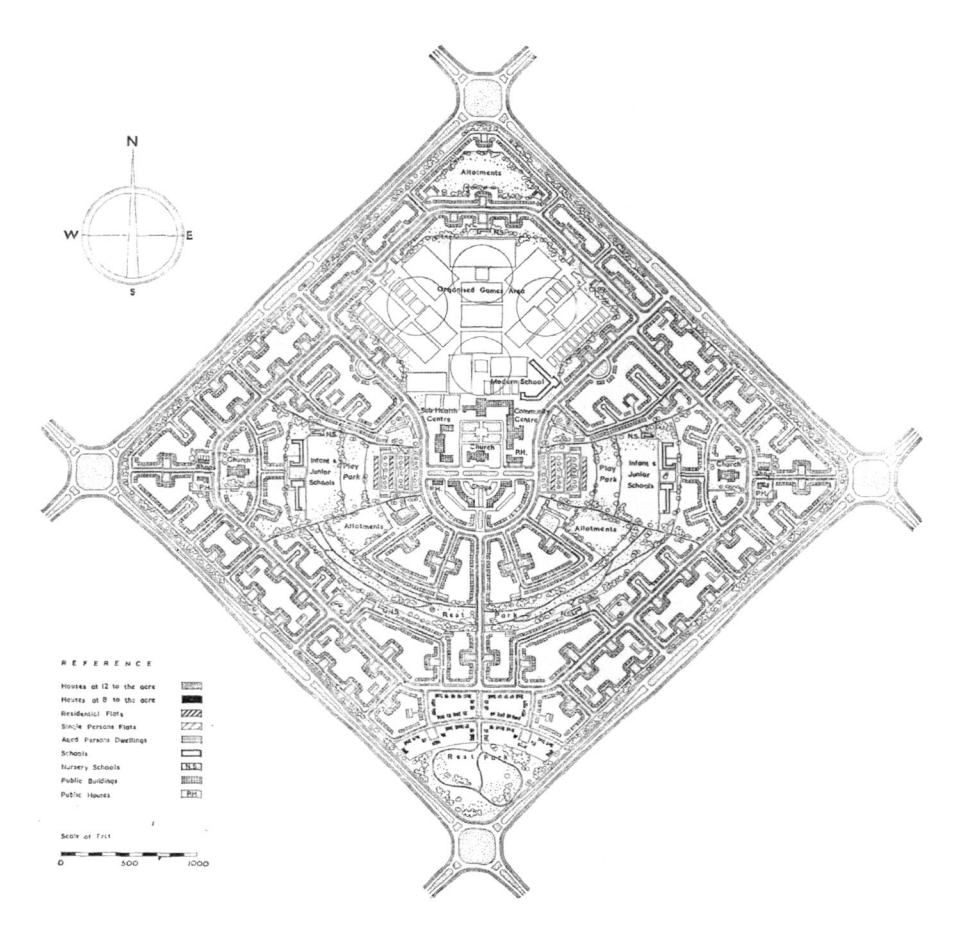

1.1 Theoretical layout for a neighbourhood centre.
[Reproduced from Nicholas, *City of Manchester Plan*, 140]

of good communal facilities".[53] The traditional village green, in this case, was to incorporate a range of such facilities, including the community centre, local shops, churches, public houses and a library. So, how were churches treated within these neighbourhood units?

In agreement with the analysis undertaken by Barlow, the 1945 City of Manchester Plan also noted the tendency of interwar estates to provide insufficient provision for churches, leading to awkwardly planned sites. Consequently, the Plan sets out a number of ideals on religious provision. Churches erected in neighbourhoods should be "their spiritual and architectural focal points, and sites in keeping with their significance should be reserved in new

53 Nicholas, *City of Manchester Plan*, 145. The 1945 plan foresaw Wythenshawe to consist of ten neighbourhoods, although in reality, Brooklands and Northenden were existing settlements that, in the end, resisted being absorbed into Wythenshawe.

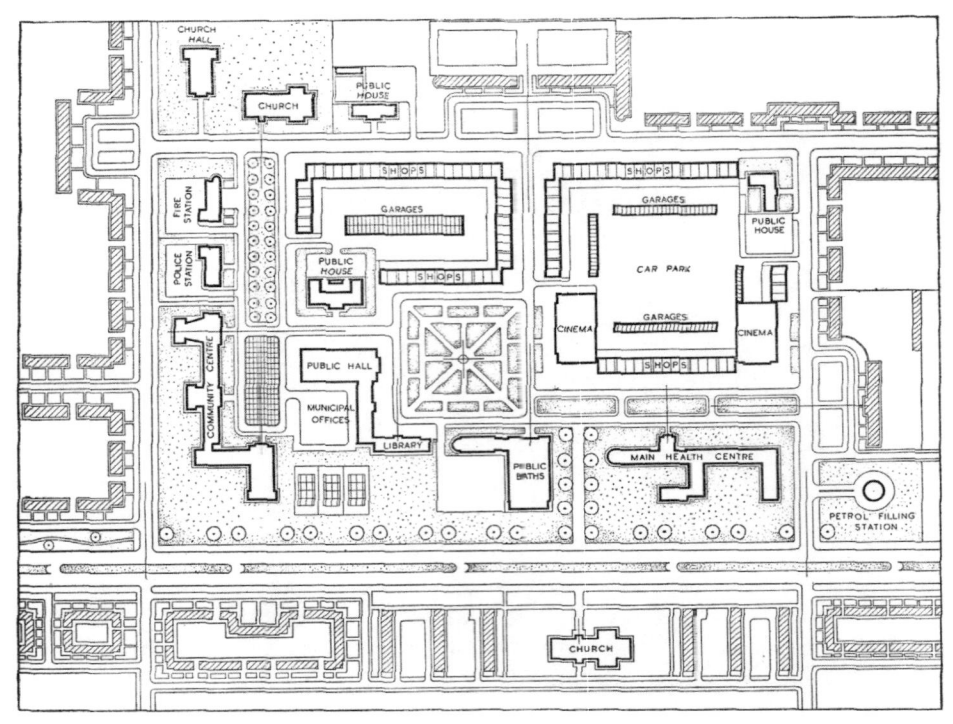

1.2 Theoretical layout for a "typical" district centre.
[Reproduced from Nicholas, *City of Manchester Plan*, 143]

development".[54] Religious life here continued to be central to community life, and idealised drawings of the neighbourhood plan showed the church directly at the centre. [Ill. 1.1] Housing areas at the extremity of the neighbourhood boundaries were further furnished with an additional public house, shops and a church. It was these buildings, where face-to-face social interaction would occur, which, it was thought, would help to develop community life in a new estate.[55] Even though the planners did not anticipate that the model neighbourhood layout could be put into practice, it served as a visual reminder of the ideals that underpinned the overall rationale and approach.

This can be contrasted with the district centre plan, which served a number of neighbourhoods, where the emphasis was on providing a wider array of shopping and entertainment facilities and ample car parking. [Ill. 1.2] Whilst it is crucial to acknowledge their idealistic nature, it seems that the municipality's visualisations of the neighbourhood and the district centre plan are at

54   Ibid., 138.
55   Greenhalgh, "Consuming Communities", 174. The concept was intended to concretise immeasurable qualities such as community and neighbourliness, although the extent to which this was ever achieved has been questioned; the blueprint provided by the municipality was contested in practice through, for example, the shopping habits that confounded the carefully worked out figures of the Manchester planners.

odds with one another in terms of planning traditions.[56] In addition, whilst it may be argued that the district centre plan shows the primacy given to commerce, it is arguable that with churches placed in neighbourhoods, close to the residents, it would be unlikely that churches would want to obtain a site in a less residential area where functions may have overlapped.[57]

In the post-1945 period, urban planning increasingly moved away from its roots in design and architecture in order to absorb thinking from quantitative social sciences, which had an impact on the allocation of sites in Manchester.[58] Typically used to identify industrial, residential and commercial needs, the same approach was applied to religious provision in the City of Manchester Plan. Nicholas undertook an analysis of the current number of churches, the number of people that each church served and the amount of land given to each church within the Manchester boundary in order to identify how many churches would be needed. He calculated that every neighbourhood unit ought to have provision for one Anglican church and one nonconformist church, whilst the Roman Catholic Church should have one place of worship for every three neighbourhoods.[59]

The question then became where to site these churches and how to allocate them to the denominations. Manchester was one of a handful of areas where the Churches Main Committee succeeded in setting up a local interdenominational committee. Once plans for Wythenshawe's north-western neighbourhood were set, in 1948, Nicholas sent the plans with potential sites indicated for churches, with the proviso that the interdenominational committee undertake the negotiations between the churches in order to decide sites.[60] [Ill. 1.3] In those neighbourhoods that were already laid out, churches

---

56 The City of Manchester Plan, 1945, was a composite document written over many years with different inputs from different people. It displays many of the incongruences and inconsistencies that have been identified in approaches to town planning in the UK in the mid-twentieth century. See Foley, "British Town Planning", 211.
57 Connelly, forthcoming.
58 Ward, *Planning in the Twentieth Century City*, 189. Michael Hebbert demonstrates that the openness to the quantitative approach in England comes from a disillusionment with land use planning, particularly on social and ecological grounds. Whilst there were a host of protagonists, the approach can be associated with planners such as Patrick Abercrombie and F. J. Osbourne. From the mid-twentieth century, collaborations (or a somewhat "unholy alliance") between traditional planners and social scientists strengthened and were formalised in policy. It may be argued that the quantitative approach gave succour to social and physical determinism in the design of new settlements. See Hebbert, "The Daring Experiment".
59 Nicholas, *The City of Manchester Plan*, 250-251. District, para 207. 0.75 acres were allocated per 1,000 people in new development areas and 0.5 acres per 1,000 people in redevelopment areas. Thoughts as to whether the churches believed this to be sufficient provision have not come to light. The figures were calculated on the basis of the number of members per denomination at the time of counting.
60 Manchester, MALS, Churches Main Committee, M196/10/4/4/1.

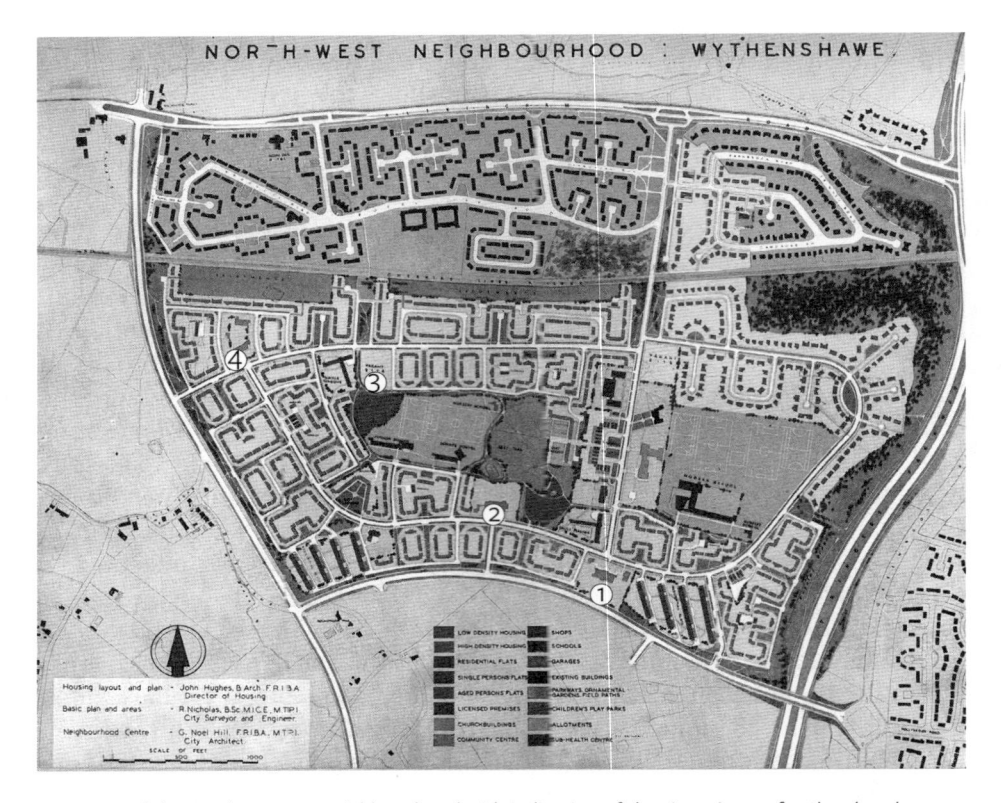

1.3 Layout of the north-western neighbourhood with indication of the sites chosen for the churches:
1) Saint Martin's Parish Church; 2) Baguley Methodist Church; 3) Baguley United Reform Church;
4) Sacred Heart and Saint Peter's Church (Catholic)
[Reproduced from Nicholas, *City of Manchester*, plate 52]

were intended to be "terminal features" — therefore given the most prominent site at the end of a long, straight road.[61] Saint Martin's Parish Church (1958), by Harry S. Fairhurst & Son, is typical in this regard by its location on an elevated site at one end of a main approach road. The other identified site, the city planners were informed, was to be taken by the Methodist Church — this was Baguley Methodist Church, which is less well-placed in terms of providing a landmark building but is set back from the housing estate and backs onto a park, lending a picturesque feel. The initial plan has one further identified site and a vacant site. Since the Roman Catholics were proposing to switch sites, the Planning Committee agreed that the Congregationalists should have the first choice of unallocated sites in that neighbourhood.[62] This became the Baguley United Reform Church to the north of the park.

61 Nicholas, *The City of Manchester Plan*, 152.
62 Manchester Archives and Local Studies, Churches Main Committee, M196/10/4/4/1.

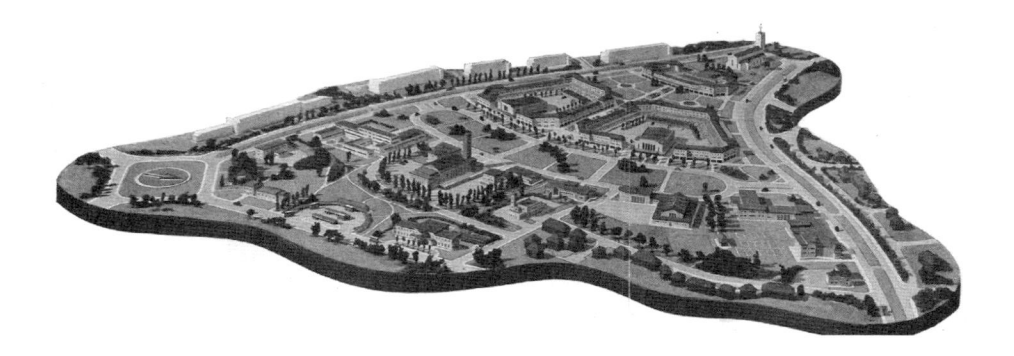

1.4 Model of Wythenshawe Civic Centre. The main church is located on the right-hand side of the model.
[Reproduced from Nicholas, *City of Manchester Plan*, plate 50]

It was, however, the civic centre that was the most important section of the Wythenshawe plan, and its evolution demonstrates how the plans moved from a "garden satellite town" to a full new town. The pre-1945 Parker plan had initially envisaged a town square to the right of Princess Parkway. By 1945, the civic centre site was enlarged to include 72 acres and shifted to the south, where a busy road could not dissect it from residential areas.[63] These 1945 plans show a civic centre with a range of classical public buildings, including shops and two theatres. Here, a parish church is shown at the end of the site, again to make a distinctive "terminal feature". [Ill. 1.4] Although plans were finessed over the 1950s, it was not until 1964, once the majority of housing was completed, that the civic centre site could be developed. By this time, the thinking envisaged a more centralised development comprising many functions, including a library and theatre, in one central complex "so that the whole Centre is seen as an obvious entity rather than a collection of individual buildings".[64] However, most churches had already been allocated sites in the neighbourhoods and district centres during the 1950s, which makes their style and siting seem incongruent with the civic centre that was eventually constructed. The churches, rather than feeding into the secular civic hub, seemed to be excluded from the centre and, in the end, addressed the neighbourhood context rather than the district centres. It is illuminating to zoom in to see how the planning debates at various scales played out in terms of the architectural concerns surrounding a Roman Catholic church in one Wythenshawe neighbourhood.

63   Deakin, *Wythenshawe*, 148.
64   Manchester, MALS, Wythenshawe Civic Centre Committee, GB127. Council Minutes/ Wythenshawe Civic Centre Committee Minutes.

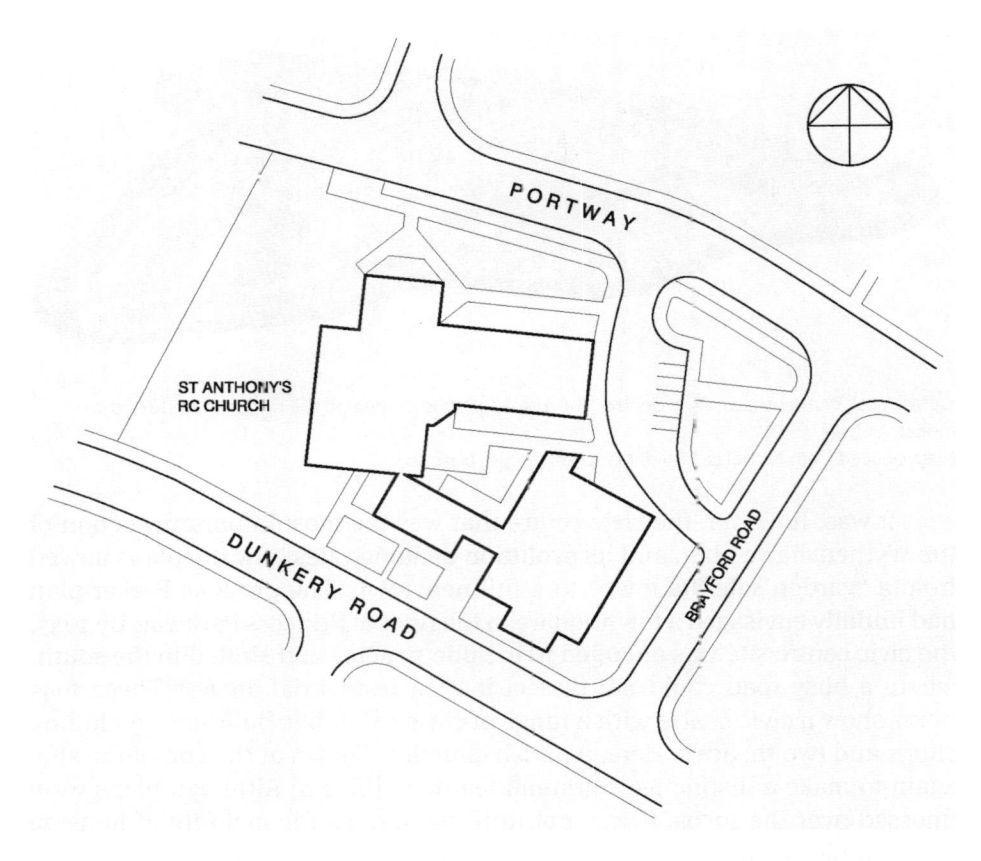

1.5: Saint Anthony's Roman Catholic Church (1960) on the map, contours of the church and the later parish centre are in bold, Woodhouse Park, Wythenshawe.
[Courtesy of Matthew Steele]

An "Out of the Ordinary" Church

The planning debates at the national and municipal levels are only one part of the story when considering the multitude of actors and negotiations that impact on church building. We will now focus our analysis on Saint Anthony's (1960), which was the closest Roman Catholic church to the civic centre site. Designed by Adrian Gilbert Scott (1882-1963), it is a landmark building placed in the neighbourhood of Woodhouse Park where three roads meet.[65] [Ill. 1.5] Two sites closer to the civic centre were reserved for the Church of England and the Methodist Church; the latter constructed their largest post-1945 church building in Saint Andrew's. The Church of England site soon housed the William Temple Memorial Church (1965) designed by George Gaze Pace (1915-1975). Whilst Pace's design departed from the Church of England's more

65 Proctor, *Building the Modern Church*, 280.

1.6 Saint Anthony's Roman Catholic Church (1960) under construction, Woodhouse Park, Wythenshawe.
[Reproduced by permission from Manchester, MALS]

traditional liturgical preferences, Gilbert Scott's proposal for Saint Anthony's harked back to traditional values even in the midst of great liturgical change within the Roman Catholic Church. [Ill. 1.6] The resultant building therefore responds to a site that addresses the mainly residential neighbourhood, but it is also indicative of a more conservative liturgical approach by the Diocese of Shrewsbury, of which Saint Anthony's was a part.[66] An exploration of Saint Anthony's is, therefore, an instructive way to view the multifarious connections between the actors involved in the final form of a church building.

The Saint Anthony's site, close to the Woodhouse Park neighbourhood centre and public house, was allocated by the city surveyors and, following an application by the incumbent parish priest, a formal licence to build was granted in 1951.[67] Saint Anthony's was one of six sites in the area and cost 2035

66 This argument is put forward by Robert Proctor in relation to the Roman Catholic churches in Manchester that were designed by the firm Reynolds and Scott. Proctor, "Designing the Suburban Church", 113-133.
67 A building licence was necessary in this period because of continuing rationing of building supplies and materials following the Second World War. This was intended to ration scarce building resources and ensure that priority buildings — such as housing and schools — could be built. The need for building licences was revoked in 1954.

pounds. The Manchester Corporation included road charges in the total cost of the site on a principle that had been agreed by the Manchester branch of the Churches Main Committee, whereby the total cost of the six sites was divided equally so that sites with a shorter road frontage subsidised sites, such as Saint Anthony's, with extensive frontages onto the road.[68]

By April 1951, Mass was formally held in a temporary construction that was informally known as "the Green Hut", which comprised two adjoined prefabricated steel Nissen huts.[69] At the time, the incumbent priest, Father Martin Kehoe (life dates unknown), had his attention attuned to the building of a parish primary school, which opened in 1954. However, he was keen to press the Bishop of Shrewsbury, John A. Murphy (1905-1995), on timings for a new church building by 1957, emphasizing that 2200 people were attending mass every Sunday, from whom sufficient funds could be raised.[70] The Green Hut itself, in a time before the public civic centre was built, was being used for a range of Catholic and non-Catholic purposes, such as a cinema and a food distribution centre.[71] This might suggest that a dual-purpose church with a community focus would have been desirable. Instead, Gilbert Scott's design for Saint Anthony's is highly traditional in liturgical arrangements and was primarily meant for worshipping; a separate parish centre did not open until 1971. This allowed for a monumental building to be designed, one that was singularly and utterly identifiable as a church and one of the largest Roman Catholic churches that had ever been built in Manchester, perhaps as a show of strength and prestige. It must be remembered that, at the time, the Roman Catholic Church in England was in a period of ascendancy in terms of rising congregations.[72]

The Bishop of Shrewsbury wanted to make use of the ample and prominent site that had been provided in the neighbourhood plans, particularly given the size of the parish and the lack of other churches in the neighbourhood. Saint Anthony's, the Bishop advised, had to be "out of the ordinary".[73] Gilbert Scott was selected as the architect who could "do justice to such a site with a noble and dignified church", with the specific suggestion that the "Gothic Revival" style exemplified in his earlier example of Saint Joseph in Upton (1954), also in the Diocese of Shrewsbury, would be appropriate for Saint Anthony's.[74]

68 Woodchurch, DSA. Letter from J. S. Montgomery to the Right Reverend J. A. Murphy, 29 April 1959.
69 Once the primary school had opened in 1954, Mass was held in the school. The Green Hut was demolished in 1958 to make way for the permanent building.
70 Woodchurch, DSA. Letter from Father Martin Kehoe to Bishop J. A. Murphy, Bishop of Shrewsbury, 20 March 1957.
71 The New Saint Anthony's Church, Woodhouse Park, Manchester. Souvenir of Solemn Opening, 3 November 1960 (Manchester: J. E. Mulligan & Co. Ltd, 1960), 14.
72 Proctor, *Building the Modern Church*, 2.
73 Woodchurch, DSA. "Summary of Bishop's Remarks on the New Church Project", c 1957, 1.
74 Ibid.

1.7. Front view of Saint Anthony's Roman Catholic Church (1960), current situation, Woodhouse Park, Wythenshawe.
[Photograph by Robert Proctor]

The Bishop even went so far as to suggest the placement of the church diagonally across the site in order to dominate both approach roads: Portway and Rudpark Road. This is the eventual form that the building took, with the main entrance towards Portway, but an equally dominant part of the building, the altar, placed towards the west to form a monumental side entrance with a tower facing Rudpark Road. In his extensive notes, the Bishop also specified that the church should not be octagonal. This could reflect a conservative approach to design but, in the Bishop's words, the expanse of the site meant that an octagonal church "might give too heavy an appearance".[75]

The allocation of a large site, close to major access roads, therefore shaped the eventual form of the building and can be considered to be another actor in the narrative. Whilst Gilbert Scott noted that "the large and open site left one exceptionally free to plan Saint Anthony's to any shape desired", a wish to interact with all of the main roads, with the feature towards Rudpark Road in addition to the main entrance, "determined the traditional Roman Cross plan, with a large open central space".[76] Saint Anthony's, whilst in very eclectic style, seems to conform to the original ideal set out in the City of Manchester Plan for a spiritual and architectural focal point to the Woodhouse Park neighbourhood. Yet this also, pragmatically, suited the needs and re-

75 Ibid.
76 Woodchurch, DSA. "The New St Anthony's Church, Woodhouse Park, Manchester". Souvenir of Solemn Opening, 3 November 1960 (Manchester: J. E. Mulligan & Co. Ltd, 1960), 7.

quirements of the parish and the Bishop of Shrewsbury for Saint Anthony's to "look like a church and to be as devotional as possible".[77] [Ill. 1.7]

There is virtually no mention of Saint Anthony's in the wider architectural press of the time, which might be considered unusual given the national prominence of Gilbert Scott's work but could simply be a result of the London-dominated architectural scene. Even so, the building was of symbolic importance to the local Roman Catholic community. The opening ceremonies were attended by 125 priests, and the 800-seat church was full for the celebrations. However, in his opening sermon, Father Kehoe was keen to impress upon the audience that the monumental church should not give the suggestion that the Diocese of Shrewsbury had disposable income:

> When you see a magnificent church like this, you might think that we are rolling in money; we are not, we are rolling in debt all over the diocese.[78]

Debt was a problem that bedevilled Saint Anthony's for many years, but the parishioners and clergy pushed on with their work. At the silver jubilee, held in 1978, it was observed that "we have a local community, almost as close-knit as a village community, in a large conurbation", which of course represented the realisation of the initial aims of the parish to have a building that was a focal point for its members in which much activity took place.[79] However, the problem of trying to maintain such a large building eventually presented itself as congregational numbers began to dwindle in the latter part of the twentieth century. Whereas the first twenty-five years of parish life could be characterised as a period of "optimism", the next twenty-five years witnessed the twin problems of a declining congregation that was also aging.[80] Today, the parish centre, which remains well used, helps to provide an income for the now Grade II listed church.[81]

Saint Anthony's construction is instructive for the myriad of actors involved in the design of one church building and the impact of wider urban planning concerns. The church's siting was the result of negotiations between the Churches Main Committee and the Manchester Corporation surveyors, including the final sum for the price of the site, which was divided up between parishes. The actual design also reflected the influences of many actors beyond the architect, particularly through the keen oversight of the Bishop of Shrewsbury. Undoubtedly, the conversations between architect and bishop were also

77 Ibid.
78 "Opening of St Anthony's, Woodhouse Park", *The Catholic Guardian*, 5 November 1960, 1.
79 Woodchurch, DSA. "St Anthony's Woodhouse Park, Silver Jubilee Brochure", 1978, 5.
80 Woodchurch, DSA. "Golden Jubilee Brochure, St Anthony's Woodhouse Park", 2003, 7.
81 The National Heritage List for England provides details of all of the protected buildings and landscapes in the country. Each building is graded according to its importance: Grade I denotes exceptional interest, whilst Grade II is of special interest.

shaped by the prominent siting at the intersection of three road frontages that seemed to demand a monumental response, one that conformed to the more picturesque ideals envisioned for the Wythenshawe estate in the 1945 City of Manchester Plan.

Conclusion

Clearly, there was much pragmatism to be found in the approach of religious organisations in obtaining and keeping key sites in the Wythenshawe estate that departed from their initial aspirations. Recognition of religious concerns was widely accepted within the national government and within Manchester. There were nevertheless problems around not only ensuring favouritism to particular denominations, but also balancing the competing concerns of secular organisations that could make equal arguments about the value of their public function. The way that the major religious organisations came together to present a coherent face to government, and to call on sympathetic ministers and civil servants, meant that they could exploit existing connections and the perceived importance of religion, even though there was a growing sense that church attendance was in decline. In addition, it could be argued that the need for prominent church sites displays an idealistic tendency towards social and physical determinism in the neighbourhood planning concept, as adopted in post-1945 English planning. The church, in this case, was a harbinger of good community spirit, even if consumer preferences would repudiate this in the late twentieth century. Here, the planners and the churches were singing from the same hymn sheet.

Various factors beyond human resources impacted on the selection and allocation of sites. Most notably, the shortage of materials and labour in the immediate post-1945 period saw some organisations constructing temporary halls, or building in stages, in order to secure the site before a permanent building could be constructed. In addition, the instrument of ecclesiastical law, which pertained only to the Church of England, was interpreted liberally by the civil servants and expanded to cover other religious organisations, albeit in a qualified way. Consequently, growing collaboration enabled the non-established religious organisations to gain concessions during the drafting of the bill for the 1947 Town and Country Planning Act.

Manchester may be an atypical case, given that the relations between the planners and the religious organisations seemed to be harmonious — except in isolated cases that usually related to compulsory purchase rather than the designation of new sites. In other English new towns, though, such as Stevenage, the interdenominational area committees begun under the Churches Main Committee were also thought to work to good effect. This may be due to the growing collaboration that was a feature of English church relations over the twentieth century. Future research could begin to compare the differences between areas where the churches worked together and those where there was little collaboration. An appreciation of the wider planning context relating to the site selection for places of worship reveals much about the social and cultural position of the English churches in the eyes of those in authority. Religious organisations seemed to enjoy a privileged role in the limited consultations that embryonic planning authorities undertook. In addition, the site allocations made by the planners could, as was the case in St Anthony's, subtly shape the final building form.

BIBLIOGRAPHY

Archives

London, Church of England Record Office, ECE/SEC/LEGN/4/2 (CERO)
London, the National Archives, HLG-71-1486 (NA)
Manchester, Manchester Archives and Local Studies (MALS)
    Churches Main Committee, M196/10/4/4/1
    Wythenshawe Civic Centre Committee, GB127
Woodchurch, Diocese of Shrewsbury Archive (DSA)

Published sources

Brown, Callum G. *The Death of Christian Britain: Understanding Secularisation, 1800-2000*, 2nd edition. Abingdon and New York: Routledge, 2009.
Chandler, Andrew. *The Church of England in the Twentieth Century: The Church Commissioners and the Politics of Reform, 1948-1998*. Woodbridge: Boydell & Brewer, 2009.
Church Assembly. *The Church and the Planning of Britain: Report of the Social and Industrial Commission of the Church Assembly 1944* [The Barlow Report]. London: The Press and Publications Board of the Church Assembly/The Society for the Promotion of Christian Knowledge, 1944.
Clapson, Mark. *Working-Class Suburb: Social Change on an English Council Estate, 1930-2010*. Manchester: Manchester University Press, 2012.
Connelly, Angela. "Places of Worship in Post-war Manchester". In: Martin Dodge and Richard Brook, eds. *The Making of Post-war Manchester*. (The Modernist Society, forthcoming)
Corkindale, J. "Land Development in the United Kingdom: Private Property Rights and Public Policy Objectives". *Environment and Planning A*, 31 (1999), 2053-2070.
Deakin, Derick. *Wythenshawe: The Story of a Garden City*. Bognor Regis: Phillimore & Co Ltd, 1989.
The Department for Chapel Affairs [The Methodist Church]. *Serving the Church: Being Guidance in the Care and Use of Methodist Church Buildings*. London: Epworth Press, 1948.
Dobb, Arthur J. *Like a Mighty Tortoise. A History of the Diocese of Manchester*. Manchester: Upjohn and Bottomley, 1978.
Dwyer, Claire; Gilbert, David and Shah, Bindi. "Faith and Suburbia: Secularisation, Modernity and the Changing Geographies of Religion in London's Suburbs". *Transactions of the Institute of British Geographers*, 38 (2013), 403-419.
Foley, Donald L. "British Town Planning: One Ideology or Three?". *The British Journal of Sociology*, 11 (1960), 211-231.
Green, Simon J.D. *The Passing of Protestant England: Secularisation and Social Change, c. 1920-1960*. Cambridge: Cambridge University Press, 2010.
Greenhalgh, James. "Consuming Communities: the Neighbourhood Unit and the Role of Retail Spaces on British Housing Estates, 1944-1958". *Urban History*, 43.1 (2016), 158-174.

Gregory, Jeremy and Chamberlain, Jeffrey Scott. "National and Local Perspectives on the Church of England in the Long Eighteenth Century". In: Jeremy Gregory and Jeffrey Scott Chamberlain, eds. *The National Church in Local Perspective: the Church of England and the regions, 1660-1800*. Woodbridge: The Boydell Press, 2003, 1-28.

Guest, Matthew; Olson, Elizabeth and Wolffe, John. "Christianity: The loss of monopoly". In: Linda Woodhead and Rebecca Catto, eds. *Religion and Change in Modern Britain*. London-New York: Routledge, 2012, 57-78.

Hastings, Andrew. *A History of English Christianity, 1920-2000*, 4th edition. London: SCM Press, 2000.

Hebbert, Michael. "The Daring Experiment: Social Scientists and Land-Use Planning in 1940s Britain". *Environment and Planning B: Planning and Design*, 10 (1983), 3-17.

Johnson, Donald Leslie. "Origin of the Neighbourhood Unit". *Planning Perspectives*, 17 (2002), 227-245.

Kitchen, Ted. "The Future of Development Plans: Reflections on Manchester's Experiences 1945-1995". *The Town Planning Review*, 67 (1996), 331-353.

Latour, Bruno. *Reassembling the Social. An Introduction to Actor-Network-Theory*. Oxford: Oxford University Press, 2005.

Miller, Mervyn. *English Garden Cities: An Introduction*. Swindon: Historic England, 2015.

Nash, David. "Reconnecting Religion with Social and Cultural History: Secularization's Failure as a Master Narrative". *Cultural and Social History*, 1 (2004), 302-325.

Nicholas, Rowland. *City of Manchester Plan: Prepared for the City Council*. Norwich and London: Jarrold and Sons, Ltd, 1945.

Nicholas, Rowland. *Manchester and District Regional Planning Proposal*. Norwich and London: Jarrold and Sons, Ltd, 1945.

Norman, E. R. "Notes on Church and State: A Mapping Exercise". In R. M. Morris, ed. *Church and State: Some Reflections on Church Establishment in England*. London: The Constitutional Unit, University College London, 2008, 9-13.

Orchard, "The formation of the United Reform Church". In: Linda Woodhead and Rebecca Catto, eds. *Religion and Change in Modern Britain*. London-New York: Routledge, 2012, 79-84.

Perkins, E. Benson. *So Appointed: An Autobiography*. London: Epworth Press: 1964.

Perkins, Chris and Dodge, Martin. "Mapping the Imagined Future: The Roles of Visual Representation in the 1945 City of Manchester Plan". *Bulletin of the John Rylands University Library*, 89.1 (2013), 247-276.

Proctor, Robert. *Building the Modern Church: Roman Catholic Church Architecture in Britain, 1955 to 1975*. Farnham: Ashgate, 2014, 278.

Proctor, Robert. "Designing the Suburban Church: the mid Twentieth-century Roman Catholic Churches of Reynolds & Scott". *Journal of Historical Geography*, 56 (2017), 113-133.

Ravetz, Alison. *Council Housing and Culture: The History of a Social Experiment*. London: Routledge, 2001.

Simon, E. D. and Simon, S. "Wythenshawe". In E.D. Simon and J. Inman, eds. *The Rebuilding of Manchester*. London, New York & Toronto: Longmans, Green and Co., 1935, 36-53.

Uthwatt, Augustus A. *Final Report: Expert Committee on Compensation and Betterment*, Cmnd. 6386. London: Her Majesty's Stationary Office, 1949.

Walford, Rex. *The Growth of "New London" in Suburban Middlesex, 1918-1945, and the Response of the Church of England*. Lampeter: Edwin Mellen Press Ltd, 2007.

Ward, Stephen. *Planning in the Twentieth Century City: The Advanced Capitalist World*. Chichester: Wiley, 2002.

Williams, Gwyndaf. "Manchester: City Profile". *Cities*, 13 (1996), 203-212.

Williams-Ellis, Clough. *England and the Octopus*. London: Council for the Protection of Rural England, 1996 [1928].

2
LYONS'S POST-WAR CHURCHES
TWO CONTEXTS, TWO CHURCHES, ONE ARCHITECT: PIERRE GENTON

JUDI LOACH AND MÉLANIE MEYNIER-PHILIP*

In the European urban context, the Diocese of Lyons provides an interesting case of planning related to church building, which also illustrates post-war changes to the process. While many of these changes were the inevitable result of the region's considerable expansion and industrialisation, the role played in this case by the Office Diocésain des Paroisses Nouvelles (ODPN, Diocesan Office for New Parishes), which the diocese set up to ensure a rational and efficacious distribution of new church buildings, was crucial. In interwar France, different dioceses had pursued separate initiatives; the Lyons diocese had established L'Œuvre du Christ dans la banlieue (The Work of Christ in the Suburbs), while its Parisian equivalent initiated the better-known Chantiers du Cardinal (The Cardinal's Construction Sites).[1] The Lyons diocese's interwar and post-war initiatives contained certain locally distinct features, most notably several movements set up by Catholics to assist the poor and the early adoption of liturgical reform by certain clergy; meanwhile, its post-war efforts were marked by the involvement of prominent Catholic individuals keen to

---

* We would like to thank Maryannick Chalabi and Olivier Chatelan for generously sharing their own archival research.
1 Debié and Vérot, *Urbanisme et art sacré: une aventure du XXe siècle*.

embrace modern art and architecture as an expression of the Church's relevance to contemporary society.[2]

Olivier Chatelan's rigorous research has provided much material concerning the ODPN and the ecclesiastical context in which churches were built in the area after the Second World War. Our own research builds on this, showing how the ODPN's guidelines were implemented differently depending on whether a specific church was built on a "greenfield" site, as part of a new development, or within the existing urban fabric.[3] We therefore present an example from each of these two contexts designed by the same architect: Pierre Genton (1924-2004), one-time assistant to both Auguste Perret (1874-1954) and Le Corbusier (1887-1965) and a nephew of Marie-Alain Couturier (1897-1954), the Dominican co-editor of *L'Art sacré*.

The ODPN, the Diocese of Lyons's "Town Planning Agency"

In the aftermath of the Second World War, France witnessed a period of comprehensive economic, demographic and urban development, including in and around Lyons. Between 1954 and 1975, the population of the Lyons metropolitan area, comprising 34 communes, grew from 724,200 to 1,055,800 inhabitants.[4] A tremendous volume of residential accommodation was built to address this growth, and the agglomeration experienced rampant urbanisation as a result. The state, in turn, developed town planning strategies that included detailed land use plans for specific districts. The Diocese of Lyons responded by creating its own "town planning agency": the ODPN.[5] Created in 1957, this replaced L'Oeuvre du Christ dans la banlieue, which had been the principal body responsible for new buildings in the parishes throughout the

---

2 The most notable movements advocating on behalf of the poor were associated with the Prado, the institution founded by Father Antoine Chevrier for juvenile welfare and education, and the magazine *Chronique Sociale*. On Chevrier, see Allioud and Désigaux, *Un fondateur d'action sociale: Antoine Chevrier*. On the early adoption of liturgical reform, see *La Maison-Dieu*, 2 (1945), 173 and 93-116; 6 (1946), 88-91; 18 (1949), 48-60; 20 (1950), 13-32; 25 (1951), 157-159; 30 (1952), 83-84. The key figure here was the abbé Remillieux. Cf. Malabre, *Le religieux dans la ville du premier vingtième siècle*.
3 Chatelan, *Les catholiques et la croissance urbaine dans l'agglomération lyonnaise pendant les Trente Glorieuses (1945-1975)*; id., *L'Église et la ville, Le diocèse de Lyon à l'épreuve de l'urbanisation (1954-1975)*.
4 Chatelan, *Les catholiques et la croissance urbaine*, 45.
5 The expression comes from Chalabi, "Les églises paroissiales construites dans la seconde moitié du XXe siècle et leur devenir", 2. As concerns the territory of the Diocese of Lyons, it should be noted that its boundaries have since changed. In 1954-1955, as a result of urbanisation along the eastern edge of Lyons, some parishes from the Diocese of Grenoble were integrated into that of Lyons. Then, in 1971, part of the Lyons diocese was split off to create the new Diocese of Saint-Etienne.

diocese since 1926.[6] The ODPN followed on the creation of the Commission d'Art sacré (Sacred Art Commission) in 1956, which was led by established architects coming, in part, from well-established architectural dynasties within Lyons.[7]

In order to understand the diocese's position here — one of straddling continuity and change — it seems important to emphasise that most of the architects hired for the church-building programme were practising Catholics and several were also heavily involved in two progressive movements: the Liturgical Movement and *L'Art sacré*, the movement affiliated with the magazine of that name. The magazine was edited by the Dominicans Couturier (an artist and previous disciple of Maurice Denis) and Pie-Raymond Régamey (1900-1996, an art historian trained under Henri Focillon). It promoted the Catholic Church's use of modern art and architecture, even if this meant employing non-Catholic artists. Meanwhile, the Liturgical Movement in France made its impact at the parish level through the Centre de Pastorale Liturgique (Liturgical Pastoral Centre), which was founded in 1943 and also had Dominicans as directors, who were in fact closely linked to those running *L'Art sacré*.[8] The strong commitment of certain Lyonese architects to these movements is evident in their buildings, which demonstrated the Church's advocacy of liturgical reforms that would later be adopted by the Second Vatican Council in the mid-1960s.[9] In Lyons, most of these reforms preceded the council's edicts, and the related architectural changes became apparent in some church buildings earlier than elsewhere. Even if the younger architects commissioned ended up designing modern buildings, however, the diocese's choices overall reflect both caution and a relatively traditional approach. This needs to be understood as a response to the immediate post-war context, during which new churches were hardly, if ever, modern, and much of the church building involved reconstructing to their pre-war glory buildings lost during the hostilities or finally realising pre-war designs left unbuilt at the outbreak of war.[10]

For its part, the ODPN relied on competencies drawn from three disciplines to achieve its aims: law, town planning and architecture.[11] It was re-

---

6   Chatelan, *Les catholiques et la croissance urbaine*, 62.
7   On the creation of the Commission d'Art sacré, see Lyons, ADL, Fonds ODPN, 1L 217, Monseigneur Mazioux to members of the ODPN, 1958. Examples of architectural dynasties in the diocese include Paul Curtelin, son of Georges Curtelin and brother of Charles Curtelin; Jean-Gabriel Mortamet, son of Louis Mortamet, himself son of Gabriel Mortamet; Marc Bissuel (1916-1989), son of Joseph Bissuel (1876-1948), himself son of Prosper-Edouard Bissuel (1840-1922), in turn nephew of Jean-Prosper Bissuel; Marc Bissuel also had an architect son, Vincent Bissuel (1942-2018). See Charvet, *Lyon artistique: Architectes*.
8   Duployé, *Les origines du Centre de Pastorale Liturgique*; Martimort, "Du Centre de Pastorale Liturgique à la Constitution Liturgique de Vatican II".
9   Loach, "The case of Lyons: 'Vatican II' before Vatican II", 89.
10   Loach, "L'invention d'un édifice-type", 412.
11   Chatelan, *Les catholiques et la croissance urbaine*, 267.

sponsible for analysing the conditions under which new construction would be carried out, but not for the execution of such schemes; instead the latter fell to parish associations, together with their "builder priests". The ODPN provided three kinds of support: legal (model contracts and explanations of current legislation), financial (potential loans, although fund-raising campaigns comprised the principal means of funding) and technical (guidelines for planning and architecture). In fact, multiple commissions worked together in sequence on the construction of new churches: first, the commission for establishing briefs; then, the technical commission and the office's own commission for sacred art, often in conflict with each other; then the financial and legal commission; and, finally, the commission for publicity.

Within the context of an exponential growth in urbanisation, the diocese embarked on a planning process for implanting future parishes across its territory. In the same way that schools and municipal infrastructures were being developed, places of worship had to be sited strategically, with parish buildings conceived as forming the heart of new districts. The rationale used by the diocese followed the commonly accepted principles advocated by Paul Winninger, who had stated in his book *Construire des églises* (1957) that the ideal ratio for parishes was to have one for every 5,000 inhabitants.[12] In Lyons, Winninger's ideas were disseminated through the diocese's weekly magazine and written about by the theologian Henri Denis (1921-2015).[13] In 1958 Monsignor Joannès Mazioux (1900-1988), director of the ODPN until 1975, stipulated that these new buildings:

> must correspond with a small number of residents, 5,000 to 10,000 on average, be no further than a kilometre apart so as to be close to all the faithful, correspond as far as possible with coherent neighbourhoods, and be located close to shopping centres, to which people are drawn through shopping, and especially be near schools.[14]

A year later Jean Capellades, one of the later editors of *L'Art sacré*, would reaffirm this in a special issue on "The Church in the City" in a more theological discourse that criticised the current church distribution for not fitting that of the populations it served.[15]

To create a strong network across their territory, the ODPN drew up a list of districts where future parish centres should be built; parish priests were then asked to find suitable sites within those districts and architects to build the centres. "Centrality" was a key determinant, at least in cases in which sites

12   Winninger, *Construire des églises*. On Winninger's ideas, see the Introduction to this book.
13   *Semaine religieuse du diocèse de Lyon*, 14 March 1958.
14   Lyons, ADL, Fonds ODPN, 1L 217, Monseigneur Mazioux to members of the ODPN, 1958. All translations are the authors' own.
15   *L'Art sacré*, 5-6 (1959), 10.

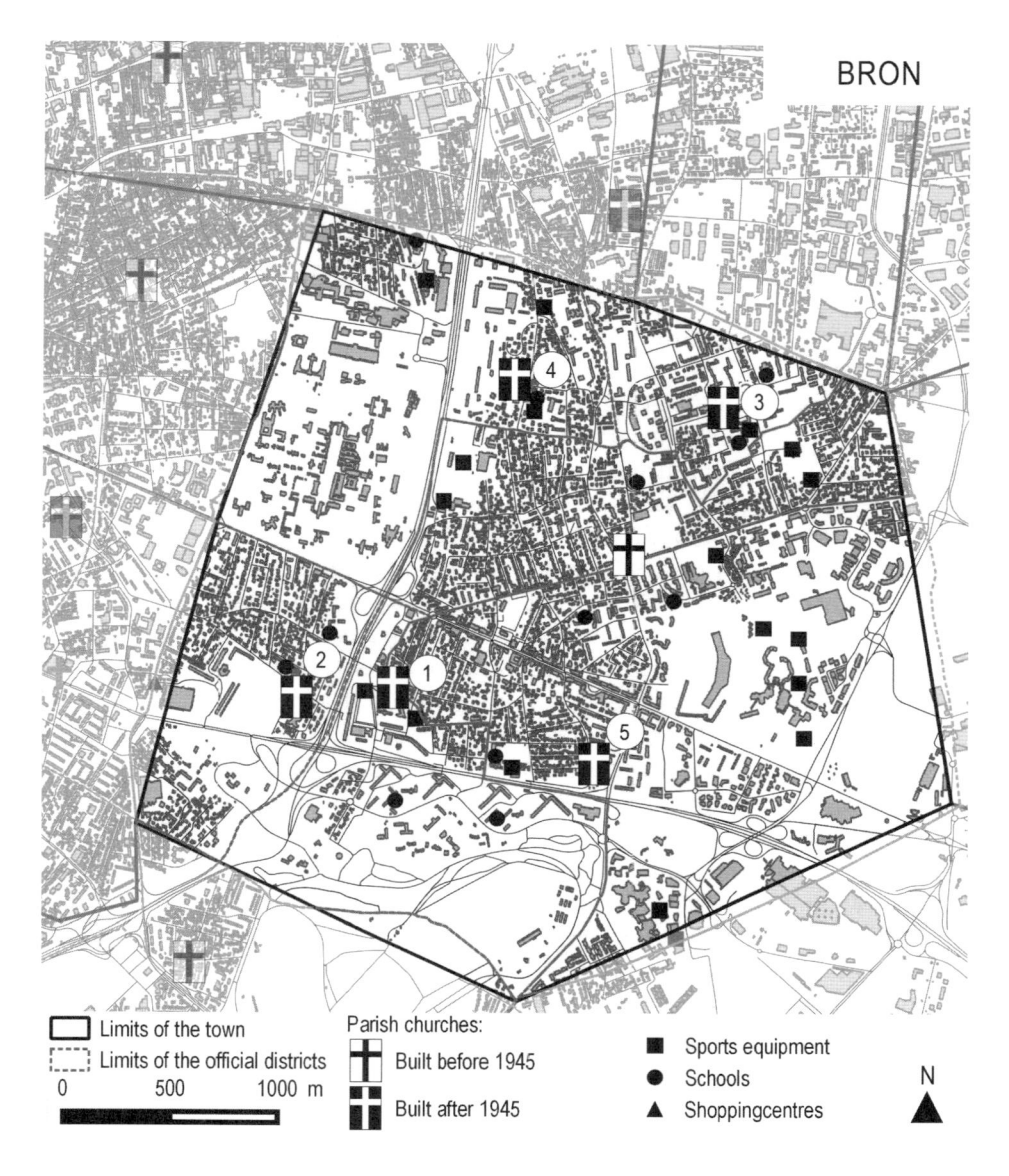

2.1 Map showing the locations of new churches built after the Second World War in Bron: Christ-Roi, by Franck Grimal, to the west (1); Notre-Dame de Lourdes, by Pierre Genton, further west (2); Saint Etienne de Terraillon, by Franck Grimal, Daniel Genevois, Roger Mermet and Marcel Sabattier, to the north-east (3); and Sainte Geneviève, by Jean-Gabriel Mortamet, to the north (4). Saint François d'Assise was planned to the south-east (5), but only a provisional chapel was ever built there.
[Drawing by Mélanie Meynier-Philip, 2017]

had not already been earmarked in the city's development plan for a new district.[16] At that time, Lyons was mostly developing eastwards. A major survey had been undertaken to locate sites for new residential areas, and in 1948, the architects René Gagès (1921-2008) and Franck Grimal (1912-2003) were commissioned to produce a planning strategy for the Lyonese region as a whole (Plan directeur du Groupement d'Urbanisme de la région lyonnaise). This would be Lyons's first local plan, inspired entirely by the Athens Charter, the influential manifesto for a functionalist city that had been issued by the Congrès Internationaux d'Architecture Moderne (CIAM) in the 1930s. The architects were to locate "any sites available and suitable for new developments" within the agglomeration, while preserving woodland.[17] They accordingly identified as potential development sites three forts (La Duchère, Montessuy and Sainte-Foy-lès-Lyon), the Tonkin military estate at Villeurbanne and the Part-Dieu barracks within Lyons. They proposed four residential neighbourhoods, of which three were soon built, two on the fort sites of La Duchère and Montessuy and the other on previously agricultural land at Bron-Parilly.[18] In addition, a new science campus, with a science university and related research institutes, was built on the site of the La Doua cavalry barracks, in Villeurbanne, and Lyons's new administrative and commercial centre was established at the former Part-Dieu barracks site, in Lyons's 3rd arrondissement.

Such a greenfield context was the case for four churches at La Duchère (an ex-fort site), as well as for the siting of churches in the earlier town plan for Bron-Parilly. According to this policy, Saint Denis, the church built for the village of Bron in the nineteenth century, did not adequately serve the post-war development, so additional church sites were allocated for the new districts. [Ill. 2.1] When it came to designating sites within areas that were already built up but still lacked sufficient churches near enough to residents, the choice of sites was more limited; this was the case in Villeurbanne, for example, a working-class, heavily industrialised district to the east of Lyons that had been growing rapidly ever since the late nineteenth century.[19] [Ill. 2.2]

In October 1960, Cardinal Pierre Gerlier (1880-1965) issued instructions to his "builder priests" advocating solid, simple and beautiful buildings, concluding that "there can be great beauty in simplicity".[20] Modern architects could interpret this as supporting their own preferred approach, but it left a broader range of approaches open. While the appointment of a com-

16 Concerning centrality, see Chatelan, *Les catholiques et la croissance urbaine*, 341. Concerning the city's development, see Chalabi, "Les églises paroissiales construites dans la seconde moitié du XXème siècle et leur devenir", 3.
17 Rey, *Lyon, Cité radieuse*, 38-39.
18 Meillerand, "Les terrains militaires", 10.
19 Meuret, *Le Socialisme municipal: Villeurbanne 1880-1982*.
20 Lyons, AD, Fonds ODPN, 1L 227, Cardinal Gerlier to "all the faithful in the diocese", 30 October 1960.

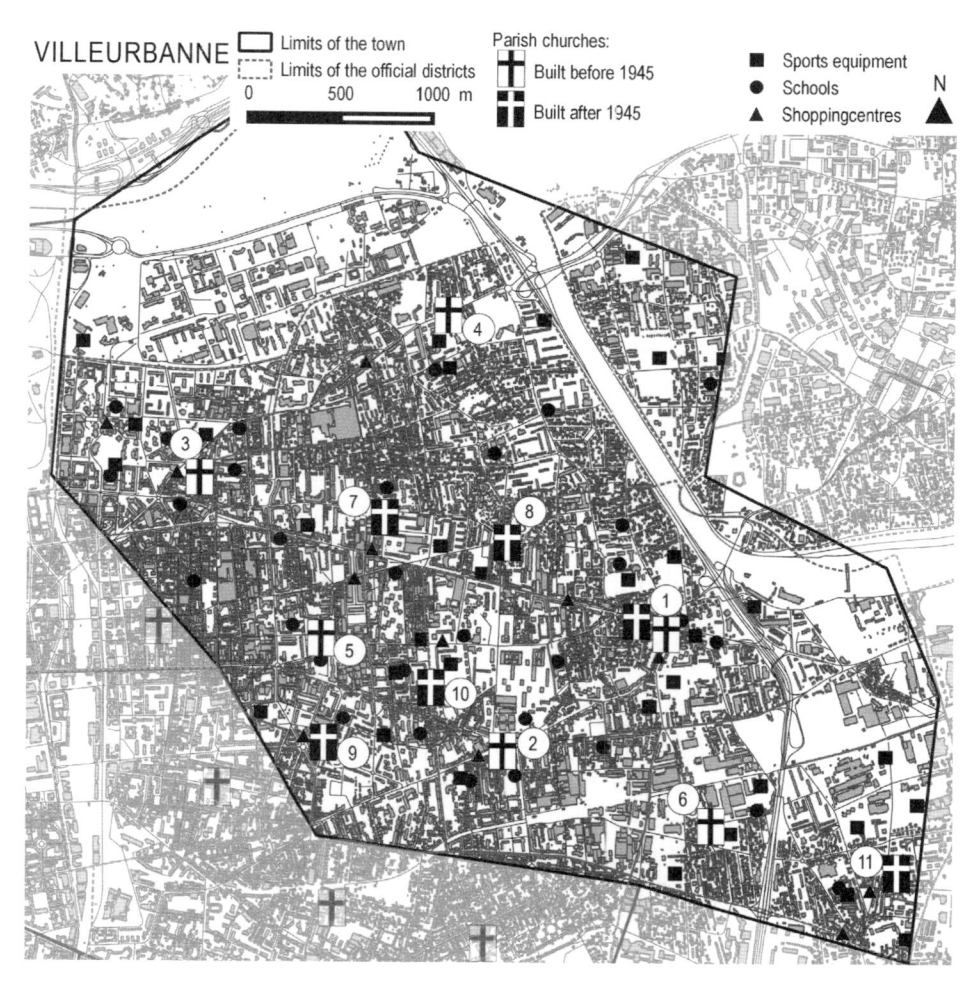

2.2 Map showing the locations of new churches built after the Second World War in relation to older churches in Villeurbanne. The small church in the village of Cusset, Saint Julian, lay on the eastern edge (1). There were two nineteenth-century churches: the Nativité de Notre Dame in Grand Clément in the old town centre to the south (2) and Sainte Madeleine in Charpennes to the west, very close to Lyons (3). In the interwar period, the growth of the Italo-Spanish population in Villeurbanne's north-east section had warranted the building of a new church in Croix-Luizet, the Sainte Famille by Louis Mortamet (4); while to the south, two parishes were founded on either side of the Nativité: Sainte Thérèse, by Louis Desvignes, to serve the new town centre of Gratte-ciel (5) and Curé d'Ars for the Cyprian district (6). The rapidly urbanising section of town between Gratte-ciel and Cusset thus lacked any neighbourhood churches, so the ODPN built Saint François-Régis, by Jean Deveraux (7), and Notre-Dame de l'Espérance, by Pierre Genton (8), in the north, spaced rationally apart; reused the private chapel of the Cœur Immaculée (unknown architect) in the Ferrandière district as a parish church (9) and established a new one, Bonne Terre (unknown architect) (10), in the south; and also established Saint Pierre Chanel, by Charles Curtelin (11), on the eastern edge, on the far side of the new bypass road in the Brosses district, towards Bron, but this was a relatively short-lived, temporary building.
[Drawing by Mélanie Meynier-Philip, 2017]

mitted builder priest was important in terms of having someone to lead the new parish's creation, the choice of architect was also a crucial factor in such initiatives, since the parish's own visual identity depended largely upon this designer. The diocese ensured a high profile for the choices they made and the outcomes by publicising all new projects undertaken or planned in the diocese, notably through *Paroisses Nouvelles,* a supplement to the diocesan magazine *L'Essor.* In it, the diocese referred to the overall church-building initiative as "L'Opération des églises nouvelles" (the New churches venture), asking on the front page whether Lyons would "succeed in this initiative". Nevertheless, by 15 March 1961, fourteen churches or chapels had been built (albeit not yet fully financed), seventy-three were under construction (to be completed within five years), seven that were considered less urgent were to be built within ten years, and thirteen further projects were under consideration.[21] This meant a total of 107 buildings, which rose to 122 in 1967.[22]

In other words, the establishment of the ODPN ensured a rational distribution of new churches across the diocese, so that all citizens were within easy reach of Catholic-run facilities. Moreover, these new facilities were sited among much-used secular ones, so that citizens would pass by them daily, such that the Church could become the living centre of each community and not just a Sunday occurrence. To this end, the related buildings had to be visible and distinctive — not merely functional boxes — yet not triumphalist like the churches of the past, expressing instead their role as "servants" to their communities. They were also to be modern enough — in form and materials — to express to the world their relevance to post-war society. The ODPN created a framework to support parishes in their church-building projects by providing financial, technical and other professional advice not otherwise available in such working-class communities and by taking responsibility for project approval, so as to prevent parishes from undertaking overambitious or otherwise unsuitable schemes. It also allocated "godparent" parishes through a diocesan network. Overall, it seems to have functioned as a safety net wherever this was needed, rather than controlling each project in detail.

The ODPN left individual parishes the freedom to appoint their own architects and develop plans with them that best fit their own procedures; inevitably, the builder priests, especially the more forceful among them (and sometimes also the architects they chose), played a key role. Consequently, some parishes continued to build according to traditional plans, while others, who had already adopted liturgical reforms, developed radically new plans that would inspire all the churches built after Vatican II, in other words, just a few years later. Likewise, each parish's choice of architect also affected their own

---

21 Situation as of 15 March 1961: Lyons, AD, Fonds ODPN, 1L 227.
22 Ibid.; see also *L'Essor Paroisses Nouvelles, Où en sommes-nous?*, supplement to no. 1.102 (8 December 1967).

building's form, materials and techniques, so that a wide variety of buildings was produced within this single diocese. As the ODPN noted at the time (1961), "Interestingly, the quest for economy has not dictated boring uniformity — the churches each have a personality of their own."[23]

Notre-Dame de Balmont (La Duchère): A Church in a Greenfield District

One of the most significant examples of a church building programme in the Diocese of Lyons — if indeed not *the* most significant — is that of the La Duchère district, and for two interdependent reasons. First, the wider project of La Duchère, launched under the mayoralty of Louis Pradel, was intended to present this particular district as a national, or even international, showcase for Lyons.[24] It was the only major reconstruction district within the city's arrondissements. That arrondissement (the 9th) was in fact Pradel's own, and its residents had originally elected him councillor. Consequently, everything was done to ensure that this development area and the town planning and architectural projects designed for it would serve as a model. Second, the Church and the diocese, being well aware of the district's national visibility, made it an exemplar of their own intervention by appointing renowned architects.

La Duchère is situated just inside the city's north-western boundary.[25] It comprises the second largest development undertaken in greater Lyons in the wake of the Second World War, after that of Bron Parilly (itself the largest such project in all France).[26] This hilltop district was the site of one of the military forts along the front line of defence implemented by General Fleury that were developed starting in 1832. This designation enabled it to retain open green spaces, and consequently landscaping potential, through the 1950s.[27] The La Duchère site was ultimately decommissioned in 1920, making available a large expanse of land close to the city centre.[28] In 1958, the architect François-Régis Cottin (1920-2013) was commissioned to build an estate for 25,000 residents on a site covering 120 hectares, with the Société d'Équipement de la Région Lyonnaise (SERL, Development Corporation of the Lyons Region) as developer.

23   Lyons, AD, Fonds ODPN, 1L 217, Minutes of meeting on Friday, 23 June 1961.
24   Louis Pradel (1906-1976), mayor of Lyons from 1957 to 1976, was involved in the inception of the major town planning and architectural projects that are now disparaged as being inappropriate for the city, such as the Part-Dieu district, the Paris–Marseille motorway cutting through the city centre via a tunnel under Fourvière and the transport interchange at Perrache.
25   *Maurice Novarina, Un architecte dans son siècle*, CAUE de haute-Savoie, 207. <expomaurice-novarina.fr>.
26   Rey, *Lyon, Cité radieuse*, 46.
27   Meillerand, "Les terrains militaires", 2.
28   Ibid., 5.

It was to be split between social and leased housing to promote greater social diversity.[29] Cottin decided to divide the site into four districts, allowing for a mixture of scales, from large blocks down to the smallest kinds of residences: Plateau, the central district; Château to the south; Balmont in the north-east; and Sauvegarde in the north-west.[30] On 20 November 1959, the detailed town plan was accepted by a decree from the Prefect of the Département du Rhône. In urban design terms, this site plan resulted in the construction of seven slab blocks and a "panoramic" tower block. As for facilities, these districts were fully up to date, with the latest schools, shopping centres and public open spaces positioned at the foot of the blocks of flats. The housing here was of higher quality than in most other projects of this type, and the district was unique among post-war developments in terms of the considerable amount of high-quality private housing it included, notably the Panoramic Tower and the Les Érables slab block.[31] As for the social housing (HLM) provided, it too was of higher quality than that of comparable projects, in terms of both the design, which was thought through to the last detail, providing for spacious duplex flats with dual exposure and unbeatable views over an extensive landscape, and the quality of materials used.

Within this context of exemplary facilities intended to serve a wide social mix, the diocese anticipated, from as early as 1957, endowing La Duchère with churches in each of its four districts, although these would comprise a single parish, Notre-Dame de la Duchère. Sites were in fact set aside for these four churches from the very first sketches for the overall plan.[32] [Ill. 2.3] Once each site had been selected and the requisite demographic, functional and financial research undertaken, the size of that church was determined according to its district's anticipated needs, using the aforementioned ODPN formula. Thus, the church for the Plateau district (1960-1968), with 9,000 inhabitants, was to accommodate 800; that for the Château district (1961-1963), with 2,500 inhabitants, 300; that for the Balmont district (1961-1964), with 5,000 inhabitants, 500; and finally, that for the Sauvegarde district (only built later, in 1971), also with 5,000 inhabitants, 500.[33] Each of these churches was to be complemented by rooms for catechism and various meetings, but there was to be a

29 This particularly French form of leaseholding — "*en accession*" — allows the lessee to buy property after a certain period of leasing it.
30 Halitim-Dubois, "De la notion de quartier à ses représentations", 64.
31 This block, also known as Barre 250, was built between 1967 and 1972 by the architect Jean Dubuisson (1914-2011). La Duchère's architectural quality has been officially recognised with the awarding of the "Label Patrimoine du XXe siècle" to several of its buildings: Dubuisson's Les Érables; Cottin's Panoramic Tower, water tower and church of Notre-Dame du Monde Entier; and Genton's Notre-Dame de Balmont.
32 Lyons, AD, Fonds ODPN, 1L 217, "Les projets des futures paroisses", undated document (deduced by Chatelan as being 1956-1957: unpublished manuscript note).
33 Lyons, AD, Fonds ODPN, 1L 184, Églises de la Duchère, Minutes of meeting of 16 February 1961.

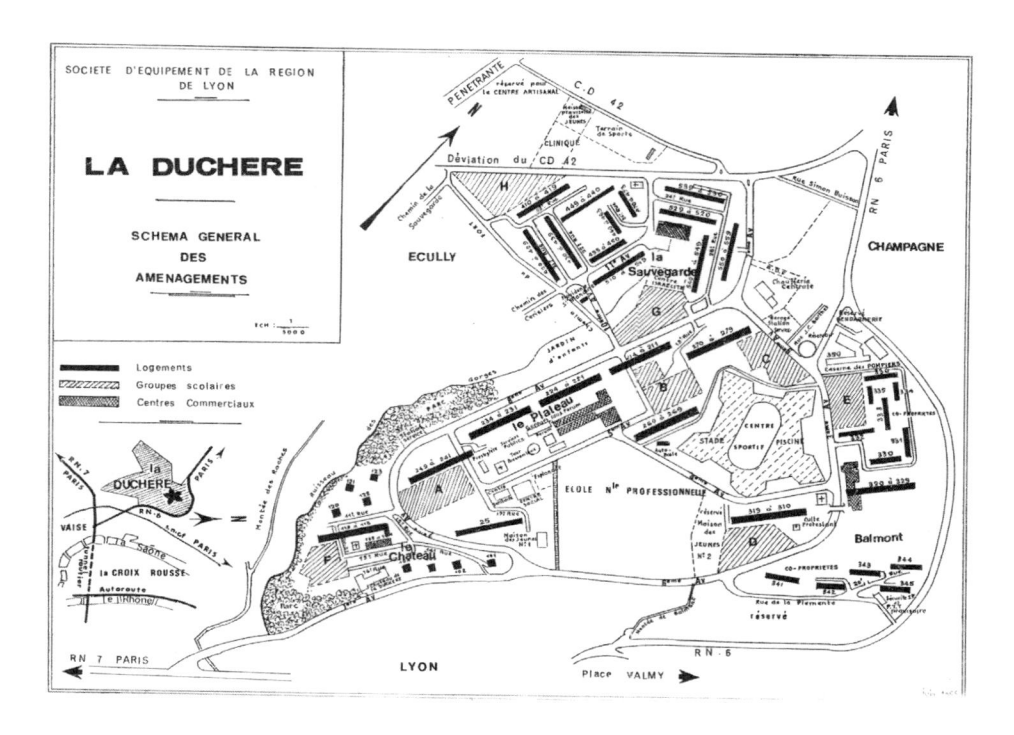

2.3 La Duchère master plan of the four districts.
[Lyons, ASAAL, Fonds François-Régis Cottin, 1-14B Q1. Courtesy of the Société Académique d'Architecture de Lyon]

single presbytery for clergy accommodation, in the Plateau district.[34] This incorporation of facilities for social activities as well as religious ones — outside Sunday services — was in response to the Church's aspiration "to be present in the world".[35] The intention was to bring the Catholic faith as close as possible to residents every day of the week, with the underlying motivation being to stave off secularisation in the surrounding areas, notably among working-class residents, many of whom were employed in the factories in Vaise, the older district at the bottom of the hill on which La Duchère stands. This was a continuation of the Church's interwar strategy, when out of concern about working-class adults turning to the Communist Party, the Church built more comprehensive parish complexes that incorporated social and sports facilities, rather than stand-alone church buildings.[36]

To comply with the ODPN's conditions, the La Duchère churches had to be built for the lowest possible cost. In providing for a total of 2100 seats

34 Ibid.
35 Capellades, *Guide des églises nouvelles en France*, 6.
36 Examples of this include the parish complexes of La Sainte Famille at Croix-Luizet (1927), Saint Antoine at Gerland (1931) and Saint-Jacques at États-Unis (1936).

across all of them, the diocesan office required them to be costed at around 1,000 francs per seat, thus a total of 2.1 million francs.[37] The use of costing by seat rather than by square metre, as was normal in the construction industry, would become a cause for dispute, notably by Genton, who claimed, "It has been proven that the greater a building's capacity, the lower its cost in relation to its size."[38] Moreover, the official cost yardstick announced in April 1963 by the Comité national de construction d'églises (National Committee for the Construction of New Churches) was in fact based on the construction industry's standard basis: "600 francs per square metre for the unfurnished building, and 800 francs per square metre fully furnished".[39] To lead this project, the diocese appointed the "formidable" abbé Louis de Galard (1906–2007), previously priest-in-charge at Saint-Pothin (1949), whose more affluent parishioners he had involved in social action.[40] He had already proved himself as the founding priest for the parish of Saint-Jacques serving Tony Garnier's États-Unis estate (1933), where he had overseen the construction of a parish centre that included social and sports facilities along with a church.[41] Furthermore, in order to guarantee that these four projects would be adequately funded, the diocesan administration also appointed a "godparent" parish for each, as was its usual practice; all of these were in relatively well-to-do districts in Lyons's then fashionable *rive gauche*, with the Rédemption in the chic district beside the Tête d'or park, for example, matched with Balmont. As part of the fund-raising campaign, a photograph of the large-scale model (2 m x 2 m) of each specific church was pinned up in the associated "godparent" church, together with essential statistics and a box for donations.[42] The planning, determined in accordance with the framework for the La Duchère project as a whole, was for "each church to open as soon as a thousand people moved into flats in that district".[43] Prior to any construction beginning, it was estimated that the groundbreaking for the Château district church would be in April 1961, followed by the Balmont church in May 1961 and the Plateau church in June 1961 and culminating with the Sauvegarde church in May 1962.[44]

37 Lyons, AD, Fonds ODPN, 1L 184, Églises de la Duchère, Minutes of meeting of 16 February 1961.
38 Lyons, APNDE, Genton to Monsieur Belland (Chair of the Association paroissiale), 21 November 1963.
39 These figures derive from the conclusions of the Comité National pour la construction des églises nouvelles, following a meeting in April 1963.
40 The French word used was "redoutable". Loach, "L'invention d'un édifice-type", 448.
41 De Galard led a community there committed to social action which included the young architect Alain Chomel (1931–2019), who would design one of the most radically modern churches in the diocese, Saint Jean Apôtre (now Notre-Dame du Liban).
42 Lyons, AD, Fonds ODPN, 1L 184, Églises de la Duchère, Minutes of meeting, 16 February 1961.
43 Ibid.
44 The anticipated consecration dates for the churches were as follows: Château, February 1962; Balmont, March 1962; Plateau, April 1962; and Sauvegarde, March 1963.

Because the churches were being integrated into the new town plan, they needed to embody the modernity of the time, so de Galard chose architects with national, or at least regional, reputations.[45] As one of Lyons's progressive clergy, he had a preference for architects who embraced liturgical reform and modern design; in this case, the ones he selected also happened to be sympathetic to Couturier and Régamey's *L'Art sacré*. Maurice Novarina (1907-2002), appointed for the first church to be built, in the Chateau district, was a Savoyard with a national reputation, notably for churches (from 1933 onwards), especially the one at Assy (1937-1950), where Couturier had persuaded a dozen of the most eminent artists of the day to contribute work.[46] Genton was allocated the second church to be built, in the Balmont district.[47] Couturier had already been promoting his work, publishing two of his student projects and other unbuilt church designs in *L'Art sacré*.[48] His appointment thus virtually assured national coverage of these first three La Duchère churches in that magazine, as well as in the professional press.[49] Cottin took on the design of the central church of the Plateau, in addition to his oversight duties for the project as a whole. He had previously built three chapels, including a parish church for the village of La Giraudière in the Monts du Lyonnais (1950-1952).[50] This became one of the most abundantly covered buildings ever in *L'Art sacré*, in part because its radically centralized plan — a square with a central altar and the congregation gathered around three sides facing the celebrant — was the earliest exemplar of wholehearted liturgical reform.[51] This initial selection of architects would indeed result in those first three parish churches obtaining greater publicity than any others in the diocese, beginning with their publication in *L'Art sacré* when two were still only in the sketch stage.[52]

45 Lyons, AD, Fonds ODPN, 1L 184, Églises de la Duchère, Minutes of meeting, 16 February 1961.
46 Including the west façade by Léger, an apse tapestry by Jean Lurçat, a crucifix by Germaine Richier, chapels by Bonnard and Matisse, a tabernacle by Braque, a baptistery by Chagall, a Madonna by Lipchitz, and stained-glass works by Rouault (the first in any church), Bazaine, Hébert-Stevens and Couturier himself.
47 Weber, "Couturier Collection at Yale University, Archival Register" (Institute of Sacred Music, Worship and the Arts, Yale University, 1994), 24; confirmed by Genton's daughter, Claire Genton, in October 2016.
48 "Un concours à l'École des Beaux-Arts", *L'Art sacré*, September-October 1951, 16-19; and two further student projects, "Une église dans les Dombes" and "La Léproserie et l'église de Djiring', *L'Art sacré*, 14, 18-26; also 'Deux projets de Pierre Genton', *L'Art sacré*, January-February 1959, 27-29.
49 "Les églises de la cité de la Duchère à Lyon", *L'Art sacré*, March-April 1961, 24-31; Behel, "L'aménagement du plateau de La Duchère à Lyon', 1, 3; "Église de Balmont à La Duchère, Lyon, France/Pierre Genton architecte", 48-50.
50 Loach, "L'invention d'un édifice-type", 412, 416-417.
51 *L'Art sacré*, September-October 1953, 26-27; *L'Art sacré*, May-June 1957, 28; *L'Art sacré*, January-February 1958, 22-25, 31.
52 "Les églises de la cité de la Duchère à Lyon", *L'Art sacré*, March-April 1961, 24-31.

Given that these first three churches were planned and designed prior to the Second Vatican Council, they were all radically original, eschewing traditional plans and forms — basilican or cruciform — and built exploiting the latest materials and construction techniques, so as to provide the Catholic Church with a modern image in keeping with the new developments in society. From the street, they each presented an innovative structure that contrasted strikingly with all the earlier churches in the agglomeration; they were all quite low-rise and lacked any bell towers or steeples. Novarina's initial design had in fact included a bell tower, as in several of his earlier churches, but this was struck out on his drawings.[53] Significantly, in 1961, the ODPN would actually require architects to obtain special permission for any bell tower, preferring them instead to exploit the building's "character" or find some more "modest" sign to express the building's function, citing not only economic, but also "theological" reasons in support.[54] In a 1959 issue of *L'Art sacré* on "The Church in the City", editor Capellades had enunciated these theological reasons for such a radical departure from custom: whereas in earlier ages churches had stood out by adopting vertical forms so as to tower above the urban fabric, within the context of new high-rise neighbourhoods, the Church could attain comparable contrast by adopting low-rise, horizontal forms, "a horizontal monumentality which is no less noble than the vertical sort".[55] Moreover, these would better express the Church's essence, freeing it from the wealth and power symbolised by the larger scale of the surrounding buildings and embodying humility instead. As Capellades wrote:

> God does not reveal himself to us as an imperious God but as a servant God, a poor and vulnerable God who comes to indicate the only way capable of freeing us from all the things that stand in our way and that suffocate us. The image offered by churches today should be that of Christ Himself: poor, welcoming, open to all, radiating love, leaving the flock to run after the lost sheep.[56]

At La Duchère, each of the first three churches responded to this dictate in different ways. Genton's Balmont church adopted an organic form, its ancillary rooms housed in a series of cylinders clustered around the liturgical space, and all at ground level, indeed partly buried in turf-covered banks.[57] [Ill. 2.4]

53   The most famous example of his bell tower use was his first church, Notre-Dame de Léman, Vongy (1933-1935), though Notre-Dame de toute Grace at Assy (1937-1946) and Notre-Dame at Audincourt (1949-1951) also contained them and each was the subject of a special issue of *L'Art sacré* (the latter: *L'Art sacré*, no. 3-4, November-December 1951). On the drawing, see Lyons, AD, Fonds ODPN, 1L 180, project dated November 1960.
54   Chatelan, *Les catholiques et la croissance urbaine*, 281.
55   *L'église dans la cité*, special issue of *L'Art sacré*, 1959, 5-6, 11.
56   Ibid.
57   Loach, "L'invention d'un édifice-type", 503-504. It is worth noting that construction of the fourth church was delayed (Ibid., 506, footnote 95).

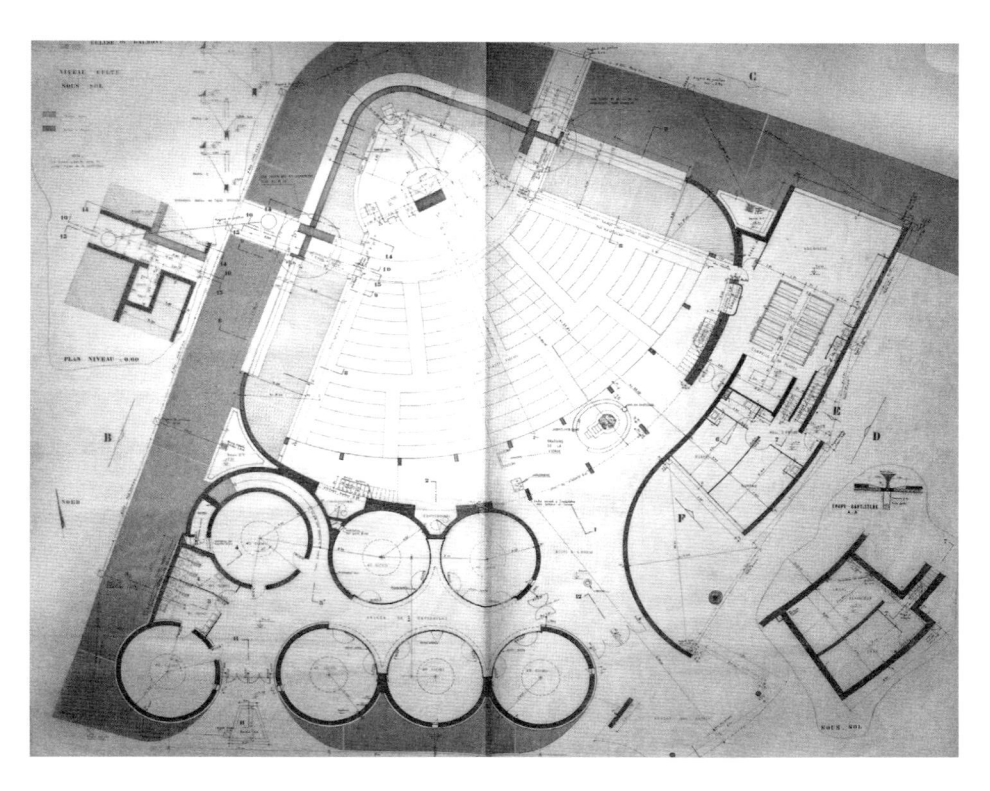

2.4 Ground floor plan of Pierre Genton's Notre-Dame de Balmont, Lyons.
[Courtesy of the Société Académique d'Architecture de Lyon]

As Genton later wrote, he designed a church which is born of the earth, which sprouts from and flourishes there, so that one can find in it the freshness, spontaneity and joy from which our life should be made.[58]

On entering each building, it was apparent that these radically innovative forms were far from arbitrary, being instead rational responses to a new function, that of the reformed liturgy. Each is compact, deriving from a centralised plan focusing on the altar in the opposite corner, facilitating optimum sight lines and hearing of the Mass and gathering the faithful together. In all three cases, the altar stood forward from the east wall, so that the priest could celebrate facing the faithful; a separate ambo within the sanctuary underlined a new emphasis on the Word; and a baptistery was sited by the entrance, dramatising the idea of baptism as a rite of entering the community.[59] Genton's fan-shaped liturgical space directed attention towards the altar at its

58 *La Duchère, Lyon*, 13; reprinted in "Église de Balmont à La Duchère, Lyon, France: Pierre Genton architecte", *L'Architecture d'Aujourd'hui*, 125 (1966), 48.
59 "La situation du baptistère", *L'Art sacré*, issue on "L'architecture et le geste rituel", 5-6 January-February 1963, 8-19.

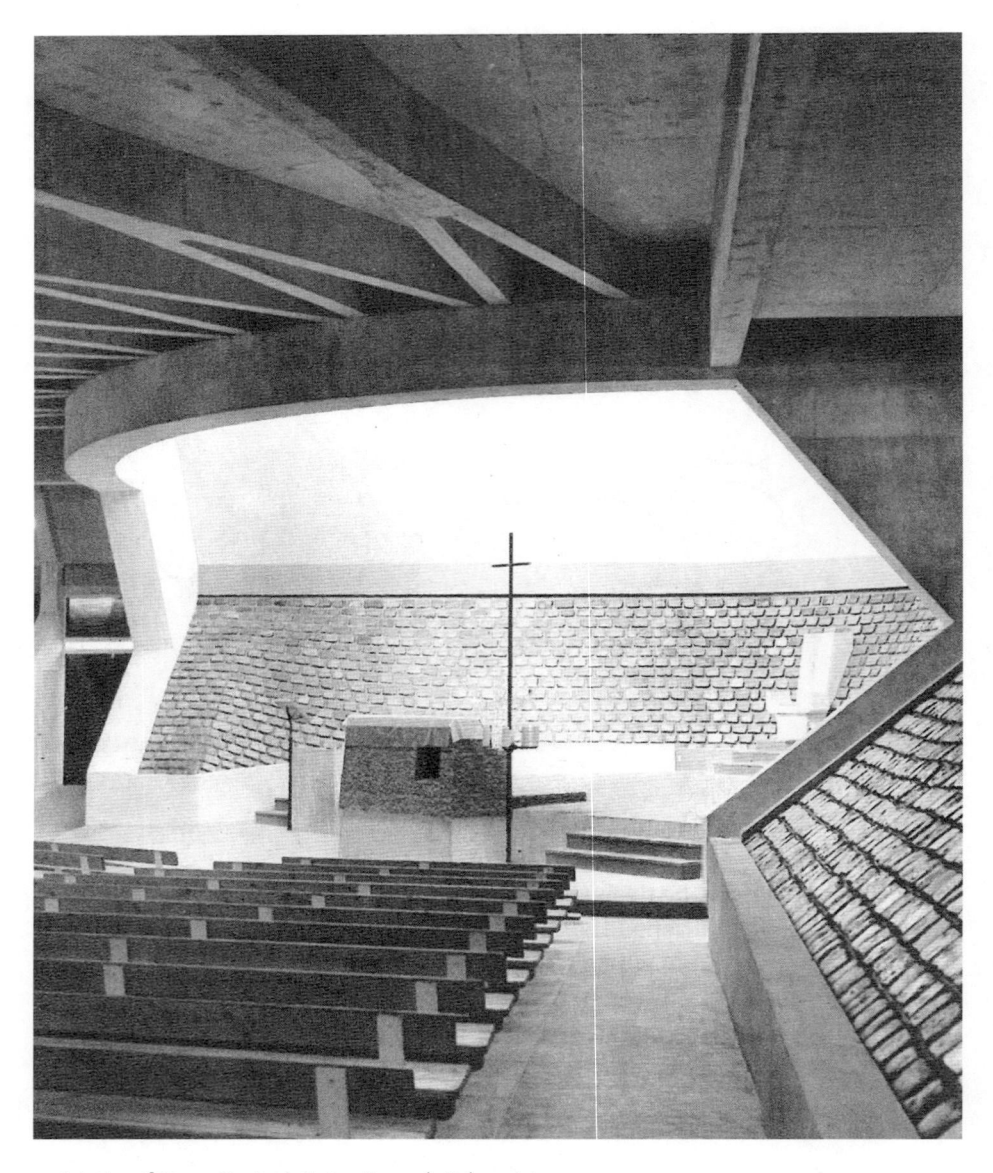

2.5 Interior of Pierre Genton's Notre-Dame de Balmont, Lyons.
[Reproduced from *La Duchère, Lyon*]

2.6 Long shot of exterior of Pierre Genton's Notre-Dame de Balmont, Lyons. [Reproduced from *La Duchère, Lyon*]

apex, opposite the entrance; this space was cave-like, with cobble-encrusted walls and daylight only entering through the sail-shaped claustra above the east end that directed light onto the sanctuary. The baptistery stood in a space of its own at the entrance and at a lower level, so as not to interrupt the main space, its font likewise of concrete cast-in-place and pebble-encrusted. All of the furnishings – including altar, ambo and font — were unquestionably modern, designed by the architect and made of the same materials as the building's interior, thus ensuring harmony. [Ill. 2.5]

The materials and techniques exploited to construct these free-form churches further demonstrated their modernity, thus connecting them with the surrounding new buildings, while their forms made them stand out. Although they all predominantly used poured-in-place concrete (like most postwar construction in France), Novarina's and Cottin's also incorporated cutting edge techniques in other materials. Novarina used a (concealed) spaceframe roof structure in metal and Cottin a glulam one, in the latter case also introducing walls where glazing slotted directly into precast concrete units, while doors pioneered structural glass. Despite the variety of modern structural systems exploited in the churches, these were used in all three cases to realise a common goal: the creation of spaces uninterrupted by structural elements that allowed the congregation to be gathered together and optimised each individual's connection with the sanctuary. The modernity of all three churches, and thereby that of the Catholic Church, was reinforced by the works of art commissioned for them; moreover, thanks in part to the exploitation of modern structural systems, most of these works were visible from the outside. The exterior of Genton's church is dominated by its claustra, for example, which is nothing less than a major abstract sculpture in untreated wood, *Signal*, by the eminent artist Etienne Martin. [Ill. 2.6]

Genton's Balmont church would be hailed in the religious and architectural press alike as among the very best built in post-war France.[60] As the comparison to his Villeurbanne church — designed to the same ODPN requirements — will show, his achievement in La Duchère was facilitated by its greenfield site: a freely chosen parcel within the district that presented a blank canvas and lacked the constraints of existing surrounding neighbourhoods, allowing for full expression of the master planner's expectations for modern design. Moreover, since the congregation was only just coming into being, he dealt mainly with a single, decisive priest, rather than with a group of parishioners not always of the same mind, not to mention neighbouring residents, as in a pre-existing urban district.

Notre-Dame de l'Espérance, in Villeurbanne, an Existing Urban District

The church of Notre-Dame de l'Espérance presents an illuminating example of the ODPN's planning principles applied within an already built-up urban district. Villeurbanne, a working-class town in its own right that abuts the eastern edge of Lyons, had experienced a period of significant expansion after the Second World War. In contrast to the church building planned for the greenfield sites in La Duchère — and indeed other new districts — this church had to be designed within the context of a pre-existing urban fabric, which at the time was a mix of factories, workshops, working-class housing and small shops, with some unbuilt plots, such as allotments, nestled in between. In 1956, a new parish was created in the Château Gaillard district, between two existing parishes: Sainte Famille at Croix-Luizet and Sainte-Madeleine-des-Charpennes. This district was not far from Villeurbanne's new town centre, Gratte-ciel, so called because its social housing — an avenue of eleven-storey blocks of flats — comprised the first skyscrapers in France (1928-1934).[61] The site for the new church was thus within walking distance of the council-built facilities there

60 "Missions et paroisses I", *Cahiers de l'Art sacré*, 7-8, March-April 1961; "Église de Balmont à La Duchère, Lyon, France: Pierre Genton architecte"; Behel, "L'aménagement du plateau de La Duchère à Lyon: Ligne basse, clocher coque, béton coloré pour L'église de Balmont".
61 Clémençon, *Les gratte-ciel de Villeurbanne*; Goujon, *Villeurbanne 1924-1934: dix ans d'administration*.

— notably, the Hôtel de Ville and Palais du Travail (containing a health centre, *salle de fêtes* and swimming pool) — as well as a school, Anatole France (opened in 1933), and was even closer to the town's sports stadium (opened in 1934).[62] The church's site thus fulfilled the ODPN's requirements of not only serving a required volume of the population, but also being close to facilities that local residents would use every day.

The local residents had first erected a chapel on a former allotment site acquired in the 1930s by the L'Œuvre du Christ dans la banlieue association. Over time, the parish became the heart of local community life; in addition to church services and catechism, it offered football, summer camps, fêtes, films and more. An ever-expanding congregation precipitated a lack of space, especially inside the chapel during large-scale celebrations. At Christmas, for example, the midnight Mass had to be moved into the nearby Imperial Cinema, and when the space used for catechism classes became too cramped, it was supplemented by converting disused railway carriages. In early 1961, Father Paul Devers (1926-2021) publicised this critical situation in an article in the first issue of the ODPN's magazine, *Paroisses Nouvelles*, backing up his argument with dramatic photos.[63]

In fact, the first sketch designs for the permanent building date from 1956, so it was actually one of the first church-building projects undertaken in the diocese after the war; yet, it would prove to be one of the slowest and was not consecrated until 1966.[64] The project's realisation was delayed by problems directly related to its urban context, as well as a lack of sufficient funding, probably due in part to the district's lesser profile. Genton's earliest surviving designs date from November 1956, even though his practice would only be officially selected in December 1958, seemingly after consideration of several other practices and after the initial "builder priest", Father Ploton, had moved on.[65] Genton's first design distributed a series of buildings across the site: the highly visible church along the street front; the presbytery and parish rooms behind it, along the site's opposite side; and another building (a crèche with club underneath) in the north-west corner. His revised design of only a few months later (February 1957) gathered all these facilities into a single building in the centre of the site, seemingly for reasons of economy.[66] His subsequent designs moved back and forth between a single building and

---

62 <http://lerizeplus.villeurbanne.fr/arkotheque/client/am_lerize/encyclopedie/fiche.php?ref=59> (accessed 15/03/2018).
63 *Si l'espérance m'était contée 1956-2006*, 16; see also Lyons, APNDE, letter dated 25 February 1961 from Monseigneur Mazioux to Paul Devers, evoking that article.
64 Lyons, ASAAL, Fonds Genton, 53.B-34.
65 Ibid., "Plan masse", dated 7 November 1956; Lyons, APNDE.
66 Lyons, ASAAL, Fonds Genton, 53.B-34, Plan dated 18 February 1957 (elevation and section for this scheme added on 21 February 1957).

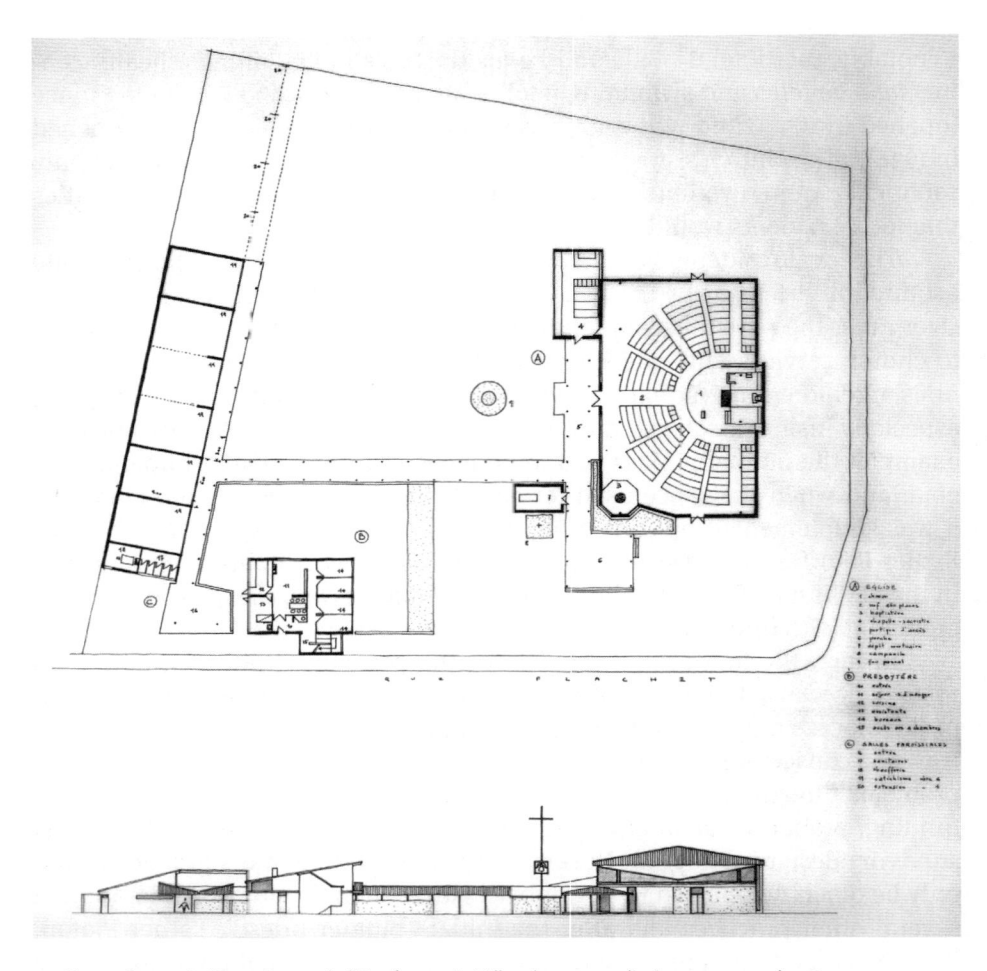

2.7 Pierre Genton's Notre Dame de l'Espérance in Villeurbanne, preliminary proposal, 1961.
[Courtesy of the Société Académique d'Architecture de Lyon]

a series of separate buildings.[67] His design of November 1961, in which the presbytery and parish rooms occupy separate buildings from the church proper, seems to have been the preferred option of both the ODPN and the parish, but residents in the adjacent block of twenty flats objected to any buildings along that edge of the site.[68] [Ill. 2.7] Therefore, in July 1962, faced with the difficulty of obtaining a building permit for this scheme, the project was redesigned, consolidating the church with all other facilities into a single, compact building at the centre of the site, so as to be as far as possible from the neighbours' existing buildings on two sides of the site; consequently, it now

67 Ibid., Plans dated September 1960 and May 1961.
68 Ibid., "Avant-projet" dated November 1961.

became a two-storey building, with the church proper above the ancillary facilities.[69] The working up of the final plans, in 1963, then progressed through a long process of deliberation on the part of the parish association and the various ODPN commissions, resulting in no fewer than eight rejected drafts.[70] The planning application was finally submitted to the *Mairie* on 14 June 1963, but the permit was only granted six months later (suggesting further objections from neighbours).[71] Construction finally broke ground in January 1964. The existing urban context and lack of a forceful "builder priest" worked together to delay the building's realisation; they also arguably enabled parishioners greater opportunity for intervention, which in turn further slowed down the process. The series of compromises all this entailed may well explain the church's more banal exterior.

Furthermore, Notre-Dame de l'Espérance seems to have suffered particular difficulties in raising the financing required. An appeal had been launched among the parishioners in 1957 for the building project, but no architect was formally appointed until late 1958, thus depriving the initial fund-raising effort of focus. As usual, the ODPN had designated "godparent" parishes as soon as the new parish's association was founded (in early 1961): Sainte-Thérèse in Villeurbanne, Saint-Genis-Laval and fourteen rural parishes around Saint Symphorien de Lay.[72] On the one hand, its "godparent" parishes were less affluent than those allocated to the La Duchére churches, and even if they had organised fund-raising for the new church, they lacked the kinds of personal connections that a powerful individual such as de Galard at La Duchère had, who still wielded influence in his old parish of Saint Pothin, which was also one of his own "godparents". On the other hand, Father Devers (the priest from 1958) refused any help offered by businessmen, notably by the industrialist Paul Berliet (1918-2012), who was digging the foundations to Genton's church at Mermoz for free, on the grounds that this was at the expense of Berliet's workers being paid properly.[73] Nevertheless, imaginative means of fund-raising included the ODPN's sale of corkscrews in the form of a modern church and the parish's organisation of fêtes (*kermesses*) with magicians, slapstick comedies and a concert in the Palais de Travail's auditorium, for which "the young troubadour" Jacques Brel offered his services.[74]

69 Ibid., Plan dated 1 October 1962.
70 Lyons, APNDE, Article 11 added by the architect in the contract signed with the ODPN, 21 January 1963.
71 Villeurbanne, Le Rize, AM, File 539-63.
72 The parishes of Saint Symphorien en Lay, Chirassimont, Cordelles, Croizet, Fourneaux, Machezal, Neaux, Neulise, Pradines, Régny, Saint-Cyr de Favières, Vendranges-Saint-Priest and Saint-Just la Pendue; cf. Lyons, APNDE.
73 Lyons, ASAAL, Fonds Genton, 53.B-P, Letter of 18 December 1963 from Paul Devers to Pierre Genton.
74 "Notre Église", *L'Essor*, 19 February 1961; Lyons, APNDE, Cahier d'annonces paroissiales de Notre-Dame de l'Espérance, no. 1 (1955/1958).

2.8 Exterior of Pierre Genton's Notre-Dame de l'Espérance, contemporary photograph. [Courtesy of Paul Devers]

From his very first sketch designs onwards, Genton thus suffered from drastic financial constraints. Fund-raising proved so difficult that in 1962, it was decided to divide the site in two and sell one half of it to fund the project.[75] While this sale helped considerably in enabling the construction of the parish complex, it also drastically reduced the buildable area, forcing a significant redesign. In the contracts executed between Genton and the Church, the ODPN set the construction budget at 1,100 francs per seat, limiting the budget for this church (to hold 525 people) to 577,500 francs.[76] Genton warned

75   2511 m² was sold, leaving 2788 m² for the parish. Letter of 2 February 1962 from E. Garnier (ODPN) to the president of the parish association, M. Belland (in which he mentions a letter of 30 January 1962 from M. Galland about the sale of the parcel; Lyons, APNDE); plan by Pierre Genton, April 1962 (Lyons, ASAAL, Fonds Genton, 53.B-Y5.4).
76   Contracts between Genton and the parish (21 January 1963) and between the parish and ODPN (24 April 1964). Such two-part arrangements were standard practice for such projects.

repeatedly that with a budget that low, it would not be possible to fulfil the brief as set. After reconsidering the costs and adopting the customary costing yardstick instead, a budget of around 700,000 francs was agreed to. In a letter to the parish association, Genton defended this higher budget, comparing the cost per square metre with that of four other churches he had already built. He claimed that the costs for those churches were "considered to be the lowest of all" for churches already built in France.[77]

As built, Notre-Dame de l'Espérance was contained within a single, two-storey building, with the church proper above all ancillary facilities. [Ill. 2.8] From outside it appeared undistinguished: a plain cuboid, its ground floor walls rendered and its first-floor ones hung with fibre-cement shingles, thus demarking the liturgical space. It did, however, thus blend into the locality, which was predominantly filled with factories, workshops and working-class housing, thereby demonstrating its intention to fulfil a "servant" role there, rather than a traditionally "triumphalist" one. While the ground floor was daylit by windows, the only wall glazing at upper level was in the north-west corner, hidden from view of the street, so that the upper walls were almost opaque; narrow, pivoting wooden shutters (no doubt inspired by those recently installed by Le Corbusier at La Tourette) stretched from floor-to-ceiling at each corner to provide ventilation.[78] An external ramp signalled the way towards the main entrance, leading up to a large porch covered by a timber roof, itself capable of sheltering parishioners before or after Mass and effectively serving as a narthex. This space also acted as a transition between the world outside and the liturgical space within; in fact, originally, the entire ramp was intended to be roofed over, so that the entrance to the church would be a passage from dark into light, but this roofing was dropped at a later stage due to a lack of funds (even after the building permit had been granted).[79]

From there, one entered the church at a corner, discovering that the internal plan was square, arranged on a diagonal, with the sanctuary in the oppo-

77   Lyons, APNDE, Genton to Monsieur Belland, 21 November 1963. This showed the cost per square metre of this church to be average: 500 francs per seat for 525 seats at Notre-Dame de l'Espérance, 410 francs per seat for 1,000 seats at his Sainte Trinité (in the Mermoz district of Lyons), 546 francs per seat for 550 seats at his Balmont church at La Duchère, 547 francs per seat for 450 seats at his Notre Dame de Lourdes at Bron and 653 francs per seat for 450 seats at his Immaculée Conception at Grand-Croix (near St Etienne). These figures derive from the analyses of the Comité National pour la construction des églises nouvelles, following its meeting in April 1963, at which the characteristics of some fifty newly built churches were compared. Ibid.
78   Lyons, ASAAL, Fonds Genton, 53.B-Y5.23, Detailed drawing of joinery by Pierre Genton, May 1963. Originally these "ventilators" were to have been narrow glass windows; these were replaced by shutters in a cost-cutting exercise.
79   Lyons, ASAAL, Fonds Genton, 53.B-Y5.27, Ramp design in the file submitted by the architect, Pierre Genton, to obtain the building permit for Notre-Dame de l'Espérance, May 1963; cf. Genton's modified ramp design at the outset of construction of Notre Dame de l'Espérance, January 1964 (Lyons, ASAAL, Fonds Genton, 53.B-Y5.29).

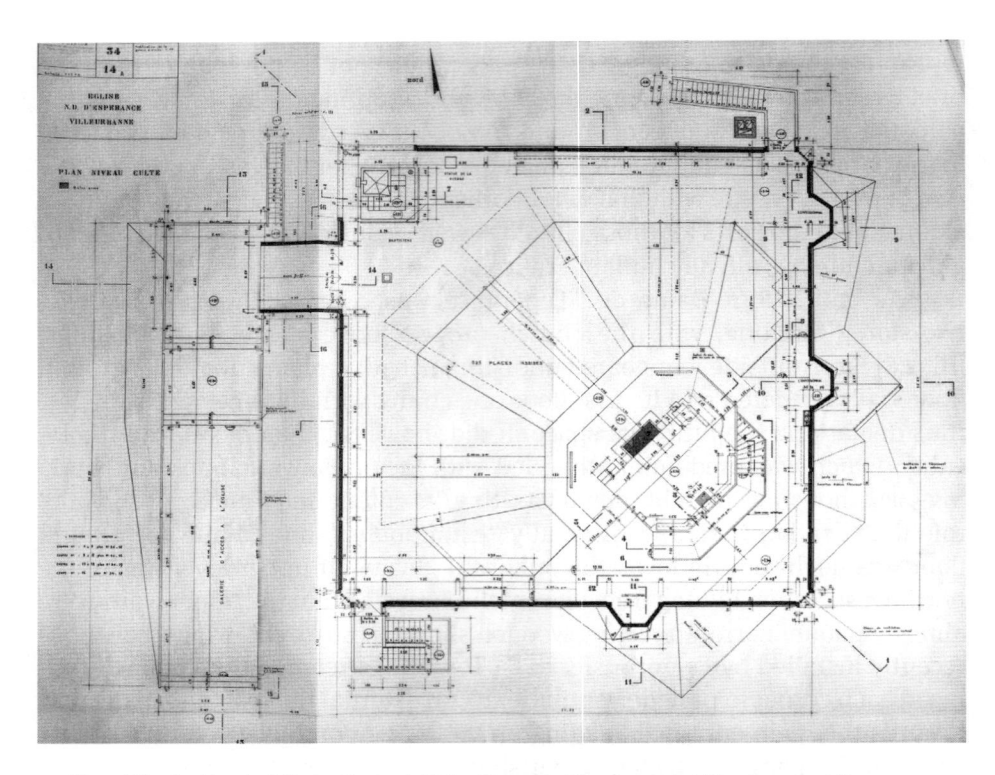

2.9 Plan of the first level of Pierre Genton's Notre Dame de l'Espérance in Villeurbanne, 1963. [Courtesy of the Société Académique d'Architecture de Lyon]

site corner; this enabled the seating to fan out around the sanctuary, gathering the congregation around it and focusing on the altar. Despite the many changes of design, Genton had always created a centralised space for liturgical use, his first two designs being for a circular building, which was replaced in all subsequent designs by a square plan.[80] [Ill. 2.9] However, he only introduced the diagonal axis in July 1962, having previously placed the sanctuary across a wall opposite the entrance, which itself often stretched along most of one side.[81] The sanctuary was emphasised by being slightly raised (on a low platform) and by having the floor slope down to it from the entrance; moreover, the principal source of daylight was through pyramidal rooflights, with the central one higher than the rest and directly above the sanctuary, so that natural light was used to create an atmosphere supportive of devotion. The secondary source of daylight was from a stained-glass window beside the entrance, which drew attention to the baptistery there, as the other main sacramental site. The internal space offered unimpeded views of the sanctuary from all

80   Lyons, ASAAL, Fonds Genton, 53.B-34, Plan dated September 1960 and 'Avant projet' dated November 1961.
81   Ibid., Plan dated July 1962.

2.10 Interior of Pierre Genton's Notre-Dame de l'Espérance, Villeurbanne.
[Photograph by Mélanie Meynier-Philip, 2016]

seats and drew the congregation together in an undivided way, because it was entirely free of any intermediary pillars; instead, the roof consisted of a space frame supported on metal pillars within the solid walls — a technical solution adopted from industrial buildings and never before exploited in such an overt manner in any church in the diocese. (In Novarina's church at La Duchère, it is hidden by a coffered ceiling in wood.) The two storeys are treated differently, indicating their different functions, with the ground floor constructed of load-bearing walls in poured concrete, whereas the upper storey walls are blockwork infill between load-bearing pillars.

Despite its tight budget, but perhaps aided by its long development, this church provided a sense of harmony and resolution, as the architecture and furnishings were all carefully considered down to the last detail, creating a coherent whole permeated with signification. The altar was carefully designed as a monolithic stone block, then implanted into the sanctuary platform so as to appear not as an independent piece of furniture, but rather as a foundation stone rooted in the ground, yet simultaneously rising up above the congregation's heads, pointing towards heaven; this sense of emerging from the ground was emphasised by the insertion of glazing into the floor around the altar, separating it from the level of the liturgical space and making it appear to be set in the ground a storey below (while also letting daylight into the sacristy below). The benches of timber slabs on concrete supports were equally complementary, being sufficiently simple not to distract from the harmony of the whole. [Ill. 2.10] Nevertheless, it is the baptistery that stands out as a unique embodiment of contemporary theological ideas about the Church's sacrament of initiation. First, it combined a pool at ground level, evoking adult baptism, together with a font at higher level, following conventional Catholic practice. Second, and most inventively, the font was filled with "celestial" water, being supplied with rainwater from the flat roof above that was conveyed indoors through metal pipes.

The first Mass was finally celebrated in the church on 11 April 1965. On discovering the interior, the parishioners' reactions included, "How well you can see here." One parishioner, catching first sight of the space frame supporting the roof, even exclaimed, "It will be fine when they take the scaffolding down!"[82] Although this church's baptistery was more innovative than any other, including Notre-Dame de Balmont's, little was published about this building. This was probably due to its later completion following so many design changes, which had been largely imposed by the site's existing neighbours. Moreover, it lay outside any highly mediatised district, such as La Duchère, lacked a priest as keen for publicity as de Galard and simply blended into its working-class district to such an extent that is was hardly noticeable.

Conclusion

In March 2000, the Association diocésaine's Conseil d'administration (Diocesan Association Executive Board) disbanded the ODPN, by which point it had made a considerable impact upon the region (the Rhône and Loire *départements*), an impact still felt today. It provided an important, innovative structure for facilitating church-building projects, in which clergy and architects worked together, exploiting strategies derived from a rational analysis of the existing situation to create buildings that supported liturgical, and thus spiritual, renewal within the Catholic Church. Because much of the Diocese of Lyons was in the vanguard of liturgical reform, and these parishes selected architects committed to modernising liturgy and architecture together, buildings with radically new plans and forms were accepted by parishes — such as the two by Genton discussed above. In the wake of Vatican II, these would prove more suitable for parish use than most earlier buildings, so that they established precedents largely adopted by churches subsequently erected in

---

[82] Commemorative booklet for the parish's fiftieth anniversary, *Si l'espérance m'était contée 1956-2006*, 19-20.

the diocese. The freedom that the ODPN left to parishes, not least in their selection of architect and design — at once following and producing an ongoing stream of modern sacred art — resulted in a variety of buildings that were often of high architectural quality, as witnessed by the official award of modern heritage status to several of them, including Genton's Balmont church. It is difficult now, virtually two generations later, to know how the ODPN's buildings were originally received, but parish archives and conversations with parishioners across Lyons suggest that initial shock soon gave way to pride, at least in part due to the strong sense of identity that their iconic forms helped engender.

Technical problems did arise, however, as with most buildings of that period, due to their somewhat experimental construction, and also the unimaginable rise in fuel costs (which led to subsequent buildings being better insulated). Nevertheless, the more serious consequences have come from demographic changes in the districts where these post-war churches were erected and where populations have evolved in ways that could not have been anticipated. While increasing secularisation across France led to a decline in congregations, this trend was accentuated from the mid-1960s onwards in working-class districts due to immigration from newly independent ex-colonies, largely comprising Muslims. Consequently, fewer churches were needed, and soon two of the four churches at La Duchère were sold or leased out, the second being Genton's Balmont church, which as early as 1993, became a centre for popularising science and then a cinema; the future of the third church there (Cottin's) has been in question.[83] At Villeurbanne, Genton's church was only closed in 2013; as yet, it is the only one of the four existing churches to be closed within that (now enlarged) parish. Perhaps its greater longevity is due in part to it having been intended to complement pre-existing secular facilities, rather than being the sole provider of them, as was usually the case for churches built on greenfield sites, where the secular social facilities were only built sometime after the housing and schools. Thus, in greenfield developments such as La Duchère, new church centres tended to supply the only social facilities around, thereby attracting all residents, not just congregation members, and in turn drawing non-Catholics into the church, a role that dissipated once the secular facilities were completed.

In the twenty-first century, the further decline in not only congregations (and therefore available finances) but also clergy has led to the amalgamation of parishes and, in turn, to the closure of churches, notably these post-war ones whose centrality within the districts they serve has rendered them

---

83   The first church to be closed was Novarina's, in 1978. It was bought by the Ville de Lyon in 1980 and converted into a Maison de l'enfance (centre for small children). Lyons, AM, 429 WP 66, convention and plans; 2069 WP 14, building permit; 2 PH 57, inauguration. Also Lyons, AD, Fonds ODPN, 1L 180.

highly attractive sites for developers. In 2018, following a massive increase in residential accommodation in Villeurbanne and consequent lack of school accommodation, Genton's church there was demolished for replacement by a school (Catholic, but therefore fee-paying).[84] Nevertheless, in general, more church buildings have been adapted to new uses than have been demolished. It is worth noting that in France, the 1905 act of separation of church and state handed ownership, and therefore financial responsibility for repair and maintenance, of all church buildings then existing to the state, whereas for later buildings, this falls to the dioceses. This makes it financially preferable for the Church to hold on to older buildings, despite the fact that these are less suitable for contemporary worship and often less well situated for congregations compared to the newer ones.

Ironically, these post-war churches' appropriateness in response to their initial brief has rendered them more vulnerable to closure and subsequent disposal than older church buildings, as they are more adaptable to new purposes. Their open plan, uninterrupted by structural supports (to optimise participation by all those present in the Mass) and eschewing traditional symbolism and form (to replace a triumphalist image with that of a "servant" church) have proved crucial here.[85] At Bron, for instance, one church was converted into a fencing club in 1997, while at least one other was leased to a Muslim congregation as early as 1979.[86]

Understandably, changes in society can require the Church, as part of it, to change, in turn forcing a reconsideration of what built form is appropriate to serve its current needs. Indeed, this had already been realised around the time of these churches' construction, with Cardinal Giacomo Lercaro (1891-1976), one of the greatest advocates at the time for introducing modern art and architecture into the Catholic Church, saying:

> We are not claiming to build churches to last through the centuries to come, but are limiting ourselves to making modest, functional churches that will serve us and which our children will feel free to rethink anew, and where necessary to abandon, or to modify as appropriate in their time and according to their religious sensibility.[87]

However, the ODPN's very success led to a problem it failed to anticipate, namely that these buildings' integration into their local communities risked engendering their disappearance, or even their radical change — a phenome-

---

84 This was despite campaigns by the parishioners and heritage organisations (including at international level) and even a certain degree of municipal support, to save this building: Meynier-Philip, "La communauté patrimoniale et les spécialistes", 79-86.
85 Meynier-Philip, "20th-century churches, a manifest of architectural flexibility".
86 Deliberation of the municipal council, April 1999 (Lyons, AM); Chalabi, "Les églises paroissiales construites dans la seconde moitié du XXe siècle et leur devenir", 24.
87 Capellades, *Guide des églises nouvelles en France*, 29.

non that can be quite traumatic for individuals. On the one hand, the ODPN's fund-raising mechanisms — engaging local parishioners (alongside wealthier "godparent" parishes) — helped create a strong sense of community within new or rapidly expanding congregations, which was further reinforced through the social activities on offer in the parish facilities. As the diocese's decisions concerning closures are imposed upon congregations, which still include some parishioners who may have sacrificially contributed towards a church's original construction, these induce resentment between parish and diocese. This will, however, become less significant as time passes and the composition of each congregation changes.

On the other hand, these modern monuments play a crucial, and under-appreciated, role for the community at large. Individuals living or working in rapidly changing districts — such as both the post-war estates now being redeveloped, like La Duchère, and the previously industrialised, now gentrifying districts, like Villeurbanne, where developers are massively replacing factories, workshops and small-scale working-class housing by blocks of middle-class flats— need landmarks such as these churches in these increasingly bland townscapes, in order to be able to identify with their locality and thus integrate with their neighbours. As such, these buildings play a crucial role in enabling ever-more-diverse populations to cohere, even when they undergo changes to their original use. Their potential for community development is enhanced by their material presence, which provides evidence — albeit fragmentary — to support the community's shared memory.

Reuse may sometimes be the best option available for such buildings and is invariably preferable to their demolition. Nevertheless, the conversion of these buildings has often been insensitive, even to the extent of obliterating their most fundamental architectural qualities. The conversion of Notre-Dame de Balmont into a cinema entailed not only the loss of an ensemble of integral, architect-designed fixtures and fittings, but moreover the obliteration of the zenithal daylighting. In any case, such conversions do not guarantee long term retention of these buildings, so essential for community identity; at La Duchère, the current construction of a new children's centre to replace that in the building Novarina designed as a church, and the forthcoming end of lease on the Genton-designed Ciné Duchère leaves both those buildings at risk. Most church buildings, even if of far lesser architectural value, usually include features and details worth preserving, not least within the context of community identity. As Luc Noppen, the respected specialist of religious heritage, noted: "The accord that their architecture effected with the functional requirements of their own specific time has today enabled their conversion but at the cost of heritage amnesia."[88]

---

88   Noppen, "La conversion des églises au Québec, Enjeux et défis", 287-289.

BIBLIOGRAPHY

Archives

Lyons, Archives diocésaines (AD), Fonds ODPN, 1L

Lyons, Archives municipales (AM), files 429 WP 66; 2069 WP; 2 PH 57

Lyons, Archives Paroissiales Notre-Dame de l'Espérance (APNDE)

Lyons, Archives de la Société Académique d'Architecture de Lyon (ASAAL), Fonds Pierre Genton, files 53.B Y3 and Y.5

Villeurbanne, Le Rize, Archives municipales (AM), files 539-63

Published sources

(Cahiers de) L'Art sacré, 1946-1963.
La Maison-Dieu, 1945-1952, 1984.

Allioud, Marius and Désigaux, Jacques. *Un fondateur d'action sociale, Antoine Chevrier*. Paris: Bayard, 1992.

Behel, Pierre. "L'aménagement du plateau de La Duchère à Lyon: Ligne basse, clocher coque, béton coloré pour L'église de Balmont". *Le Journal du bâtiment et des travaux publics*, 16 (May 1963), 1 & 3.

Blanchet, Christine and Vérot, Pierre. *Architecture et Arts Sacrés de 1945 à nos jours*. Paris: Archibooks, 2015.

Capellades, Jean. *Guide des églises nouvelles en France*. Paris: Le Cerf, 1969.

Caussé, Françoise. "La critique architecturale dans la revue *L'Art Sacré* (1937-1968)". *Livraison de l'histoire de l'architecture*, Vol. 2, n°1 (2001), 27-36.

Chalabi, Maryannick. "Les églises paroissiales construites dans la seconde moitié du XXème siècle et leur devenir: l'exemple de Lyon". *In Situ, revue des patrimoines* (2009): <http://insitu.revues.org/5887>.

Charvet, Étienne-Léon-Gabriel. *Lyon artistique, Architectes, Notices biographiques et bibliographiques avec tables des édifices et la liste chronologique des noms*. Lyons: Bernoux & Cumins, 1889.

Chatelan, Olivier. *Les catholiques et la croissance urbaine dans l'agglomération lyonnaise pendant les Trente Glorieuses (1945-1975)*. Unpublished doctoral thesis in history, Université Lumière Lyon 2. Lyons, 2009.

Chatelan, Olivier. *L'Église et la ville, Le diocèse de Lyon à l'épreuve de l'urbanisation (1954-1975)*. Paris: L'Harmattan, 2012.

Clémençon, Ann-Sophie, ed. *Les gratte-ciel de Villeurbanne*. Besançon, 2004.

Debié, Franck and Vérot, Pierre. *Urbanisme et art sacré: une aventure du XXe siècle*. Paris: Critérion, 1991.

La Duchère, Lyon. Lyons: Lescuyer, c 1965-1967.

Duployé, Pie, O.P. *Les origines du Centre de Pastorale Liturgique, 1943-9*. Mulhouse: Salvator, 1968.

"Église de Balmont à La Duchère, Lyon, France: Pierre Genton architecte". *L'Architecture d'Aujourd'hui*, 125 (April-May 1966), 48-50.

Goujon, Lazare. *Villeurbanne 1924-1934: dix ans d'administration*. Lyons: Ass. typograph., 1934.

Halitim-Dubois, Nadine. "De la notion de quartier à ses représentations: l'exemple de La Duchère". *Bulletin du Centre Pierre Léon d'histoire économique et sociale*, (1995), 63-70.

Loach, Judi. "The case of Lyons: 'Vatican II' before Vatican II". In: Andrea Longhi, ed. *Architettura e liturgia: Autonomia e norma nel progetto*. Bologna: Bononia University Press, 2017, 89-103.

Loach, Judi. "L'invention d'un édifice-type du mouvement moderne à propos des églises catholiques construites à Lyon après la guerre". In: *Archives et architecture: Mélanges en mémoire de François Régis Cottin*. Lyons: Société d'histoire de Lyon, 2015, 481-529.

Malabre, Natalie. *Le religieux dans la ville du premier vingtième siècle: La paroisse Notre-Dame Saint-Alban, d'une guerre à l'autre*. Unpublished doctoral thesis, Université Lumière Lyon 2, 3 vol. Lyons, 2006.

Martimort, Aimé-Georges. "Du Centre de Pastorale Liturgique à la Constitution Liturgique de Vatican II". *La Maison-Dieu*, 157 (1984), 15-32.

Meillerand, Marie-Clotilde. "Les terrains militaires comme ressort de l'urbanisation au XXe siècle dans l'agglomération lyonnaise". *In Situ*, 16 (2011).

Meuret, Bernard. *Le Socialisme municipal: Villeurbanne 1880-1982*. Lyons: Presses universitaires de Lyon, 1982 (OpenEdition books 2019).

Meynier-Philip, Mélanie. "La communauté patrimoniale et les spécialistes, une alliance édifiante? L'exemple d'une communauté qui se mobilise pour la défense successive de deux églises à Villeurbanne", in Myriam Joannette and Jessica Mace, eds. *Les communautés patrimoniales*. Québec: Presses universitaires de Québec, 2019, 65-90.

Meynier-Philip, Mélanie. "Étude historique, analyse architecturale et évaluation patrimoniale de l'église Notre Dame de l'Espérance". In: Mélanie Meynier-Philip. *Entre valeur affective et valeur d'usage, quel avenir pour les églises paroissiales françaises? La région urbaine Lyon - Saint-Etienne interrogée par le référentiel du "Plan églises" Québécois*. Doctoral thesis, Université Lumière Lyon II, École nationale supérieure d'architecture de Lyon. Lyons, 2018, 585-615 (<https://tel.archives-ouvertes.fr/tel-02020281/document>).

Meynier-Philip, Mélanie. "20th-century churches, a manifest of architectural flexibility. Study on the metropolis Lyon Saint-Etienne". Paper given at the colloquium "L'avenir des églises", National School of Architecture of Lyons, 20-22 October 2016.

Minard, Claire. *Le rôle de la lumière dans l'œuvre de Pierre Genton*. D.E.A dissertation in History of Art, supervised by Dominique Bertin, Université Lyon 2. Lyons, 1996.

Noppen, Luc. "La conversion des églises au Québec, Enjeux et défis". In: Lucie K. Morisset; Luc Noppen, and Thomas Coomans. *What future for which churches?* Québec: Presses de l'Université du Québec, 2006, 277-300.

"Paroisses Nouvelles, Où en sommes-nous?". *L'Essor*, 08/12/1967.

Rey, Jacques. *Lyon, Cité radieuse*. Lyons: Libel, 2010.

Si l'espérance m'était contée 1956-2006. Villeurbanne: Parish Notre-Dame de l'Espérance, 2006.

Sterken, Sven. "A House for God, or a home for His people? The church-building activity of Domus Dei in the Belgian Archbishopric (1952-82)". *Architectural History*, 56 (2013), 387-425.

Stroik, Duncan G. "Church architecture since Vatican II". *The Jurist: Studies in Church Law and Ministry*, 75, 1 (2015), 1, 5-34.

Winninger, Paul. *Construire des églises*. Paris: Le Cerf, 1957.

3
CONSTRUCTING COUNTRY, COMMUNITY AND CITY
ALVAR AALTO'S LAKEUDEN RISTI (1951-1966)

SOFIA ANJA SINGLER

Alvar Aalto (1898-1976) promoted the impression of novelty: a cross-shaped bell tower was, he asserted, unprecedented in architectural history. As he stated in his project description:

> The history of architecture does not recognise the cross-shaped tower, and as author, I am aware that this may lead to treacherous frontiers, as is always the case when symbol and construction are brought together.[1]

Since its completion in 1960, the 65-metre eponymous bell tower of Lakeuden Risti (The Cross of the Plain) has peered over the flatlands of Ostrobothnia as a monumental emblem visible several kilometres away. Its formal-typological curiosity is not its only noteworthy quality, however: the seemingly straightforward symbolism belies the complex palimpsest of ecclesiastical, historical, architectural, economic and political narratives that shaped it. [Ill. 3.1] The project illustrates how national and municipal governments, town and regional planning agencies, business and industry, and local congregations — in addition to architects and church officials — sculpted Finnish post-war ecclesiastical architecture and presents examples of the precise ways in which they did so.

The visual novelty of a cross-shaped tower paralleled the newness of the conditions under which it was constructed, for Finland went through large-scale cultural upheaval in its transformation from a remote agrarian society

---

[1] Aalto, *LAKEUKSIEN RISTI*, 3. Unless otherwise noted, all translations are the author's own.

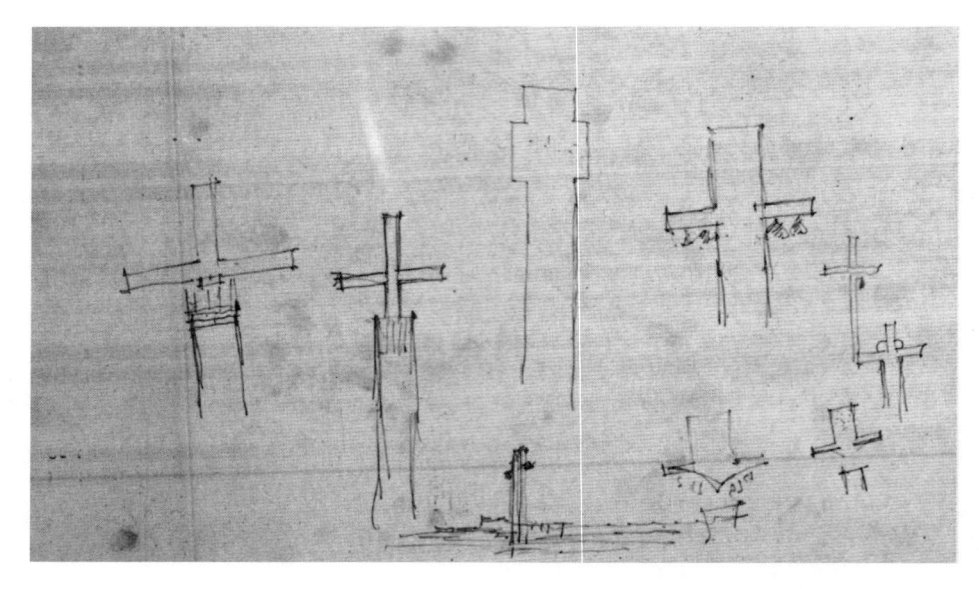

3.1 Sketches of the bell tower for Lakeuden Risti (1951-1966) in Seinäjoki, Atelier Alvar Aalto, 1951. [Courtesy of the Alvar Aalto Museum Archives, Jyväskylä]

to an industrial European nation during the 1950s and 1960s.[2] Lakeuden Risti stands as an architectural metonym that marks not only Christ's passion but critical developments in Finnish post-war society. It highlights how liturgical reform alone, a major consideration in post-war architectural history, is insufficient for explaining the era's religious architecture without reference to broader sociocultural milieux, particularly urbanisation. Because the Finnish Lutheran Church's aesthetic ambitions were linked to national modernisation projects and materialised at a scale broader than individual church buildings, it becomes necessary to consider ecclesiastical architecture in relation to the urban. Recent scholarship on post-war religious architecture has begun to extend enquiry beyond liturgical renewal, aesthetics and form to the develop-

[2] The year 1952 is regarded as a turning point in the historiography of Finland; it was the year that the last war reparations to the Soviet Union were paid off, Helsinki hosted the Olympics and Armi Kuusela was crowned Miss Universe. Claims for a renewed sense of cultural autonomy prevailed as ties to the Soviet Union were loosened; furthermore, with the spread of American youth culture (including brands like Coca-Cola) and increased trade and political connections to central and southern Europe, the national identity of Finland grew increasingly Westernised and decreasingly isolated. Architecturally, the 1950s and 1960s defined an era of significant projects in housing, institutional buildings and infrastructure. Indeed, the 1950s have been called the "golden era" of Finnish culture, art and architecture, following on the "pioneers' era" of the 1930s and "reconstruction era" of the 1940s. Most architectural histories align in the depiction of the 1950s as a period of intensely innovative building that continued into the 1960s, even if attitudes toward the long-term success of the decades' projects vary. Hakli, *Romantiikkaa, förtitalismia vai inhimillistynyttä funktionalismia?*, 109-112; Helander, *Suomalainen rakennustaide*, 5.

3.2 Exterior view of Lakeuden Risti (1951-1966), Seinäjoki, with the low volumes of the parish centre in the foreground and the church and bell tower behind them.
[Photograph by Eva and Pertti Ingervo, c 1966. Courtesy of the Alvar Aalto Museum Archives, Jyväskylä]

ment of ecclesiastical (infra)structures as outcomes of complex interactions between religion, architecture, planning and politics. Lakeuden Risti is a particularly relevant example: although it is linked to the liturgical and religious policies of its time, it is equally, if not more, illustrative of the industrial, economic, urban and planning discourses that surrounded its inception.[3]

Aalto was awarded the commission for a church and parish centre in Seinäjoki, Ostrobothnia, in 1951. [Ill. 3.2] The architecture of the resultant ecclesiastical complex, Lakeuden Risti (1951-1966), was influenced by European Protestant, Finnish governmental and Ostrobothnian regional policy, politics and public discourse simultaneously. Many national church architectural paradigms were developments of German and Swedish Protestant, and sometimes Catholic, guidelines, whereas national planning drew primarily from American and British models. Such national-level strategies laid out the general direction of development for Aalto's project, but were selectively reinterpreted or rejected according to the ambitions of municipal and parish officials, who in turn were responding to the local population's and congregation's reactions.

In addition to shedding light on the factors and actors that influenced the design of post-war churches, Lakeuden Risti suggests that ecclesiastical com-

---

3 The need to situate transnational post-war architectural and planning discourse in local contexts, particularly through the consideration of actors other than architects and planners themselves, has been acknowledged in contemporary scholarship. Wakeman, "Rethinking Postwar Planning History", 155-156, 160.

missions provided Aalto a fruitful realm within which to develop his modernism. Lakeuden Risti is considered one of Aalto's most ambitious projects, and its role in securing him subsequent commissions for the multiple buildings of the adjacent civic centre is broadly acknowledged.[4] The relevant account of Lakeuden Risti acting as a forerunner to an entire portfolio of civic buildings and public spaces deserves to be further qualified, however. More than a transactional stepping stone into further commissions for the Aalto atelier, Lakeuden Risti warrants consideration as a religious urban scheme per se; its status as a project of national religious architecture is inextricably intertwined with the politics of planning and the development of the resultant civic centre. Lakeuden Risti's role as antecedent to further urban projects is, in large measure, what qualifies its status as a religious building: during the intense reconstruction efforts of the 1950s and 1960s, Finland's national church collaborated with the state to build country, community and city in unison.

The Gunpowder Village's Dream of Provincial Glory: The Bid for the Diocesan Seat

It was the declarations of parochial, and subsequently, municipal, independence in Seinäjoki in the nineteenth century that sowed the seeds for the church competition of 1951. Lakeuden Risti was the culmination of Seinäjoki's decades-long search for municipal independence and identity, as well as a manifestation of its ambitious, albeit ultimately unsuccessful, bid for a diocesan seat.

Evidence of temporary settlement in today's Seinäjoki dates back to the twelfth century, with the first permanent farming communities being founded along the area's fertile riverbanks in the sixteenth century. In 1557, the region was home to three taxable farmsteads that cultivated rye and barley.[5] The area then experienced a surge of growth and wealth in the first half of the nineteenth century, 1798 having marked the founding of a successful iron ore mine, Östermyra, by which name the region subsequently became known, which led to the country's first gunpowder factory opening there in 1825. Triumph was short-lived, however. As mineral raw materials diminished and the invention of dynamite effectively put an end to gunpowder sales, Östermyra's industrial success faltered in the 1860s. Nervous for the future, industrialists began to

---

4   Aalto won commissions for the adjacent library, town hall, theatre and police headquarters after the completion of the church and parish centre. Charrington, *The Makings of a Surrounding World*.

5   The settlement history of the Seinäjoki region is summarised in Lahti, ed., *Seinäjoen rakennuskulttuuria*.

campaign for the foundation of an independent parish.[6] More than a reflection of support for the Church, though, the industrial parties' funding of the parish project was a strategy to facilitate the establishment of a new municipality, through which it would be easier to secure protection of commercial privileges than in broader, regional decision-making bodies. An independent parish, of which a church was not only an emblem but a legal requirement, was a prerequisite to establishing a new municipality — thus, the funding of new churches was directly in industrial parties' own interests.[7] Since waning industrial success meant there were insufficient funds to erect a new church, an old gunpowder shed — owned by Russia — was consecrated as the church of Törnävä, named after the farmland by which it stood.[8] The intense lobbying campaign, spearheaded by the industrialist family Wasastjerna, ultimately led to the founding of a new parish called Seinäjoki in 1863.[9]

Using its newly-founded parish as leverage, Seinäjoki successfully applied to the Finnish Senate for status as an independent municipality (*itsenäinen kunta*) in 1868. Seinäjoki's special rank as an independent municipality in a province otherwise comprised of officially unrecognised villages attracted new businesses to the town. In the 1870s, the Senate further designated it a "railway municipality" (*rautatieyhdyskunta*) for the province; the railway tracks through the town were completed in 1882. As railway workers flocked to the area, other industries followed. In the 1920s, following the Finnish Declaration of Independence in 1917, Seinäjoki experienced a veritable population boom, leading to the foundation of new schools, banks and cooperatives in the vicinity of the railway centre. Thanks to this growth, Seinäjoki was granted market town (*kauppala*) status in 1931. The surrounding villages were joined into a rural municipality (*maalaiskunta*) enveloping the market town at its centre. Since the old gunpowder church was now located in the surrounding rural municipality, the market town launched a campaign to build a new church in its industrial–commercial nucleus.[10]

---

6   Previously, the unrecognised villages were part of the Nurmo chapel parish (a smaller type of parish, without a church proper) in the ecclesiastical district of Lapua.
7   The Church Act of 1869 stipulated that each parish have a church of its own. The Settlementtiliitto (Finnish Federation of Settlement) — originally the Teollisuusseutujen Evankelioimisseura (Evangelical Society of Industrial Regions), founded in 1918 — was a particularly active supporter and funder of parish churches throughout the 1920s and 1930s. Knapas, "Kirkkoja viideltä vuosikymmeneltä", 9.
8   From 1809 to 1917, Finland was an autonomous Grand Duchy in the Russian Empire, ruled by the Emperor as Grand Duke.
9   The importance of the physical church building must not be underestimated. Having denied Seinäjoki's first application for a parish of its own, the Senate only accepted a revised version that listed the church building as grounds for the foundation of a new parish. Alanen, *Seinäjoen historia*.
10 Aaltonen, *Näkyyhän se varmasti*, 13-20.

The plans for a new church were never solely premised on establishing a place of worship closer to the railway tracks, however; from the outset, they were also linked to the municipality's ambition to become the seat of a new diocese. In the 1940s, Finland's national Lutheran Church decided to redistribute the archdiocese of Turku (Åbo), which was burdened by an excessively large administrative area. The proposal to establish a new diocese to alleviate Turku's workload sparked a long and bitter battle between Seinäjoki and other municipalities in Southern Ostrobothnia, the province where the new diocese was to be founded.[11] The municipal governments of competing towns such as Vaasa and Lapua caricatured Seinäjoki as a "dirty knot of railway tracks", justifying their superiority by their longer histories as market towns and even the purported piety of their respective populations.[12] Seinäjoki, in turn, branded its railway town status a strength — for example, a senior member of the local parish council, the headmaster Reino Ala-Kulju, reminded the national media of how "when Saint Paul spread the Gospel, he was sure to prioritise centres of traffic and business as places to linger in".[13]

The construction and expression of a particular "local identity" for Seinäjoki thus became a key concern in the church competition of 1951. The winning design had to crystallise Seinäjoki's projected role as the religious centre of the province and propel its success in the bid for the diocesan seat. A parish building committee was appointed to oversee the competition and eventual construction of the church.[14] Forty-five entries were submitted, five of which were disqualified for not following the competition rules. One of the disqualified entries was a submission titled Lakeuksien Risti ("The Cross of the Plains"), which was rejected because it exceeded the competition site boundary by twenty metres. The top three proposals were all submitted by architectural students. Ultimately, however, the jury decided not to commit to any of those three, choosing instead to award the commission to "Lakeuksien

---

11   As capital of the province, Vaasa had been assumed to be the natural choice for the diocesan seat at the XVI Church Meeting (1948), where the need for a new diocese was first recognised. At the meeting of 1953, however, this assumption was questioned due to Vaasa's coastal location, which some committee members feared would be too peripheral. *Suomen evankelis-luterilaisen kirkon kirkolliskokouksen pöytäkirjat ja liitteet* (1948, 1953).
12   Aaltonen, *Näkyyhän se varmasti*, 22.
13   Ibid., 28.
14   Parish building committees were introduced in Finland as specialist subcommittees of parish councils after the Declaration of Independence in 1917. Building committee members were appointed by the parish council, which typically aimed to include, in addition to select parish councillors themselves, other laypersons representing a range of professions and education levels. The members of the building committee set up for Seinäjoki's church competition of 1951 included farmers, train guards, businessmen and teachers, many of whom also sat on the municipal council. Heikkilä, "Kirkon rakentamisen ohjausjärjestelmät", 71; Aaltonen, *Näkyyhän se varmasti*, 48.

Risti", despite its rule-breaking plan.[15] The sealed envelope that accompanied the suite of drawings revealed the designer's identity: Atelier Alvar Aalto, Helsinki.[16]

It is significant that Aalto was chosen despite formal disqualification — the anonymity of the selection deserves to be questioned, for the highly idiosyncratic register of Aalto's architecture would have been recognisable to architects, including those who sat on the jury. Members of the jury, of course, explained the decision as being based on architectural merit, but the atelier's reputation would have been too valuable to pass up. Aalto's fame in both international and national arenas, as well as his presidency of the Finnish Association of Architects, SAFA (1943-1958), would have made his appointment a strategic move in the parish's quest to win the diocesan seat.[17] It is possible that the parish had considered hiring Aalto directly, but acquiesced in the architectural establishment's demands for a fairer process. The building committee in Seinäjoki abandoned their original intent to organise an invited competition for a shortlist of up to seven preselected architects in response to SAFA's recommendation that an open, anonymised competition be hosted instead. Since the late 1920s, church commissions in Finland had been awarded almost solely through open competitions; the competition format was instituted as the modus operandi for building churches in order to ensure pluralism in the country's extremely polarised architectural field. The change had been prompted by Carolus Lindberg's editorial in *Arkkitehti* in 1922. A subsequent policy proposal, presented to SAFA in 1925 by Pauli Blomstedt, Hilding Ekelund and Yrjö Laine, lamented the dichotomous "traditionalism versus functionalism" debate that defined and confined ecclesiastical architecture.[18] The policy proposal was backed by the Ministry of Education; it is likely that governmental support fortified SAFA's position in the ecclesiastical architectural realm, allowing the association to leverage considerable power in the national church's building matters.

After various financial and administrative delays that followed the competition, the Aalto office was commissioned in 1956 to develop the winning

15 The first prize went to Pekka Pitkänen and Olli Vahtera, the second to Christer Bärlund and the third to Eero Eerikäinen and Martti Jaatinen. The competition jury reserved the right to select any of the entries, not just the prizewinners, for realisation. *Seinäjoen seurakunnan kirkon ja sen ympäristön asemakaavan piirustuskilpailu: kilpailuohjelma*.
16 Aalto was assisted by atelier members Alice Asher, Jaakko Kaikkonen, Erkki Karvinen, Lorenz Moser, Elsa Mäkiniemi (whom Aalto married in 1952), Eduard Neuenschwander, Ulrich Stucky and Olavi Tuomisto. After completion, the singular form Lakeuden Risti ("The Cross of the Plain") replaced the project's original name Lakeuksien Risti ("The Cross of the Plains").
17 Aalto's fame is known to have bumped up his position in other competitions, too, including the Lutheran cemetery competition in Lyngby-Taarbaek, Denmark. Pakoma, "Cemetery and Chapel of Rest, Lyngby-Taarbaek".
18 Dhima, *Tila tilassa*, 10-11.

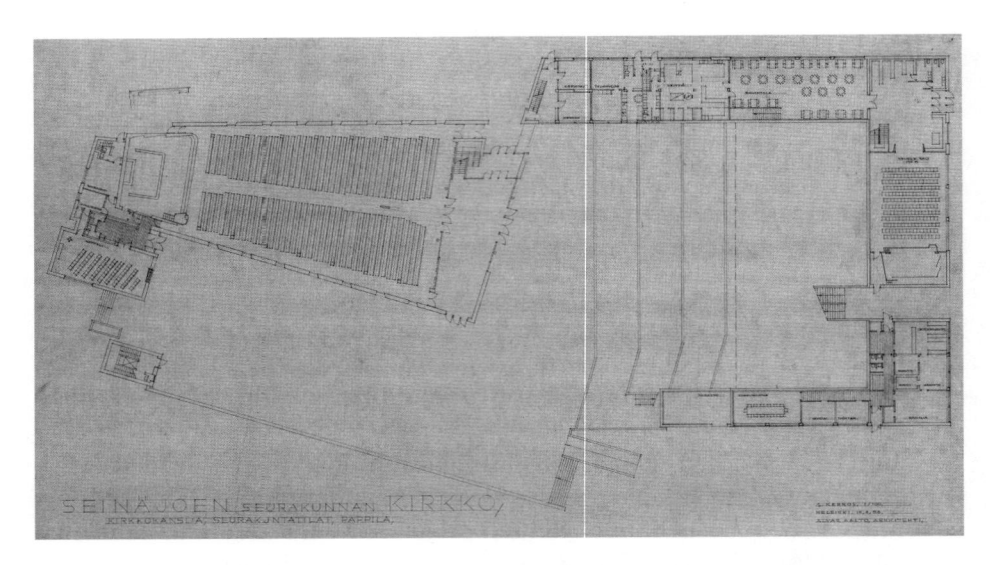

3.3 Ground floor plan of Lakeuden Risti (1951-1966) in Seinäjoki, Atelier Alvar Aalto, 1960. Original at 1:100. [Courtesy of the Alvar Aalto Museum Archives, Jyväskylä]

scheme further and delivered final construction drawings the following year. Construction of the church began in 1958 and was completed in 1960; the parish centre was built between 1964 and 1966. [Ill. 3.3] The U-shaped parish centre encloses a stepped outdoor piazza for up to 3,000 people and is punctuated by an uncovered staircase that opens up a direct axis to the main entrance of the church. The church seats 1400 people, with monumental columns holding up the ceiling and defining narrow aisles on either side of the nave. The floor slopes subtly toward the altar, endowing the nave with an almost imperceptible, yet effective, sense of processional gravitas. [Ill. 3.4] In line with the interior spaces' white plaster uniformity, the exteriors of both the church and parish centre are of white rendered brick, although in Aalto's original scheme, the façade would have been dark granite; he was forced to settle for the former as a result of the value engineering. Lakeuden Risti is Aalto's second church project following a seventeen-year hiatus during which his atelier designed no religious projects at all.[19]

The monumentality of Lakeuden Risti certainly accounts for its air of grandeur, likely explaining why it was long erroneously called a cathedral

19 Aalto's religious oeuvre may be considered to consist of two main "periods": the early classicist and functionalist church renovations and competition entries of the 1920s and 1930s and the major churches and parish centres of the 1950s and 1960s in Finland, Germany and Italy. Aalto's post-war "return" to sacred architecture began with a competition entry for a church and parish centre in Lahti in 1950, but its execution was delayed until the 1970s. Kolmen Ristin Kirkko (The Church of the Three Crosses, 1955-1958) in Imatra was actually the first of Aalto's post-war churches to be fully realised, given that Lakeuden Risti's construction took until 1960.

3.4 Interior view of nave, Lakeuden Risti (1951-1966), Seinäjoki.
[Photograph by Mikko Merckling, c 1990. Courtesy of the Alvar Aalto Museum Archives, Jyväskylä]

(including by Aalto himself).[20] The lingering of the incorrect term is also a remnant of the loss of the bid for the diocesan seat, perhaps steeped in some obstinacy: the Church never defined Lakeuden Risti as the seat of the bishopric, but locals kept the label nonetheless. Ultimately, the town of Lapua won the bid, and Lakeuden Risti remained a parish church rather than a cathedral. Although the project did not transform the municipality into the "religious capital" of the province in terms of the bishopric, it illustrates the story of intense urban development that pushed Seinäjoki to become the province's first city in 1960.

"Toward the People": Post-war Ecclesiastical Architectural Ambitions

Having lost significant land area to the Soviet Union in the 1940s, Finland remained an agrarian economy until the 1950s.[21] The 1950s and 1960s marked a period of substantial government policies implemented to transform Finland into a modern Nordic social-democratic welfare state, a process support-

20   Schildt, ed., *Alvar Aalto: The Complete Catalogue*, 50.
21   Having declared independence from Russia in 1917 and fought a civil war in 1918, Finland waged three more wars between 1939 and 1945: the Winter War (1939-1940) and the Continuation War (1941-1944) against the Soviet Union and the Lapland War (1944-1945) against Germany. It remained independent and unoccupied throughout these wars but lost more than a tenth of its land area to the Soviet Union.

ed and pushed forward by the country's national church.[22] The Constitution Act of 1919 and the Freedom of Religion Act of 1923 declared the state to be non-confessional but granted the Lutheran Church national church status.[23] Although the Church remained legally and administratively autonomous, its special relationship to the state allowed it, amongst other privileges, to collect church tax. In the post-war years, the Church's desire to maintain national church status, on the one hand, and the state's ambition to foster a strong national identity among its people, on the other, led to mutual collaboration; their shared determination to articulate progressiveness was materially expressed in the construction of religious centres as part of new master plans.

Finland had been left heavily divided into Reds and Whites after the civil war in 1918 but was united in fighting against the Soviet Union during the Second World War. The national church has been credited as a significant agent in bringing the population together after the civil war; common religious background was qualified as a unifying force for a population antagonistically divided by class, education and social status.[24] The Church's role as guardian of a "shared cultural tradition" was highlighted anew in the reconstruction efforts of the 1950s, when it sought to expand its network of churches all over the country as an expression of its national reach. Typically, this ambition was manifest in the siting of new churches, placed tactically in the commercial centres of newly urbanised neighbourhoods. The Church had to take care, however, not to appear ostentatious; post-war ecclesiastical design had to balance the ambition to communicate the Church's dominion over the country with humble acknowledgement of the financial precariousness of the reconstruction era. Hence, the prime siting of new churches was coupled with meek massing and form.[25]

Having gained market town status, Seinäjoki seized the opportunity to construct a new church closer to the railway centre. The new building was envisioned from the outset as more prominent and monumental than the old "gunpowder church". The parish council stipulated in the competition require-

22 The term "Nordic" refers to Finland, Sweden, Norway, Denmark and Iceland. "Scandinavian" is sometimes mistakenly used as a synonym for "Nordic", although it refers to the three kingdoms of Sweden, Norway and Denmark.
23 Kääriäinen, Niemelä and Ketola, *Moderni kirkkokansa*, 133. The Lutheran Church retains its national church status today.
24 Klinge, *Vihan veljistä valtiososialismiin*; Murtorinne, *Yleiskatsaus*.
25 Formal simplicity and lack of ornamentation were, of course, typical attributes of Lutheran architecture even before the post-war years' economic situation pushed expression to become barer than before. It is commonly accepted that Finnish church architecture developed primarily from German Protestant roots filtered through Sweden between the sixteenth and nineteenth centuries, but it is unclear how directly German thought influenced Finnish ecclesiastical architecture in the twentieth century. The extent to which church officials or architects would have been familiar with theorists and practitioners such as Otto Bartning or Rudolf Schwarz or the Protestant Church architectural congregations held in Germany remains to be determined. Dhima, *Tila tilassa*, 13.

ments that the winning design articulate the "distinguished cause of a potential cathedral".[26] At the same time, however — mirroring the cautiousness of the national church — the council was careful not to brand the project a display of excess luxury. The parish's church tax percentage was lowered for the duration of the building project in order not to anger congregation members and to demonstrate solidarity in the face of economic hardship. That decision may even be considered a trade-off that allowed for more monumentality architecturally; parishioners were more accepting of grandeur when it felt fairly funded and when their financial involvement consisted more of donations than taxes. Ultimately, Aalto's design still went through several cycles of value engineering. Most significantly, the black granite originally envisioned for the façades was rejected in favour of white rendered brick due to congregation members' perception of granite's opulence. Twisting a well-known aphorism on the fear of God to reflect its members' own sensitivity to public reception, the building committee's internal meeting notes remarked, "Fear of parish members is the beginning of wisdom."[27]

The expression of meekness was not only a product of economic austerity, but also a manifestation of ongoing developments in the architectural, liturgical and religious discourse of the Church. In the wake of an unprecedented need for construction and reconstruction throughout Europe, congresses in both the Catholic and Protestant Churches were summoned to define the direction of post-war church architecture.[28] The Evangelische Kirchbautagung (Protestant Congress) ratified the Rummelsberg Programme in 1951, which overturned the Eisenach Regulations of 1861 and revoked the Church's official preference for "Christian style", that is, architecture developed from early Christian, Romanesque and Gothic churches.[29] Instead, Christian expression was to mirror its own time. The Programme, adopted by the Finnish national Lutheran Church, advocated for a longitudinal plan that culminated in an

---

26   *Seinäjoen seurakunnan kirkon ja sen ympäristön asemakaavan piirustuskilpailu: kilpailuohjelma.*
27   The aphorism, "The fear of God is the beginning of wisdom" (*Herran pelossa viisauden alku*), originally a verse from Proverbs 9. 10, was well-known in Finland from welcome signs nailed above church doors. Aaltonen, *Näkyyhän se varmasti*, 59.
28   The First Congress on Church Architecture was held in Hanover in 1947, followed by the First Protestant Congress on Church Architecture in Berlin in 1948, chaired by theologian Oskar Söhngen. The proceedings of the congresses were documented in the journal *Kunst und Kirche* (1957-1968); the last Protestant Congress was organised in 2002 in Leipzig. In Finland, J. S. Sirén discussed the findings of the Congresses in the journal *Arkkitehti* and also included them in his teaching at the Helsinki University of Technology, although the extent to which architects more broadly were familiar with them is unknown. Söhngen, *Evangelische Kirchbautagung in Berlin 1948*; Sirén, "Kirkkorakennustaiteemme arkkitehtooninen moraali", 26-30.
29   Heyer, *Evangelische Kirchenbautagung in Rummelsberg 1951.*

3.5 Interior view looking toward pulpit and altar, Lakeuden Risti (1951-1966), Seinäjoki.
[Photograph by Kalevi Mäkinen, c 1960. Courtesy of the Alvar Aalto Museum Archives, Jyväskylä]

altar and pulpit, preferably complemented by a baptismal font or organ, the latter being more common in all the Nordic countries.[30]

Lakeuden Risti, like all of Aalto's post-war churches, visually emphasises the triad of altar, pulpit and organ in accordance with the Lutheran focus on the sermon and hymns.[31] Furthermore, its architectural language resists conforming to any stylistic category, instead combining elements of different periods and movements into an idiosyncratic formal expression — the project has been called modernist, constructivist, expressionist and romanticist all at once.[32] [Ill. 3.5] The aesthetic register that resists easy categorisation reflects both the architect's and the Church's search for new form. The pulpit, for example, is a severe, straight-hewn mass, above which its sculptural sounding board, a majestic marble wing, splays out towards the congregation in a manner that recalls no obvious ecclesiastical precedent. Furthermore, in lieu of a painted altarpiece, an unadorned six-metre cross towers above the altar, reiterating the bell tower's cross motif. The altar cross was simultaneously less traditional than mainstream altar paintings and more straightforwardly Christian than many contemporaneous abstract pieces, a quality that would have bolstered the parish's theological credibility during the bid for

30 Schwebel, "An Aversion to Grand Gestures", 213-215.
31 Miller, "Aalto's Religious Architecture", 11.
32 Schildt, ed., *Alvar Aalto: The Complete Catalogue*, 50.

the diocesan seat. Unlike his early-career classicist designs, none of Aalto's post-war churches contain traditional altarpieces; the timber cross features in his Lutheran projects in Finland and Germany, as well as in his only Catholic church, in Italy. The bareness of Aalto's post-war church interiors — not uncommon among contemporaries — can be read in terms of both a typically modernist ambition for simplicity of form and a characteristically Protestant conviction that church art and architecture ought to veer away from visual opulence in order to support believers in their search for the spiritual above the material.[33]

Originally a Catholic reform, but quickly adapted by the Protestant Church, was celebrating the Eucharist *versus populum*, where officiating clergy face the congregation rather than the apse.[34] Architecturally, this was manifest in the apse no longer being separated from the nave; the altar area being set only marginally higher or at the same level as the congregation space; and the pulpit being lowered closer to the pews. Although Lakeuden Risti predates the Church's official promotion of Mass *versus populum*, in many respects it lent itself to the reformed liturgy: it has no separate apse; its altar area sits three low risers from the nave; and the pulpit is elevated only slightly. The altar, however, was not designed for celebrating *versus populum*; the timber cross attached to the altar table prevents the celebration of the Eucharist with the celebrant facing the congregation.[35]

Ultimately, the Church's drive to bring itself physically and metaphorically closer to people extended from liturgy "toward the people" to a new building type that would sit "among the people" in the city: the parish centre. Based on the Norwegian "working church" model, parish centres strove to secure the presence of religion in the day-to-day life of newly urbanised neighbourhoods.[36] They were also a vehicle for the Church to ensure continu-

33 Kuorikoski, *Modern Church Architecture in View of Theological Aesthetics*.
34 Protestants were quick to link celebrating Mass *versus populum* to Luther's *Deutsche Messe* (1526), which recommended that clergy face the congregation during readings. The practice was formally recommended by the national Lutheran Church's worship guide, *Päiväjumalanpalveluksen opas* (1971). Dhima, *Tila tilassa*, 23-24.
35 Interestingly, the altar area was large enough to accommodate another table between the altar and the railing; once a liturgy celebrated *versus populum* was adopted, the secondary table could be used for the distribution of the Eucharist facing the congregation.
36 The Norwegian "working church" (*arbeidskirke*) stemmed from nineteenth-century seamen's churches, whose missionary and teaching spaces were often connected to the main worship space with sliding doors, creating the model for what later became known as "multipurpose church spaces" (*flerbruksrom*). In the post-war period, working churches aimed not just to link the worship space to everyday functions, but to diminish its importance, an ambition fortified particularly in the build-up to the student protests of 1968. The working church was considered "a service institution in line with other public resources (…); functionality, accessibility and ordinariness were characteristic." Den norske kirke, ed, *Kunsten å være kirke–om kirke, kunst og kultur*, 146; Knapas, "Kirkkoja viideltä vuosikymmeneltä", 10-11.

ity of building activity, since the erection of parish centres — devoted to work, socialising and hobbies — provoked less opposition than the construction of new churches.[37] Generally, in the post-war decades, theological and existential debates on religion in Finland were peripheral to the discourse on the Church's public role; religion was discussed more in terms of social cohesion stemming from tradition than as a search for religious truths, a focus crystallised in the parish centre building type.

At Seinäjoki, the competition brief of 1951 highlighted the importance of the parish centre as an equal building to the church proper.[38] As parishioners expressed concern over the construction costs of the church, the building committee was quick to highlight the social function of the parish centre, reassuring the congregation that the complex was more a space for collective pastimes than intended for strictly religious praxis. Since the town was young, it lacked central spaces for clubs and societies; the committee characterised Lakeuden Risti as a shared cultural venture that would promote local socialisation. In Aalto's completed design, the parish centre is such an integral part of the project that the complex would be rendered wholly other in its absence. Unlike all other entries, Aalto's scheme linked the parish centre directly to the church proper, rather than hiding it beneath or behind (many competing proposals relegated the parish centre to a basement space, for example).[39] The piazza enclosed by Aalto's parish centre harks back to Ostrobothnian Midsummer (*juhannus*) customs of dancing and socialising outdoors during the summer solstice. The way in which the parish centre roots itself in the celebration of Midsummer, a pagan holiday later Christianised into the Nativity of Saint John, echoes the Church's focus on community. Although he remained silent through the church architectural debate of the 1950s and 1960s — likely due in equal measure to his disinterest in faith and an intentional tactic to remain publicly neutral, just as he had done with regard to international and national politics — Aalto's earlier writings on the importance of congregating together for ritual activities can be linked to broader modernist justifications of religion as a productive framework for post-war community construction.

The focus on community was also linked to an interpretation of Jesus as a revolutionary. Particularly in the run-up to the student protests of 1968, modernist artists' highlighting of "Christ the anarchist" became a way to consciously draw from the political content of Christianity without renouncing it

---

37 Schwebel, "An Aversion to Grand Gestures", 219.
38 *Seinäjoen seurakunnan kirkon ja sen ympäristön asemakaavan piirustuskilpailu: kilpailuohjelma*. In the 1950s, the National Church Board urged parishes to fund housing rather than churches, with the recommendation that where there was a demonstrable need for worship space, parish centres be preferred over churches. Nikula, "Building for the State Church", 239.
39 *Lakeuden Risti: Kirkkokilpailun piirustusten kopioita 1952* (Seinäjoki Parish Archives).

altogether.[40] Anarchist apologias for the Church argued for the relevance of religion as an antidote to hierarchical power structures, inequality and consumerism. In Finland, the movement referred to the socialist anarchist Jean Boldt, who had famously invaded Helsinki Cathedral in 1917 to demonstrate that ostentatious churches were only hindrances to selfless charity, which ought to happen in the streets instead.[41] It is likely that the Church's promotion of community-centred life would have appealed to Aalto, who elaborated on such themes in his speeches and writings; furthermore, even if not directly linked to religious ideology, his appreciation of the Russian anarchist Pjotr Kropotkin (1842-1921) can be considered relevant.[42] Parish centres became material manifestations of the Church's increasingly decentralised power structure; simultaneously, as focal buildings in the new neighbourhood plans, they were evidence of town planning's growing focus on the "local character" of separate areas of the city.

In its echoing of modernist arguments for the rebellious agency of religion, Lakeuden Risti was consciously characterised as a somewhat "anarchist" venture by the local parish council, despite the fact that it was planned and executed in line with the national church's building policy. One member of the Seinäjoki Chamber of Commerce, which liaised closely with the church building committee, declared, "[It is] certainly a foolhardy project, but God blesses daredevils."[43] In essence, an establishment project was depicted as a courageous anti-establishment venture in order to appeal to the area's industrial workers, whose attitudes toward municipal and ecclesiastical power hierarchies were tense. Local legend recalls the anecdote of the bricklayers intentionally making Aalto's bell tower 10 cm taller than planned in order to immortalise the locals' audacity in the final building.[44] The building committee appointed the journalist Veli Kaakinen as propaganda officer to ensure that media coverage would highlight the egalitarianism of the project. Kaakinen's regular columns in the local paper, *Etelä-Pohjanmaa*, kept parishioners up-to-date on construction, consistently characterising each milestone as a collective success and making sure to thank project members, from construction workers to parishioner donors, for their devotion to the shared cause. The topping-out ceremony was even called "a family celebration".[45] The project's

40 Köykkä, *Sakeinta sumua käskettiin sanoa Jumalaksi*, 137-143.
41 Nyström, *Poikkeusajan kaupunkielämäkerta*, 135-141.
42 Pelkonen, *Alvar Aalto: Architecture, Modernity and Geopolitics*, 121; Schildt, *Alvar Aalto: His Life*, 42-43. Aalto atelier member Veli Paatela recalled: "I was present once when someone asked [Aalto] whether he was a communist. He replied, 'I'm not a communist.' 'Well, are you a Bolshevik?' 'No, I'm an anarchist.'" Quoted in Charrington, *The Makings of a Surrounding World*, 85.
43 Aaltonen, *Näkyyhän se varmasti*, 58-59.
44 Ibid., 71.
45 Ibid., 70.

"rebellious" public image also helped reinforce the perception of Seinäjoki's purported uniqueness in the province, relevant to its ambition to win the diocesan seat: Lakeuden Risti was portrayed as a daring scheme that crystallised, in Aalto's words, the "underlying religious tone" of the region.[46]

The Church and the City: Post-war Planning Paradigms

In 1960, the national church's newspaper, *Helsingin kirkkosanomat* (Helsinki Church News), was renamed *Kirkko ja kaupunki* (The Church and the City). The new name captured religious officials' interest in the urban. At the onset of a new decade of urbanisation, the city became a critical consideration for the Lutheran Church — and given its status as national church, its aesthetic programme was inherently linked to urban design and planning.

Town planning in Finland had relied on and reinforced the Lutheran Church's social responsibility since the nineteenth century, even prior to its national church status. In the 1860s, part of local industrialists' motivation for lobbying for the founding of the Seinäjoki parish had been to fulfil their responsibility for helping the poor. Since the wealthy were seen to have a moral duty to care for those suffering from the famines of the mid-1800s, the idea of a parish was welcomed by factory owners in acknowledgment that it would assume responsibility for the philanthropic endeavours needed in the community. Town planning was introduced as a formal discipline in Finnish architectural education in the early years of the twentieth century by Otto-Iivari Meurman (1890-1994), professor at the Helsinki University of Technology, who promoted it as a fundamentally social or even sociological discipline — a notion that assumed the Church's involvement in national planning, if indirectly.[47] Highlighting planning more as a socio-political than compositional exercise, and thus critiquing nineteenth-century aestheticist planning ideals, Meurman's focus struck a chord during the Finnish housing shortages of the 1920s and 1950s.

Echoing nineteenth- and early-twentieth-century precedent, the post-war emphasis on the Church's philanthropic mission led again to industrial and municipal parties' lobbying for ecclesiastical buildings in the new master plans. Allowing the Church to acquire key plots in and near town centres took up valuable commercial space but was ultimately favourable to businesses and town officials, since the Church's presence decreased the social responsibility assigned to them. At Seinäjoki, the plot purchased for the new church occupied a prominent site close to the railway station. Remarkably, townsmen and

---

46   Aalto, *LAKEUKSIEN RISTI*, 3.
47   Korvenmaa, ed., *The Work of Architects*. One of the first teachers of the new discipline was Carolus Lindberg, whose town planning class Aalto took in 1920.

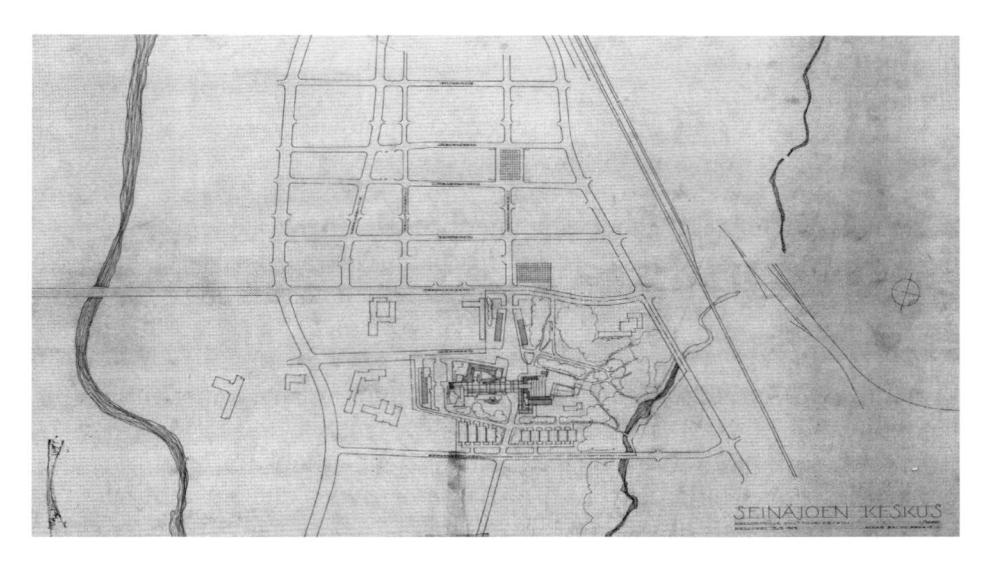

3.6 Town plan depicting the site of the civic and cultural centre in Seinäjoki, Atelier Alvar Aalto, 1965. Original at 1:2000. The commercial city centre is in the north and Aalto's civic and cultural centre in the south. In the Aalto ensemble of buildings, the civic buildings are in the west and the ecclesiastical complex in the east.
[Courtesy of the Alvar Aalto Museum Archives, Jyväskylä]

municipal officials unanimously accepted the sale of the plot to the Church, despite its advantageousness for commercial use. The very concept of the Nordic social-democratic welfare state was rooted in Lutheran thought, and the Church played a fundamental role in the development of the welfare system as part of post-war modernisation.[48] Ecclesiastical buildings might thus be considered physical products of state–church collaboration in the construction of Finland's welfare provision. Their presence in town centres was ensured by centralist planning ideals, which, in opposition to the decentralist planning of the 1940s, advocated for compact commercial centres surrounded by residential, work and leisure areas; new churches and parish centres would thus simply be woven into the new downtown business districts.[49]

Although the church plot at Seinäjoki stood in close vicinity to the commercial downtown, it was not directly within it. [Ill. 3.6] The site was not quite greenfield, either, although it sat on marshland just outside the commercial street grid; it was neither far enough away to be considered a rural setting nor close enough to be downtown. This "both–and" quality of the plot may help explain certain formal aspects of the church; it is not as anonymous as

48 Hiilamo, *The Evangelical Lutheran Church of Finland and the Welfare State at the Time of Crises*; Nelson, *Lutheranism and the Nordic Spirit of Social Democracy*.
49 Meurman, building on the theories of Patrick Geddes, Ebenezer Howard and Lewis Mumford, argued the case for Finnish decentralised planning in his seminal textbook *Asemakaavaoppi* (Town Planning), 1947.

the typical "downtown church" of the 1950s, but instead expresses an ecclesiastical legibility more commonly associated with countryside churches. Most churches and parish centres erected in town centres could only be recognised as such thanks to simple crosses fixed somewhere on their plain concrete or brick façades. The campaign to win the diocesan seat demanded from Lakeuden Risti a somewhat anomalous level of grandeur, which was more comfortably expressed from the edge of the commercial centre than from within it. Although the parish building committee deemed the competition site "ungrateful", its deviance from the typical paradigms of downtown plot and countryside landscape seems to have provided a fruitful interstice within which to productively mediate between ambitions of anonymity and monumentality.[50]

Town-scale planning alone was insufficient in tackling post-war challenges, however. The urgent need to house evacuees and rebuild the areas destroyed in the wars against the Soviet Union and Germany in the 1940s led to new planning paradigms, including the first regional and neighbourhood planning policies.[51] Regional planning as a discipline arose in response to the Settlement Act of 1936, which stipulated that evacuees be housed proportionally around the country; Seinäjoki welcomed a significant number of evacuees within a few years. There had already been a need to highlight the unity of the province given Seinäjoki's envied position as the area's only independent municipality, and this need became more urgent as war evacuees arrived. The town — and by extension, its parish — now had to unite the identities of several different religious groups, language factions and geographic identities into a shared community. Church and municipal officials alike recognised the differences between the religious groups in the province; for example, all four major revival groups — the Awakened (*herännäiset/körtit*), the Knee-Prayers (*rukoilevaiset*), the Laestadians (*lestadiolaiset*) and the Evangelicals (*evankeliset*) — coexisted in the region.

The physical scale of Lakeuden Risti, then, can be considered in relation to its duty to unite; wishing to welcome members from all over the province to worship together, the building committee would have been willing to accept a larger scale for the church than in pre-war years. The clearest architectural manifestation of this ambition was Aalto's open-air piazza; with capacity to

50   *Seinäjoen kirkkokilpailun arviointi.*
51   A seminal law passed to assist evacuees was the Act on the Acquisition of Land for Settlement Purposes (1924), more commonly known as "Lex Kallio" after its proponent Kyösti Kallio, who later became president of the republic. Lex Kallio improved the conditions of tenant farmers by facilitating the acquisition of land for settlement and cultivation purposes. It was repealed and replaced in 1938 by the Settlement Act (1936, implemented in 1938), whose impact was short-lived due to the wars that broke out immediately afterwards. This was followed by the Rapid Settlement Act (1940) and the Land Acquisition Act (1945), which sought to advance and accelerate settlement and land acquisition for evacuees of the Winter and Continuation Wars.

3.7 An outdoor service in the piazza of Lakeuden Risti (1951-1966), Seinäjoki.
[Photographer unknown, n.d. Courtesy of the Alvar Aalto Museum Archives, Jyväskylä]

hold up to 3,000 people, it was a literal expression of the "open arms" attitude projected by the majority church to its revival movements in the region. [Ill. 3.7] As Aalto wrote, "The site plan and plan are derived from the fact that Southern Ostrobothnia is a province of many great religious meetings and groups."[52] Despite being protest movements rooted in seventeenth-century German pietism, the revivalist groups never separated from the Lutheran Church; the tolerance or even acceptance of revivalists has been considered a key strategy by which the majority church managed to maintain its national church status. In essence, its willingness to allow criticism within its own circles diminished the risk of protesting factions breaking off.[53]

In order to avoid the concentration of evacuees in towns only, the first regional plans were aimed at the economic and urban development of rural areas.[54] This development of the countryside was also a product of necessity, though, since Finland was forced to restructure its industry in order to meet the war reparations demanded by the Soviet Union. The so-called Wood Republic had to expand its focus from timber manufacturing to ships and locomotives, in line with the Soviet stipulation that no more than a third of reparations be wood-processed goods.[55] Seinäjoki's position as the central railway nexus of Western Finland was critical as Finnish industry became modernised

52   Aalto, *LAKEUKSIEN RISTI*, 1.
53   Markkola and Naumann, *Lutheranism and the Nordic Welfare States in Comparison*, 11.
54   Rautsi, "The Alternative", 6-8; Norvasuo, "Alvar Aalto and the Industrial Origins of Finnish 1940s Community Planning", 234–236.
55   Myllyntaus, "Technological Change in Finland", 47.

in the 1950s and 1960s; it became a powerful regional centre of commerce. Like many of the churches erected in the 1950s, Lakeuden Risti was envisioned as an inherently urban edifice from its inception — it would express Finland's modernity, revived economy and urbanisation with a tenor of confidence. The bell tower was considered a symbol of religious unity, intertwined with industrial pride:

> The municipal officials of Seinäjoki hammered a gigantic railway nail into the clay of the flatlands — as both a church tower and a representation of the area's economy.[56]

In addition to regional planning, the post-war years saw the introduction of another new planning scale: that of the neighbourhood. On the one hand, reconstruction and the rehousing of evacuees had called for a focus on the regional level, but on the other, a more localised scale than that of the town was deemed necessary.[57] If, at a regional scale, churches such as Lakeuden Risti were charged with the responsibility of acting as unifying centres for different religious groups, at the neighbourhood scale, it was through parish centres that the Church was to insert itself into the life of newly urbanised towns. Lakeuden Risti crystallises the ambitions of both scales, demonstrating how ecclesiastical commissions operated within regional and neighbourhood realms simultaneously. The parish centre of Lakeuden Risti, with its low-lying mass, regularly fenestrated elevations and simple corridor plan, is a typical example of the humble, "anonymous" urban parish centres the Church had advocated for, whereas the monumentality of the church proper relates to regional planning efforts that assigned Seinäjoki the role of economic and industrial "province leader".

The Church acted as a sympathetic patron that allowed Aalto to further his thinking on planning and urban design. It has been argued that Aalto's urbanism took a sharp departure from mainstream CIAM ideals in the post-war years; indeed, his focus on monumental civic centres was an anomaly among the "technological romanticism" of rationalist planning.[58] Aalto had been an

56 Aaltonen, *Näkyyhän se varmasti*, 11.
57 Meurman introduced the neighbourhood scale as a development of the "node model" of his pre-war planning theory; the concept originated in Sweden. Although neighbourhood planning was developed concurrently with regional planning, the two remained distinctly separate. Norvasuo, "Alvar Aalto and the Industrial Origins of Finnish 1940s Community Planning", 231-232.
58 St John Wilson, *The Other Tradition*, 6-9. Aalto was invited to join the Congrès Internationaux d'Architecture Moderne (CIAM) by his friend, Swedish architect Sven Markelius, who had been present at the founding of the organisation at La Sarraz in 1928; Aalto participated in CIAM conferences from 1929 onwards. CIAM, steered by leading modernists of different nationalities until its dismantling in 1959, aimed to promote and develop the principles of the Modern Movement in architectural, urban and design praxis.

active member of CIAM in the 1930s, devising Corbusian town plans with "the ardour of the newly-converted".[59] Although he was no longer active in CIAM in the post-war years, nor involved in its successor Team X, his continued emphasis on landscape and infrastructure was rooted in early CIAM discourse. It may thus be more accurate to consider Aalto's urbanism as neither a development nor rejection of CIAM models, but a blending of these two positions. Revisions to the Athens Charter, such as Lewis Mumford's and José Lluis Sert's promotion of "centres of community life" (meant to mitigate the fragmentation of neighbourhood life), were not dissimilar to Aalto's and the national church's visions of the ideal town and the role of the parish centre therein.[60]

Lakeuden Risti was an opportunity for Aalto to explore the construction of a sense of community through urbanism and planning. His emphasis on what he termed "harmonisation" can be read as a mediation between the aesthetic planning of Eliel Saarinen (1873-1950) and the programmatic planning of the functionalist–rationalists that dominated the Finnish scene from the 1950s onward.[61] As early as 1930, referring to his friend and mentor Gunnar Asplund's (1885-1940) work, Aalto had defined the "democratisation of art and the creation of harmonious life" as the highest ambition of modern architecture, which he clarified was "not just about compositions in stone, glass and steel (…) but flowers, fireworks, happy people and clean tablecloths".[62] In the ecclesiastical context, the concept of harmony linked to the Church's promotion of "valuable everyday life" as the driving force of post-war community construction efforts. Whereas town councils often favoured rationalist proposals focused on re-densifying city centres through commercial activity, the Church advocated for non-commercial public space within the new master plans. If the design of churches gave Aalto the opportunity to pursue his thinking on monumentality, the parish centre provided a more direct chance to further ideas of "harmonious" collective living in an urban setting. Acknowledging the technical and economic pressures of the reconstruction era, Aalto declared that, despite the undeniable necessity to mass produce and rationalise, "the construction of buildings and community should support man's dwelling and harmonious life".[63] The overlaps in religious, national and municipal planning ambitions created suitable frameworks for Aalto to develop his architectural register in Lakeuden Risti.

59 Schildt, ed. *Alvar Aalto: The Complete Catalogue*, 30.
60 Mumford, "CIAM Urbanism after the Athens Charter"; Sert, "The Human Scale in City Planning".
61 See, for example, Aalto, "Valtakunnansuunnittelu ja kulttuurimme tavoitteet". Aalto's theory of harmonisation has been considered a precursor to the planning discourse of the 1970s and 1980s, which substituted mid-century models of architect-centric design with more dispersed models of planning undertaken by many different parties working in collaboration.
62 Aalto, "Stockholmsutställningen", 72.
63 Aalto, "Taide ja tekniikka", 176.

Following the church competition, the town council of Seinäjoki sponsored two further competitions for a civic centre and town hall to be erected directly opposite Lakeuden Risti. Aalto took part in the competitions and again, despite not winning, received the commissions — it is commonly acknowledged that Aalto's role as architect of Lakeuden Risti secured his position as designer of the subsequent civic and cultural projects. Ultimately, the Aalto atelier went on to create an entire monumental centre, including a library, theatre and administrative office block. [Ill. 3.8] The ensemble — commonly known as the "Aalto centre" (*Aalto-keskus*) in contrast to the commercial "town centre" (*keskusta*) by the railway station — remains one of three realised town centre plans in Aalto's oeuvre, the other two being Rovaniemi and Alajärvi.[64] Lakeuden Risti is rightly considered the trigger to a decades-long project in planning, urban design and architecture, but further research is needed to elucidate the links between the initial ecclesiastical commission and the following decades' civic centre development. The urban qualities and implications of Lakeuden Risti, even before the competition for an adjacent civic centre was envisioned, deserve acknowledgment in their own right; analyses of post-war planning and urbanism must recognise the urban agency of religious complexes in themselves, not just as stepping stones to other urban projects.

Conclusion

Lakeuden Risti illustrates how national ambitions of modernisation were expressed and executed, as well as liberally reinterpreted or even contradicted, at a local level. Lakeuden Risti selectively deviated from national church and state ambitions to adhere to the ideological and pragmatic demands imposed upon it by its immediate context, particularly municipal politics. For instance, although Lakeuden Risti's value-engineered material palette and focus on social mission over aesthetics illustrate the Church's "voluntary relinquishment of self-representation", the express pride in its unusually tall bell tower and

---

64 The most recent addition to the Aalto centre is the new city library, Apila ("Clover"), by Finnish studio JKMM (2012), which connects to Aalto's library (1965) through a subterranean tunnel. The town centre has grown and densified considerably since the 1960s; most notably, its nineteenth- and early-twentieth-century single- and double-storey timber blocks have been replaced by multi-storey shopping centres and office buildings. The area west of the railway station remains the town's commercial nucleus to this day. Seinäjoki's post-war growth is currently being studied in more depth; an ongoing research project at the University of Helsinki's Ruralia Institute, *Seinäjoen kaupunkiajan historia* ("The History of the City of Seinäjoki", 2017-2020), is charting the city's development from 1960 to today.

3.8 Exterior view of the civic and cultural centre in Seinäjoki. In the foreground, to the left, the theatre; in the middle ground, to the left, the town hall, and to the right, the library; in the background, the parish centre and church. Collectively, these buildings, along with the police headquarters and an administrative office building (not pictured), are known as the "Aalto centre".
[Photograph by Teuvo Kanerva, c 1979. Courtesy of the National Board of Antiquities, Helsinki]

its compositional sophistication were commonly lauded as qualities that duly glorified Seinäjoki.[65]

Aalto's appointment as architect of the project is, in itself, indicative of how national and local interests were cross-pollinated, sometimes self-contradictorily, in the development of Lakeuden Risti: he was simultaneously characterised as a global cosmopolitan and a local farmstead boy. By the 1950s, Aalto's office had acquired a "signature register" admired widely in Finland and abroad. His international fame undoubtedly attracted both the national Church, intent on communicating its contemporary relevance through architectural means, and the local parish, determined to brand the project an expression of local talent, resulting in the characterisation of the globally-renowned architect as a "born and raised" local. Aalto was born in Kuortane, a small village some forty kilometres from Seinäjoki, but moved to the town of Jyväskylä at the age of five. He was widely known as a Jyväskylä native, particularly since it was at the Jyväskylä Lyceum that he received his education

65 Schwebel, "An Aversion to Grand Gestures", 219.

and founded his atelier. Such facts were set aside as Aalto was characterised as a "homeboy" under the auspices of the building committee's propaganda. Aalto was no passive agent in the branding process himself: he emphasised how he had "personally witnessed the great religious festivities of Southern Ostrobothnia" and recounted that it was "a study of the region's general ambiance (...) that led to this particular form [of Lakeuden Risti]".[66]

Lakeuden Risti demonstrates how the local execution and reinterpretation of national-scale church architectural policy transcended a contextualism understood as stylistic or formal references to built fabric: the political milieu of the diocesan seat competition shaped the building even more than the architectural surroundings. The need to acknowledge the contributions and influence of actors other than architects and planners in shaping post-war buildings and cities has already been highlighted in contemporary scholarship. That point is corroborated by the extent to which Lakeuden Risti's design was influenced by non-architectural agents. In addition to supporting narratives of international and national religious architectural policies being selectively adapted at local levels throughout Europe, Lakeuden Risti also calls attention to the necessity of investigating what exactly is meant by "local" in the post-war context. It is sometimes used synonymously with "municipal" but would benefit from being considered in terms of, for example, local religious context (e.g. revivalist groups operating within a national church) or particular parts of town (e.g. differences between commercial centres and greenfield plots). An analysis of such "spheres of local" could be enriched by comparison to pre-war and interwar projects, particularly as cultural historians have suggested that the renewed focus on the "local(s)" in post-war Finland was a product of the population having been united in the battles against the Soviets and Germans.

Aalto's interest in ecclesiastical projects has been explained in large measure by the creative freedom, scale and programmatic complexity offered by such commissions, yet artistic ambition alone remains insufficient in describing the complex relationship between Finland's most renowned architect and its national church. Aesthetic studies have benefited from considering Aalto's oeuvre in relation to the artistic and art philosophical debates that preceded and paralleled them; analyses of Aalto's curvilinear formal language, material palette and detail motifs, for example, have illuminated links between his built and textual output and contemporaneous aesthetic discourse. A similar process of considering Aalto's ecclesiastical works in relation to the religious, political and urban debates of their time is necessary for understanding the influences that shaped them. His suaveness in social arenas is well-known; it is a common quip, typically issued with a derogatory undertone, to point out that Aalto's clients ranged from Communist clubs to the Church. More than a laissez-faire attitude toward clients' agendas or uncritical greed for new com-

66   Aalto, *LAKEUDEN RISTI*, 1, 3.

missions, however — Aalto did, after all, also refuse clients — his sustained relationship with the Church warrants consideration as a conscious partnership that benefited both parties. If Aalto found in the Church a patron sympathetic to many of his design ambitions, the Church found in him an architect capable of promoting an image of its modernity. Their relationship, as evidenced by Lakeuden Risti, was mutually symbiotic.

Although an analysis of Lakeuden Risti's inception and construction poses more questions than answers, it demonstrates how complex the milieux that shaped post-war religious architecture were. To interpret projects such as Lakeuden Risti solely or even primarily with reference to liturgical reform, as was common in scholarship on religious modern architecture until recently, would be remiss. Liturgy, in Lakeuden Risti as well as Aalto's later religious projects, was a natural component of the building brief, but far from a key "design driver" that would have decisively shaped the resultant architecture. More significant were the local sociocultural milieux that framed the inception of religious commissions in local parishes, and above all, the mutual affinity between Aalto and the national Church, which drew from a set of shared ambitions and values, from a commitment to developing contemporary form to an appreciation of religion as a vessel and embodiment of collective cultural tradition. In a polemical essay on the condition of ecclesiastical art, published three decades before the church competition at Seinäjoki, the young Aalto declared that in a:

> simple unpretentious room (…) one single detail, a crucifix on a grey limestone wall, heightens the atmosphere of devotion and is a hundred times more beautiful than columns and ornamental flourishes framing an altarpiece many metres high.[67]

In other speeches and writings, Aalto focussed on the importance of gathering together for ritual activity and the role of church buildings as visual markers in urban centres. Indeed, his discussion of community and the city are not dissimilar from the Church's own discourse. The emphasis on simplicity of form, social belonging and the urban can be linked both to architectural modernism and twentieth-century Protestant thought: ambitions to construct country, community and city were, after all, concerns shared by both modern architects and the national church in post-war Finland.

---

67   Aalto, *Kirkkotaiteestamme*, 38.

BIBLIOGRAPHY

Acknowledgments

The author is grateful to Timo Riekko at the Alvar Aalto Museum Archives and Riikka Jäsperlä and Riitta Kjäll at the Seinäjoki Parish Archives for their help in the archival research conducted for this essay in the summer of 2017; to Dr Maximilian Sternberg for his insightful comments and criticism; and to the participants, respondents and organisers of the Territories of Faith conference in July 2017 for many invaluable reflections both on this essay and on religious modern architecture at large. Dr Timo Marjomäki deserves special thanks for arranging the first of many site visits to Seinäjoki in 2010.

Archives

Jyväskylä, Alvar Aalto Museum
- 1015 original drawings and sketches
- 323 photographs
- Written archival sources filed in the folder Seinäjoki: kirjeenvaihto

Seinäjoki, Parish Archives
- 9 original drawings
- 5 photographs
- written archival sources filed in the following folders:
  . Lakeuden Ristin rakentamista ja kunnossapitoa koskevia asiakirjoja, 1951-1982
  . Lakeuden Ristin rakentamista koskevaa kirjeenvaihtoa 1957-1961
  . Kirkon rakentamisen rahoitus 1957-1966
  . Joitakin kirjeenvaihtoja kirkkokilpailun tiimoilta
  . Lakeuden Risti: Kirkkokilpailun piirustusten kopioita 1952

Published sources

Aalto, Alvar. "Kirkkotaiteestamme". In: Göran Schildt, ed. *Näin puhui Alvar Aalto*. Helsinki: Otava, 1997, 37-38.

Aalto, Alvar. *LAKEUKSIEN RISTI*. Project description. Seinäjoki Parish Archives, n.d.

Aalto, Alvar. "Stockholmsutställningen". Interview in Åbo *Underrättelser*, 22.5.1930. In: Göran Schildt, ed. *Näin puhui Alvar Aalto*. Helsinki: Otava, 1997, 71-73.

Aalto, Alvar. *Taide ja tekniikka*. Inaugural lecture at the Academy of Finland, 3.10.1955. In: Göran Schildt, ed. *Näin puhui Alvar Aalto*. Helsinki: Otava, 1997, 172-177.

Aalto, Alvar. "Valtakunnansuunnittelu ja kulttuurimme tavoitteet". Lecture at the Finnish Cultural Foundation, 27.2.1949. In: Göran Schildt, ed. *Näin puhui Alvar Aalto*. Helsinki: Otava, 1997, 168-171.

Aaltonen, Markus. *Näkyyhän se varmasti: Alvar Aalto ja Seinäjoki*. Jyväskylä: Veterator, 2004.

Alanen, Aulis. *Seinäjoen historia I, Vuoteen 1931 eli kunnan jakautumiseen kauppalaksi ja maalaiskunnaksi*. Seinäjoki: Seinäjoen kaupunki, 1970.

Charrington, Harry. *The Makings of a Surrounding World: The Public Spaces of the Aalto Atelier*. Thesis (PhD). London School of Economics and Political Science, 2008.

Den norske kirke, ed. *Kunsten å være kirke–om kirke, kunst og kultur*. Oslo: Verbum, 2005.

Dhima, Sari. *Tila tilassa: Liturgian ja tilan dialogi alttarin äärellä*. Thesis (PhD). University of Helsinki, 2008.

Hakli, Olli. *Romantiikkaa, förtitalismia vai inhimillistynyttä funktionalismia? Suomen jälleenrakennuskauden arkkitehtuurihistoriografia*. Thesis (MA). University of Helsinki, 2012.

Heikkilä, Markku. "Kirkon rakentamisen ohjausjärjestelmät". In: Arto Kuorikoski, ed. *Uskon tilat ja kuvat: Moderni suomalainen kirkkoarkkitehtuuri ja -taide*. Helsinki: Suomalainen Teologinen Kirjallisuusseura, 2008, 67-89.

Heikkilä, Pekka. *Tyrvään paratiisi ja passio*. Documentary (48 min). The Communications Centre of the Evangelical Lutheran Church of Finland and YLE, 2012.

Helander, Vilhelm. *Suomalainen rakennustaide*. Tampere: Kirjayhtymä, 1987.

Heyer, Walther. *Evangelische Kirchenbautagung in Rummelsberg 1951*. Berlin: Arbeitsausschuß des Evangelischen Kirchbautags, 1952.

Hiilamo, Heikki. *The Evangelical Lutheran Church of Finland and the Welfare State at the Time of Crises*. Unpublished manuscript. Helsinki: Social Insurance Institute of Finland, 2012.

Kääriäinen, Kimmo; Niemelä, Kati and Ketola, Kimmo. *Moderni kirkkokansa: Suomalaisten uskonnollisuus uudella vuosituhannella*. Kirkon tutkimuskeskuksen julkaisuja, 82. Jyväskylä: Gummerus, 2003.

Klinge, Matti. *Vihan veljistä valtiososialismiin. Yhteiskunnallisia ja kansallisia näkemyksiä 1910- ja 1920-luvuilta*. Porvoo: Söderström, 1972.

Knapas, Marja Terttu. "Kirkkoja viideltä vuosikymmeneltä". In: Marja Terttu Knapas, ed. *Suomalaista kirkkoarkkitehtuuria 1917-1970*. Helsinki: Museovirasto, 2006, 6-12.

Korvenmaa, Pekka, ed. *The Work of Architects: The Finnish Association of Architects, 1892-1992*. Helsinki: The Finnish Association of Architects and the Finnish Building Centre, 1992.

Köykkä, Arto. *Sakeinta sumua käskettiin sanoa Jumalaksi: Uskonnollinen kieli Pentti Saarikosken tuotannossa*. Thesis (PhD). University of Helsinki, 2016.

Kuorikoski, Arto. *Modern Church Architecture in View of Theological Aesthetics*. Lecture at the international symposium "500 Years of Protestant Church Architecture", Helsinki, Finland, 31 October–1 November, 2017.

Lahti, Tellervo, ed. *Seinäjoen rakennuskulttuuria: Asutus, kulttuurimaisema ja vanha rakennuskanta*. Seinäjoki: Seinäjoen Historiallinen Yhdistys ry, 2002.

Lehtosalo, Mari. *Kirkollisen lasimaalauksen kulta-aika Suomessa: Suosion taustan tarkastelua*. Thesis (MA). University of Jyväskylä, 2008.

Markkola, Pirjo and Ingela K. Naumann. "Lutheranism and the Nordic Welfare States in Comparison". *Journal of Church and State*, 56 (2014), 1, 1-12.

Miller, William C. "Aalto's Religious Architecture". *Faith and Form*, VIII (1975), 10-13.

Mumford, Eric. "CIAM Urbanism after the Athens Charter". *Planning Perspectives*, 7 (1992), 4, 391-417.

Murtorinne, Eino. "Yleiskatsaus. Kirkon seitsemän vuosikymmentä". In: Markku Heikkilä and Eino Murtorinne, eds. *Kirkko suomalaisessa yhteiskunnassa 1900-luvulla*. Hämeenlinna: Kirjapaja, 1977, 7-25.

Myllyntaus, Timo. "Technological Change in Finland". In: Jan Hult and Bengt Nyström, eds. *Technology and Industry – A Nordic Heritage*. Nantucket: Science History Publications USA, 1992, 29-52.

Nelson, Robert H. *Lutheranism and the Nordic Spirit of Social Democracy: A Different Protestant Ethic*. Aarhus: Aarhus University Press, 2017.

Nikula, Riitta. "Building for the State Church: Church Architecture in Finland 1950-2000". In: Wolfgang Jean Stock, ed. *European Church Architecture 1950-2000*. Munich and New York: Prestel, 2002, 236-245.

Norvasuo, Markku. "Alvar Aalto and the Industrial Origins of Finnish 1940s Community Planning". *Planning Perspectives*, 31 (2016), 2, 227-251.

Nyström, Samu. *Poikkeusajan kaupunkielämäkerta: Helsinki ja helsinkiläiset maailmansodassa 1914–1918*. Thesis (PhD). University of Helsinki, 2013.

Pakoma, Katariina. "Cemetery and Chapel of Rest, Lyngby-Taarbaek". In: Aila Kolehmainen and Esa Laaksonen, eds. *Drawn in Sand – Unrealised Visions by Alvar Aalto*. Helsinki: Alvar Aalto Museum and Alvar Aalto Academy, 2002, 48-49.

Pelkonen, Eeva-Liisa. *Alvar Aalto: Architecture, Modernity and Geopolitics*. New Haven and London: Yale University Press, 2009.

Rautsi, Jussi. "The Alternative: Alvar Aalto's Urban Plans, 1940-1970". *Habitat International*, 12 (1988), 1, 5-21.

Schildt, Göran. *Alvar Aalto: His Life*. Translated by Timothy Binham and Nicholas Mayow. Jyväskylä: Alvar Aalto Museum, 2007.

Schildt, Göran, ed. *Alvar Aalto: The Complete Catalogue of Architecture, Design and Art*. New York: Rizzoli, 1994.

Schildt, Göran, ed. *Näin puhui Alvar Aalto*. Helsinki: Otava, 1997.

Schwebel, Horst. "An Aversion to Grand Gestures: Theological and Liturgical Perspectives on Protestant Church Architecture". In: Wolfgang Jean Stock, ed. *European Church Architecture 1950-2000*. Munich and New York: Prestel, 2002, 212-223.

Seinäjoen seurakunnan kirkon ja sen ympäristön asemakaavan piirustuskilpailu: Kilpailuohjelma. Competition brief. Seinäjoki Parish, 1951.

Seinäjoen kirkkokilpailun arviointi. Evaluation of the competition entries (internal notes of the parish building committee). Seinäjoki Parish, 1951.

Sert, José Luis. "The Human Scale in City Planning". In: Paul Zucker, ed. *New Architecture and City Planning*. New York: Philosophical Library, 1944, 392-413.

Sirén, Johan Sigfried. "Kirkkorakennustaiteemme arkkitehtooninen moraali". *Arkkitehti*, 3-5 (1948), 26-30.

Söhngen, Oskar. *Evangelische Kirchbautagung in Berlin 1948 – Ein Bericht*. Berlin: Evangelische Verlagsanstalt, 1949.

St John Wilson, Colin. *The Other Tradition of Modern Architecture: The Uncompleted Project*. London: Academy Editions, 1995.

Suomen evankelis-luterilaisen kirkon kirkolliskokouksen pöytäkirjat ja liitteet. Minutes of the Synods of the Evangelical Lutheran Church of Finland. Turku, 1948, 1953.

Wakeman, Rosemary. "Rethinking Postwar Planning History". *Planning Perspectives*, 29 (2014), 2, 153-163.

4
FAITH IN A DIVIDED CITY
CHURCH BUILDING IN BERLIN AND THE 1957 INTERBAU EXHIBITION

MARINA WESNER*

In the limited space of a divided post-war Berlin, two opposing political systems clashed repeatedly, resulting in a permanent state of competition that was reflected in the city planning. The eastern part of the city was the capital of the socialist GDR and in need of an outward appearance to match that status, while the other half of the city was meant to serve as a showcase for the Western world and as such reflect its values. In the 1950s, the architectural embodiments of these two sets of ideals were the buildings on Stalinallee in East Berlin and those of the West Berlin Interbau exhibition of 1957 in the Hansaviertel neighbourhood. Besides the opposing political systems, values and social and human ideals, attitudes towards religion also differed widely in the East and the West — from which a concomitantly divergent means of dealing with both existing and new churches developed. The approaches and decisions that emerged from these different attitudes are evident to this day in the cityscape.

The first section of this chapter will provide an overview of religiosity and church architecture in each half of the city, before focusing on West Berlin and, more specifically, the Interbau Berlin exhibition of 1957. Among the buildings constructed for the exhibition in the southern part of the historic Hansaviertel were two churches: the Protestant Kaiser-Friedrich-Gedächtniskirche (Emperor Frederick Memorial Church) and the Catholic St.-Ansgar-Kirche (Saint Ansgar's Church). Interbau also featured a special exhibition on "The City of Tomorrow". The aim here is to explore how the *Zeitgeist*, opposing notions of

* Translated from the German by John Owen and Sven Sterken.

social utopia and the diverging attitudes of religious leaders impacted church building in Berlin, before zooming in on how it was dealt with in the framework of Interbau's vision of the city of the future. Finally, we ask what place these two churches occupy in the architectural historicgraphy of the post-war period and what role is left for them to play in the contemporary city.

The Christian Churches and the Division of Berlin

After the Battle of Berlin in April 1945, Nikolai Erastowich Bersarin (1904-1945) became head of the Soviet garrison. His famous "Order Number One" stipulated, amongst other things, that church services were allowed until nine o'clock in the evening. In so doing, Bersarin was abiding by the decisions of the Allied forces who had decided back in 1944 to restore church life after the war and grant churches independence over their own affairs. The significance of this was that their wider social and socially integrative roles could be upheld, and the more general right to religious freedom could be respected.[1]

How the Churches were to fulfil this mission was another question altogether. In the first place, most of their buildings had been destroyed or damaged beyond repair.[2] Further, despite the existence of a communal city council in the early post-war period, Berlin had been definitively divided with the founding of the Federal Republic of Germany (FRG) on 23 May 1949 and the German Democratic Republic (GDR) on 7 October 1949. As a result, Protestant congregations and Catholic parishes were divided and often no longer had access to their own churches. Examples of this include the parishes of St. Michael (Catholic), whose area became divided by the border between Mitte (East Berlin) and Kreuzberg (West Berlin), and the Protestant Martin-Luther parish, which became divided between Pankow (East Berlin) and Gesundbrunnen (West Berlin). The most well-known example was perhaps the Versöhnungskirche (Church of the Reconciliation) along Bernauer Strasse: it became located within the Soviet sector, with most of the parishioners living in the neighbouring French sector. When the Berlin Wall was constructed in 1961, the church became isolated from both sides and fell into the so-called Todesstreifen, the heavily guarded no-man's-land between East and West. [Ill. 4.1]

After the war, therefore, both Christian denominations needed to not only reconstruct their buildings, but also revise their organisational structures in

---

1   Maser, *Kirchen in der DDR*, 20.
2   Cante, *Sacralbauten*, 207. It is estimated that 309 of the 342 pre-war churches and synagogues in Greater Berlin had been destroyed or damaged during the war.

4.1 The Versöhnungskirche along Bernauer Strasse shortly after construction of the Berlin Wall (1961), which isolated it in the so-called Todesstreifen.
[Contemporary postcard. Collection of the author]

order to continue offering essential services and pastoral care.³ The hierarchical structure of the Catholic Church required no fundamental reorganisation because, at least in theory, it had maintained control over its own affairs in the Reich Concordat of 1933. After the division, the Bishopric of Berlin comprised territory in two different countries and remained a suffragan bishopric to the Archbishopric of Breslau until 1972. The official bishop's seat was St.-Hedwig-Kathedrale (Saint Hedwig's Cathedral) in East Berlin, even though his official headquarters was in West Berlin; his administrative offices had premises in both parts of the city.

The situation of the Protestant Church was considerably more complicated. The National Socialist dictatorship's idea to set up a universal Protestant Reichskirche had divided the twenty-eight Landeskirchen (state churches) into the Deutsche Christen (German Christians) who followed the dictatorship and the Bekennende Kirche (Confessional Church) who opposed it. In 1948, the various Landeskirchen were reunited in the Evangelische Kirche Deutschland (German Protestant Church, hereafter EKD). However, cooperation among them became increasingly difficult, and in 1957, the EKD suffered a serious schism after it signed the Military Chaplaincy Agreement with the West German government, providing for pastoral care for the military. Accusing the EKD of favouring the Western powers, the GDR leadership forced the East German Landeskirchen to withdraw from it. Cross-border cooperation became so difficult that in 1969, a Bund der Evangelischen Kirchen in der DDR (Association of Protestant Churches in the GDR) was formed.

The Churches' different situations were also reflected in the role and self-image of their leaders. The Protestant Bishop Otto Dibelius (1880-1967), who had revived the Protestant Konsistorium as soon as possible in May 1945, was the most outspoken of them, developing an overtly critical attitude towards the GDR regime.⁴ In 1949, for example, he decentralised the church administration by moving parts of it to East Berlin in an attempt to counteract its increasing separation from the West. At the same time, he was anxious to support the churches in the Soviet sector financially for as long as possible, assuming that the Socialists would sooner or later prevent the Church from doing its work. The downside of this positive discrimination, however, was

---

3 "Protestant" in this context refers to what might be called both "*Evangelisch*" and "*Protestantisch*" in German. It is worth noting that Berlin has been predominantly Protestant since the seventeenth century. It was not until the eighteenth century that the first Catholics came to the city, and they have always been in the minority, at about ten percent of the population (even up until the present day).

4 Since 1925, Dibelius had been the Generalsuperintendent (General Superintendent) of the Landeskirchen with responsibility for Berlin. As a result of a series of conflicts with the National Socialists, he resigned in 1933 and became involved with the Bekennende Kirche from that point on. He was bishop of the Berlin Landeskirchen until 1966 (in practice, after 1961, this meant of West Berlin).

that it became harder for the congregations in West Berlin to receive funding from their own synod. Dibelius's Catholic counterpart, Bishop Wilhelm Weskamm (1891-1956), was less forthright. Manoeuvring with greater care during his short tenure (1951-1956), he was essentially preoccupied with rebuilding St.-Hedwig-Kathedrale, which had been left in near total ruins by the Allied bombing in 1943. He was succeeded by Julius Döpfner (1913-1976), who left Berlin after only a couple of years, whereupon Alfred Bengsch (1921-1979) became the new bishop in 1961, only three days after the erection of the Wall. Continuing the diplomatic course of his predecessors, he was given monthly permission to cross the Wall to minister to the eastern portion of his flock — contrary to Dibelius, who fiercely fought the Communist rule until his death in 1967.

Although freedom of religion and conscience, as well as a ban on discrimination against Christians, were inscribed in the constitution of the GDR, the state promoted an atheist world view and actively restricted the social role of the churches. However, the Protestant and Catholic churches were the only large organisations in the GDR which were not directly answerable to the Sozialistische Einheitspartei Deutschlands (SED, the Communist party), which gave them freedoms not granted to other institutions. As a result, the Protestant Landeskirchen and the Catholic bishoprics on both sides of the border were able to continue working together for a considerable time. The Referat für Kirchenfragen (Department of Church Affairs) gradually took a dim view of these developments, however.[5]

The relationship between church and state changed constantly over the lifespan of the GDR. After the state had failed to win the churches over to the socialist system (based on having a common enemy in fascism), it started censoring them more. At the third party conference in 1950, for example, the SED emphasised the state's right to promote "dialectical materialism as the philosophical world view of the working classes" in schools — famously summarised by Marx's dictum that "it is not the consciousness of men that determines their being, but, on the contrary, their social being that determines their consciousness".[6] Although in 1958, a group of SED leaders were instructed by Moscow to cease indiscriminately persecuting Christians — for fear that religious radicalism would result in opposition movements — political pressure was ramped up in the 1960s with an increase in repressive measures. In November 1962, for instance, the Referat für Kirchenfragen suggested banning West German church council members from entering the GDR as part of a move to convince its own citizens to convert to the "correct" faith. Moreover,

5 Berlin, LA, Akte C Rep. 104/95, *Die Arbeit des Referats Kirchenfragen des Magistrats* (1953-1962).
6 Karl Marx, *Zur Kritik der Politischen Ökonomie*, preface, 1859, Marx-Engels Werke 13, 9. All quotes have been translated from the German original.

parents could be penalised if their children did not take part in the *Jugendweihe*, a secular, socialist form of confirmation. After Erich Honecker (1912-1994) became the new GDR leader in 1971, a slight easing set in, for it became clear that the attempts to bring the churches in line with Socialism had failed thus far. Nevertheless, churches were requested to renounce their negative views of Socialism and support the state's humanitarian and peace goals.[7] This upswing in relations culminated in a meeting between Honecker and a delegation of the German churches at which the religious freedom guaranteed by the constitution was confirmed, along with the churches' role in society, under the slogan "The Church in Socialism" (which also became the title of a church magazine). With hindsight, all this was highly significant, for in the course of the 1980s, the churches offered shelter to opposition elements and dissidents and thus contributed to the collapse of the GDR.[8]

The institutional development sketched above was reflected in not only the relatively low number of churches built in East Berlin, but also the official urban planning policies. For example, church buildings were not mentioned in either the famous Sechszehn Grundsätzen des Städtebaus ("Sixteen Principles of Urban Design", the socialist counterpart to the Athens Charter of the Congrès Internationaux d'Architecture Moderne, or CIAM) or the Aufbaugesetz, a general policy document on the planning of cities in the GDR. This omission was officially endorsed by Lothar Bolz (1903-1986), the Minister for Construction, during a speech in 1950:

> We do not intend to alter the appearance of our cities beyond recognition, nor to offer up a new entirely uniform design, but we do want to enliven them with a new spirit. We do not need cities whose centre is defined by a palace and its lord. We also do not need cities whose appearance is designed by stock exchanges, banks and their masters. Neither barracks nor bureaux de change should shape our cities' image. Instead, it should be creative people's great social buildings which put them as the masters of the political economic and cultural life of their homeland.[9]

Although one can clearly understand that church buildings, too, would be considered symbols of the old social order, they were not explicitly mentioned, allegedly so as to not upset the large part of the population that still adhered to Christian denominations. Nonetheless, it was clear that in the regime's mind, the city centre of Berlin was supposed to represent the new socialist order; thus, there was no room for religious buildings. This had already become clear in 1949 with the blasting of the Georgenkirche (Saint George's Church) near the city centre; officially demolished for its ruinous state, its destruction was

---

7 Henkys, "Eine neue Qualität", 12-13.
8 Israel, *Zur Freiheit berufen. Die Kirche in der DDR*.
9 Bolz, *Von deutschem Bauen. Reden und Aufsätze*, 21.

clearly ideologically motivated. Indeed, as Walter Ulbricht (1893-1973, then secretary-general of the SED and GDR leader between 1960 and 1971) made clear in his famous "Tower Speech" on the occasion of the inauguration of the model city of Eisenhüttenstadt (formerly Stalinstadt) in 1953: "Yes! We'll have towers, for example a tower for the town hall, a tower for the cultural centre. We can't have other towers in the socialist city."[10]

Despite the 1958 instructions from Moscow to stop repression, it became ever harder for parishes to get permission or even support for building projects. The difficult situation the churches found themselves in becomes clear in the arguments used in a reply by the planning administration to the Konsistorium's proposal with regards to the future pastoral needs of Berlin. Stating bluntly that the number of inhabitants in East Berlin would continue to decrease in the near future, it said that no new churches were deemed necessary.[11] Nonetheless, there were several instances where the state contributed to the maintenance or construction of new churches, especially in the course of the 1970s, when the GDR leadership gradually softened its stance towards the Church. In 1972, for example, a considerable budget (55 million deutschmarks) was made available to revert surviving churches of historical or architectural importance to normal parish usage. Further, as a result of increasing international pressure, the SED leadership allowed the Protestant Church to erect a total of fifty-five new buildings (mainly churches and community centres) in the new towns that were planned, as part of a special building programme entitled "Churches for New Cities", and initiated a parallel programme for the Catholic Church. Ironically, perhaps, the first such project was a new community centre in Eisenhüttenstadt.[12]

In terms of financing, the official policy was that new church buildings were to be paid for by donations to the EKD. In reality, large sums were donated by the West German churches, but often this money was diverted to other aims, such as financing Honecker's social reform programs. The relative boom in church building in new housing areas in Berlin was therefore not only related to a relaxation of the GDR's policies, but also an indication of the regime's need for foreign currency. This becomes clearest when looking at the situation for the Catholic Church, which cleverly capitalised on its minority position and structural ties across the intra-German border through the so-called LIMEX programme (named after the state's foreign trade company). The idea was that finances would be secured from West Germany, but building

10 Ulbricht, quoted in Kitschke, *Die Kirchen der Potsdamer Kulturlandschaft*, 22-23. See also <https://kirchensprengung.de/kirchensprengung-home> (last accessed 03/07/2020).
11 Berlin, LA, Akte C, Rep. 104, No. 574, Städtebauliche Stellungnahme zum Bedarfsplan der evangelischen Kirche zur Errichtung kirchlicher Gebäude in der Berliner Innenstadt, 1 November 1960.
12 Scheffler, "Devisenbeschaffungs programm Kirchenbau".

4.2 The Catholic Kirche Maria, Königin des Friedens in Berlin-Biesdorf by Architektenkollektiv Rodnick, Laute and Limberg (consecrated 1983). The first church in East Berlin to be built as part of the LIMEX programme.
[Photo courtesy of the Bundesarchiv (183-1984-0926-300 / Junge, Peter Heinz / CC-BY-SA 3.0)]

materials would be procured in the GDR.[13] The first church built under this scheme, St. Marien, was consecrated on 1 April 1978 in Premnitz (Westhavelland). In Berlin, the first LIMEX church was the Kirche Maria Königin des Friedens (architect Ralf Rufnick, built 1982-1983). [Ill. 4.2] Nevertheless, despite this financial opportunism, church building remained a marginal activity in East Berlin. In fact, far more buildings were demolished than built anew, with the total number of Protestant churches decreasing by fifteen units between 1945 and 1989, to eighty-six in total. The Catholics were only slightly better off: their total number of churches rose from thirty-one to thirty-four. The effect of the official politics of discouraging churches thus became clearly visible in the urban landscape.

In fact, before the Second World War, there had been an equal density in terms of churches across Berlin. This shifted massively during the division, however, with many more churches built in the western part of the city. As mentioned before, right after the war, it was understood that the role of the churches needed to be strengthened and their infrastructure rebuilt quickly. To this effect, the World Council of Churches initiated a program of so-called *Barackenkirchen*: provisory church buildings that consisted of serial pre-produced wooden barracks. Two examples were built in West Berlin, namely the Alt-lutherische Freikirche (Old Lutheran Free Church) in Steglitz and the Kirchsaal der evangelischen Brüdergemeine (Brethren Church) in Neukölln. Another initiative was Otto Bartning's (1883-1959) Notkirchen-Programm (Emergency Churches Programme), which proposed a more durable solution based on prefabricated structural systems. Realised in great numbers across Germany from 1947 to 1950, its application in Berlin remained limited, one example being the Offenbarungskirche (Church of the Revelation) in Friedrichshain. The fact that Protestant churches weren't considered sacred spaces (contrary to Catholic ones) and the crucial role they played in creating a sense of community amongst the population in the early post-war days may explain why, at a later stage, many churches were effectively conceived of as community centres, providing space for community activities, offices, kindergartens or mini-clubs, as well as charitable associations.

In general, places of worship in West Berlin in the post-war period fall into four groups. To start with, a number of iconic churches were built that attracted national and international attention, such as the much-debated Kaiser-Wilhelm-Gedächtniskirche (Protestant) by Egon Eiermann (1904-1970) and St.-Agnes-Kirche (Catholic) by Werner Düttmann (1921-1983). Both of these churches are typical of the way Berlin chose to deal with its war wounds in the early 1960s: Eiermann's expressionist treatment of the church ruin became one of the most provocative architectural statements of the decade, while St. Agnes illustrated how the radical restructuring of certain parts of the city was

13 Scheffler, "Devisenbeschaffungs programm Kirchenbau".

erasing its own past. The latter church was meant as a replacement for a 1920s chapel, but the parish had to negotiate for several years to obtain a new site amidst a new housing estate featuring 3,000 apartments.[14] In an attempt to counteract the prevailing amnesia, Düttmann situated the church on the main street cutting through the settlement, opposite a planned village green, as a reminiscence of traditional village structures. Further examples of this type of "monumental" church are Maria Regina Martyrium (built 1960-1963) by Hans Schädel (1910-1996) and St.-Canisius-Kirche (built 1954-1957 and destroyed by fire in 1995) by Reinhard Hofbauer (1907-1976). At the same time, numerous churches damaged during the war were renovated and rebuilt. Examples are the Protestant Epiphanien-Kirche (Epiphany Church) (rebuilt in 1957-1960 by Konrad Sage) and the Catholic St.-Norbert-Kirche (rebuilt in 1961 by Hermann Fehling (1909-1996), Daniel Gogel (1927-1997) and Peter Pfankuch (1925-1977)). Beyond that, some smaller churches and community centres were built that catered to the parishes that had been separated by the division of Berlin.

Finally, a significant number of new churches were also built to heighten the ecclesiastical offer in residential areas, including the large new housing estates that arose in Berlin. For example, in Gropiusstadt (realised between 1962 and 1975), three Protestant churches and one Catholic church were built at precisely determined locations: the former three are each 1.5 km to 2 km apart, and almost all of the churches are situated in the immediate vicinity of an underground station. Schädel's and Hermann Jünemann's (1936-2019) St.-Dominicus-Kirche (Catholic, built 1975-1977) demonstrated what a truly modern church building could become: positioned in the middle of a square plan and dramatically lit by a skylight in the truncated dome above it, the altar was the focus of attention, with the pews for the faithful grouped in a circle around it.[15] Clearly distinct from this strictly symmetrical setting, the imposing bell tower bore an incision covered by an attached plate — suggesting as a sign of hope that the as-yet-divided diocese remained united under the cross.[16] Despite its modest size, tailored to the small proportion of Catholics living in the area, the church formed a clearly distinguishable urban landmark and introduced a sense of human scale to the anonymous high-rises of Gropiusstadt. With its stylistic, liturgical, communal and urban qualities, this church possessed an almost prototypical character, and two identical counterparts were built at around the same time (St.-Markus-Kirche in Berlin-Spandau and Kirche Zu den heiligen Märtyrern von Afrika (Church of the Holy Martyrs of Africa) in Berlin-Lichtenrade).

14   Berlin, Pfarrarchiv St. Hedwig, 07-20-28-0097-09-001/ -003/ -004.
15   Between 1948 and 1985, Schädel planned over eighty churches (some of them rebuilt), making him one of the most important church architects of the post-war period in Germany. See Lenssen, *Aufbruch im Kirchenbau: die Kirchen von Hans Schädel*. Jünemann was the building director for the Berlin diocese.
16   Streicher and Drave, *Berlin. Stadt und Kirche*, 10.

Summarising, the building activity of the congregations in West Berlin can be said to represent a normal distribution curve (when expressed in numbers, counting only new buildings). Right after the war, in the late 1940s, only a few churches were built — mostly Catholic. During the following decade, by contrast, more than fifty new buildings were realised: "pure" liturgical churches at the onset, but gradually more and more community centres — the majority of which were Protestant. The peak of construction activity was reached in the 1960s, with almost seventy buildings, eighty per cent of which were to serve Protestant congregations. From the 1970s on, production slowed down to just over thirty buildings, still significantly Protestant (seventy-five per cent). Finally, in the 1980s, the only new churches being built were for Catholic parishes. Although it is clear from these numbers that the Protestant congregations built a significant number of churches in the post-war era, their impact on the Berlin cityscape remains limited because the majority of the production was relatively straightforward, with only a few notable exceptions. The Catholic parishes, by contrast, built considerably less, but on the whole, their buildings were more innovative and daring.

The Hansaviertel: A "Shop Window for the West"

As in no other city in Europe, the polarised ideological climate of the early 1950s reflected itself in Berlin's post-war transformation, for architecture and urban planning were actively called upon by both the East and the West as instruments and expressions of their vision of society. In West Berlin, the most important instance of this merging of planning and ideology was the reconstruction of the southern part of the nearly completely destroyed Hansaviertel, which became a projection surface for ideological, architectural and cultural values. What makes it interesting for our discussion is the fact that the new development also featured two church buildings, one Protestant and one Catholic. The main questions, then, involve the extent to which these buildings expressed or contributed to Interbau's overall vision and what this tells us about the place of religion in this self-image of the "free" West.

The Hansaviertel lies between the Spree and the Großer Tiergarten and was originally developed in 1874. An arc-shaped railway viaduct soon divided it into a northern and southern part, without creating all too much of a rupture, though. The area quickly developed into a sophisticated city district; by 1900, 18,000 people lived there, with around 3,500 in the southern part. A large proportion of these were wealthy families, with many businesspeople and artists, including, at some point, Rosa Luxemburg and Walter Benjamin. The diversity of the population was reflected in not only the wide range of building styles along the district's broad, green streets, but also its provision of religious buildings: a Protestant church (the Kaiser-Friedrich-Gedächtniskirche) was built early on, followed by various synagogues and, finally, in 1925, a Catholic chapel (St. Ansgar). In the interwar period, Berlin's structural lack of living space and the impact of the global financial crisis affected the Hansaviertel particularly hard, resulting in the subdivision of most of the houses and a steep increase in population. During the war, the area was hit by massive bombing raids on the nights of 22 through 24 November 1943, resulting in the near total destruction of its southern section — only 21 of the 161 pre-war buildings survived — and completely dislocating the district's built and social fabric.

The idea of holding an architectural exhibition (a format that had quite a long tradition in Germany, including the one in Stuttgart in the 1920s that spawned the famous Weissenhofsiedlung) was first put forward in the West Berlin Senate in 1951, when the Senatsbaudirektor (principal government planner of Berlin), Ludwig Lemmer (1891-1983), proposed that the city outdo the Constructa fair in Hanover that had taken place earlier that year.[17] This move was part of a national competition at the time between cities to become the new capital of West Germany and meant to boost Berlin's image and self-confidence. The Hansaviertel was considered as a site for the competition after administrators of the Tiergarten district, to which it belongs, sought to organise a planning contest to remedy the enormous housing shortage there. This was not approved by the Senate, however, which suspended all building activity in the area until 1953, when it announced an urban planning competition for the reconstruction of the entire Hansaviertel. Meant as a response to the building of Stalinallee in East Berlin (today, Karl-Marx-Allee), an unabashed showcase of socialist urban development, the project received an even more important international and ideological dimension when the American administrators pressured the Senate to scale it up into an international showcase of living and dwelling in the Free West. Thus, the idea for the International Building Exhibition Interbau was born.

Participants in the competition had an almost blank canvas at their disposal — a fact that perhaps explains the high number of entries (ninety-eight). Although there were many foreigners amongst them, the first prize went to a trio of Berlin architects: Gerhardt Jobst (1888-1963), Willy Kreuer (1910-1984) and Wilhelm Schließer (life dates unknown). Their entry was praised for its "confident hand", its "completely novel, grand composition" and its emphatic

---

[17] Lemmer studied with, amongst others, Paul Bonatz (1877-1956) in Stuttgart and worked as an independent architect before becoming appointed as the Magistratsbaudirektor (City Architect) of Berlin. In 1951, he became Senatsbaudirektor and taught at the Hochschule für bildende Künste in Berlin.

use of the topographical features of the Tiergarten park and the Spree river.[18] Furthermore, its grouping of buildings was described as "beautiful, without a discernible overarching scheme, and sophisticated". With its loose overall structure, composed of free-standing buildings in a green environment, the scheme perfectly mirrored the modernist planning principles embodied by CIAM's Athens Charter, as well as its underlying disdain for the closed city blocks of the nineteenth-century industrial city. This was no coincidence, of course — for in the post-war world, architectural modernism had become the preferred paradigm in the Western world, and was understood to be the self-evident expression of its core values of freedom, economy and progress. Jobst, Kreuer and Schließer's landscaped, non-hierarchical design wonderfully embodied these ideals. Meanwhile, the planning of the Interbau 57 started under the guidance of Bartning, who in the meantime had become president of the Association of German Architects.

The imposition of a new urban morphology was not the only way the area's past was annihilated; its original property structure was also entirely erased, since most owners were bought out (or had their land expropriated) so that the parcels could be regrouped into bigger lots prior to selling them on to investors and private companies. It is significant, both in the framework of our investigation and as a token of the stabilising role played by the Church after the war (Protestant, in this case), that the sole parcel not affected by any such form of reorganisation was that of the Gedächtniskirche. Finally, to avoid the need for major thoroughfares, the street layout in the southern part of the Hansaviertel was completely redesigned. Of the three roads that once intersected in its central square, Hansaplatz, only Altonaer Strasse was kept, despite predictions that the car to person ratio would rise from 1:16 (one car for every sixteen inhabitants) to 1:5 shortly. The planners wisely proposed instead providing ample public transportation nearby (e.g. a U-Bahn station was built there) and keeping cars away from residential areas as much as possible.[19] The result was a totally new district that stood out in the first place through its green, landscaped character, punctuated here and there by tower blocks or low-rise apartment buildings. Generally speaking, the built density was highest in the area next to the railway arc and decreased towards the border with the Tiergarten, with some sort of urban centre located around Hansaplatz. Despite this massive reduction of built space, though, the number of inhabitants in the new Hansaviertel remained about the same as before. [Ill. 4.3]

18 Quotes are from *Bauwelt*, 1954, 3, 45. At the moment of the competition, Jobst taught urban design at the Technische Hochschule in Berlin. The Zentralinstitut für Städtebau (Central Institute for Urban Design) was founded under his leadership in 1949. Kreuer worked originally in Cologne for, amongst others, Dominikus Böhm, until 1937, when he relocated to Berlin, taking up a job under Werner March. From 1951 on, he also taught at the Technische Universität Berlin.
19 Otto, *Die Stadt von morgen*, 64-69.

4.3 Aerial view of the Hansaviertel from 1962, with most buildings completed. The Kaiser-Friedrich-Gedächtniskirche can be seen at the bottom right; Sankt-Ansgar-Kirche is to the left of the intersection (middle of the image).
[Courtesy of the Landesarchiv Berlin (F Rep. 290 No. 0083467). Photograph by Karl-Heinz Schubert]

The ambition (and supposed success) of the undertaking was to illustrate that West Berlin was viable as an economic entity on its own and that it was supported in this endeavour by the entire free world. For the city's inhabitants, it represented encouragement in their struggles for freedom and progress. Thus, as a symbol of freedom, and a contrast to the state-controlled uniformity of Stalinallee, the Hansaviertel would stage and celebrate the plurality of styles, typologies and shapes that followed naturally from a context of unrestrained freedom and prosperity. To this effect, a wide range of modernist architects from all over the world were given almost free reign to develop their views on the contemporary dwelling and materialise them on-site. What had been lauded initially as one of the main qualities of the urban master plan —

namely, that it would harness individualist excesses in the architectural fabric — now ironically became a major problem, however. Indeed, the quest for an overall uniformity in building shapes and sizes contradicted Interbau's fundamental premise: to demonstrate individuality through a wide range of very different architects.[20] No fewer than fifty-three architects and ten landscape designers were invited to contribute to Interbau: nineteen from outside Germany, sixteen from West Germany and eighteen from West Berlin. Curiously, all the non-residential buildings were entrusted to well-established German architects from Berlin: the two churches went to Lemmer, the Senatsbaudirektor, and Kreuer, a partner of the team that won the urban design competition; the municipal library was entrusted to Düttmann; and the only school in the area was given to Bruno Grimmek. As to the reason for this restricted access to public commissions, we can only speculate, but it suggests that the room for experimentation at Interbau was limited to the realm of private dwellings.

When Interbau finally opened on 6 July 1957, only a third of the planned buildings were effectively finished. This did not affect its success, however; in the course of three months, it drew over a million visitors. The observation crane and chairlift were very popular amongst the visitors, who could also view a number of model apartments and be impressed by their modern conveniences, such as central heating. The new residential blocks (to the extent they were completed or even partially built at the time of the show) constituted only one facet of Interbau, however; the accompanying events and temporary exhibitions may have been an ever bigger attraction. Alongside a large number of pavilions representing West Germany's various federal states, Interbau featured a temporary hall with a futuristic space-frame roof that housed an exhibition called "The City of Tomorrow" — which was, apart from its content, also groundbreaking as an avant-garde demonstration of visual communication.[21]

The exhibition was curated by the architect Karl Otto (1904-1975) and consisted of two parts.[22] The first part focused on theoretical approaches to modern architecture and urban planning, posing questions about how future societies would want to live. Considering the city as the logical habitat of the future, it asked how one should grapple with its inherent issues, such as lack of space, traffic congestion, pollution and noise, before suggesting possible solutions. The exhibition explicitly renounced the dense city models of the nineteenth century, with their tenement blocks, rear courtyards and narrow alleyways (which were further identified as the very reason for societal disorder, along with the traditional mixing of living, working, recreation and trans-

20 *Verordnung Hansaviertel*, 16–17.
21 Wagner-Conzelmann, *Die Interbau 1957*.
22 Otto studied under Hans Poelzig (1869-1936) and worked in Mies van der Rohe's (1886-1969) studio. As director of the Berliner Hochschule der bildenden Künste in 1955, he led his own practice alongside teaching and designed a large number of school buildings.

portation), and presented an alternative model: a more dispersed, structured urban landscape that would foster social bonding and family values. As its basic tenet, the exhibition's narrative held that people wanted to live *with*, and not merely *next to*, one another, and the topic of human relationships (then also among CIAM's main preoccupations) occupied central stage. As it was stated, the living conditions in future cities ought to protect and shape individuals, families and neighbourhood communities, in order for society "to re-discover an orderly structure"[23]. In such an environment "the shared responsibility of each individual towards the wider community would flourish in accordance with true democracy".[24] Further, in acknowledgement of the central role it plays in people's well-being and man's most basic needs, nature was also accorded due attention. Relating it to the central theme of the exhibition in his essay in the exhibition catalogue, Otto stressed that the core of future cities would need to consist of healthy, open, green spaces, with a skeleton of green corridors emanating from their centres to integrate them more fully into their surroundings. This was no less than a reversal of traditional urban form. Indeed, as Otto wrote:

> The green space as the centre of the city takes the place of the built, constructed central points of previous eras (church, palace, etc.). The design of the green centre can take any form. At its edges, the buildings of government, administration, church and society can develop.[25]

Thus, in the city of the future, civic and collective values were no longer expressed through buildings such as the town hall, the cathedral or the market, but by the democratic, egalitarian green spaces that grouped them together.

This inversion of the town centre was also a recurrent feature in the series of plans for the rebuilding of cities across Germany that were shown in the second part of the exhibition. In striking contrast with the setting most Germans had known in their youth, churches occupied only a peripheral position in most of these plans, if present at all. Only one proposal explicitly capitalised on the structuring capacity of church buildings, namely a detailed study for a satellite town near Aachen by Erich Kühn (1902-1981).[26] Inspired by the then-ubiquitous concept of the neighbourhood unit, his proposal was for a city of 200,000 inhabitants, composed of five units of 40,000 each, and fur-

23 Message on one of the exhibition panels; quoted in: <https://hansaviertel.berlin/en/interbau-1957/die-stadt-von-morgen/> (accessed 18/06/2020).
24 Quoted from the catalogue in <https://hansaviertel.berlin/en/interbau-1957/die-stadt-von-morgen/> (accessed 18/06/2020).
25 Otto, *Die Stadt von morgen*, 49.
26 Ibid., 87-98. Kühn studied in Munich and Berlin and mainly worked in public service. At the end of his professional career, he became dean of the Rheinisch-Westfälische Technische Hochschule in Aachen from 1965 to 1967.

ther subdivided into units of 10,000, 2,500 and 650.[27] As Kühn explained, the size, spatial organisation and scale of these subdivisions derived from their basic public amenities for religion, education and administration, essential instruments in creating a sense of community. The units of 10,000 inhabitants were key, according to Kühn — large enough to be considered "small cities", they formed the essential building blocks of his urban constellation. Interestingly, Kühn derived the number of inhabitants and size per unit from what he considered to be the "ideal catchment area" of the largest of these amenities, namely the church. Stating that the ideal size of a parish was 5,000 inhabitants — a number frequently put forward in the literature on parish planning at that time — and that in the Aachen region, both Christian faiths were equally represented, Kühn straightforwardly deduced that 10,000 people was the ideal size for his basic units and that both denominations would have to be located in the geographical centre.

In most other city plans, the distribution of churches seemed to follow a more administrative logic, determined by federal statistics about the number of dwellings needed to make public amenities (for education, culture, religion and so forth) economically viable. In one proposal for an extension of Bremen, for example, the author quite optimistically proposed one church per neighbourhood unit of 2,000 flats, but by positioning them more towards the edges of these neighbourhoods, he failed to capitalise on the churches' spatial and social structuring capacity.[28] Even so, the proposals on display at the "City of Tomorrow" exhibit offered a salient expression of how during the 1950s, urban form, life style and social values were seen as an indivisible whole. The question now becomes how the two churches in the Hansaviertel fit in with that picture.

The Interbau Churches

The original, neo-Gothic, Kaiser-Friedrich-Gedächtniskirche in the Hansaviertel was built in 1895 by Johannes Vollmer (1845-1920) in remembrance of the so-called "99-day Emperor", Friedrick III, father of Emperor William II.[29] [Ill. 4.4] The church was slightly offset at the intersection of Lessingstrasse and Händelallee, orientated north–south (instead of east–west), and its prominent steeple — set laterally from the church body in the axis of Lessingstrasse — gave it a strong visual presence from Hansaplatz and far beyond. With the neighbourhood severely damaged in the bombing raids of November 1943, community and parish life came to a complete standstill after the majority

---

27 Otto, *Die Stadt von morgen*, 93.
28 Ibid., 173.
29 Gundermann, "Hundert Jahre Kaiser-Friedrich-Gedächtniskirche".

4.4 The original Kaiser-Friedrich-Gedächtniskirche in the Hansaviertel by Johannes Vollmer (built 1892-1895).
[Contemporary postcard. Collection of the author]

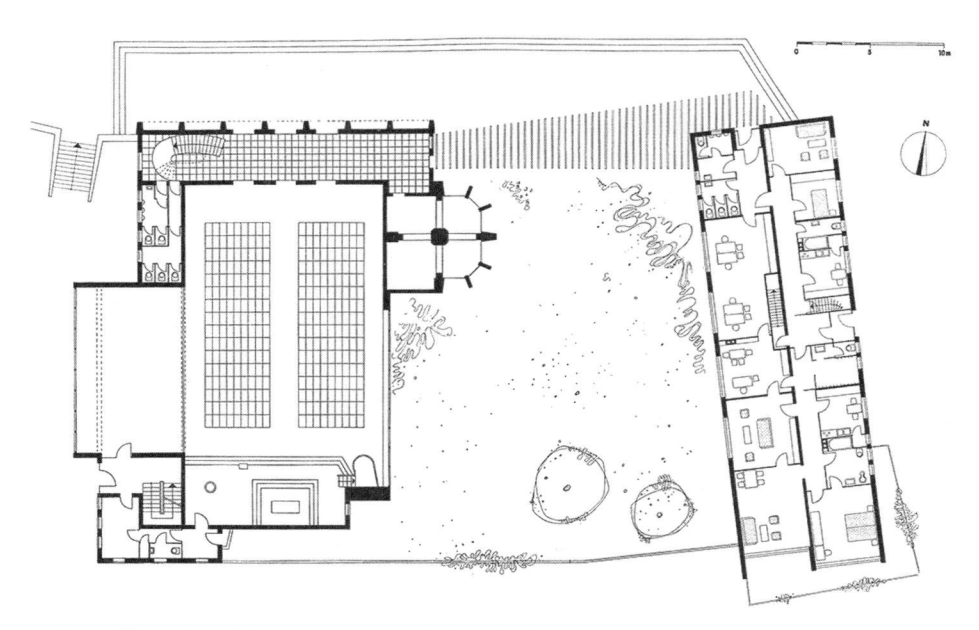

4.5 Ground floor plan of the new Kaiser-Friedrich-Gedächtniskirche and community spaces by Ludwig Lemmer (built 1955-1957).
[Reproduced from *Interbau Berlin 1957*]

of the residents left the area. It was only in 1947, under the impetus of the dynamic pastor Fritz Schmidt-Clausing (1902-1984), that initiatives were taken to bring the church and its congregation back to life. One of the pastor's ideas was to ring the church's sole remaining bell in honour of the prisoners of war that returned from Russia; with the Hansaviertel being situated close to the Russian sector, this gesture did not go unnoticed in the early days of the Cold War and drew attention to the forlorn congregation. Once the Berlin Senate decided to rebuild the Hansaviertel from scratch, the church ruins were cleared away, after the congregation received confirmation from Bartning — himself a devout Protestant and influential church designer — that a new church would be erected on exactly the same site as part of Interbau. Apart from the symbolical significance, there were also economic and administrative reasons for this: the congregation owned the land, which allowed for the foundations of the old church to be reused.

The new church was a simple, single-nave construction designed by Lemmer. [Ill. 4.5] Determined by the footprint and orientation of the old church, its entrance lay to the north, where three two-leaf doors lead to a wide atrium; from there, one could either progress into the church, climb the open stairwell that gave access to a gallery along the western wall of the nave or access the base of the steeple. Although the proportions of the church space proper were almost the same as the historical building, the original cross-shaped floorplan (where the arms were used as assembly rooms) was not kept: the choir was only half as deep and now asymmetrically positioned; the western arm made way for a weekday chapel (underneath the gallery); and a huge stained-glass wall replaced the eastern arm of the cross. In typically Protestant fashion, the main liturgical elements (altar, pulpit, lectern and font) were grouped closely together, with an emphasis on the pulpit, dramatically positioned next to the glass wall and elevated from the choir by a set of five steps. Lemmer used all the architectural means at his disposal to focus attention on this part of the interior: the pews (seating 230) were orientated parallel to the altar in two rows, thus strongly emphasising the axial orientation of the interior, and the large window in the eastern façade and slightly tilted roof (the wall height ranges from 9 m to 11 m) added to this sense of expansion of the space towards the altar. This progression from darkness to light, or from everyday preoccupations into the realm of the spiritual, was a symbol of hope in the war-ravaged context of Berlin.[30] Further differences from the original building were to be found outside. Particular importance was given, for example, to the forecourt of the church. Contrary to the old situation, where two steps led up to the church, the new building featured a generous rising plateau from the street level to serve as a place for informal assembly or formal celebration on particular occasions. Totally different in terms of scale, position and form — as if to visually articulate its secular, auxiliary status — a new vicarage and community centre with spaces for youth and families were also built; the pergola linking it to the church also acted as a divider between the public domain and the church courtyard, thus contributing to its secluded feel and reflecting its status as a safe haven for the young families that would come to populate the new Hansaviertel.

The level of Schmidt-Clausing and Lemmer's ambitions with the Gedächtniskirche can perhaps best be measured against its huge steeple. Originally meant to be freestanding and 80 m high — the height of the original tower — it was eventually reduced to 68 m, the same height as the Siegessäule (Victory Column) in the nearby Tiergarten. [Ill. 4.6] Just like the old spire, but now articulated as an open tower constructed from rods of reinforced concrete (nicknamed "*Der Seelenbohrer*", or "Soul-driller"), the height and unique shape of the tower not only secured its visual presence across a considerable distance, but also imbued it with political meaning. Indeed, Schmidt-Clausing, never too shy when it came to promoting his congregation, wanted it "to shine across to the Eastern sector of Berlin".[31] This "promotional" aspect of the church was also reflected in its materiality. Apart from a reinforced concrete frame, the predominant material used in its construction was, quite surprisingly for a

---

30 <https://www.ev-gemeinde-tiergarten.de/page/45/die-geschichte-der-kaiser-friedrich-ged%C3%A4chtniskirche> (accessed 18/06/2020).
31 Cante, *Sakralbauten*, 215.

4.6 View of the new Kaiser-Friedrich-Gedächtniskirche with its imposing tower.
[Contemporary postcard. Collection of the author]

church, aluminium. This was a new, experimental building material at the time, and its application in the building industry was heavily promoted by West German and Swiss companies, who donated over 30 tonnes of it for use in almost every part of the building: from the corrugations and cross of the steeple to the window frames, railings, pulpit, lectern, organ casing, gallery decoration and ceiling. Schmidt-Clausing's proposal for a huge aluminium cross in the forecourt of the church — jokingly referred to as "Saint Aluminium" in a promotional leaflet — was ultimately rejected, though.[32]

An ambitious project such as this naturally comes with a huge cost, and the congregation was only able to carry its financial burden by spreading it across a large number of shoulders. Schmidt-Clausing himself played an important role in this, for he understood how to mobilise people and organisations for his pastoral project. The church was thus financed through numerous donations, loans and subsidies. Alongside more conventional funding sources such as the Berliner Stadtsynodalausschuss (Council of Protestant Churches of Berlin) and the GARIOA emergency aid program (set up by the United States to prevent starvation in the occupied zones after the war), there were more unusual donors, such as the governments of various federal states and mayors from a number of important German cities. The altar bible, for example, was donated by Federal President Theodor Heuss and the altar crucifix by Prince Louis Ferdinand and Princess Kira of Prussia. The Hanseatic cities of Bremen, Hamburg and Lübeck donated the three bells, while the Federal Government offered to pay for the cross on top of the steeple. The large stained-glass window in the weekday chapel (designed by Willy Fries, 1881-1965) was donated by Dibelius and the Protestant Hilfswerk Berlin, while the huge glass wall in the opposite façade (designed by Georg Meistermann, 1911-1990) was funded by a group of cities and companies affiliated with the North Rhine-Westphalia State Government. In addition, the states of Baden-Württemberg and Hesse, and even Lemmer himself, funded specific artworks (namely, a series of figures by Ludwig Peter Kowalski (1891-1967) for the round windows), while the three main entrance doors were donated by the city of Bonn.

Although of a predominantly symbolical nature, all this generosity was still very important, for it underscored the political importance attached to this church as a symbol of a free, Christian Germany. There was also a downside to it, however, for most of the donors then wished to have a say in the choice of artists or the design of their gift. As a result, the church contained not only a high number, but also a great variety of artworks from many different artists. [Ill. 4.7] This contrasted with the Protestant idea of restraint; moreover, the modern, expressionist depiction of some biblical scenes caused some controversy. Fries's stained-glass window, for example, was criticised for not only its pessimistic undertone, but also the fact that it depicted a cru-

---

32 *Aluminium und die Kaiser-Friedrich-Gedächtniskirche*, 2.

4.7 Interior view towards the altar of the Kaiser-Friedrich-Gedächtniskirche. The large mosaic at the back was designed by Hans Stocker and Ludwig Lemmer. From the pulpit, one can address the faithful seated in both the gallery and the day chapel.
[Postcard. Collection of the author]

cifixion scene with soldiers resembling those of the Reichswehr. The contrast with Meistermann's "light wall", entitled *Sieg des Lichts* (Victory of the Light), was somewhat awkward, to say the least. Despite the involvement of so many actors, though, design and construction of the church proceeded swiftly, and it was consecrated on 10 July 1957, almost exactly two years after the laying of the foundation stone and just four days after the opening of Interbau.

While the Gedächtniskirche came about relatively smoothly, the same cannot be said for its Catholic counterpart, which could not simply be rebuilt on its old site. The original congregation had been founded in 1925 as a dependence of the parish of St. Sebastian, with the faithful convening in a garage at the back of a house on Altonaer Strasse, which was transformed into a chapel dedicated to Saint Ansgar, patron saint of the North. That site of worship was relatively short-lived, however; the chapel was destroyed in the air raids of November 1943. Still, the street-side house remained intact, and this became the congregation's new home after a chapel was arranged in the basement. The newly appointed parish priest, Bernhard Schwerdtfeger (1914-1981), did not let the grass grow under his feet: as soon as he heard about the redevelopment of the Hansaviertel (made public in March 1951), he went to the Tiergarten Town

Hall to inquire whether a Catholic church had been included in the plans. This being the case, the persuasive and indefatigable Schwerdtfeger managed to gain the support of various important participants in the Hansaviertel project, such as Lemmer and Bartning, as well as his own superiors within the Catholic hierarchy, in particular, Deputy Secretary Georg Banasch (1888-1960) and, importantly, his Protestant counterpart, Schmidt-Clausing. Schwerdtfeger's efforts quickly paid off: in early 1954, the Interbau organisers committed themselves to the construction of a Catholic church in the centre of the district. After various locations had been examined, the choice fell upon a site at the corner of Altonaer Strasse and Klopstock Strasse, close to the original site of the pre-war chapel. However, unlike the Protestant congregation, the Catholic community did not own the plot, a fact that would delay the project until April 1956, when the owner of Klopstock Strasse 39 finally gave in. Once the purchase was finally concluded, the plot was cleared of everything except the two adjacent houses, for they contained the temporary chapel and the priest's flat.

Quite surprisingly perhaps, by this point, an architect for the church's design had long since been chosen. In his very first meeting with Schwerdtfeger, Banasch had suggested entrusting Kreuer — part of the team of architects that had won the urban design competition — with the task. This was not a self-evident choice, given that although he was an established architect (e.g. having designed the iconic Amerika Gedenkbibliothek), Kreuer had not previously designed any religious buildings. Nonetheless, his initial sketches (although designed without a particular site in mind) were quickly approved by the church board and the commission was formalised in August 1954.

Just like its Protestant counterpart, St.-Ansgar-Kirche consisted of two parts: the church proper and a secondary building with clergy accommodations, rooms for parish associations and youth clubs and a parish hall with a capacity of 150. The two volumes were connected by a sacristy and enclosed a courtyard, which was also accessible/visible from the street. [Ill. 4.8] For the rest, Kreuer's approach was very different from Lemmer's. Contrary to the static, shoe-box shape of the Gedächtniskirche, St. Ansgar's was defined by a sweeping parabola, materialised as a blind concrete wall on the side of the adjacent S-Bahn and through a series of staggered windowpanes on the side facing the courtyard. Seating 250, the church space was directly accessible from the street, without an atrium separating the interior from the street side. Once inside, the focus of attention was, of course, the altar zone, articulated through simple architectural means: located in the vertex of the parabola, it was slightly raised and visually set apart from the main space through a different ceiling treatment. Kreuer envisaged his church as a *Gesamtkunstwerk* (a total work of art), meaning that all the elements and materials were to form part of a uniform, premeditated scheme, instead of being added a posteriori as had been the case in the Protestant church. To this end, he worked closely

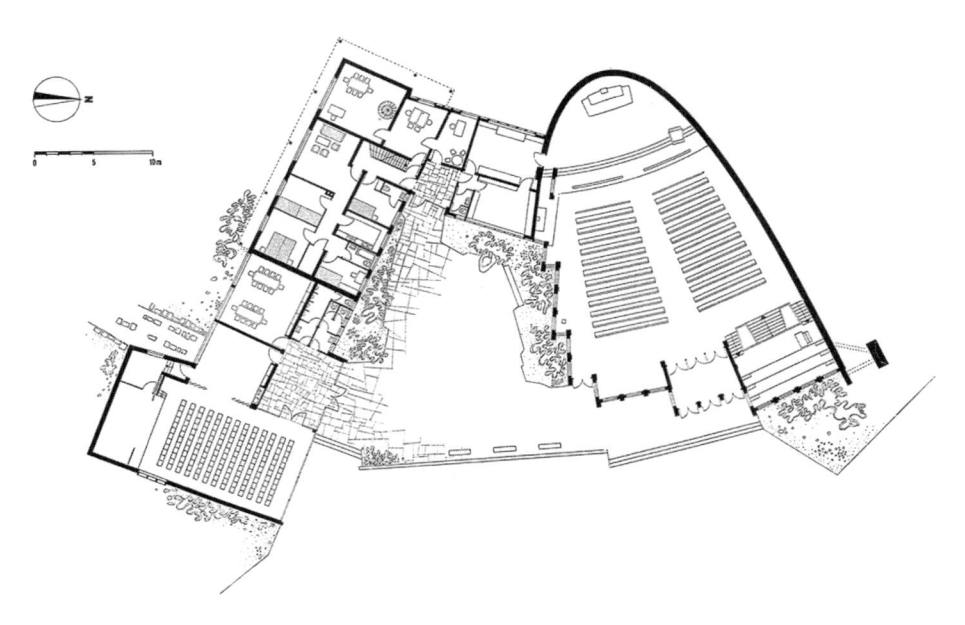

4.8 Ground floor plan of Sankt-Ansgar-Kirche and community rooms by Willy Kreuer (built 1954-1957). [Reproduced from *Interbau Berlin 1957*]

with only two artists: Kowalski (who had also contributed to the Gedächtniskirche) and Gabriel Schrieber (1907-1975). The latter designed the portals in wrought copper that were funded by the three Hanseatic cities (Bremen, Lübeck and Hamburg) and depict scenes from the life of Saint Ansgar. Originally, a gold tabernacle stood on the simple, grey-green syenite altar, with a dark *stucco lustro* crucifixion scene as a backdrop, also designed by Schrieber — a powerful ensemble whose expressive power was lost, however, when the altar was moved away from the wall and the tabernacle removed according to the post-conciliar guidelines. [Ill. 4.9] The same artist also designed the baptismal font in rose quartz, which, with its wrought silver lid, constitutes the brightest point in the church. The only other artwork is a monumental depiction by Kowalski of the Stations of the Cross on the windowless, parabolic wall. A final difference between the two Hansaviertel churches is their spires. Unlike the Gedächtniskirche, St.-Ansgar-Kirche is located near the Hansaviertel's high rises, a backdrop that would make even the tallest spire look pointless. Kreuer therefore conceived of it more as a sculptural signpost from which a cross protrudes. [Ill. 4.10]

Despite the church's relative simplicity, its construction cost a lot of blood, sweat and tears. Shortly after the foundation stone was laid on 21 October 1956, the main contractor filed for bankruptcy, forcing the parish committee to raise the necessary funds to pay the construction workers' outstanding salaries. The rest of the cost of construction was covered by loans and sub-

4.9 Interior view towards the altar of the Sankt-Ansgar-Kirche by Willy Kreuer (built 1954-1957), after the liturgical rearrangement following the Second Vatican Council.
[Postcard. Collection of the author]

sidies from various parties, such as the GARIOA rebuilding fund, the Berlin Senate, the lottery and the federal Ministerium for Gesamtdeutsche Fragen (Ministry for Pan-German Affairs), but the parishioners had to also cover interior decorations. Their efforts paid off: just over a year later, on 1 November 1957, the church was consecrated by Bishop Döpfner — well after Interbau had closed on 29 September.

Any discussion about the Hansaviertel churches cannot avoid the question of whether they were able to live up to the multiple expectations for them. Throughout the various phases of its design, the Gedächtniskirche project was covered several times in the German architecture magazine *Bauwelt*.[33] In 1954, the magazine published a model of the church, commenting that, although not uncontroversial, it was a satisfying proposal in many regards, one that would soon catch the eye of the world and provide a clear focal point in the vast area of the new Hansaviertel, since "thanks to its slender spire, it would be able to hold on against the tall residential buildings."[34] Reviewers also stated that the architect had skilfully managed to make the best of the constraints

33 *Bauwelt*, 52 (1954), 1023; 36 (1956), 879; 24 (1957), 588.
34 *Bauwelt*, 52 (1954), 1023.

4.10 Sankt-Ansgar-Kirche at the corner of Altonaer Strasse and Klopstock Strasse by Willy Kreuer (built 1954-1957).
[Postcard. Collection of the author]

imposed upon him by the existing foundations. As we can derive from these high-flung comments, expectations for the new Hansaviertel churches were high. There were various reasons for that: the context of Interbau, both as an ideological vehicle and a world showcase for modernist architectural ideals; the symbolical meaning of the two churches as expressions of freedom of conscience in the West and unity between the two Christian denominations; their role as architectural and artistic models of modern religiosity; and finally, the reputation of the architects involved.

Nonetheless, the project seems to have met with quite some disapproval initially because it overturned the Protestant ethos of modesty and parsimony — a failure that, as we have seen, may have derived from competing visions between the overambitious pastor, the various donors, the political aspirations for the project and the Interbau affiliation. The resulting lack of sympathy became painfully apparent in the year of its consecration, when the Evangelische Kirchenbautagung (Protestant Church's Building Conference) took place in Berlin in September 1957 as part of Interbau, under the title "Church

Architecture in the City of the Future".³⁵ Quite surprisingly, the programme of tours did not include the Kaiser-Friedrich-Gedächtniskirche, and neither Schmidt-Clausing nor Lemmer were invited to speak. Instead, Gerhard Langmaack (1898-1986), a Hamburg architect, gave a speech on "Church Architecture in the City of the Future", in which he concluded:

> No directly valid example for our main theme of church architecture in the city of the future can be found in the Interbau, in either the approach to city planning as a whole or in the organisation of parishes, ... Unfortunately, there is no evidence of any deliberate intellectual grappling with our set of central questions throughout the entire Interbau.³⁶

What makes this all the more remarkable is that the conference took place within walking distance of the newly built church and that Bartning — who had actively supported its construction — was also present. Federal President Heuss is also reported to have said that he was relieved that the church's steeple had finally not been built as planned originally. He suggested that building a church as a conscious provocation to the Eastern sector contradicted its basic significance as a place of peace and conciliation. If such a perception were to take hold, it would be hard to shake off and could be a cause of problems in the future.³⁷

While the Protestant church had to deal with a great deal of criticism, or indeed contempt, St. Ansgar encountered less criticism — partly, perhaps, because it remained more under the radar given that only a minority of the population in Berlin was Catholic. Nonetheless, the depiction of the Stations of the Cross did arouse some disapproval.³⁸ Moreover, when a well-attended service was held in the church in late 1957 to commemorate the opening of the new Bundestag, then-Chancellor Konrad Adenauer is reported to have expressed to Bishop Döpfner his hope that "the reconstruction of Saint Hedwig's [the historic Berlin cathedral] would be more successful than the newly built Saint Ansgar's church".³⁹

Given the high profile of both churches, such public expressions of disapproval must have been quite embarrassing for their designers, Lemmer and Kreuer. But perhaps their participation was also part of the problem: although both were established architects, neither had experience with church design or working with congregations and ambitious pastors — a fact that helps explain why their designs failed to resolve the tensions mentioned above. This

---

35 Heyer, *Evangelische Kirchenbautagung Berlin 1957. Der Kirchenbau in der Stadt der Zukunft*; <http://kirchbauinstitut.de/die-50er-jahre/> (accessed 18/06/2020).
36 Heyer, *Evangelische Kirchenbautagung Berlin 1957*, 60-61.
37 Berlin, ELA, 898, Gemeindeheft zum 100-jährigen Jubiläum, 14.
38 *1957-1982 - St. Ansgar im Hansaviertel Berlin-Tiergarten*, 11.
39 Ibid.

claim is supported by the fact that their involvement allegedly derived primarily from their positions as Senatsbaudirektor and winner of the urban design competition, respectively, along with the decision to reserve the public buildings at Interbau for local architects. If this is true, these commissions constitute another illustration of the firm ties that existed at the time between the political establishment in Berlin and the architectural profession.[40] Whatever the reason, Lemmer's design, in particular, presented an uncomfortable and unresolved tension between innovation and tradition, given that the use of modern construction techniques, new materials and avant-garde art could not conceal the fact that, in liturgical terms, the church remained a very traditional *Wegekirche*. Whether this was the result of the constraints imposed upon the architect (e.g. the foundations of the old church) or derived from deliberate choices remains unclear. It is perhaps precisely because of this ambivalence that the building hardly features in the historiography of post-war church building in Berlin, where it became quickly overshadowed by the polemics about the reconstruction of the nearby Kaiser-Wilhelm-Gedächtniskirche on the Kurfürstendamm. Built between 1959 and 1963 by Eiermann, its radical concept (leaving part of the church in ruins and adding a radically modern addition) made it an internationally acclaimed symbol for the hopes and hardships of Berlin's inhabitants.[41]

Conclusion

As a divided city, Berlin's relationship to its church buildings developed differently on opposite sides of the Wall. It was not just in their different approaches to urban planning or the aesthetics of public buildings that the opposing political systems and their competitive attitudes were expressed. Churches, too, were part of this spatial and visual rhetoric, because their presence (or absence, in the case of East Berlin) had a significant impact on the new cityscape. Whereas in East Berlin, church spires were seen as undesirable symbols of a conquered system, in the West, they represented a society which held freedom as its core belief. Similarly, whereas in West Berlin, equipping new residential complexes with churches seemed almost self-evident, in the East, any such notion was subject to years of arduous wrangling. As we have seen,

40 Heischkel, *Bauen in West-Berlin 1949-1963*.
41 In Biedrzynski's *Kirchen unserer Zeit* there is a very positive account of St. Ansgar; the Gedächtniskirche is mentioned only in passing. Schnell's *Der Kirchenbau des 20. Jahrhunderts in Deutschland* mentions St. Ansgar but not the Gedächtniskirche. Finally, in Weyres and Bartning's *Kirchen: Handbuch für den Kirchenbau* Berlin is mentioned hardly at all. In a recent contribution, Krauskopf calls both churches "prototype buildings for the church architecture of tomorrow" but does not develop this assertion any further (Krauskopf, "Architects Debate Contemporary Church Building").

both the Catholic bishopric and the Protestant Landeskirchen did their best to maintain the unity of their organisations and cooperation across the city, though for the Protestant Church, the effort was doomed to failure when its East German branch had to leave the EKD.

In retrospect, it seems astounding how much effort and money was invested in the building, rebuilding and restoration of the churches of Berlin after the war. This testifies to their importance as symbols of hope, freedom and courage in a city where the contrasting dynamics of economic prosperity and totalitarian repression rubbed against one another. While today, both of the Hansaviertel churches have become recognised for their artistic and cultural value, the sociocultural profile of Berlin has altered to such an extent that it poses bigger challenges for the traditional faiths (Catholicism and Protestantism) than ever before. In the first place, just like anywhere else, church membership is rapidly dwindling, forcing congregations to merge and share resources. This inevitably leads to the question of which churches should be kept and which altered, or even demolished. Unsurprisingly, the latter option is only envisaged for the more recent, modern churches, which makes them all the more vulnerable — even more so as it becomes increasingly difficult for parishes and congregations to bear the high cost involved in their maintenance. This was illustrated by the demolition in 2005 of the St.-Johannes-Capistran-Kirche in Berlin-Tempelhof, a brutalist structure designed by Reinhard Hofbauer. Both St. Ansgar and Gedächtniskirche have undergone substantial restoration in recent years, safeguarding them for the near future. Such campaigns come at a high cost, however, and illustrate how the future of any church building is extremely dependent on the goodwill of its congregation and the wider public. Raising awareness and creating public support for this heritage, both amongst the congregations and the wider public, is thus of paramount importance. Otherwise, people will keep on feeling like outsiders in their own church. It is to be hoped that the current bid to have both the Hansaviertel and Karl-Marx-Straße adopted on the UNESCO World Heritage List may increase public interest and awareness and thus safeguard both sites for future generations.

BIBLIOGRAPHY

Archives

Berlin, Diözesanarchiv (DA)
- DAB X: Q-IV-St-A-006

Berlin, Evangelisches Landeskirchliches Archiv (ELA)
- 3/1401 – Kaiser-Friedrich-Gedächtniskirche
- 3/1402 – Kaiser-Friedrich-GED
- 17/34 – Nachlass Oberbaurat Berndt, Fritz
- 898 – Kirchen Berlin West

Berlin, Landesarchiv (LA)
- Akte C Rep. 104/Nr. 95, Die Arbeit des Referats Kirchenfragen des Magistrats (1953-1962)
- Akte C Rep. 104, Nr. 574, Kirchliche Bauvorhaben (Akten des Magistrats von Berlin)

Published sources

1957-1982 - St. Ansgar im Hansaviertel Berlin-Tiergarten. Gemeindeblatt. Berlin, 1982.

Aluminium und die Kaiser-Friedrich-Gedächtniskirche. Düsseldorf: Aluminium-Zentrale, 1957.

Artikeldienst Interbau. *Internationale Bauausstellung Berlin 1957*. Berlin, 1957.

Biedrzynski, Richard. *Kirchen unserer Zeit*. Munich: Hirmer Verlag, 1958.

Bolz, Lothar. *Von deutschem Bauen. Reden und Aufsätze*. Berlin: Verlag der Nation, 1951.

Cante, Marcus. ed. *Sakralbauten*. Berlin und seine Bauten, VI. Berlin: Ernst & Sohn, 1997.

Greschat, Martin. *Der Protestantismus in der Bundesrepublik Deutschland (1945-2005)*. Kirchengeschichte in Einzeldarstellungen, IV/2. Leipzig: Evangelische Verlagsanstalt, 2010.

Gundermann, Iselin. "Hundert Jahre Kaiser-Friedrich-Gedächtniskirche". Der Bär von Berlin. 44 (1995), 71-90.

Heischkel, Henriette. *Bauen in West-Berlin 1949-1963. Die Rolle der Bauverwaltung im Spannungsfeld von Kunst und Politik*. Berlin: Mann Verlag, 2018.

Henkys, Reinhard. "Eine neue Qualität". *Kirche im Sozialismus*, 2 (1978), 9-16.

Henneken, Marianus, ed. *75 Jahre St. Ansgar im Hansa-Viertel. 1926-2001*. Fredersdorf-Vogelsdorf: Servi-Verlag, 2001.

Heyer, Walter. *Evangelische Kirchenbautagung Berlin 1957. Der Kirchenbau in der Stadt der Zukunft*. Neunte Tagung für evangelischen Kirchenbau vom 5. bis 9. September 1957. Berlin: Arbeitsausschuß d. Evang. Kirchbautages, 1957.

Hummel, Karl-Joseph and Kißener, Michael, eds. *Die Katholiken und das Dritte Reich: Kontroversen und Debatten*. Paderborn: Verlag Ferdinand Schöningh, 2009.

Interbau Berlin 1957: Internationale Bauausstellung im Berliner Hansaviertel, 6. Juli - 29. September. Official catalogue. Berlin, 1957.

Israel, Jürgen, ed. *Zur Freiheit berufen. Die Kirche in der DDR als Schutzraum der Opposition 1981-1989*. Berlin: Aufbau-Taschenbuch-Verlag, 1991.

Janiszewski, Bertram. *Das alte Hansa-Viertel in Berlin. Gestalt und Menschen*. Berlin: Pro Business, 2014.

"Die Kaiser-Friedrich-Gedächtnis-Kirche". In: Fritz Schmidt-Clausing. *Das Hansa-Viertel. Von den Schöneberger Wiesen zur Stadt von morgen*. Berlin, 1957, 28-33.

"Kirchenbau in der DDR. Wille gegen Widerstand." <https://www.monumente-online.de/de/ausgaben/2017/3/DDR-Kirchen.php#.XZzg7WYuA2w>. Last accessed 03/11/2021.

Kitschke, Andreas. *Die Kirchen der Potsdamer Kulturlandschaft*. Berlin: Lukas Verlag, 2017.

Krauskopf, Kai. "Architects Debate Contemporary Church Building: Post-War German Sacred Architecture, 1945-60". In: Kathleen James-Chakraborty and Lisa Godson, eds. *Modern Religious Architecture in Germany, Ireland and Beyond. Influence, Process and Afterlife since 1945*. New York: Bloomsbury, 2019.

Kühl-Freudenstein, Olaf and Boge, Ruth. *Kirchenkampf in Berlin 1932-1945, 42 Stadtgeschichten*. Berlin: Institut Kirche und Judentum, 1999.

Lenssen, Jürgen. *Aufbruch im Kirchenbau: die Kirchen von Hans Schädel*. Würzburg: Freunde Mainfränkischer Kunst und Geschichte, 1989.

Maser, Peter. *Kirchen in der DDR. Niemals voll in das Regime integriert*. Erfurt: Landeszentrale für Politische Bildung Thüringen, 2018.

Nicolaus, Herbert and Obeth, Alexander. *Die Stalinallee. Geschichte einer deutschen Straße*. Berlin: Verlag für Bauwesen, 1997.

Otto, Karl. *Die Stadt von morgen. Gegenwartsprobleme für alle*. Berlin: Mann, 1959.

Preuschen, Henriette von. *Der Griff nach den Kirchen. Ideologischer und denkmalpflegerischer Umgang mit kriegszerstörten Kirchenbauten in der DDR*. Thesis (D. ing.). Forschungen und Beiträge zur Denkmalpflege im Land Brandenburg 13. Worms: Werner, 2011.

Roeder, Hans-Jürgen. "Zwischen Anpassung und Opposition". *Kirche im Sozialismus*, 6 (1976), 27-38.

Scheffler, Tanja. "Devisenbeschaffungsprogramm Kirchenbau". *Bauwelt*, 27 (2015), 30-33.

Schmiechen-Ackermann, Detlef. *Anpassung, Verweigerung, Widerstand. Soziale Milieus, politische Kultur und der Widerstand gegen den Nationalsozialismus in Deutschland im regionalen Vergleich*. Berlin: Gedenkstätte Deutscher Widerstand, 1997.

Schnell, Hugo. *Der Kirchenbau des 20. Jahrhunderts in Deutschland*. Munich-Zurich: Schnell & Steiner, 1973.

St. Ansgar und die Interbau (1957). Berlin: Regina-Druck, 1957.

Streicher, Gebhardt and Drave, Erika. *Berlin. Stadt und Kirche*. Berlin: Morus-Verlag, 1980.

Verordnung über die Erhaltung der städtebaulichen Eigenart aufgrund der städtebaulichen Gestalt für das Gebiet „HANSAVIERTEL" im Bezirk Mitte von Berlin. Berlin, 2018.

Wagner-Conzelmann, Sandra. *Die Interbau 1957. Städtebau und Gesellschaftskritik der 50er Jahre*. Berlin: Imhof Verlag, 2007.

Weyres, Willy and Bartning, Otto. *Kirchen: Handbuch für den Kirchenbau*. Munich: G.D.W. Callwey, 1959.

EXPERTISE

5
RETHINKING THE URBAN PARISH
FRANÇOIS HOUTART, THE CENTRE DE RECHERCHES SOCIO-RELIGIEUSES AND THE 1958 PASTORAL PLAN FOR BRUSSELS

EVA WEYNS AND SVEN STERKEN

In considering the sweeping changes in pastoral approaches in post-war Europe, it is worth exploring the dynamics behind the establishment in 1956 of the Centre de Recherches Socio-Religieuses de Bruxelles (CRSR), a study centre for socio-religious research founded in Brussels by Canon François Houtart (1925-2017). The institutional and intellectual reasons behind the CRSR provide a typical instance of the then-increasing reliance of diocesan authorities on exterior expertise in dealing with the demographic, cultural and economic challenges of post-war society. This, in turn, must be understood against the backdrop of the institutionalisation of sociology as an academic discipline in its own right in Belgium and elsewhere. It was Houtart's conviction that the traditional territorial parish was no longer the right framework for urban mission in the rapidly expanding agglomerations. Instead, he proposed a new type of pastoral unit, and a rigorous planning method for its establishment, based on his expertise in the sociology of religion, urban planning and pastoral theology.

After outlining the framework for these new pastoral planning concepts and methods, we move on to an examination of how they were implemented in the CRSR's 1958 Pastoral Plan for Brussels (Étude de l'équipement paroissial de la région Bruxelloise). Based on a meticulous investigation of the religious landscape in the Belgian capital, the Plan proposed a thorough, long-term re-organisation of the pastoral infrastructure there. However, as we illustrate by looking into the foundation process for three new parishes recommended in the Pastoral Plan, its overall impact remained limited. As we posit, fundamental discrepancies between the theoretical premises of the Plan and the reality on the ground provoked a conservative reaction amongst the diocesan authorities and local clergy alike, thereby hampering its operational value. This was, in fact, not too surprising, given that fundamentally, Houtart's critique of the singular, territorially defined parish existentially questioned a cornerstone of the Catholic edifice.

The Centre de Recherches Socio-Religieuses de Bruxelles

During the tenure of Joseph-Ernest Van Roey (1874-1961), Archbishop since 1926, the demography of the Belgian archdiocese changed rapidly under the influence of expanding economic centres like Antwerp and Brussels and the industrialisation of formerly rural zones like the Campine area. The resulting social and spatial changes required new strategies to maintain a Catholic presence, which explains the existence of several, often overlapping, consultative bodies within the archdiocese during the 1950s. The most visible of these bodies was the diocesan building agency Domus Dei. Founded in 1952, it focused on fund-raising and public awareness and provided assistance to parish priests in dealing with architects and contractors.[1] Quickly becoming a model in its genre, it played an important role in the renewal of post-conciliar church architecture in Belgium. Also created at that time was the Commission Consultative des Biens Ecclésiastiques (Advisory Committee for Ecclesiastical Goods, further referred to as the "Commission"). Presided over by Vicar-General Paul Schoenmaeckers (1914-1986), it met on a weekly basis and oversaw the so-called "temporal" aspects of the diocese, such as the construction or restoration of churches, and the financial situation of parish councils.[2] Whereas at the onset the Commission functioned primarily as the internal, operative branch of Domus Dei, over time it grew in size and importance, assuming more responsibilities along the way. This was certainly the case after the influential Vicar-General Paul Theeuws (1914-1993), chairman of the Commission Diocésaine des Monuments (Diocesan Committee for Monuments, a mixed committee of both clerics and laypeople advising on the design and restoration of churches), started attending the meetings. In the rapidly changing social and spatial context, more and more issues arose that required a broader long-term vision on pastoral care on the scale of the entire archdiocese.

In this context, the rapidly expanding field of sociology seemed an attractive resource, for it provided essential information about people's spatial behaviour, spiritual needs, economic situation and so forth. In particular, the

[1] Sterken "A House for God or a Home for His People?".
[2] Malines, AAM, Canon Jozef Billiauw Fund, Records of the Commission Consultative des Biens Ecclésiastiques, 1953-1964.

sociology of religion had been thriving in Belgium under the impulse of Canon Jacques Leclercq (1891-1971).[3] The specific chair for this discipline that was created at the Université catholique de Louvain in 1946 soon enjoyed a solid international reputation. The first group of graduates from that programme subsequently founded the Centre Belge de Sociologie Religieuse with the aim of fostering research in the field and promoting its application. The fact that well-known figures in the field such as Louis-Joseph Lebret (1897-1966), Jean Labbens (1921-2005) and others presented their research at the Centre testifies to its international position. Nevertheless, although it originally gave the Centre its formal approval and called upon its expertise, the Belgian episcopate soon decided to establish a more permanent institution of its own, entrusting the coordination to Houtart, then secretary of the aforementioned Commission.

Born in 1925 as the eldest of fourteen children in a prominent family, Houtart was ordained as a priest in 1949 and became a chaplain for the Jeunesse Ouvrière Chrétienne (Young Christian Workers) in Brussels.[4] As he encountered the religious indifference of the working classes in the Belgian capital, he asked himself, "How is it possible that the working class sees Christianity as an enemy, given its message of human emancipation?"[5] In his view, two forces were reinforcing one another here, namely industrialisation and urbanisation — a hypothesis he examined in his graduate thesis at the Université catholique de Louvain (where he read Social and Political Sciences between 1949 and 1952 under Leclerc, amongst other professors), which demonstrated how since the nineteenth century, the Church had not kept up with the urban development of the Belgian capital and had almost systematically neglected to provide pastoral care in the working class districts.[6]

In 1952 Houtart left for the United States on a Fulbright scholarship to study at the University of Chicago, the cradle of urban sociology. Again, the urban parish was central in his preoccupations: not only did he join a local congregation, he also established maps of all the parishes in the city, charting their foundation in relation to its demographic evolution. Contrary to Brussels, he found that in Chicago, the greatest number of religious institutions were to be found in the working-class neighbourhoods, showing that the North American Catholic Church had adapted more successfully to the social composition of modern cities.[7] During his stay in the United States, Houtart not only met with Andrew Greely and Joseph Fichter — both leading religious sociologists — but also became acquainted with the two key protagonists of

3   Chalon, "Implantation de la Sociologie Religieuse en Belgique".
4   For an introduction to Houtart's life and work, see Pérez, *The Decline of Certainties*; Chatelan, "Michel Quoist, François Houtart".
5   Pérez, *The Decline of Certainties*, 36.
6   Ibid., 37. The thesis was published as: Houtart, *Les paroisses de Bruxelles (1803-1951)*.
7   His findings were published as: Houtart, *Aspects sociologiques du catholicisme américain*.

the so-called Chicago school, namely Robert Ezra Park and Louis Wirth. Park's original contribution was a study of the behaviour of social groups with a view to understanding their distribution in the urban system.[8] As he stated, local communities constituted key elements in the urban fabric, for they acted as a link between the individual and the larger urban realm. From Park, Houtart retained two essential principles: namely, that cities were to be regarded as a social organism; and that the potential of the Catholic parish to effectively foster a sense of community depended on its potential to adapt to the realities of the modern metropolis. One such "reality" had been highlighted by Wirth in his classic essay "Urbanism as a Way of Life" (1938), in which he stated that modern city life produced a sociocultural environment fundamentally different from rural or pre-industrial settlements.[9] Although Wirth wrote that family bonds and solidarity weakened in an urban context, he saw this as the ultimate condition of modernity. His belief that, as a sociologist, his role was to understand and address the problems brought about by this new condition must have inspired Houtart to consider the problem of urban religion through the lens of applied sociology. As Houtart came to understand, beyond a purely pastoral issue, the religious apathy of the working classes was a symptom of a deeper sociological problem in the first place, namely the lack of group identity.

Upon his return, Houtart obtained a degree in urban planning at the Institut Supérieur d'Urbanisme Appliqué in Brussels, then under the direction of the French urban theoretician Gaston Bardet (1907-1989). [Ill. 5.1] A fierce opponent of the functionalist CIAM (Congrès Internationaux d'Architecture Moderne) doctrine, Bardet championed a more sociologically inspired form of urban planning based on Marcel Poëte's ideas of the city as a living organism, the principles of the Chicago school and a Christianised interpretation of the neighbourhood unit.[10] According to Bardet, a town was to be regarded as a federation of communities of varying scales. In particular, he distinguished three types of social groupings (*échelons*): the *échelon patriarcal*, the *échelon domestique* and the *échelon paroissial*.[11] Scales of community rather than spatial categories, the *échelons* reflected Bardet's understanding of the urban environment as a social rather than a physical construct.

Given his background in sociology, urban planning and parish administration, Houtart was ideally positioned to lead the newly created CRSR. It became operational in 1956 and was modelled after similar centres abroad, such as the Dutch Katholiek Sociaal-Kerkelijk Instituut (Catholic Social-Ecclesiasti-

8   Goist, "City and 'Community'".
9   For an introduction to Chicago sociology, see Plummer, "Introducing Chicago Sociology".
10 Sterken and Weyns, "Urban Planning and Christian Revival".
11 Bardet, *Pierre sur pierre*.

5.1 The 1951 summer school of the Institut Supérieur d'Urbanisme Appliqué in Brussels. François Houtart is the fourth person from the left in the back row.
[KADOC-KU Leuven, Wilfried Wouters Archive]

cal Institute, or KASKI).[12] Its primary vocation was to pursue applied research: "The fundamental purpose of the Centre for Socio-religious Research is (...) to help the Church in its continuous effort to adapt its activities to the evolution of the society in which it lives."[13] The fact that this advisory role was also endorsed by the assembly of superiors of the religious orders (representing over ninety institutions) and the National Secretariat of Catholic Education — the most powerful educational body in Belgium at the time — illustrates the high hopes vested in the CRSR. Whereas its institutional blueprint derived from KASKI's pragmatism, its conceptual orientation was more inclined towards the French tradition of, for example, Gabriel Le Bras and Fernand Boulard, who studied religious issues not as an end in themselves, but as phenomena within a broader, more scientific perspective of urban and rural sociology. Therefore, although Houtart always stressed that the raison d'être of religious sociology resided in its apostolic application, he was no less demanding in terms of method of inquiry, quality of results or critical distance.[14]

12 CRSR, "Rapport au Conseil de Gestion"; Chalon, "Implantation de la Sociologie Religieuse en Belgique"; CRSR, "Bilan van 5 jaar aktiviteit, 1956-1961"; Dingemans, "Le Centre de Recherches Socio-Religieuses de Bruxelles"; Houtart, "Le Centre de Recherches Socio-Religieuses de Louvain".
13 CRSR, "Bilan van 5 jaar aktiviteit, 1956-1961", 3. Unless otherwise noted, all translations are the authors' own.
14 Chatelan, "Michel Quoist, François Houtart", 228.

The CRSR very quickly put itself on the map and became a model in its genre. From the onset the centre was very productive: in the first three years of its existence, it issued no fewer than forty-five reports on a variety of topics, such as the distribution and redistribution of parishes in the Brussels agglomeration (cf. further in this contribution); the current state of the religious orders; the problem of vocations in relation to the changing demography of the country; and the strategic location of new hospitals and schools of the Catholic network.[15] Houtart also seized every occasion to put his centre at the forefront and expand the frontiers of his discipline. For example, at the World's Fair in Brussels in 1958, he hosted an international conference on parish planning (attended by over one hundred experts) that propelled the CRSR into the heart of the international scene.[16]

Rethinking the Urban Parish

In the post-war period, the "spiritual misery" of the modern metropolis, as revealed for example by Pierre Lhande in the Parisian suburbs, seemed to have become accepted as a given in the ecclesiastical milieu, proving the inevitably secularising effect of mass urbanisation.[17] Various sociologists of religion, and Houtart in particular, contested this idea, for in their view, it had less to do with the phenomenon of urbanisation per se than with the inadequacy of the existing pastoral framework. Houtart therefore set out to uncover the specificities of the new urban realm and understand its pastoral repercussions, with a view to proposing alternative, more contemporary, ways of urban religiosity. Developing this agenda in an impressive array of articles, he often took a deliberately polemic and even provocative stance, becoming increasingly impatient with the Church leaders' navel-gazing. Nevertheless, upon closer inspection, one notices that, in fact, Houtart developed a quite nuanced and systematic take on the issue.

Laid out in its modern form during the Council of Trent (1545-1563), the Catholic parish was a clearly defined territorial entity, equipped with its own church, parish hall, school and community facilities. Autonomous and autarkic, it comprised all the Christian faithful living within its area, under the supervision of a parish priest and a number of assistants.[18] This pastoral framework stemmed from a time when work, family and social life all occurred within the same geographical area. In the twentieth century, by contrast, cities had expanded into ever-growing urban agglomerations, where mobil-

---

15 Dingemans, "Le Centre de Recherches Socio-Religieuses de Bruxelles".
16 On the 1958 colloquium, see the introduction to this book.
17 Lhande, *Le Christ dans la banlieue*.
18 Spicer, *Parish Churches in the Early Modern World*.

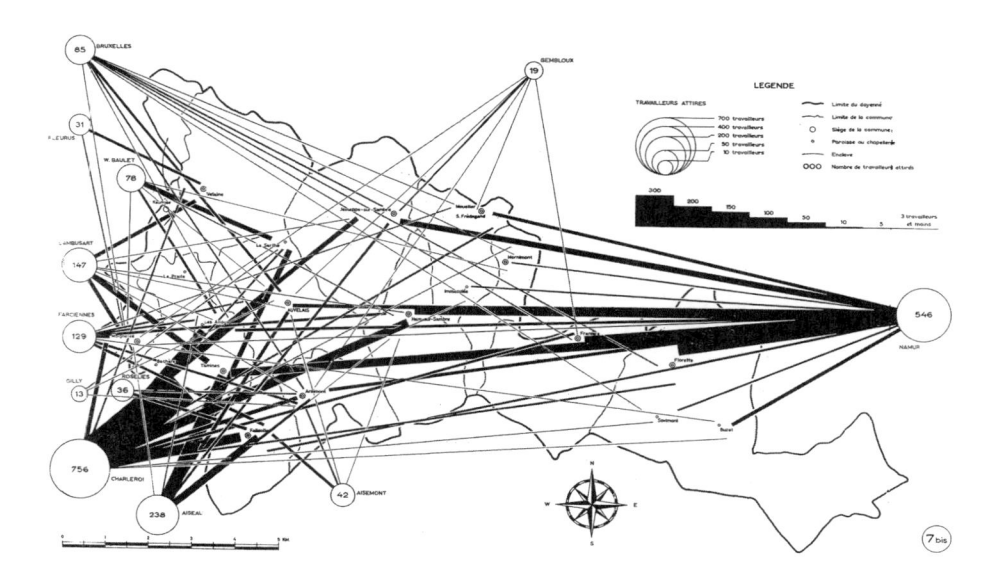

5.2 Deanery of Auvelais, main outlying centres of attraction for the population, 1957.
[Louvain-la-Neuve, UCL, Archives of François Houtart, BE A4006 FI 289 - R-043, report 37: CRSR, "Etude socio-religieuse du doyenné d'Auvelais", June 1958, map 7bis]

ity and differentiation had become the norm, both on the geographical and the social plane. Urban dwellers increasingly lived at the intersection of various sociocultural milieus and spent much of their time commuting between them — a phenomenon saliently illustrated by the 12,000 people transiting into Brussels every day.[19] [Ill. 5.2] While in earlier times the neighbourhood had constituted the central framework of daily life, in modern cities, the places of dwelling, working and leisure had now become scattered. As a result, social intercourse was no longer confined to those living close to the family home, but increasingly subordinate to "functional" relationships linked to the spheres of work, leisure and education; the home and the neighbourhood were thus no longer the sole places where people picked up ideas.[20] In other words, the specific qualities of the parish as a stable, homogenous, territorial unit were defeated in the metropolis.

For pastoral sociologists like Houtart, the conclusion was simple: whereas the equation between religion, community and territory might still make sense in rural areas, it was simply naïve to hold on to it in the unstable context of the modern city. This led to the inevitable question of whether the territorial

19 Houtart, "Faut-il abandonner la paroisse dans la ville moderne?", 606-607; Houtart, "Dimensions nouvelles de la paroisse urbaine", 386.
20 Houtart, "Faut-il abandonner la paroisse dans la ville moderne?", 606-607; Remy, "Consequences socio-culturelles de la concentration urbaine"; Remy, "Les institutions ecclesiastiques en civilisations urbaine et industrielle". Rémy, who had a background in economics, was one of Houtart's closest collaborators at the CRSR.

parish was still adequate for the urban pastorate. In Houtart's view, that was clearly not the case. In the first place, the urban parish was pastorally inefficient, for it had become too big: in world capitals like Paris or Brussels, parishes numbered 12,000 inhabitants on average, with excesses of up to 30,000 inhabitants.[21] Under such conditions, the parish lost its meaning and became a purely "administrative" entity. The parish was thus also failing to fulfil its mission from a sociological point of view. As research had shown, in many cases, the core group of committed parishioners was generally very small (three to five per cent of the inhabitants) and belonged to the "petite bourgeoisie". With such a limited group determining its identity and politics, the parish became an exclusive, rather than inclusive, institution, leaving out the majority of the less-educated, but far more mobile, urban masses.[22] As Houtart concluded, "The very essence of parish life, namely personal relationships and the existence of a community, has almost completely disappeared."[23] Indeed, without its integrative social mission, a parish was no longer a "group" in the sociological sense of the term, but simply a "social agglomerate".[24] Finally, there were also economic reasons for dismissing the traditional parish: despite its ever-bigger size, it was still too small to provide a meaningful offering for education, social work or associative life on top of its pastoral mission — although many a priest prided himself on his primary school or sports field as an expression of his courage and independence. This, Houtart claimed, was precisely the problem: the parish clergy enjoyed a great deal of autonomy (perhaps too much), and rather than cooperating with neighbouring colleagues, they often considered them competitors. For him, it was therefore clear that, by reason of its pastoral, social and economic inefficiency, "pastoral work on a purely territorial basis is (…) clearly inadequate."[25]

But, as Houtart hastened to add, this failure was not related to the parish per se; it also had to do with the fact that parishes were now being confronted with problems for which they were never conceived.[26] Whereas he saw no reason to simply abolish the institution, a status quo of current policies was also out of the question. In any case, as Houtart stated, the parish was not an absolute "theological fact".[27] Rather, he stressed its historical nature. As society had evolved significantly since the parish had been canonically coded in the Council of Trent, a readjustment was in place. Moreover, the parish was also a "social fact", for it involved a group of people sharing a set of religious

---

21   Houtart, "Faut-il abandonner la paroisse dans la ville moderne?", 605.
22   Houtart, "L'aménagement religieux des territoires urbains", 523.
23   Houtart, "Faut-il abandonner la paroisse dans la ville moderne?", 610.
24   Houtart refers here to Fichter, *Social Relations in the Urban Parish*.
25   Houtart, "Vers une pastorale urbaine", 288.
26   Houtart, "Faut-il abandonner la paroisse dans la ville moderne?", 605.
27   Houtart, "L'aménagement religieux des territoires urbains", 517.

and moral values — which were subject to change, as well.[28] It was not up to society to bend itself to the prerequisites of the parish, he asserted, but rather, the other way around. The parish was thus not to be *abolished*, but *adapted* to the reality of the day. If not, it would quickly become superfluous, for the secularising effect of mass urbanisation was being felt more and more each day. Truly *missionary* parishes were therefore needed, based on a common liturgy, worship practice and charity, rather than a shared territory.[29] Or, as Houtart added:

> The greatest danger (...) would be to live as if we were still in Christendom. (...) The apostolate in the big cities is a conquest to be achieved day after day, with appropriate methods, and does not consist in serving only the people who continue to gravitate towards the parish.[30]

Such an *apostolat de quartier*, tailored to the various sociocultural milieus in the city, required smaller and simpler parishes. Following the then generally accepted theoretical "optimum", Houtart accepted 5,000 inhabitants as a workable size — with the caveat that it was, in fact, still too much for a single pastor.[31] Rather than competing with one another, he therefore suggested that the local clergy work in teams; with some administrative support, this could broaden the capacity of a single parish to 8,000 souls.[32] Parishes also needed to be limited in geographical terms: ideally, the church should be no farther away than a fifteen-minute walk for its congregants (approx. 500 m). With regard to this latter point, Houtart's advice was simple: big churches required big parishes and hindered the creation of new ones. He therefore advocated more modest, cost-efficient buildings, seating 500 to 600, made using modern building techniques and with a limited lifespan of 75 years. This pragmatic stance towards church architecture was a clear departure from the emphasis on monumental edifices embraced by many parish priests hoping to make a lasting mark at the culmination of their careers.

At first sight, Houtart's vision of the parish seemed completely at odds with the prevailing ecclesiastical policies. This had to do with the fact that in searching for an alternative, he had drawn inspiration not from pastoral theology, but from contemporary urban planning, and more specifically, from the then-ubiquitous concept of the "neighbourhood unit". That was hardly surprising, given that he had studied, as we have seen, under Bardet, one of the principal proponents of this idea in the francophone world.[33] It indeed

---

28   Houtart, "Dimensions nouvelles de la paroisse urbaine", 384.
29   Houtart, "L'aménagement religieux des territoires urbains", 527.
30   Houtart, "Faut-il abandonner la paroisse dans la ville moderne?", 613.
31   On the optimum size of the parish, see Debié and Vérot, *Urbanisme et art sacré*, 152-153.
32   Houtart, "Le planning des paroisses urbaines", 112.
33   Houtart, "Faut-il abandonner la paroisse dans la ville moderne?", 611.

seemed an ideal match: comprising up to 10,000 inhabitants, the neighbourhood unit provided its inhabitants with all the necessary amenities within walking distance. No longer having to cater to these aspects, the parish priest could thus focus entirely on his apostolic mission instead. Further, neighbourhood units were always conceived as interrelated parts of a bigger ecosystem, sharing large-scale amenities such as hospitals, secondary schools and sport stadiums. That, too, was instructive for the urban pastorate: if parishes collaborated, they could share expertise and infrastructure, allowing certain parish priests to become specialists in certain aspects of the urban pastorate. To this effect, the pastorate's future unit should no longer be the individual parish, but the agglomeration as a whole.[34] Or, as Houtart stated:

> It is no longer possible to consider the parish as an island in the middle of the city. It forms a part of a whole that exceeds territorial boundaries (…). The basic unit from which we have to start is the city or the agglomeration.[35]

Although Houtart thus maintained the institutional role of the parish, the way he conceived of its spatial and material dimension represented a sea change. As he made clear in various essays, the mere multiplication of churches — the solution advocated by Paul Winninger in his widely circulated pamphlet from 1957, *Construire des églises* — would no longer do.[36] Instead, "pastoral planning" was to become the norm: a premeditated strategy based on clear, long-term goals, such as a more rational distribution of efforts, finances and infrastructure, as well as a specialisation and professionalisation of the clergy. Yet, as Alexandre Sokolski, one of Houtart's collaborators, observed, "Planning has its exigencies."[37] To be sure, it required rigour and method, which explains why the CRSR went to such great lengths in developing a detailed, step-by-step plan for the establishment of new parishes.[38] Its statement that "planning is the result of sociological and physical knowledge in service of an overall action plan" revealed once more the influence of the Chicago school upon Houtart and his team.[39] Indeed, their emphasis on surveying and the gathering of "hard facts" as a prerequisite for action and design transpired in the exhaustive enumeration of elements of inquiry in the plan. A survey of the current and future availability of human resources was to be undertaken first, because, as Houtart observed, "without priests, there is no point in providing parishes".[40] Also, the financial means of the faithful were to be taken into

34 Houtart, "L'aménagement religieux des territoires urbains", 524.
35 Houtart, "Dimensions nouvelles de la paroisse urbaine", 392.
36 Winninger, *Construire des églises*.
37 Sokolski, "Plan d'étude", 121.
38 Sokolski, "Plan d'étude"; Sokolski, "Methode de Planning Paroissial Urbain".
39 CRSR, "Etude de l'équipement paroissial de la région Bruxelloise. Volume I", 5.
40 Houtart, "Le planning des paroisses urbaines", 108.

consideration, since building a church imposed a heavy burden upon them. Then, a detailed study of the spatial and social characteristics of the area under study needed to be conducted. Here, the CRSR followed Bardet's "social topography", a specific mapping method that allowed for detailed registration of the social composition of a certain area and an assessment of the impact of geographical obstacles or cultural differences on its distribution.[41] Further, existing or planned developments needed to be taken into account, as well as the existing provision in pastoral infrastructure.

On the basis of all this information, it became possible to divide the urban agglomeration into *zones* based on clear differences in building density or major geographical elements, such as rivers, woods, industrial areas and so forth. The zone still being too large to be analytically meaningful, it was to be further subdivided into *sectors*, areas that formed a logical unity and whose borders were determined by smaller infrastructural elements, such as arteries, railway tracks, parks, large building complexes, etcetera. In pastoral terms, a sector designated a group of parishes for which the construction of a new church or a change in boundaries in one affected all the others. Sectors were more than just the sum of individual parishes, though; the idea was that by sharing infrastructure, expertise and resources, priests could specialise in a certain task (e.g. catechesis, liturgy or accounting) and provide this service for several parishes at once. Finally, a hierarchy between sectors was also to be established: the higher the increase in population (density) and the farther the distances between the existing churches, the more urgent a sector's restructuring became. Priority sectors were subsequently scanned in great detail based on their morphological, social and cultural specificities, on the basis of which specific pastoral measures were then proposed — varying from opening up a private chapel (belonging to a convent or a school) or increasing the frequency of services, to establishing a new parish from scratch. Thus, as Sokolski summarised the goals of the CRSR's parish planning method, a powerful tool was now available, with a dual significance: for those involved in church building (architects, diocese, etc.), it constituted a rational support for sustainable planning; for the local clergy and the laity, it provided an apostolic instrument that uncovered the social and cultural physiognomy of the parishioners and allowed the pastoral offering to be more easily tailored to their specific needs.[42]

---

41   Sterken and Weyns, "Urban Planning and Christian Revival", 111-112.
42   Sokolski, "Plan d'étude", 126-127.

5.3 Base map of the Brussels region, 1958.
[Louvain-la-Neuve, UCL, BE A4006 FI 289 - R-048, report 42: CRSR, "Etude de l'équipement paroissial de la région Bruxelloise. Cartes", October 1958, unnumbered map]

The CRSR's 1958 Pastoral Plan for Brussels

The parish planning method described above is best exemplified by the CRSR's study of the pastoral infrastructure of the Brussels agglomeration commissioned by the archdiocese in 1955.[43] This comprehensive study — which took three years to complete and resulted in a two-hundred-forty-page report, including twenty-three maps — provided a meticulous description of the capital's physiognomy and charted a course for its further pastoral development. Its object of study was the area within the future ring road (constructed from 1962), comprising the nineteen municipalities that together make up the Brussels agglomeration. [Ill. 5.3] In accordance with the blueprint sketched above, the report discussed a great number of topics, such as the geographical conditions (relief, hydrography, green spaces); the demographic evolution of the capital since the early nineteenth century and the migratory movements to, from and within the capital; the density and sociological composition of the population; and, of course, the prevalent language (Brussels is Dutch–French bilingual, with a clear dominance of the latter at the time). The degree of detail is overwhelming at times: for example, details are provided for all nineteen municipalities within the Brussels agglomeration about the Christian Democrat Party's popularity in the previous two elections (1952, 1958) — concluding that it was slightly on the rise in the Brussels region.

Of the ninety-six parishes in the Brussels agglomeration, the majority had been erected in the latter half of the nineteenth century, corresponding with the industrial expansion of the area. [Ill. 5.4] In the decade after the Second World War, only a handful of new parishes (four) had been erected. In terms of population, 12 parishes numbered between 15,000 and 20,000 inhabitants; 8 between 20,000 and 25,000, and 2 even had over 25,000 souls, namely Saint-Croix in Ixelles (31,000) and Saint-Gilles in Saint-Gilles (26,200). Further, the report also gave a detailed breakdown of the numerous congregations present in the agglomeration and an overview of convent chapels open to the public. An analysis of overall church attendance (twenty-three per cent on average in the agglomeration) led to the unsurprising result that it was feeblest in the municipalities along the rivers Zenne and Maalbeek, as well as in the commune of Molenbeek — three areas designated as "proletarian". Equally unsurprising, religious observance was highest in the bourgeois areas south-east of the centre. Finally, in terms of human resources, the availability of the clergy was studied in great detail and broken down in terms of workload, age, language and provenance. In 1958, 314 priests served the 990,000 inhabitants of the agglomeration; mathematically, this resulted in an average of 3,165 souls

---

43   CRSR, "Etude de l'équipement paroissial de la région Bruxelloise. Volume I"; CRSR, "Etude de l'équipement paroissial de la région Bruxelloise. Volume II"; CRSR, "Etude de l'équipement paroissial de la région Bruxelloise. Cartes".

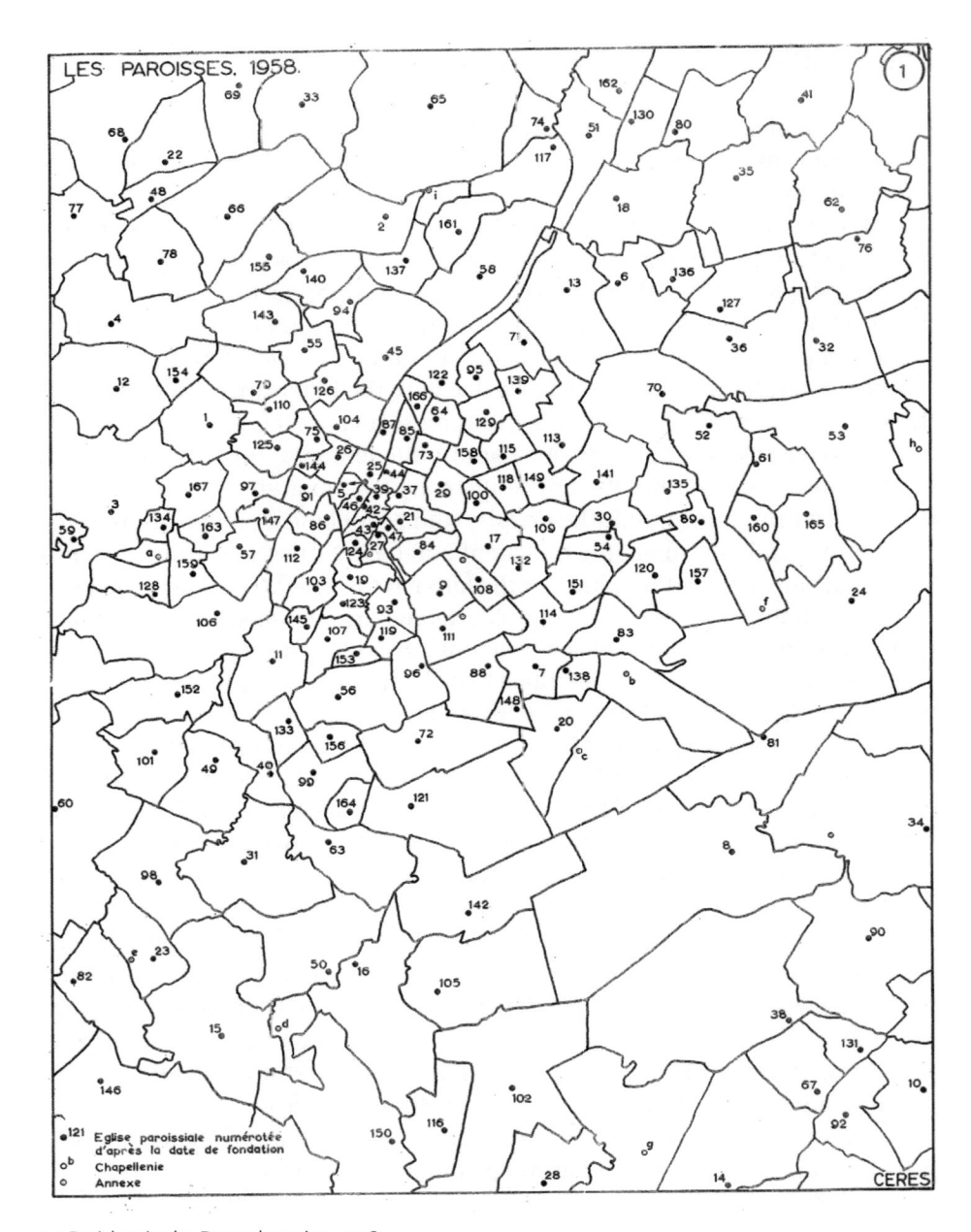

5.4 Parishes in the Brussels region, 1958.
[Louvain-la-Neuve, UCL, BE A4006 FI 289 - R-048, report 42: CRSR, "Etude de l'équipement paroissial de la région Bruxelloise. Cartes", October 1958, map 1]

5.5 Zones and sectors of the Pastoral Plan for Brussels, 1958.
[Louvain-la-Neuve, UCL, Archives of François Houtart, BE A4006 FI 289 - R-048, report 42: CRSR, "Etude de l'équipement paroissial de la région Bruxelloise. Cartes", October 1958, map 8]

per priest, but in reality this was much higher in the central parishes. The conclusion was alarming: reducing the workload to manageable terms (2,000 parishioners per priest) meant that no fewer than 350 new priests had to be recruited.

Subsequently, the agglomeration was divided into zones and sectors. [Ill. 5.5] One central zone of high-built density was identified, as well as four suburban zones in full expansion; an additional residential zone outside the agglomeration was also integrated into the study.[44] The larger zones were further subdivided into a variable number of sectors: the central zone, for example, was divided into ten sectors; most of the others, into two to five. The rule was that the denser an area, the more subdivisions. Two types of areas requiring special attention were defined. In the first place, each parish was given a score based on two parameters: church attendance and population density — highlighting especially the overpopulated parishes with a high degree of absenteeism, such as Saint-Gilles, with 26,000 inhabitants and 13.90 per cent church attendance. On this basis, twenty-three "areas with pastoral need" (*zones de besoin pastoral*) were determined, mostly located in the municipalities within the nineteenth-century belt around the centre, such as Saint-Gilles and Anderlecht. These areas did not necessarily require new infrastructure, but were thought to benefit from organisational or managerial changes, such as different hours of worship or the use of a convent chapel. By contrast, the second type of areas, called "areas without pastoral provision" (*zones non-desservies paroissialement*), where additional infrastructure was deemed necessary, were determined in a different way, namely on the basis of geographical criteria and sociographic data (graphical representation of all the sociological data gathered in the previous phases of the study). In principle, this classification pertained to all the areas that did not fall within a theoretical radius of 500 m around an existing church building (1000 m for the less densely built up areas). After interpolation with the sociographic analysis, this resulted in no fewer than forty-two areas with insufficient access to places of worship. [Ill. 5.6] Unsurprisingly, most of them were located in the low-density municipalities of the second ring around Brussels, such as Forest and Uccle. In measuring the urgency of intervening in a particular zone, the CRSR considered the data gathered during the preliminary research, taking into account factors that required immediate action, such as language issues or overpopulation. In total, the study concluded, there was a need to establish at least six chapelries and fifty parishes, which corresponded to the construction of six chapels and forty-three churches and the conversion of seven convent chapels into parish churches.[45] Moreover, thirty-four of these construction projects needed to be realised within the next ten years.

---

44 CRSR, "Etude de l'équipement paroissial de la région Bruxelloise. Volume I", 10.
45 Ibid., 133.

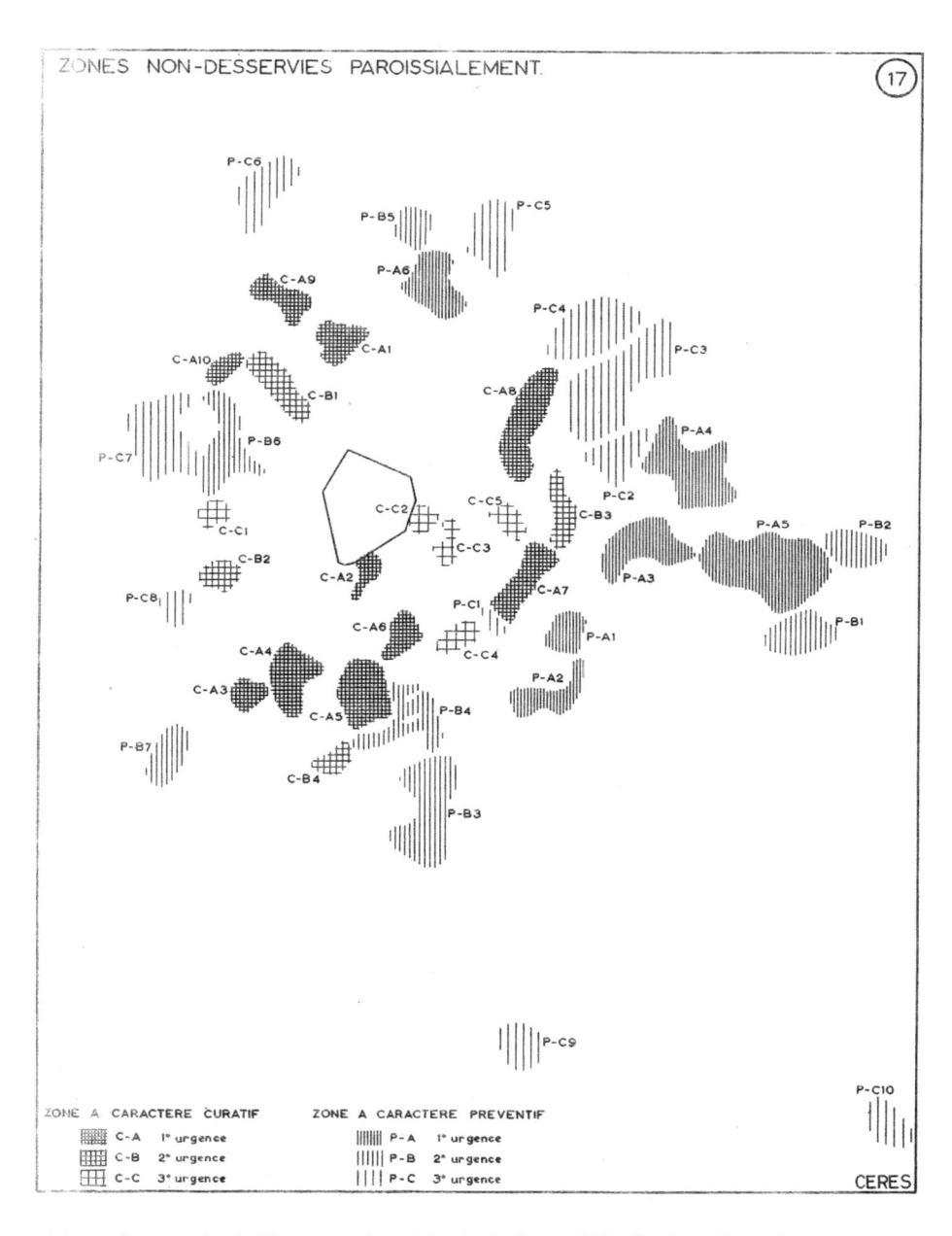

5.6 Areas designated as lacking pastoral provision in the Pastoral Plan for Brussels, 1958.
[Louvain-la-Neuve, UCL, Archives of François Houtart, BE A4006 FI 289 - R-048, report 42: CRSR, "Etude de l'équipement paroissial de la région Bruxelloise. Cartes", October 1958, map 17]

The Pastoral Plan for Brussels was a remarkable document in many ways. In the first place, the breadth of the documentation and rigour with which it was interpreted benefited amply from Houtart's multidisciplinary background. Indeed, his intimate knowledge of the religious landscape in the capital, the evolution of which he had investigated for his graduation thesis in sociology, as well as his previous professional experience in dealing with parish councils as secretary at the archdiocese, provided a critical lens when interpreting the raw data.[46] Further, raised in a privileged milieu but having worked as a chaplain amongst the working classes, he intimately knew the pastoral needs of both ends of the social ladder. Finally, his time at the Institut Supérieur d'Urbanisme Appliqué had helped him also to become acquainted with urban planning methods. The two-step procedure he proposed was based, in fact, on the new spatial planning legislation that was about to be introduced in Belgium; it, too, made a distinction between more open-ended regional plans (laying out the general principles) and local plans on a more detailed scale. The fact that many of the Pastoral Plan's documents resembled the 1958 Regional Plan for Brussels then under study is no coincidence since Houtart was closely related to the firm that designed it, Groupe Alpha.[47]

Second, the Plan was proposing an approach to pastoral care its intended readership was clearly not acquainted with, for the lengthy introduction discusses in great detail the merits, goals and methods of the study, amply justifying its objectives and elaborating at great length on the meaning and need of "planning". This very notion must indeed have been alien to most diocesan actors, for in general, pastoral provision proceeded in an ad hoc, bottom-up manner. In most cases, requests came from a local priest or a group of laypeople asking for a new church or a readjustment of their parish's boundaries if the area had expanded too far. The result of this policy was that in many cases, churches were built on sites that were ill-located or too expensive. Further, another noteworthy feature of the Pastoral Plan was its scale, which reached the height of ambition. Although the CRSR had applied its parish planning method before in smaller cities, like Tournai, the Brussels agglomeration signified the litmus test for it. In particular, it enabled verification of the centre's central contention: namely, that pastoral care must be planned on a regional scale — in contrast to the traditional approach, which, as we have seen, remained within the boundaries of a single parish.[48] Moreover, CRSR's "testing"

46 Houtart, *Les paroisses de Bruxelles (1803-1951)*.
47 On Alpha's 1958 development plan for Brussels, see Ryckewaert, *Building the Economic Backbone of the Belgian Welfare State*, 185-194. Further research is needed to determine the nature of the collaboration between Houtart and Groupe Alpha in the context discussed here. One link is certain, namely to Jean Gilson; he was secretary of the ISUA when Houtart studied there. Houtart also refers to the group in Pérez, *The Decline of Certainties*, 37.
48 An example of this approach is discussed in Weyns and Sterken, "Constructing a Genius Loci: The St Pius X's Church in Wilrijk, 1957-1967".

of its planning principles in Brussels was also of symbolical significance. On the national level, the capital region was increasingly becoming the flywheel in the country's modernisation; the ring road soon to be built along its contours would also become the central hub in the Belgian highway network. In addition, in 1958, the year the study was presented, the eyes of the world were focused on Brussels as it hosted the World's Fair — an event that signalled the start of the city's development into a tertiary centre of international importance.

The fact of considering the problem of the urban pastorate on the scale of the agglomeration certainly had the advantage of bringing to light all its shortcomings at once, but that did not mean they could also all be addressed simultaneously. The idea of categorising the pastoral sectors according to the urgency of their needs was therefore a logical move. As we have seen, this hierarchy derived from a mixture of qualitative and quantitative criteria.[49] The almost bureaucratic rationality of the method remained thus tempered by the lens of interpretation. In conclusion, we can therefore say that the Pastoral Plan for Brussels illustrates the CRSR's balanced assessment of the territorial parish. Although in its recommendations, the report distanced itself clearly from its traditional concept, the parish remained a crucial anchor point for pastoral care in its institutional guise — albeit in a modified form: no longer autarkic, but part of a larger ecosystem of zones and sectors; no longer autonomous, but in continual interaction with its neighbours. The plan was certainly innovative, but did it also enable the actors on the ground to put through the ideas it stood for?

Assessing the Pastoral Plan: Planning versus Pragmatism

After completion, the CRSR's reports were usually assessed by the Commission, which then decided which recommendations would be further investigated: sometimes this led to commissioning the CRSR to further study parish boundaries and potential sites; on other occasions, the parish priest would be informed directly about the proposals and asked to check for sites suitable for church building. Thus, the Commission weighed the CRSR's advice and the needs of local actors, ultimately deciding itself which new parishes would become established. In hindsight, this allows for an initial assessment of the Pastoral Plan's operational qualities. In the first place, the Plan's recommendations were mostly applied at the level of the parish. Second, in comparing the CRSR's proposals to the number of effectively established new parishes in the Brussels region, it becomes immediately apparent that many of its ambitions were not realised: only sixteen of fifty proposed new founda-

49   CRSR, "Etude de l'équipement paroissial de la région Bruxelloise. Volume I", 113-128.

tions were effectively put through. Nonetheless, most of the parishes that were established after 1958 are located in areas pinpointed by the CRSR, such as the municipalities along the Senne Valley. It would be too simple to base our evaluation of the Pastoral Plan solely on quantitative criteria, however; the fact that its recommendations were not followed in terms of numbers, does not mean that they had no impact. In order to assess its operational qualities, this section therefore analyses the foundation of three parishes in the Brussels agglomeration, each time highlighting a different aspect of the process: Saint-Bernard in Saint-Gilles, where a convent chapel was converted into a parish church; Saint-Marc in Uccle, a case that illustrates the often quite mundane discussions about borders and purchasing rights; and Saint-Luc in Anderlecht, a site that had already caught Houtart's eye in his 1952 historical survey of the parish landscape in Brussels.

The first case is situated in Saint-Gilles, a municipality that had 56,500 inhabitants at the time. Located on the slopes south of Brussels, it featured the highest percentage of built-up surface in the region (sixty-seven per cent). Although in demographic decline during the post-war years, its two existing parishes were busy improving their infrastructure in the 1950s: the historical parish of Saint-Gilles built a new parish hall, while the younger parish of Sainte-Alène, established in 1912, was still in the process of finalising its church. By the 1960s, two new parishes were created: Saint-Bernard (1968) and Jésus Travailleur (Jesus the Worker, 1970). Created at the request of the parish priest of Sainte-Alène, the latter offered an example of the old bottom-up mechanism mentioned in the previous section. The fact that it was not included in the CRSR's Pastoral Plan may have to do with the fact that its foundation was already long under way and a plot had already been purchased. By contrast, the establishment of Saint-Bernard was a direct result of the CRSR's efforts, whereby the north-east side of the municipality, known as "Le Haut de Saint-Gilles", had been designated a "Zone non-desservie paroissialement" (number C-A2) because of its isolated character, population density (346 inhabitants per hectare of built surface), high number of inhabitants per parish (26,200 for Saint-Gilles) and wanting religious practice (15 per cent of the population). The report recommended converting the existing, Neo-Gothic chapel of the Carmelites, built by architect Émar Collès in 1891 on the Rue de la Source, where some 200 people attended Sunday Mass each week, into a proper parish church.[50] [Ill. 5.7]

What seemed a straightforward solution in theory, resulted in a long and difficult process of negotiation. The Commission adopted the CRSR's recommendation to establish a new parish for 8,000 people in the Haut de Saint-Gilles. Despite the presence of an existing convent chapel, it was decided that a proper parish would be established, with its own dedicated par-

---

50 CRSR, "Etude de l'équipement paroissial de la région Bruxelloise. Volume II", 14-16.

5.7 Frontal view from Rue de la Source, Saint-Gilles, showing the former chapel of the Carmelites (Émar Collès, 1891) on the left, 1956. It was transformed into the Saint-Bernard church in 1966, with the entrance gate, bell tower and cloister wing shown on the right demolished sometime in the 1960s.
[© KIK-IRPA, Brussels, Belgium, cliché B165939]

ish priest. Joseph Kempeneers (1909-1992), the newly appointed dean of the Brussels south-east deanery and parish priest of Saint-Gilles's main parish, was appointed to the task by Archbishop Van Roey in 1959. Although initially receptive to Kempeneers's proposal to buy the chapel for conversion, the Carmelites' prioress subsequently objected that the hums of praying and singing parishioners would negatively affect the order's contemplative nature. At the request of the Commission, Kempeneers therefore investigated the possibility of constructing a church building at another location. The heavily built-up character of the area, however, meant that real estate prices were high, which reduced the options; also, there was a risk that the new location would be too close to some other existing parish church or the existing chapel. Kempeneers therefore persisted in the original plan and continued to explore various options, such as buying the chapel from the prioress; separating the chapel from the convent (and providing a new chapel for the latter); and appealing to the prior general. Finally, in 1963, a solution presented itself after a property in the convent's city block was put up for sale. This time, the congregation agreed to Kempeneers's suggestion, and in 1965, a new wing was realised on the acquired property according to a design by local architect Willy Reyns, which included a sober chapel with brick walls and abstract stained-glass windows. Following the wishes of the prioress, the old cloister wing along the street front was subsequently demolished to create a neater separation between the future parish church and the convent. Thus, Kempeneers's persistence and creativity led to a win-win situation: the community of the faithful now had a proper parish church at its disposal, while the Carmelites could continue their mission in peace in a modernised convent.

Anecdotal though it may seem, this case illustrates how the CRSR's parish planning method deviated from the customary bottom-up process by which new parishes were usually created. Rather than the local community or the parish priest, this time it was the diocese that took the initiative, on the recommendation of the CRSR — although it should be noted that the latter was not involved in following up on its own recommendations. Further, the example also shows that there were limits to implementing the CRSR's proposals. As was the case here, the fact of working in the existing fabric sometimes caused pastoral strategies to become entangled with various types of agency (in this case of a religious order and private proprietors), leading to complex and lengthy negotiations. This case thus helps us understand why no other conversions of convent chapels into parish churches, an option repeatedly proposed by the CRSR in its Pastoral Plan, were realised.

Whereas in Saint-Gilles, the CRSR's involvement had remained limited to making the initial suggestion, in the second case, in Uccle, it became an active agent throughout the process. Uccle is a large, wealthy municipality in the suburban area south of Brussels. With only 66,400 inhabitants at the time, it was characterised by its low-density development (principally detached houses and residential blocks), almost no public housing and a booming real estate market in the residential sector. In pastoral terms, the CRSR had identified one "Zone non-desservie paroissialement" (C-A5) there in need of urgent action, along with three other similarly designated areas with a lower degree of urgency. In the end, though, the Commission decided to only act on the advice for the most urgent area, establishing the new parish of Saint-Marc in 1965. This remaining the only real change in the parish landscape of Uccle after 1958, it illustrates how the CRSR's idea of classifying the various pastoral areas according to their urgency often worked against it in reality.[51] Located in the centre of Uccle, in-between the parishes of Saint-Pierre (18,000 inhabitants), Saint-Job (12,000 inhabitants) and Notre-Dame du Rosaire (8,000 inhabitants), the C-A5 area was typically bourgeois, with a rather high level of church attendance (22-45 per cent).[52] It nonetheless required urgent action because of the relatively long distances between the existing churches and the expected population boom (ten per cent growth was expected within five years). Similar to the previous case, Houtart first proposed converting an existing chapel because the more urgent needs elsewhere in the agglomeration did not justify heavy expenditure here.[53] The chapel of the Institut des Dames de Marie, a boarding school for girls strategically located between Saint-Pierre and Notre-Dame du Rosaire, seemed a perfect fit.

In an additional report from 1961, however, the CRSR changed its mind: it now not only recommended the construction of an additional place of worship, but also suggested drawing the boundaries of the new Saint-Marc parish in such a way that, in terms of population at least, the surrounding parishes would become of equal size. Keeping the theoretical optimum of 5,000 inhabitants in mind, the new parish would help restructure the parish landscape in Uccle by limiting the number of souls per parish to between 5,000 and 13,500. As explained before, such intentions invariably met with resistance from the local clergy. Here, the parish priest of Notre-Dame du Rosaire complained that the CRSR had only taken into account "a theoretical population figure and not considered at all the distinct physiognomy of a living parish. (...) Executing the plan like this will require a brutal reconversion of the existing parish structures."[54] At this point, the archdiocese stepped in to mediate in the territorial dispute between the various parishes. [Ill. 5.8] This being not uncommon, it is nonetheless striking that after that point, the CRSR was no longer involved.

51 Besides the establishment of Saint-Marc, a new church was built for Notre-Dame de la Consolation in 1975, but that parish had existed since 1895.
52 CRSR, "Etude de l'équipement paroissial de la région Bruxelloise. Volume II", 17-18.
53 Letter from François Houtart to Vicar-General Schoenmaeckers, 28/03/1960 (Malines, AAM, File on the Saint-Marc parish, Uccle).
54 Note from the Notre-Dame du Rosaire parish, n.d. (Malines, AAM, File on the Saint-Marc parish, Uccle).

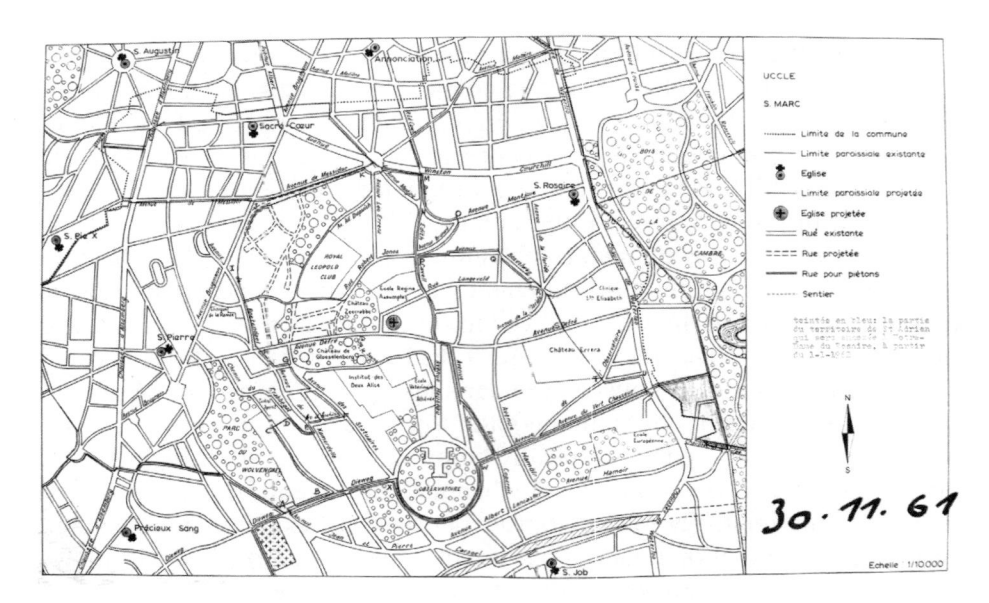

5.8 Proposal for the parish boundaries of the Saint-Marc parish: the site for the new church is marked with a cross in a circle, 1961.
[Malines, AAM, File on the Saint-Marc Parish, Uccle]

Vicar-General Schoenmaeckers finally forced a breakthrough: to compensate for having to cede part of its territory to the new parish of Saint-Marc, territory from another parish would be attached to Notre-Dame du Rosaire. Mundane as such transactions may seem, they bring to light the downside of the Catholic parish's territorial nature: once drawn, its boundaries quickly became absolute, and any change in them touched upon the pride of the community and the sovereignty of the local parish priest.

The next step involved finding a suitable site for the new parish church. To this effect, the archdiocese originally appointed the architect and urban planner Léon De Keyser (life dates unknown), with a view to obtaining a preliminary agreement with the municipality prior to purchasing a plot.[55] The land purchase proved difficult, however, since most proprietors preferred to maximise their gain by developing apartment buildings on their land. The newly appointed chaplain, Joseph Jourdain (1924-2016), eventually managed to strike a deal for two adjacent plots on Avenue De Fré, a busy road at the heart of the new parish, and immediately hired his own architect, André Milis (°1927). [Ill. 5.9] Together, they developed a detailed programme for a large church, the scale of which (seating 1,000) reflected the unbridled expansionism of the period. Concerned with such considerable expenditure, and follow-

---

55 Except for the fact that he studied at the ISUA under Bardet, and that he established himself in Ganshoren during the 1960s, we were unable to find any further details about this architect.

5.9 Frontal view from Avenue De Fré, Uccle, of the Saint-Marc church (1970) by André Milis. Photo from the 1970s. The presbytery was later built on the plot to the left of the church.
[Uccle, Parish Archives of Saint-Marc, donation of parish priest Joseph Jourdain]

ing the CRSR recommendation of a capacity of 700, the Commission requested a smaller alternative be built on only one of the plots. Despite the fact that Jourdain persisted in his vision, and even obtained a substantial donation from a local entrepreneur allowing him to purchase both plots, the Commission stood its ground and sent Milis back to the drawing board. The latter dutifully and skilfully acquitted himself of the task, resulting in the dedication of the church in 1970: accommodating the parish rooms and a weekday chapel on the ground floor and stacking the church space proper on the first floor of a rectangular brick volume, Milis managed to fit the extensive programme on only one of the two plots, leaving the other free for the later construction of the presbytery. [Ill. 5.10]

Just like in the previous case, conclusions can be drawn from this anecdote, for it illustrates the overt pragmatism with which the diocese (and the Commission in particular) treated the CRSR's recommendations. Not only did the centre's proposal for the reordering of parishes in Uccle become adapted to the wishes of dissatisfied clergy, the initial objections (by both the CRSR and the diocese) against investing heavily in this area evaporated once Jourdain secured funds to buy the land. Furthermore, as in the previous case, the coming about of Saint-Marc illustrates how strongly the establishment of a new parish depended on the perseverance and commitment of local actors — although it is not always clear whether they acted out of Christian zeal or personal ambition.

5.10 Interior of the Saint-Marc church (1970) in Uccle by André Milis.
[Photograph by Eva Weyns, 2019]

The third case is situated in Anderlecht, which lies in the south-eastern part of the agglomeration, between the Brussels–Charleroi canal (the agglomeration's industrial axis) and the then-planned ring road. With over 92,000 inhabitants, it was one of the most populous municipalities of Brussels at the time and experiencing expansion. Apart from its historic core around the church of Saints-Pierre-et-Guidon, Anderlecht consisted of a dense nineteenth-century built fabric that included a number of large-scale housing developments from the 1950s and 1960s, amongst the largest in the agglomeration. Its typically working-class mentality was reflected in the consistent socialist majority on the city council. For the archdiocese, and Houtart in particular, both of these aspects were of great concern, together with the overburdened Saints-Pierre-et-Guidon parish (24,000 souls). Houtart held the area close to his heart, since he had worked there as a chaplain and studied it as part of his degree in social sciences in the early 1950s. Indeed, he had already put together a note for the archdiocese at that time proposing that the existing parish be split in two.[56] After having determined various 'Zones non-desservie paroissialement' (C-B2, C-C1 and P-C8) in the region in its Pastoral Plan, the CRSR published two further reports on Anderlecht in 1958, recommending the construction of six places of worship — a high number derived not only from the expected population boom, but also as part of a strategy to counter the

---

56 Houtart, "Note sur l'éventuelle création d'une paroisse Bd. Aristide Briant à Anderlecht", n.d.; letter from Houtart to the Archdiocese, 07/04/1952 (Mechlin, AAM, File on the Saints-Pierre-et-Guidon parish, Anderlecht).

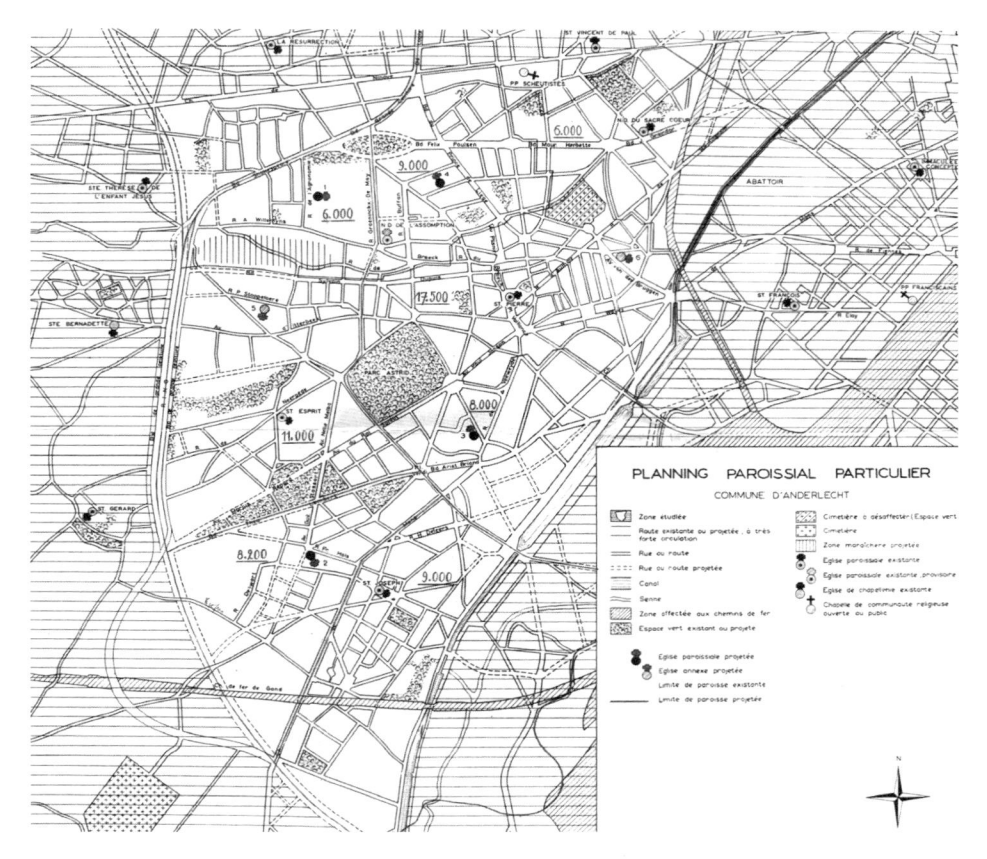

5.11 Pastoral Plan for the municipality of Anderlecht, 1958. The existing and proposed infrastructure are indicated by different symbols.
[Malines, AAM, report 39: CRSR, "Planning paroissial particulier. Anderlecht", August 1958, annex]

traditionally low rate of religious practice in the area (twelve to twenty-five per cent). [Ill. 5.11] Clearly, it was all hands on deck to re-Christianise Anderlecht — and by extension the worker population in the Belgian capital.[57]

Although here the CRSR's proposals thus arose out of a real urgency, once more, the local clergy opposed its plans, which partially explains why it took until 1965 before only one single new parish, dedicated to Saint Luke, became established in the area designated as C-B2. Apart from that, little changed in the parish landscape of Anderlecht after 1958, other than the building of a new church in the existing parish of Notre-Dame de l'Assomption and a little chapel of ease in the Vogelenzang neighbourhood of the Saint-Gérard parish

[57] The reports suggested specific sites for these places of worship that needed to be acquired in the near future. See CRSR, "Planning paroissial particulier. Anderlecht", 21; CRSR, "Planning particulier de l'enseignement gardien et primaire catholique. Anderlecht"; CRSR, "Etude de l'équipement paroissial de la région Bruxelloise. Volume II", 10-11, 68.

in the 1960s — the latter of which had not even been mentioned in the Pastoral Plan since there were no plans for that area at that point, a fact that, in turn, indicates the speed of residential development in Brussels in the 1960s.

Despite the rational basis of the proposed new parish boundaries — taking into account a busy road and geared towards anchoring the parish in the existing urban fabric — one local parish priest stated:

> Little by little, the geographical districts constitute moral entities: the old quarters (...) have their own physiognomy; the new districts are under the influence of a double factor, notably the price of the land and the building regulations.[58]

Further, the high density of churches proposed by the CRSR was also brought into question, given the proximity between the existing church buildings. More important perhaps, apart from the disruption of the parishioners' habits, was the notion that it would bestow upon them a heavy financial burden. Indeed, in an urban context where competition for land was high, the density of pastoral provision aspired to by the CRSR was unrealistic. This is corroborated by the fact that less than a year after the publication of the Pastoral Plan, various proposed church sites were already no longer available.[59] Part of the plot for the projected Saint-Luc church had, for example, been purchased by the municipality with a view to creating access to a park. Thus, by the time the archdiocese was ready to take action, some of the CRSR's proposals were already obsolete.

Apart from illustrating the speed of urbanisation in the Brussels area, this case also reveals a more fundamental weakness of the CRSR's parish planning method: the sites it earmarked for church construction were not anchored in municipal spatial planning tools, such as the Special Zoning Plans that had become compulsory since 1946.[60] As a stopgap measure, the archdiocese wrote to the Anderlecht municipal council, arguing that "churches and schools are institutes of public utility that should be provided for in the development plans for new neighbourhoods, along with shopping centres, playgrounds and access roads".[61] It soon became apparent that this would

---

58 Letter from the parish priest of Saints-Pierre-et-Guidon, 22/07/1959 (Malines, AAM, File on the Saint-Luc parish, Anderlecht).
59 *Note sur Anderlecht*, 27/05/1959 (Malines, AAM, Canon Jozef Billiauw Fund, Records of the Commission Consultative, 1953-1964).
60 The Act of 1946 obliged municipalities to establish Master and Special Zoning Plans with a functional zoning for their territory. The application of this law, however, was limited. It was not until 1962 that a more elaborate planning framework was implemented on a national scale.
61 *Note sur Anderlecht*, 27/05/1959 (Malines, AAM, Canon Jozef Billiauw Fund, Records of the Commission Consultative, 1953-1964).

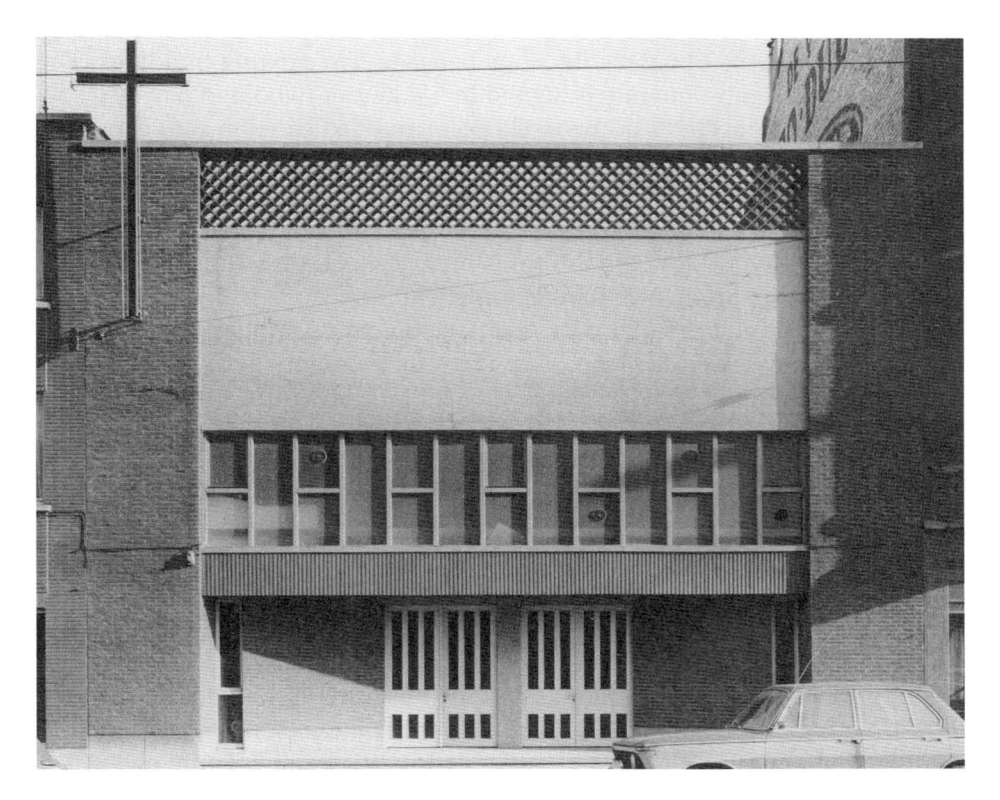

5.12 Front façade of the Saint-Luc church (1961) by Léon De Keyser, along Chaussée de Mons, Anderlecht, 1972.
[© KIK-IRPA, Brussels, Belgium, cliché M084097]

not work here: not only did the municipality have a strong tradition of letting out parts of its territory on a long-lease basis rather than selling them, the socialist council may well have been opposed to encouraging Catholic influence amongst its voters for ideological reasons.[62] The archdiocese did not let this interfere with its intentions, though, and instead adopted a more pragmatic course. As in Uccle, additional expertise was called in, this time in the figure of Jacques Vandermeeren (1920-2004). A founding partner of Groupe Structures, one of the country's largest architectural firms at the time, he also worked for the municipal council as a consultant surveyor. In this double capacity, Vandermeeren negotiated with potential sellers, checking their options with Anderlecht's urbanism department. Although finding a site not too close to an existing church proved difficult, he successfully arranged the acquisition of a

62 Report of the Commission, 15/04/1959 (Malines, AAM, Canon Jozef Billiauw Fund, Records of the Commission Consultative, 1953-1964.). Our hypothesis is corroborated by the fact that in municipalities with a political majority of Christian Democrats, such as Woluwe-Saint-Lambert, the archdiocese was indeed able to have sites reserved for church building in the Special Zoning Plans.

small plot along the Chaussée de Mons between two existing buildings. The church that was subsequently designed by De Keyser (who had played a role similar to Vandermeeren's in the Uccle case) and dedicated in 1961 consisted of a straightforward rectangular worship area that, together with the sacristy, occupied the entire plot on the ground floor and a meeting room with a small kitchen on the second floor along the street side of the parcel only. [Ill. 5.12]

The banality of this church unmistakably illustrates that particular visions of parish planning also had an impact at the typological level. As mentioned above, given the rapid pace of change in cities, Houtart had proposed building churches for a lifespan of no more than seventy-five years. Further, as the introduction of pastoral zones allowed for the centralisation of certain parish activities, smaller churches could be built that would in turn encourage the participation of the faithful in the liturgy.[63] While this clearly did away with the notion of the church as a monumental structure built for eternity, Saint-Luc illustrates that the alternatives often emanated from circumstantial pragmatism rather than well-deliberated theological reflection. Moreover, this case shows that the CRSR's recommendations in terms of parish boundaries and size were first and foremost theoretical in nature and often did not withstand the reality check once they were being implemented. Indeed, the Pastoral Plan's operational qualities were substantially hindered by its underestimating of the impact of private and public interests. Dealing with the complex dynamics of real estate, municipal politics and planning administrations required specific expertise that only architects, urban planners and real estate agents could bring. The fact that the CRSR's proposals were not really anchored in the municipal planning procedures further weakened its ambitions; indeed, despite its intention to act proactively, it was often faced with a fait accompli.

Conclusion

After their problematic implementation in Anderlecht, the Commission grew increasingly impatient with the CRSR's recommendations. Confronted with ever-dwindling financial and human resources (the number of vocations started to decrease from the early 1960s onwards), it began to question the desirability of multiplying the number of parishes. In an internal memo, the question was raised of whether it would not be more advisable to foster collaboration between the parish clergy rather than continue creating new pastoral units:

---

63 Houtart, "Le planning des paroisses urbaines", 115; CRSR, "Etude de l'équipement paroissial de la région Bruxelloise. Volume I", 62-63.

> Cannot the existence of a separate meeting for the parish priests of Anderlecht, under the chairmanship of the parish priest of Saint-Pierre, lead to the experience of a true inter-parochial coordination, perhaps releasing us from creating new parishes?[64]

Thus, the Commission arrived at the same conclusion as the CRSR, namely that the principal weakness of the existing pastoral landscape was perhaps not the size of the parishes, but the total lack of cooperation between them. As a matter of fact, the principal merit of the Pastoral Plan — and perhaps of the CRSR in general — seems to reside in the fact that it made the diocesan leadership understand that the economic, societal and political evolutions occurring required profound and all-encompassing measures. Hence, in 1960, the number of deaneries (a group of parishes) was augmented, following the recommendations made by the CRSR on that topic in 1955 — although the idea of matching their boundaries with those of the municipalities emanated in fact from the Commission.[65] An even more fundamental reorganisation took place after Archbishop Leo Suenens (1904-1996) took office in 1961: the northern part of the archdiocese was split off and established as the Diocese of Antwerp, while the remaining territory was subdivided into so-called vicariates.[66] Hierarchically situated between the diocese and the deaneries, these new territorial entities reflected the linguistic, economic and political individuality of the various regions within the archdiocese. The concept of the "sectors" as defined in the Pastoral Plan, whereby various parishes were grouped together and hierarchically situated in-between the deaneries and the parishes proper, was not implemented until the 2000s, in the form of "pastoral units" — this was no longer to foster collaboration, however, but rather a way of rationalising an overly fine-grained parish landscape that no longer corresponded to the limited number of worshippers.

The increasingly distant attitude of the archdiocese towards the CRSR reflected the progressively difficult position of the centre towards the mid-1960s. Confronted with the incessant demand by dioceses, institutes and congregations for clear-cut, practical advice in the short term, the researchers at the CRSR became increasingly frustrated in their ambition to gain academic credibility for the field of the sociology of religion — a feeling they shared with

---

64 *Note sur Anderlecht*, 21/06/1959 (Malines, AAM, Canon Jozef Billiauw Fund, Records of the Commission Consultative, 1953-1964).
65 Report of the Commission, 02/03/1960 (Malines, AAM, Canon Jozef Billiauw Fund, Records of the Commission Consultative, 1953-1964); CRSR, "Projet de redistribution des doyennés de la région bruxelloise"; Gevers, "Hoogtepunt en einde van een tijdperk".
66 Kenis, "Kerk als minderheid in een pluralistische samenleving. Het aartsbisdom onder Leo Jozef Suenens en Godfried Danneels (1961-2009)".

their colleagues abroad.[67] The fact that the centre derived its income almost exclusively from research commissioned by Catholic patrons did not help in this respect. Although Houtart felt compelled to pose fundamental scientific and pastoral questions, he soon found that the CRSR was not the right forum for doing so:

> We depended on the requests of bishops or religious organisations. Generally, those who entrusted us with the research had their own ideas about reality. When they asked us for a study, it would often be more to prove the validity of their own ideas than to find out what was really happening. Although there were no conflicts at the beginning, the situation became increasingly difficult.[68]

Not only did the researchers at the CRSR increasingly feel harnessed by the applied perspective of their work, they also realised that the Catholic leadership ignored some of their most fundamental messages. After the establishment of the linguistic frontier in 1962 — which divided the country into two separate linguistic (but also, in fact, cultural) spheres — the Belgian Catholic Church held on to its national unity, issuing uniform pastoral guidelines for the entire country, thus totally contradicting the CRSR's fundamental recommendation that matters of faith belonged to the cultural sphere and should therefore be regionalised. In such a context, aggravated even further by the difficult financial situation of the Belgian episcopate, the paradoxical nature of an "embedded" research institute like the CRSR became all the more clear. It soon started negotiating with the Université catholique de Louvain, which has accommodated it from 1964 on. The archdiocese, for its part, took a pragmatic route and decided to no longer invest in prospective studies, but in the services of freelance consultants (such as the "architect-businessman" described in an internal memo) in the search for suitable building plots for realising its pastoral intentions.[69]

---

67 Houtart, "Le Centre de Recherches Socio-Religieuses de Louvain"; Ziemann, *Encounters with Modernity*, 94-98.
68 Pérez, *The Decline of Certainties*, 87-88.
69 Report of the Commission, 20/01/1961 (Malines, AAM, Canon Billiauw Fund, Records of the Commission Consultative, 1953-1964).

BIBLIOGRAPHY

Acknowledgments

The authors are grateful to Gerrit Vanden Bosch and Annelies Tambuyser at the Archives of the Archdiocese of Malines-Brussels and Cathy Schoukens at the Archives of UCLouvain for their generous assistance with the archival research; and also to Jan De Maeyer and Peter Heyrman for their insightful feedback on the text.

Archives

Louvain-la-Neuve, Archives of UCLouvain (UCL)
 - Fund François Houtart: Reports of the Centre de Recherches Socio-Religieuses
 - Outgoing correspondence of the Centre de Recherches Socio-Religieuses
Mechlin, Archives of the Archdiocese of Malines-Brussels (AAM)
 - Canon Jozef Billiauw Fund, Records of the Commission Consultative des Biens Ecclésiastiques, 1953-1964
 - Parish Files of Saint-Bernard, Saint-Gilles, Sainte-Alène, Saint-Marc, Saint-Luc, Saints-Pierre-et-Guidon parishes

Published sources

Bardet, Gaston. *Pierre sur pierre: construction du nouvel urbanisme*. Paris: Editions LCB, 1945.
Chalon, P. "Implantation de la Sociologie Religieuse en Belgique". *Social Compass*, 6 (1 January 1959), 155-164.
Chatelan, Olivier. "Michel Quoist, François Houtart. Deux itinéraires entre sociologie religieuse et désir de l'Amérique Latine (années 1950-1960)". *Revue d'histoire ecclésiastique*, 112, 1-2 (2017), 215-238.
CRSR. "Bilan van 5 jaar aktiviteit, 1956-1961", 1961.
CRSR. "Etude de l'équipement paroissial de la région Bruxelloise. Cartes", October 1958.
CRSR. "Etude de l'équipement paroissial de la région Bruxelloise. Volume I", October 1958.
CRSR. "Etude de l'équipement paroissial de la région Bruxelloise. Volume II", October 1958.
CRSR. "Planning paroissial particulier. Anderlecht", August 1958.
CRSR. "Planning particulier de l'enseignement gardien et primaire catholique. Anderlecht", August 1958.
CRSR. "Projet de redistribution des doyennés de la région bruxelloise", June 1955.
CRSR. "Rapport au Conseil de Gestion", June 1956.
Debié, Frank, and Vérot, Pierre. *Urbanisme et art sacré: une aventure du XXe siècle*. Paris: Critérion, 1991.
Dingemans, Louis. "Le Centre de Recherches Socio-Religieuses de Bruxelles". *Social Compass*, 8 (6 January 1961), 177-186.
Fichter, Joseph H. *Social Relations in the Urban Parish*. Chicago (Ill.): University of Chicago Press, 1954.
Gevers, Lieve. "Hoogtepunt en einde van een tijdperk. Het aartsbisdom onder kardinaal Van Roey (1926-1961)". In: Jan De Maeyer, Eddy Put, Jan Roegiers, André Tihon, and Gerrit Vanden Bosch, eds. *Het Aartsbisdom Mechelen-Brussel: 450 jaar geschiedenis*. Vol. 2. Antwerp-Leuven: Halewijn-KADOC, 2009, 173-253.
Goist, Park Dixon. "City and 'Community': The Urban Theory of Robert Park". *American Quarterly*, 23 (1971), 1, 46-59.
Houtart, François. *Aspects sociologiques du catholicisme américain: vie urbaine et institutions religieuses*. Collection de sociologie religieuse 4. Paris: Edouvrières, 1957.
Houtart, François. "Dimensions nouvelles de la paroisse urbaine". *Nouvelle revue théologique*, 80 (1958), 4, 384-394.
Houtart, François. "Faut-il abandonner la paroisse dans la ville moderne?" *Nouvelle revue théologique*, 6 (1955), 602-613.
Houtart, François. "L'aménagement religieux des territoires urbains". *La Revue Nouvelle*, 14 (December 1958), 12, 517-527.
Houtart, François. "Le Centre de Recherches Socio-Religieuses de Louvain". *Social Compass*, 16 (9 January 1969), 3, 402-404.
Houtart, François. "Le planning des paroisses urbaines". In: F. Boulard, J. H. Fichter, Fr. Houtart, G. Laloux, H. Mendras, and D. Szabo, eds. *Paroisses urbaines, paroisses rurales*. Paris: Casterman, 1958, 104-120.
Houtart, François. *Les paroisses de Bruxelles (1803 - 1951): législation - délimination - démographie - équipement*. 2e ed. Leuven: UCL, Institut de recherches économiques et sociales, 1955.
Houtart, François. "Vers une pastorale urbaine". In: François Houtart and Jean Remy. *Milieu urbain et communauté chrétienne*. Tours: Mame, 1968, 288-299.

Kenis, Leo. "Kerk als minderheid in een pluralistische samenleving. Het aartsbisdom onder Leo Jozef Suenens en Godfried Danneels (1961-2009)". In: Jan De Maeyer, Eddy Put, Jan Roegiers, André Tihon, and Gerrit Vanden Bosch, eds. *Het Aartsbisdom Mechelen-Brussel: 450 jaar geschiedenis*. Vol. 2. Antwerp-Leuven: Halewijn-KADOC, 2009, 255-317.

Lhande, Pierre. *Le Christ dans la banlieue: enquête sur la vie religieuse dans les milieux ouvriers de la banlieue de Paris*. Paris: Plon, 1927.

Pérez, Carlos Tablada. *The Decline of Certainties. Foundig Struggles Anew. The Biography of François Houtart*. Panama: Ruth Casa Editiorial, 2018.

Plummer, Ken. "Introducing Chicago Sociology: The Foundations and Contributions of a Major Sociological Tradition". In: Ken Plummer, ed. *The Chicago School: Critical Assessments*. 1: *A Chicago Canon?*. London: Routledge, 1997, 3-44.

Remy, Jean. "Consequences socio-culturelles de la concentration urbaine". *Social Compass*, 7, (1960), 4, 307-311.

Remy, Jean. "Les institutions ecclesiastiques en civilisations urbaine et industrielle". *Social Compass*, 13, (1966), 1, 39-52.

Ryckewaert, Michael. *Building the Economic Backbone of the Belgian Welfare State: Infrastructure, Planning and Architecture 1945-1973*. Rotterdam: 010 Publishers, 2011.

Sokolski, Alexandre. "Methode de Planning Paroissial Urbain". *Social Compass*, 7, (1960), 4, 313-324.

Sokolski, Alexandre. "Plan d'étude du secteur urbain en vue d'un planning paroissial". In: F. Boulard, J. H. Fichter, Fr. Houtart, G. Laloux, H. Mendras, and D. Szabo, eds. *Paroisses urbaines, paroisses rurales*. Paris: Casterman, 1958, 121-136.

Spicer, Andrew. *Parish Churches in the Early Modern World*. Farnham: Ashgate, 2016.

Sterken, Sven. "A House for God or a Home for His People? The Domus Dei Church Building Action in the Belgian Archbishopric". *Architectural History*, 56 (2013), 387-425.

Sterken, Sven and Weyns, Eva. "Urban Planning and Christian Revival. The Institut Supérieur d'Urbanisme Appliqué in Brussels under Gaston Bardet (1947-1973)". In: Ákos Moravánszky and Judith Hopfengärtner, eds. *Re-Humanizing Architecture. New Forms of Community, 1950-1970*. East West Central. Re-Building Europe, 1950-1990 1. Berlin-Basle: Birkhäuser-De Gruyter, 2016, 243-254.

Weyns, Eva, and Sterken, Sven. "Constructing a Genius Loci: The St Pius X's Church in Wilrijk, 1957-1967". In: L. Rosas, A. Sousa, and H. Barreira, eds. *Genius Loci: Lugares e Significados / Places and Meanings*, Vol. 1. Porto, 2017, 251-263.

Winninger, Paul. *Construire des églises: les dimensions des paroisses et les contradictions de l'apostolat dans les villes*. Rencontres 49. Paris: Cerf, 1957.

Ziemann, Benjamin. *Encounters with Modernity: The Catholic Church in West Germany, 1945-1975*. New York: Berghahn Books, 2014.

6
CATHOLIC PARISHES IN THE LISBON MASTER PLAN OF 1959
THE LEGACY OF THE SNIP AND THE MRAR

JOÃO ALVES DA CUNHA AND JOÃO LUÍS MARQUES

Similar to other European capitals, Lisbon faced a demographic boom in the 1950s that resulted in a lack of sufficient public housing and produced intermittent slums along the city's periphery. The Catholic hierarchy of the Lisbon diocese quickly realised that a challenge of this magnitude could only be dealt with through a coordinated plan for the entire diocese, preferably in conjunction with the master plan for the agglomeration being developed by the civil authorities. This resulted in pastoral and administrative reforms that were introduced in the City of Lisbon in 1959. In assessing this joint effort by the ecclesial and civil authorities, we focus here on two of the principal actors: Cardinal D. Manuel Gonçalves Cerejeira (1888-1977), who secured political support for the plan's realisation, and Manuel Falcão (1922-2012), an ordained priest and rising star in the then-emerging field of the sociology of religion, who provided the scientific underpinnings. Equally important was an organisation they founded to coordinate the massive church-building programme emanating from the reforms, the Secretariado das Novas Igrejas do Patriarcado (SNIP, Secretariat for New Churches in the Patriarchate), which in turn benefited greatly from the thinking and input of members of the Movimento de Renovação da Arte Religiosa (MRAR, Religious Art Renewal Movement), founded in the early 1950s.

As we show below, there was much room for experimentation, despite the conservative climate in Portugal at the time under the dictatorial regime.[1] This had to do with not only Cerejeira's surprisingly broad views on modern art and architecture, but also the fact that, despite their peripheral position, several members of the SNIP were in close contact with the most progressive church architects of the day. As the evolution of the SNIP makes clear, this exchange went well beyond a passing formal acquaintance. Whereas in its early years, the secretariat's concerns revolved around architectural and liturgical innovation, the scale of the problem and urgency of pastoral needs led it to adopt a broader, more sociologically and anthropologically informed, response to creating a strong Church presence in the rapidly expanding periphery of Lisbon. In addition to facilitating individual architectural works, the SNIP produced a prototype for a *capela-salão* (chapel hall), a flexible infrastructure aimed at fostering a sense of community amongst urban dwellers. This is amply illustrated in the two case studies presented below, for the churches of Sagrado Coração de Jesus and Nossa Senhora da Conceição, Olivais Sul, which underscore the contributions of an important, but understudied, actor in the debate about church and city planning in post-war Portugal and beyond.

Cardinal Cerejeira, Manuel Falcão and the Parish Remodelling of 1959

Cerejeira was appointed Bishop of Lisbon in 1928 and, as was custom, immediately became cardinal, despite his young age.[2] He would soon prove a conservative advocate of the Estado Novo (New State), the regime that evolved from the Ditadura Nacional (National Dictatorship) formed after the coup d'état of 28 May 1926. Deeply rooted in Catholic social thought, the doctrine of Estado Novo was developed and embodied by António de Oliveira Salazar (1889-1970), who ruled over Portugal between 1932 and 1968. Underpinned by nationalist and autocratic ideologies, it fostered a corporatist organisation of the economy and society at large, the regime's initial goal being to create stability after the unsteady years of the Portuguese First Republic (1910-1926). To this effect, Salazar restored the influence of powerful institutions, particularly the Catholic Church, which had been strongly persecuted in the First Repub-

---

[1] This article is a synthesis of material from the doctoral research carried out by the authors: da Cunha, *MRAR e os anos de ouro na arquitetura religiosa em Portugal no século XX* (2014), and Marques, *A igreja na cidade, service e acolhimento, arquitectura portuguesa 1950-1975* (2017).

[2] On Cerejeira, see Falcão, "O Cardeal Cerejeira, Pastor da Igraeja Lisbonense"; De Azevedo Maera, "Lisboa No Tempo do Cardeal Cerejeira, Historia Religiosa".

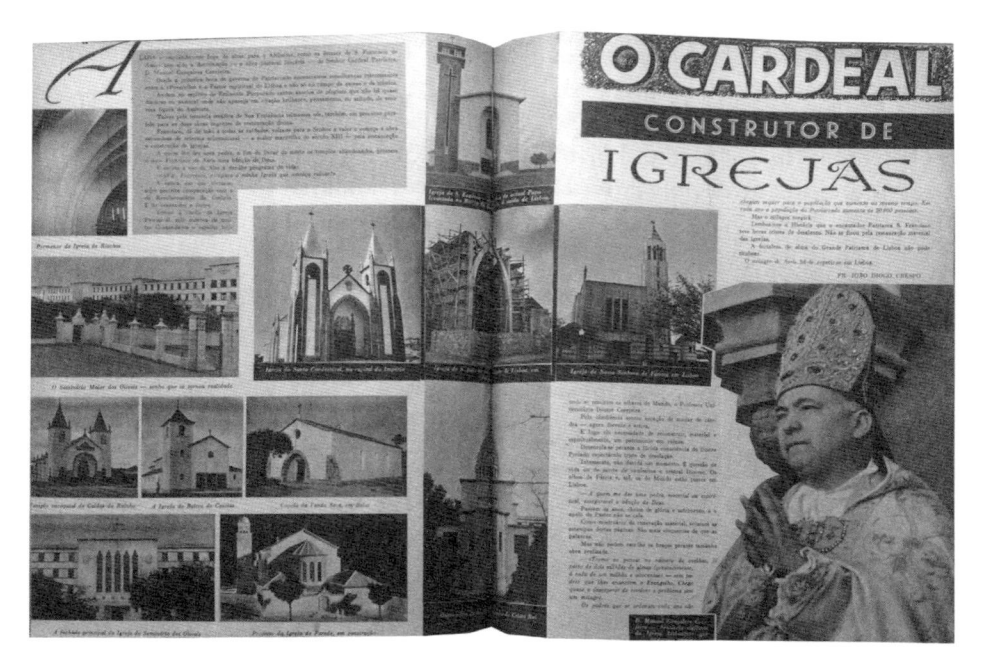

6.1 Press clipping showing Cardinal Cerejeira, "builder of churches".
["O cardeal construtor de igrejas", 12-13. Courtesy of the MRAR Archive]

lic.³ For its part, the Catholic hierarchy was eager to re-establish its influence in Portuguese society; Cerejeira, in particular, considered it his mission to rebuild the Diocese of Lisbon and re-Christianise Portuguese society. United by a strong personal friendship, moreover, Salazar and Cerejeira shared interests, ideas and beliefs — a convergence of positions succinctly captured in the regime's slogan, *Deus, Pátria e Família* ("God, Nation, Family"). This mutual agency found its consecration in the Concordat that was ultimately signed between the Estado Novo and the Vatican in 1940.⁴

Although his cardinalate (which lasted forty-eight years, making it one of the longest in history) has been interpreted as the embodiment of the social, political and cultural conservatism prevalent at the time, Cerejeira himself seems to have been surprisingly open to modern impulses in religious art

3   There is an abundance of literature on the relationship between the Portuguese state and the Catholic Church. See, for example, Cerqueira, "L'Église catholique et la dictature corporatiste portugaise"; Pinto and Rezola, "Political Catholicism, Crisis of Democracy and Salazar's New State in Portugal"; Almeida, "Progressive Catholicism in Portugal: Considerations on Political Activism (1958-1974)". On the use of architecture by the Estado Novo, see Almeida de Carvalho, "Ideology and Architecture in the Portuguese 'Estado Novo': Cultural Innovation within a Para-Fascist State (1932-1945)".
4   Although based on the principle of independence between church and state in religious and political matters, it stipulated, amongst other things, that while bishops were appointed by the Holy See, their final nomination required the government's approval.

and architecture. From the start of his tenure, he promoted the construction of new religious infrastructure such as the Lisbon Seminary (1932-1951) and the parish church of Nossa Senhora de Fátima (1933-1938), which were designed by the modernist architect Porfírio Pardal Monteiro and written about in the French architectural magazine *L'Architecture d'Aujourd'hui*.[5] [Ill. 6.1] In 1938, Cerejeira's broad vision of artistic affairs also came to the fore in a statement published in the magazine *Arquitectos*, in which he replied to the controversy surrounding the modern design of the church of Nossa Senhora de Fátima by declaring, "As for being modern, we do not even realise it could be something else. All forms of art in the past were modern in relation to their time."[6]

Cerejeira was certainly not expressing the opinion of most dignitaries at the time. Although the regime had allowed modernist tendencies in numerous public works in its early days, its ever-increasing conservatism made the repudiation of tradition conceptually untenable.[7] Gradually, the forms and principles of the Modern Movement became dismissed as unadaptable to the local climate and "national character", and the movement was deliberately discredited by branding its adherents as socialists or communists — and thus enemies of the state. Instead, a state-sanctioned "*Portuguesismo*" became the norm for all public buildings starting in 1940. The state became a very active patron of architecture through its Ministério das Obras Públicas (Ministry of Public Works), directed by the energetic Duarte Pacheco, enthusiastically promoting a rhetoric of monumentality for its larger buildings and a romanticised version of the local vernacular for the lesser buildings in the provinces. A major impetus for the construction industry had come from the *Plano Nacional das Casas Económicas* (National Plan for Affordable Dwellings) in 1933, which was the beginning of an active state policy to address the unrelenting migration from rural areas to major cities.[8] To ease the transition for these segments of the population and prevent further uprooting, large housing schemes were developed whose planning and architectural style mimicked that of rural villages. Interestingly, the official guidelines concerning the layout of such neighbourhoods stressed the importance of communal facilities, particularly places of worship.[9] The paradigm that best corresponded with the acculturating ambitions of these schemes, as well as their underlying ideology, was,

5 "La cité religieuse"; "Église Notre-Dame de Fatima à Lisbonne". On the polemics spurred by this modern church, see Santos Costa, "A Igreja de N. Senhora de Fatima em Lisboa e a arte moderna em Portugal" and Cunha, "A igreja de Nossa Senhora de Fátima, em Lisboa: novidade e tradição na arquitectura e liturgia de uma obra singular".
6 Cerejeira, "Sua eminência o cardeal patriarca". Unless otherwise noted, all translations are the authors' own.
7 Pereira, "Die Architektur des Regimes 1938-1948".
8 Ramos, Gonçalves and Silva, "From the Late 19th Century House Question to Social Housing Programs in the 30s".
9 Legislative Decree no. 28:912, I series, no. 186, Ministério das Obras Públicas e Comunicações, 12 August 1938.

6.2 Wide shot of the Santo Eugénio church (Fernando Peres Guimarães, architect) in the Encarnação public housing development, Lisbon, 1951.
[Courtesy of the SNIP Archive]

unsurprisingly, that of the garden city. As the Encarnação allotment in Lisbon (1951) illustrates, this paradigm perfectly captured the Portuguese preference for detached houses and deference to the Church, as well as educational institutes, as their compass in moral and religious matters. [Ill. 6.2]

In 1953, the Cardinal once again touched upon the issue of religious art and modernity. Referring to the ongoing debate about this in the French magazine *L'Art sacré*, he stated:

> The Church has never officialised a style (...). Not only does the Church not condemn the modern, but it has welcomed it at all times. Weren't the consecrated works of the past always modern in their time?[10]

Two years later, Cerejeira returned to the subject once more. On 2 October 1955, at the inauguration of the monumental church of São João de Brito in the recently developed Alvalade neighbourhood, he delivered a speech entitled "The New Churches of the Patriarchate". Its central topic was the structural lack of churches in the Lisbon diocese — a problem that had grown increasingly worse throughout his tenure: whereas in 1935, there had been a pastoral deficit of fifteen churches, that number rose to forty-three in 1948, and by 1959, it was estimated that seventy churches and one hundred fifteen chapels were needed.[11] In light of the pastoral challenge this represented, it became clear

10   Cerejeira, "Pastoral sobre Arte Sacra".
11   Cerejeira, "Ainda o problema do Clero"; Id., "O grave problema das igrejas no Patriarcado".

that church building was a matter of not only architectural style, but also pastoral necessity and building economy. Cerejeira admitted that the twenty-one new parish churches that had been consecrated in the first twenty-five years of his tenure were largely insufficient to cover the ever-increasing pastoral needs of the expanding urban agglomeration. The stakes were high, for it was the Christian soul of Portugal that was in peril:

> Now the point is not to go "spreading Christianity" in Africa; the tragic point is that it must be done here, in the capital of this Nation (and its environs), which has spread the Faith to all parts of the world. (…) It is necessary and urgent, if we want to save the Christian soul of Portugal, to build at least 26 more churches (this is the minimum number, imposed by the demographic chart of the Patriarchate), all, I repeat, all intended to constitute religious centres of new parishes.[12]

And he went on to state:

> A parish church is not just a place of worship. As I said above, it is, rather, the living cell of the Christian community. It does not accomplish its mission if it is not a centre of worship, yes; but it must also be one of teaching, of apostolate, of beneficence, of recreation. As a living cell, it forms, cultivates, develops, defends and diffuses integral Catholic life.[13]

Whereas in his previous allocutions, he had discussed church building only from the perspective of religious art, he now underscored its pastoral role. In order to re-Christianise Portuguese society – and the urban masses in Lisbon in particular – in his view, parish infrastructure had to encompass more than just a place for worshipping; facilities such as a presbytery, a parish hall and a playground and rooms for catechesis and welfare services were deemed equally essential. The financial means of the Portuguese Church and parish communities were largely insufficient to cover the existing deficit, however, and the diocese also lacked personnel to staff these new outposts. For the Cardinal, it was clear: the seriousness and urgency of the situation required a coordination of efforts. Hence, in that same address, he called upon the state for help, recalling that in previous times, "the State has not been indifferent to the tragic problem, contributing in many cases with its share of co-participation."[14] In 1956, Cerejeira asked Salazar in a private message on a postcard for his "decisive support for the work of the new churches to be built in the Patriarchate."[15] This postcard reveals not only the complicity between the two, but also the urgency of implementing a concerted territorial policy to combat

---

12 Cerejeira, "As igrejas novas do Patriarcado".
13 Ibid.
14 Legislative Decree no. 28:912, I series, no. 186, Ministério das Obras Públicas e Comunicações, 12 August 1938.
15 Brandão, *Salazar - Cerejeira a 'força' da Igreja*, 102-103.

the presence of Protestant communities on the city's periphery — a situation identified by the Cardinal as a growing threat.

To get a better grip on the situation, the diocese conducted a survey in 1955 in all the churches of Lisbon to gauge Sunday attendance (the first of its kind in Portugal). This was overseen by Falcão, whose career had been intertwined with Cerejeira's from the start. Trained as an engineer at the Instituto Superior Técnico in Lisbon, Falcão then entered the Lisbon Seminary (founded by Cerejeira in 1931) and was ordained as a priest by the latter in 1951.[16] Falcão went on to teach at his Alma Mater and developed a great interest in the then-emerging field of religious sociology through his active participation in the Conférence Internationale de Sociologie Religieuse (CISR), about which he reported in the Lisbon Seminary's student periodical, *Novellae Olivarum*.[17] It was in fact with a group of students from the seminary that Falcão carried out the 1955 survey, which examined the religious behaviour of the population according to gender, age group and place of residence. Its goal was to grasp the physical and social reality of the 332 parishes of the most populous diocese in the country and thus gain an insight into the religious state of the diocese, so as to serve "as a powerful stimulus to a more conscious, enlightened, more adapted and more effective pastoral zeal".[18]

The survey's outcomes seemed to corroborate Falcão's intuition. Contrary to the widespread image of Lisbon as a city of intense piety, the religious fervour in the capital turned out to be far weaker than expected: on average, only twenty per cent of the adults in the Diocese of Lisbon went to Mass every Sunday, despite the fact that missing it was considered a grave sin. The survey also showed a marked difference in both geographical and social terms between the 49 (out of 332) parishes situated in the capital and those in the rest of the patriarchate and brought to light the steep increase in population in the urban agglomeration around Lisbon (reaching over 200,000 in the 1940s) as a result of the incessant influx from rural areas. Those strong migratory movements produced a new, uprooted and impoverished urban proletariat that was characterised by severe social, moral and religious disorientation. Dramatic as it was, Falcão understood that this phenomenon was not unique

---

16   Biographical details can be found at <https://www.agencia.ecclesia.pt/noticias/documentos/curriculum-de-d-manuel-Falção-19222012/> (accessed 09/07/2019).
17   For example, in May 1956, Falcão and five other Portuguese representatives participated in the 5th International Conference on Religious Sociology in Louvain. On the origins of the sociology of religion in Portugal, see Pereira Coutinho, "Sociologia e antropologia da religião em Portugal" and Ferreira, *A Sociologia em Portugal: da Igreja à Universidade*. The main means of dissemination for Catholic sociologists were the journal *Lumen* (official organ of the Portuguese Episcopal Conference) and the magazine *Novellae Olivarum*, edited by the Lisbon Seminary.
18   Falcão, "Sondagem à assistência à missa dominical no Patriarcado de Lisboa", 68. See also Falcão, "Assistência à missa dominical no Patriarcado de Lisboa". Falcão discussed the 1955 survey in "A prática dominical no Patriarcado de Lisboa em 1955", 3-18.

to Lisbon or even Portugal; it was symptomatic of the fact that in a rapidly urbanising society, the traditional parish was losing its integrative capacity. This situation differed greatly from previous times, when there had been an institutional coincidence between church and society, whereby the parish provided not only a religious, but also a civic framework for its inhabitants; throughout one's life, sacramental moments were also intense moments of sociability, without which one could simply not be part of the local group.[19] This changed radically in the twentieth century, and even more drastically so in the post-war era. Whereas in rural areas, the ecclesiastical boundaries might still coincide with civil parishes, this was no longer the case in cities like Lisbon. As Falcão stated in an essay published in 1958 under the title "The Parish, Its Crisis, Its Value", this dichotomy was more than an administrative problem, for it revealed that the urban population no longer found an immediate inspiration for its profane activities in religion or worship.[20]

This situation required a different approach than rigidly holding on to the traditional territorial parish as a stable Christian matrix. Indeed, the modern city concentrated populations but decentralised their lives: one's place of residence no longer corresponded to that of one's workplace or social activities. Echoing a common trope within CISR circles at that time, Falcão concluded that this condition required a new view of the urban pastorate: in a de-Christianising society, the urban clergy had to become missionaries in their own neighbourhood, and urban parishes had to be conceived in such a way that they provided groups of city dwellers with the necessary support and infrastructure to become truly Christian communities. Apart from the gap between the existing parish division and the reality of social communities, the survey also revealed another, perhaps more surprising, fact: namely, that newly opened churches attracted the faithful in sharply higher percentages than neighbouring, older churches — regardless of whether they were modern or traditional in style. This revealed the attractive power of new architecture, which could thus be an important instrument of evangelisation. This hypothesis was verified by Falcão for a small number of new churches — in particular, in the largest parish of Lisbon, São João de Deus, where a new church had been inaugurated in 1953.[21]

The increasing disproportion in the number of inhabitants per parish was of particular concern to Cerejeira. As he noted in a pastoral letter in 1959,

19 Clemente, "As paróquias de Lisboa", 392-393.
20 Falcão, "A paróquia, sua crise, seu valor".
21 Falcão also referred in the article to the new parochial churches of Benedita, Alcobaça (1955, architect Lucínio Cruz); Silveira, Torres Vedras (1955, architect Inácio Peres Fernandes); Bárrio, Alcobaça (1947, engineer Eduardo Alberto Henriques dos Reis); Riachos, Torres Novas (1949, architect Inácio Peres Fernandes); and Vilar, Cadaval (1953, architect unknown). Falcão, "Sondagem à assistência à missa dominical no Patriarcado de Lisboa".

the average population per civil parish of Lisbon was 18,500.[22] This number, the Cardinal underscored, was well above the number of 5,000 that had been suggested as the ideal urban parish by the French cleric Paul Winninger in his highly influential book *Construire des églises*.[23] Cerejeira also referred to Pope Pius XII, who had proclaimed in 1952 that parishes with more than 10,000 inhabitants were overburdened; the Pontificia Commissione Centrale per l'Arte Sacra had therefore suggested splitting up a parish when it represented 12,000 or more inhabitants. In any case, as Cerejeira stated by quoting Winninger, parishes of 15,000 souls were "monsters" and "agents of de-Christianisation". He therefore declared a "struggle against the megalopolis", following the example of some of his colleagues elsewhere in Europe. As he mentioned in his pastoral letter, valuable and successful examples of how to proceed could be found in Cardinal Verdier's Chantiers du Cardinal church-building campaign in Paris; the Comitato pro Templi Nuovi, an office to promote the establishment of parish centres formed by Cardinal Montini in Milan; the Domus Dei organisation created by Cardinal Van Roey in Brussels and the strategy developed by Cardinal Lercaro in Bologna.

It was not only the Church that felt the need to adjust its structures to the unavoidable urban and demographic transitions under way, however. The civil authorities, too, had been struggling to keep up with the pace of the capital's evolution. Attempts to develop a master plan for channelling the city's future growth started in 1938, resulting in the 1948 plan by Étienne de Groër.[24] This soon proved obsolete, though, for it had been based on predictions that no longer held stake. So in 1954, a special department was established within the municipal administration, the Gabinete de Estudos de Urbanização (Urbanization Studies Office), with the aim of revising the 1948 plan. Although the resulting Plano Diretor de Urbanização de Lisboa (Lisbon Urbanization Master Plan) from 1959 retained most of de Groër's principles (e.g. a radiocentric road network around a central axis; decreasing population densities from the centre to the periphery), it proposed important changes such as building a bridge over the Tague river (fostering the urbanisation of the proximate riverbanks) and constructing various motorways — thus revealing the growing emphasis on motorised and individual transportation.

---

22 Cerejeira, "O grave problema das igrejas no Patriarcado".
23 Winninger, *Construire des églises*. Cerejeira was aware of this publication, for he explicitly referred to it in a pastoral letter: "In 1957, in a book that made a great sensation, about the size of parishes and the contradictions of the apostolate in the cities, — a real cry of alarm! — Paul Winninger, the superior of the Seminary of Philosophy in Strasbourg, was not afraid to write, at the conclusion of his long, well documented inquiry: 'Building churches doesn't solve anything immediately (...).'" Cerejeira, "O grave problema das igrejas no Patriarcado".
24 On the de Groër Plan, see Cadernos do Arquivo Municipal no 9, 2014, 183-190. Online at <https://issuu.com/camara_municipal_lisboa/docs/cad09/145> (accessed 09/07/2019).

Cerejeira took advantage of this momentum to push through the urgently needed parish reform. Issuing a decree to this effect in March 1959, he wrote:

> The preparation of the Lisbon Urbanization Master Plan has given us the opportunity of putting the problem of the parish division of Our City in a wider context. In fact, only such a plan would allow us to look not only at the present situation, but at the future with certainty, and to foresee the general lines of the division of a city that, once the urbanisation foreseen for the present urban area has been completed, will have 1,100,000 inhabitants.[25]

As it turned out, the parish remodelling and the capital's administrative reform went hand in hand, with technicians on the Lisbon City Council and members of the diocese (Falcão in particular) working closely and successfully towards re-establishing the lost correspondence between the civil and ecclesiastical divisions of the city. Endorsing their efforts, Cerejeira wrote:

> The major drawbacks of the situation so far are no longer being felt, and it is even possible and easy to carry out, in successive phases, the perfect correspondence of the civil and religious divisions. We are pleased to see this happy outcome, which it would not be possible to obtain so fully and swiftly if the Authorities who contributed to it did not have a clear vision of the harmony of interests which in this and in many areas are common to the Church and the State.[26]

This "happy outcome" did not come overnight; it was the result of a long, systematic process. To start with, a series of studies had to be performed, including a statistical analysis of each parish that included the context of its foundation, its boundaries, the number of inhabitants it served, an inventory of its places of worship and their location and some critical observations regarding its pastoral needs. Based on these data, a detailed map of the city was drawn up on a 1:10,000 scale, indicating the exact position of all Lisbon's churches and chapels. A circle with a radius of 500 m indicated the part of the city each of them served, covering an area roughly equivalent to ten minutes' walking time. [Ill. 6.3] Although this was, of course, an abstract exercise, for it did not consider the topographical reality of the city, it revealed that some important areas were not covered by the existing pastoral network, while others had an oversupply of churches. On this basis, a number of new parishes were created on the basis of the geographic, demographic and socio-economic realities of the city. To honour the quite varied social topography of the city, the planners sought to "delimit the area of the parishes by the natural or urban divisions, so that each one can achieve, as far as possible, the ideal of

25 Cerejeira, "Decreto Patriarcal - Remodelação Paroquial da Cidade de Lisboa".
26 Cerejeira, "O grave problema das igrejas no Patriarcado".

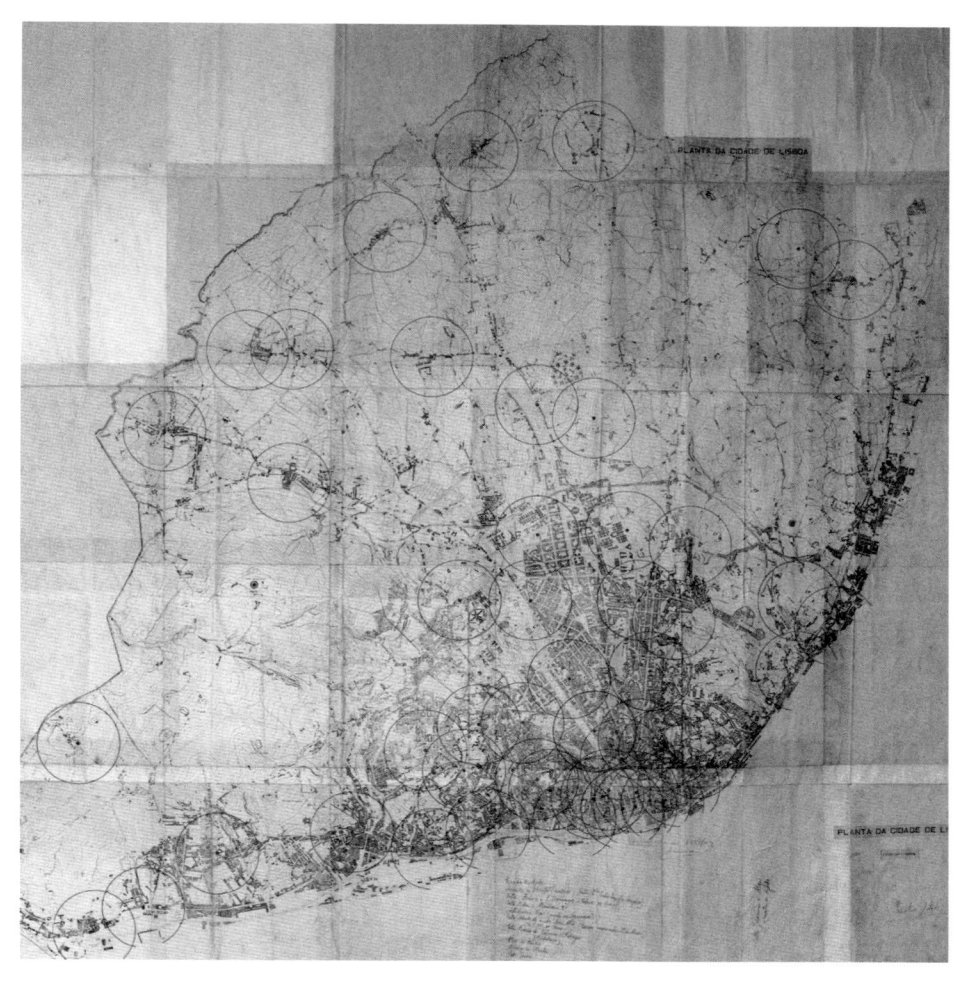

6.3 Lisbon's parish city plan study from the 1950s showing the location of existing churches and chapels in the capital. The circled areas represent a maximum of ten-minutes' walking distance from the place of worship in the centre.
[Courtesy of the SNIP Archive]

human and Christian community".[27] Interestingly, the city's administration reasoned along similar lines, preferring demographic homogeneity to social diversity. Underscoring this partnership between church and state in the civil administrative map reform of 1959, some of the patron saint names belonging to churches were reinstated for civil parishes in the city centre. This emphasized the historical Portuguese Christian identity and reversed the secular actions of the First Republic by which the names of some of the old civil parishes in Lisbon had been changed to remove any religious references. Despite their

27   Ibid.

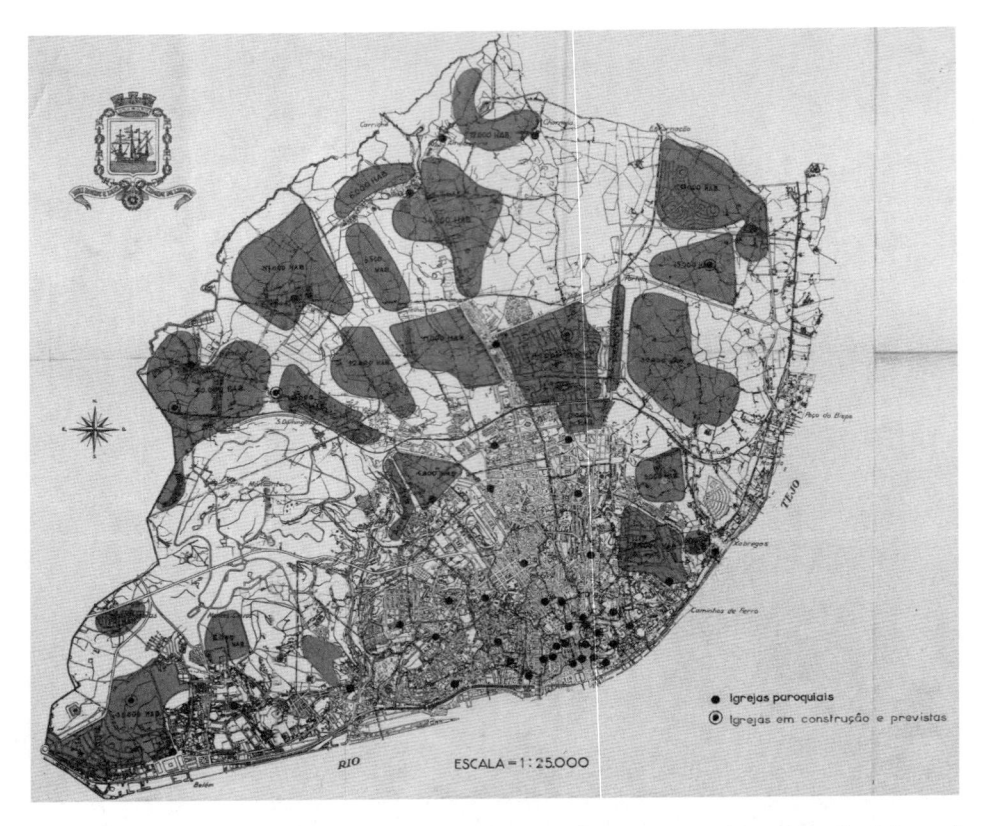

6.4 Lisbon's parish city plan from 1959 showing the new parish boundaries, with locations of existing and future churches. Areas of population growth are marked in red in the original document (here in grey), according to the forecasts by Étienne de Groër.
[Courtesy of the SNIP Archive]

overall concurrence, however, the two parties – the diocesan experts and the city's administration – could not agree upon a set number of inhabitants per parish; unlike the city, the diocese favoured the concept of smaller communities, regardless of the staffing constraints it faced. To serve the pastoral needs that had been identified, it estimated that the forty-nine existing parishes would need to be reconfigured into a total of eighty-three over the long term. As a result, the new administrative and religious matrices for Lisbon did not correspond exactly, since some civil parishes consisted of two religious ones.

Realising that such a reform could not be pushed through all at once, the diocese decided to implement the new parish subdivision in three phases. First, fifteen new parishes were created by splitting up, uniting or eliminating existing ones (two were united with two others and one was eliminated), bringing the total number to sixty-one. To this effect, eighteen new churches were to be built in the City of Lisbon in the following decades. An "ideal" location was suggested for each of them, based on a metric whereby all parishioners would have equivalent travel times — an ambition that was, of course, hard to realise in the more densely built-up parishes, where available building land was scarce. In a second phase, nine more parishes would be created, with the aim of reducing the overall average to about 12,000 souls per parish. The third and final phase was supposed to focus on the areas to be urbanised according to the new master plan and was to result in the creation of yet another thirteen new parishes. Thus, based on the prediction that by the mid-1960s Lisbon would comprise 1.1 million people, it was believed that the average number of inhabitants per parish would not exceed 13,000.[28] [Ill. 6.4]

MRAR and SNIP: New Expertise for New Solutions

While the parish reshuffling of 1959 tackled the pastoral problem on an urban scale, the question remained as to how it should be faced at the local level. Indeed, as Cerejeira stated in his 1959 pastoral letter entitled "The Serious Problem of Churches in the Patriarchate of Lisbon", the numbers were seriously daunting: one hundred fifteen chapels and seventy new churches were needed immediately throughout the diocese, twenty-four of them in the city alone. As the Cardinal admitted, this was a Herculean task that would indeed be discouraging "were it not about the life and death of the Church in the Patriarchate".[29] An undertaking of this magnitude required a new, and radically different, approach to church building. As Cerejeira stated:

> The material conditions of the Catholic milieu (generally poor) and the spirit of the time impose a revision of the modern-day church. It is no longer possible to think about churches that impose themselves by their measure of sumptuosity. Whether due to the cost or the number of churches to be built, the means are lacking. Added to this is the urgency of construction. But even if the means abounded, such churches, especially in the working areas growing around Lisbon, would not be the most suitable today for bringing the Christian message to souls. A stream of evangelical purification permeates our time, which is translated into liturgical worship, sacramental life, authenticity of witness. The simple church — I would even say Franciscan: clear, cheerful, welcoming and authentic — corresponds better to the contemporary state of mind. Several people, such as Father Régamey in France, have been struck by the need for this type of renewal. It easily leads to the possibility of the economical church, more on the scale of the common man, who will not feel estranged in it.[30]

28 The 1959 plan was revised and adapted in the decades that followed to accommodate the urban growth being witnessed, but the goal of the eighty-three planned parishes was never fully realised.
29 Cerejeira, "O grave problema das igrejas no Patriarcado".
30 Ibid.

This again reveals how well-informed Cerejeira was of what was happening in other European countries and how he wished to develop similar expertise in his own diocese:

> To this end a group of architects was organised in Milan, as in Bologna, for the study of one or more standard solutions of a general nature. Perhaps, in Lisbon, a similar measure is necessary, given the greatness of the problem of the new churches.[31]

That opened the door for the creation of a new diocesan body whose mission it would be to coordinate this vast church-building programme:

> This work of building the new churches will certainly require some steps to be taken at the diocesan level, such as by the Secretariat for New Churches and the Commission of Sacred Art, for a good organisation, direction and accomplishment of everything pertinent to the matter at hand.[32]

Indeed, the urban, architectural, technical and legal challenges ahead could only be addressed by competent experts from outside the Church. Thus, on 6 January 1961, Cerejeira issued a decree creating the Secretariado das Novas Igrejas do Patriarcado (SNIP), justifying this decision on the basis of the magnitude and specificity of the mission at hand:

> The construction programme itself, especially with regard to the size of the church and the number and nature of the annexes, should be carefully thought out. There is also the need to guide and assist the works of conservation, renovation and restoration of ancient churches. This work poses problems of unity and architectural adaptation, purity and harmony of style, liturgical and pastoral functionality, which require special technical and artistic preparation.[33]

He acknowledged that the scale and complexity of this task "have weighed on and sometimes crushed the parish priests of the Patriarchate", so that it was a matter "of justice, charity and prudence to free them as much as possible of occupations and concerns which technicians might take upon themselves".[34] The Cardinal explained the mission of the SNIP accordingly:

> Like similar offices in foreign dioceses with the same problems, it encourages, coordinates, guides and accompanies initiatives and activities related

31 Cerejeira, "O grave problema das igrejas no Patriarcado".
32 Ibid.
33 Cerejeira, "Decreto de criação do Secretariado das Novas Igrejas do Patriarcado".
34 Ibid.

to the planning and construction of places of worship and other buildings necessary to the life of the diocesan Church.[35]

He went on to acknowledge that although he had felt the need for such a body for a long time, it was not until this point that there was a group of both priests and lay people available who had sufficient competence regarding such matters, namely from the Movimento de Renovação da Arte Religiosa (MRAR).

Founded in 1953, the MRAR gathered together architects, artists, historians and priests committed to conferring greater dignity and artistic quality to religious art and architecture in Portugal. The members of this group shared a modern take on their respective professions, and opposed the traditionalist tendencies promoted by the regime. Devout Catholics themselves, they particularly questioned what they called the inauthenticity of the official religious architecture, with its "particular demands of truth, harmony and dignity".[36] Based on their avid faith and fed by the spirit of mission and militancy typical of the Juventude Universitária Católica (Catholic University Youth), the MRAR's members felt it was their duty to strive for a true renovation of religious art and architecture. As Nuno Teotónio Pereira (1922-2016), one of its founding members, phrased it in 1959, "The idea of reforming the MRAR was not born: it imposed itself on us. It had to be."[37] Apart from a sense of vocation, they also shared a deep sense of responsibility, for, as Pereira put it, to remain silent "would be to betray the vocation of architects and Catholics".[38] Another person, in addition to Pereira, whose involvement was instrumental in the MRAR's founding was João de Almeida (1927-2020). In 1949, at Cerejeira's recommendation, Almeida moved to Paris, where he met, amongst others, the Dominican friars Marie-Alain Couturier and Pie-Raymond Régamey, directors of the hugely influential periodical L'Art sacré. After a year of studying in the libraries and museums of Paris under their guidance, Almeida moved to Basel, where he worked in Hermann Baur's atelier.[39] During this period, the young Portuguese architect had the opportunity to make numerous trips to various Swiss and German cities, visiting the works of other leading architects who were modernising religious architecture, such as Fritz Metzger, Ernst Gisel and Rudolf Schwarz.

The many pictures and stories of his experiences Almeida brought with him upon his return to Lisbon in the autumn of 1952 had a profound impact on his colleagues from the MRAR and the Olivais Seminary, where he was studying and where he created the Equipa de Arte Sacra (Sacred Art Team), an infor-

35 Ibid.
36 Pereira, "A Arquitectura Cristã Contemporânea".
37 Pereira, "Conversando com o arquitecto", 4.
38 Pereira et al., *Exposição de Arquitectura Religiosa Contemporânea*, Exhibition catalogue (Lisbon. MRAR Archive, April 1953).
39 Cunha, "João de Almeida", 8.

6.5 The exhibition "Arquitectura Religiosa Contemporânea" (Contemporary Religious Architecture) at Galeria de São Nicolau, Lisbon, 1953.
[Courtesy of the MRAR Archive]

mal student discussion group. Both groups felt some sort of kinship with the Swiss churches. According to Nuno Portas (°1934), who would later become president of the MRAR, this had to with the fact that they had "transposed the principles of architectural functionalism into the building of worship".[40] These "perfect liturgical mechanisms", as Portas liked to call the Swiss churches, inspired the young MRAR members to such an extent that in the exhibition on religious architecture they organised in Lisbon in 1953, the last section was devoted entirely to Swiss and German examples. [Ill. 6.5] That was only the first of many exhibitions, conferences and initiatives organised by the MRAR in the fifteen years of its existence for the purpose of educating its members and sensitising the clergy, as well as the general public, to a modern aesthetic in terms of liturgy, art and architecture.

After this initial phase, the MRAR became particularly influenced by the initiatives being undertaken in the Diocese of Bologna after one of its most committed members, Diogo Lino Pimentel (1934-2019), spent a year (1959) at the Centro di Studio e Informazione per l'Architettura Sacra under the supervision of Giorgio Trebbi (1926-2002) and Glauco Gresleri (1930-2016).[41] Upon his return, Pimentel stated:

40 Portas, "Arquitectura Religiosa Moderna em Portugal", 22.
41 Gresleri et al., *Chiesa et quartiere*.

> A new perspective came to me, which consists of having acquired the notion of the fundamental importance of the sociological–urbanistic issues present in relation to the design of the sacred buildings.[42]

In Bologna, he had been able to visit the many church construction sites, particularly Gresleri's Beata Vergine Immacolata, which Pimentel found the most interesting.[43] Pimentel also collaborated with Gresleri on a project for a small rural church on the outskirts of Florence and with Trebbi on the church of San Pio X in Bologna. These experiences, combined with numerous meetings and discussions at the diocesan offices in Bologna, proved invaluable for Pimentel's personal education and subsequently for the MRAR's direction, given that Pimentel went on to become one of its most prominent members.

In the meantime, Falcão had been formally appointed director of the SNIP in 1961 by Cardinal Cerejeira and was responsible for coordinating its three divisions. The "technical" division was directed by Pimentel; it handled all matters related to planning, architecture and technical issues, as well as executing exhibitions and other initiatives of the "propaganda" division. That division was led by Almeida, and its mission was to undertake initiatives to arouse public interest in the new churches campaign and organise fund-raising campaigns, the most important of which was the annual church-building day: one Sunday a year, all the money collected at every Mass in the diocese was allocated to the construction of the multitude of churches and chapels needed. [Ill. 6.6] Inspired by the example of Bologna, the SNIP maintained a constant dialogue with society at large in a quarterly newsletter. Entitled *Novas Igrejas* (New Churches), this short-lived magazine (only eight issues appeared between 1961 and 1963) sought to foster reflection and knowledge among both the clergy and the faithful with regard to religious art and architecture, as well as the liturgical ministry. It was a very costly and time-consuming affair, however, and the initiative folded in 1963, and was replaced only in 1968 by an information leaflet (a single sheet folded in three) with a run of over 375,000 copies. This later incarnation accompanied the annual fund-raising campaign and provided insightful information about the financial situation of the church-building programme, the envisaged architectural solutions and their pastoral concepts. Maintained for over twenty years, that publication constitutes an invaluable source for the architectural and religious historiography of Portugal since the late 1960s. The final division of the SNIP was the administrative division headed by the priest João Trindade, who collected and administered the Fund of the New Churches of the Patriarchate, studied and proposed the distribution of subsidies for land and works and directed or carried out transactions related to the acquisition of land.

42   Pimentel, *Relatório* (Lisbon, SNIP Archive, March 1960).

novas igrejas do patriarcado

1968

Construir igrejas majestosas foi, noutros tempos, uma das formas mais expressivas de glorificar a Deus. A catedral ou a grande basílica, edificadas por gerações sucessivas no coração das velhas cidades, mais do que um espaço para congregar e abrigar os que oravam, eram a sua própria oração feita monumento.

Hoje, a renovação litúrgica pôs em relevo uma nova dimensão da oração da Igreja, a que esses tempos não foram muito sensíveis: a da participação consciente e activa de todos os fiéis na liturgia. Por outro lado, sente-se hoje que a oração litúrgica se deve projectar na vida, numa irradiação de fé e caridade, o que, no mundo moderno, significa espírito de verdade e de justiça, contributo para o desenvolvimento dos povos e luta pela paz verdadeira...

Por isso, as novas igrejas, já não serão monumentais e majestosas como as de outros tempos, que isso seria contradizer a própria realidade da Igreja dos nossos dias. Serão a *casa* que congrega e abriga o «Povo de Deus», reunido para a oração que é a Igreja actuando como servidora dos homens. Exprimir e servir essa realidade, é o que se pede à arquitectura sacra de hoje.

No Patriarcado, novos bairros e povoações inteiras, abrangendo milhares de cristãos, não dispõem ainda duma igreja, dum lugar de culto e oração, no qual se reunam para a missa, para escutarem a palavra de Deus, para receberem os sacramentos, para conviverem e organizarem as suas actividades de apostolado, formação, caridade e ensino.

No *primeiro domingo de Janeiro de 1968*, a todas as missas celebradas no Patriarcado, serão recolhidos os contributos em dinheiro de toda a diocese para o Fundo das Novas Igrejas. Destina-se este fundo, através da manutenção de serviços, de subsídios e empréstimos, a conseguir que, onde quer que façam falta, surjam as igrejas e capelas necessárias, ou se adaptem as existentes carecidas de restauro ou remodelação.

Estamos no «Ano da Fé». Que a generosidade do nosso contributo seja expressão da consciência de que ele é uma forma de ajudar eficazmente a manter e desenvolver a fé cristã na diocese a que pertencemos.

6.6 Cover of the leaflet *Novas Igrejas do Patriarcado* (New Churches of the Patriarchate), 1968.
[Courtesy of the SNIP Archive]

Churches in the City, for the City: Sagrado Coração de Jesus and Nossa Senhora da Conceição, Olivais Sul

Initially, the SNIP continued along the lines of the MRAR, adopting in particular the idea of a standard programme for guiding the construction of new churches. In 1964, together with the Comissão de Arte Sacra (Diocesan Commission for Sacred Art, created in 1963), it proposed a preliminary document, "Regulamento de construção e restauro de igrejas" (Regulations for the Construction and Restoration of Churches), which would later be developed into the "Programa-base para a construção de novas igrejas" (Preliminary Programme for the Construction of New Churches), published in 1966. The document started by defining the broad architectural characteristics of a building, before introducing each of the elements that compose a church, stating that "as a work of architecture, it can only be modern" — an expression used often by the MRAR.[44] Beyond the formal and functional aspects, however, the guidelines aimed to effect a new form of presence for the Church in the city, in search of a contemporary means by which the Church could relate to the world – a Church that, following Christ, "did not come to be served, but to serve" (Matthew 20. 28). Therefore, the Church, "instead of imposing itself, should rather propose itself to the world; likewise, the church building must insert itself discreetly into the urban fabric".[45]

In Portugal, this idea made its debut in the design competition held for the new church of the Sagrado Coração de Jesus, in the Marquês do Pombal district of Lisbon. Although initiated by the MRAR in collaboration with Falcão in 1957, the competition was eventually organised by the SNIP in 1962 after it had been delayed due to a renegotiation of the building plot.[46] The design competition concerned a modern parish church of 1,000 seats and a large parish complex with different facilities. The brief reads:

> In order to be a modern church in the sense that it is intended for the People of God of today, it must respond to the noblest needs and aspirations of men of our time: an urgent desire for community life; craving for truth and authenticity; desire to move from the superficial to what is central and essential; ambition for clarity, brightness and visibility; vehement longing for silence and peace, warmth and security.[47]

---

43 Ibid.
44 SNIP, "Programa de construção de novas igrejas", 26.
45 Ibid., 27.
46 On the Sagrado Coração de Jesus competition and the project built, see "Concurso de anteprojectos para a Igreja Paroquial do Sagrado Coração de Jesus e seus anexos".
47 SNIP ed., *Programa de construção da igreja paroquial do SS. Coração de Jesus e de seus anexos [1957]. Competition brief*, 4 (Lisbon, SNIP Archive, 1962).

6.7 Rendering of the Sagrado Coração de Jesus church (1962-1970) in Lisbon (Nuno Teotónio Pereira and Nuno Portas, architects).
[Courtesy of the MRAR Archive]

The jury, which included the well-known Swiss architect Hermann Baur, awarded the first prize to Pereira and Portas, whose proposal presented itself as a building "able to welcome and to be contaminated by the city". According to the authors, the basis for their design had been the question "How is the Church 'communicating' with the street, with the city?"[48] [Ill. 6.7] This was interpreted on two levels in terms of layout. As opposed to the traditional central siting and dominant occupation of the lot, the built volumes of the church and parish centre were pushed to its edges, creating a permeable public space that formed a welcome distraction from the monotonous urban grid in the area. In addition, this public square bridged the height difference (approx. 10 m) between the Camilo Castelo Branco and Santa Marta streets through a succession of outdoor terraces. Thus, the various components of the parish complex (restaurant, library, medical facility, cinema, conference room and kindergarten) could be accessed through a new pedestrian street that, in the imagination of the architects, would become a place for dialogue and

48 Pereira, *Ante-projecto da igreja do Sagrado Coração de Jesus*, 1 (Lisbon, SNIP Archive, 1962, 4).

6.8 Interior of the Sagrado Coração de Jesus church (1962-1970) in Lisbon (Nuno Teotónio Pereira and Nuno Portas, architects).
[Photograph by Hugo Casanova, 2020]

interaction between citizens — believers and non-believers alike — and attract people beyond the parish proper. In this manner, rather than dominating its surroundings, the church infused them with social impulses, proposing a new interpretation of the place of the sacred in the contemporary urban environment. All this was expressed architecturally with great skill; the designers were widely acknowledged for the way in which they had managed to carefully insert a large volume on such a small plot in a densely built-up area and for the poetic dialogue between the "brutalist" articulation of the bare concrete volumes, as well as the restrained mastery of the detailing. [Ill. 6.8]

Nevertheless, despite its success, it was clear that this was too much of a one-off project to be repeatable. Moreover, the Roman Catholic Liturgy was undergoing fundamental reforms. For the SNIP's directors, it was plain: a true rethinking of the church typology was needed; the ancient models could no longer be the answer; it was time to put "new wine into new wineskins" (Matthew 9. 17). From now on, the SNIP would align its research and actions along two axes. First, instead of encouraging the search for specific architectural solutions, as it had been doing, it would endeavour to put architecture — as a field of expertise — at the service of the pastoral needs raised by the new times. Second, in its search for such prototypical solutions, it would align itself with the directives of the Second Vatican Council, which stated that there could be much spiritual richness in material poverty.

Based on these points of departure, a prototype called the *capela-salão* (chapel hall) was developed in 1967, whose primary purpose was to provide accommodation for a large variety of groups and activities, enhancing communal and spiritual life in dialogue with the city.[49] The SNIP started looking for an efficient, cost-effective construction scheme that could serve as a basis for different formal interpretations. The solution was a simple plan composed of a small space exclusively for prayer, directly connected to a second, larger, multifunctional space that functioned as an extension of the first, permitting larger assemblies. [Ill. 6.9] During non-liturgical times, the latter was an independent space, available for meetings, courses, socialising, parties, games, catechesis, etcetera. As the SNIP described this solution:

> The *capela-salão* is indeed the house where a particular Christian community meets, whether for prayer or for activities of a formative, cultural or even social nature. This typology seems to be a truly up-to-date and appropriate solution to certain settings.[50]

This proposal also seemed perfectly suited to the times, as it invited Catholic communities to use the church space with complete freedom (i.e. without the sacred/profane distinction). This plan resulted in a set of projects that used this community-building design as a starting point and then assumed diverse external configurations according to the needs of each place, site conditions or urban setting. More than thirty *capelas-salão* were built in twenty years, including in dioceses other than Lisbon, attesting to the widespread interest generated by the SNIP's proposal among highly diverse communities.

The success of this typological solution led to the adoption of a similar scheme in several projects for larger parish churches, such as the church of Nossa Senhora da Conceição in Olivais Sul, the first major social housing development of Lisbon; it was "the laboratory of an enlightened modern attitude that prolonged the quality of urban values at the scale of architecture".[51] Part of the extensions planned in the 1959 master plan for Lisbon, Olivais Sul comprised approximately 8,000 housing units for 38,000 inhabitants. Faithful to the principles of the Athens Charter, it was conceived of as a self-contained neighbourhood in a green setting. Its most unique aspect was that it featured designated residential blocks for specific professions (teachers, po-

49 Marques, "Entre lo provisional y lo definitivo".
50 SNIP, ed., *Novas igrejas do patriarcado* (Lisbon, SNIP Archive, 1968).
51 Ana Tostões, Editorial, *DOCOMOMO Journal*, (2016) 55 ('Modern Lisbon' theme issue), 3.

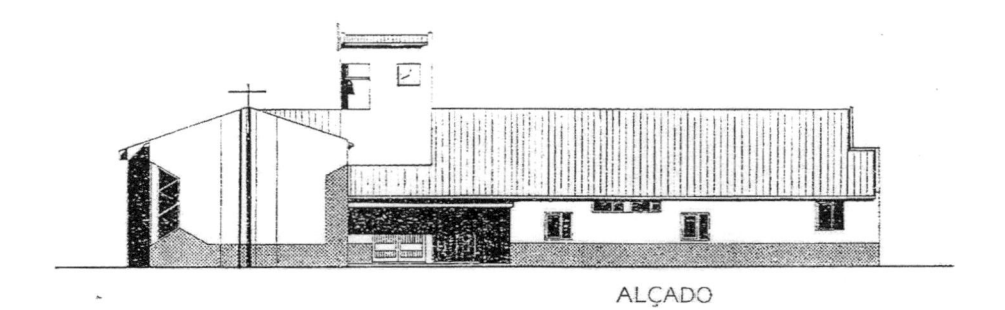

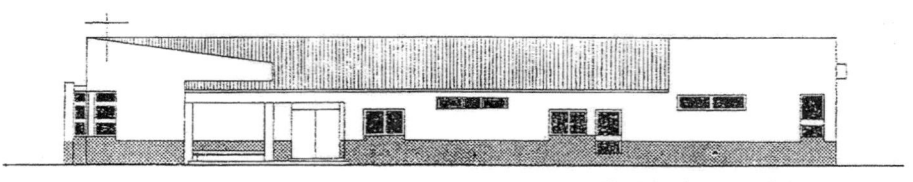

CATHOLIC PARISHES IN THE LISBON MASTER PLAN OF 1959 213

ALÇADO

ALÇADO (VARIANTE)

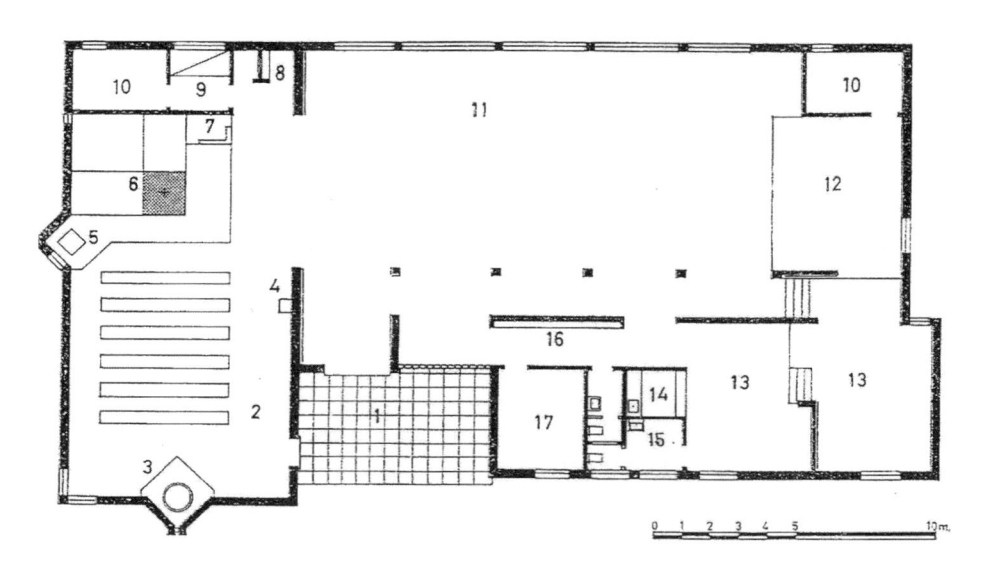

6.9 Plan and possible façades for the *capela-salão* (1969).
[Courtesy of the SNIP Archive]

6.10 Rendering of the courtyard of the Nossa Senhora da Conceição church in Olivais Sul (1970-1988) (Pedro Vieira de Almeida, architect).
[Courtesy of the SNIP Archive]

licemen, judges, etc.), for they were funded by different government institutions. Whereas such social and typological variety led to a "social mix" for the area as a whole, the individual parts consisted of mentally isolated cells with homogenous populations. In such a context, collective amenities such as schools, and certainly also churches, were paramount to fostering the intended process of socialisation.

The first of the three parishes projected for Olivais Sul under the 1959 diocesan plan was only formally established in 1967, when a provisional chapel was built there. Until then, the faithful had gathered in the basement of a residential building, and later in a primary school. In 1970, the SNIP launched a design competition for one of the three worship venues planned for the area. The brief was for a seating capacity of 500 (with an additional 500 standing-room places), with the usual array of meeting rooms, and was, in this respect, little different from the standard programme drafted by the SNIP in 1966. The winning proposal by Pedro Vieira de Almeida (1933-2011), who was also involved in the design of the Sagrado Coração church, proposed an architecture that would "empower community relations" through its capacity

6.11 Interior of the Nossa Senhora da Conceição church in Olivais Sul (1970-1988) (Pedro Vieira de Almeida, architect).
[Photograph by Hugo Casanova, 2017]

to become appropriated by the parishioners.[52] [Ill. 6.10] Only then could this church building make a difference. Or, as Vieira de Almeida stated:

> Given the particular urban situation of Olivais, a set of object-buildings with which it is difficult to dialogue, we tried to take advantage of a building that refused to be one more object, a building that internalises itself by structuring for and by itself a life and animation that the neighbourhood does not propose.[53]

Rather than pertaining to just a building, therefore, the competition project was conceived of as "a set of facilities, living by itself and by itself enabling a way of living".[54] Imbued with the spirit of the times, the church building was intended to be "a system and not a form". To this effect, Vieira de Almeida slotted the large volume of the church into the sloping site, giving it an almost

52   Marques, *A igreja na cidade, service e acolhimento, arquitectura portuguesa 1950-1975*, 447-483; Lopes Dias, *Teoria e Desenho da Arquitectura em Portugal 1956-1974: Nuno Portas e Pedro Vieira de Almeida*, 170-172.
53   Almeida, *Nova igreja de Olivais Sul* (Lisbon, SNIP Archive, 1970); <https://www.paroquiaolivaissul.pt/quem-somos/a-paroquia> (accessed 10/07/2019).
54   Pimentel et al., *Relatório do júri - Concurso de esbocetos para a nova igreja de Olivais Sul*, 9 (Lisbon, SNIP Archive, 1970).

industrial expression in terms of scale and materials (exposed concrete). Its overall presence is nonetheless introverted. Indeed, on the exterior, the discreet, unadorned entrance is marked only by a cross; and in the interior, the spaces live from the light, even though they have no direct relationship with the street outside. At the entrance, a wide staircase leads to the upper level, which features the sacred space itself where the Masses are held, with the altar in its centre. [Ill. 6.11] This floorplan also features various modules that define the circulation spaces and spaces for contemplation. The latter include the two courtyards that serve to illuminate the interior space, with the aid of skylights over the aisles in the church space and a glass brick wall that filters light into the interior. By emphasising the horizontal plane in the building's layout, and its modular conception, Vieira de Almeida consciously stepped away from the church as a dominant symbolic reference in the area, proposing instead a very direct application of the post-conciliar concept of a church as an intrinsic, living part of the city. Indeed, the blending of the Olivais Sul church with its surroundings, the multiple passageways that intersect it and the manifold informal open spaces in the interior that act like little squares make for a public interior that almost feels like a city within a city. Interestingly, this capacity for becoming appropriated — or even inhabited, one could say — derived from the simple logic of the building's structure with narrow and wide modules corresponding to paths and permanent spaces.

In its report, the jury, which included some former members of the MRAR who now held important diocesan positions, such as Pimentel, lauded the urban qualities of the proposal, recognising the interior streets' potential for social encounter, and the versatility of both the celebration space and the multi-purpose room. As the jury stated, the proposed design "brought order and rigor, promoting unity between constructive structure and distribution of the programme".[55] Additionally, and not unimportantly in light of the restricted financial means, the project allowed for a phased construction — thus also effectively responding to an important premise of the programme. For all these reasons, in the words of the jury, Vieira de Almeida's proposal was "like an oasis in Olivais Sul".[56] Nevertheless, difficulties related to the funding of the project and profound political changes significantly delayed its construction, which explains why the ground breaking ceremony did not occur until 6 January 1980 and it took another eight years for the church, dedicated to the Virgin of the Immaculate Conception, to be consecrated.

---

55 Pimentel et al., *Relatório do júri - Concurso de esbocetos para a nova igreja de Olivais Sul*, 9 (Lisbon, SNIP Archive, 1970).
56 Ibid.

Conclusion

The two case studies discussed here — Sagrado Coração de Jesus (1962) and Nossa Senhora da Conceição Olivais Sul (1970) — can rightfully be considered as milestones in the development of religious architecture in Portugal in the twentieth century. Such emblematic projects do not come into being in isolation, however. As we have seen, both churches were the fruit of a long and complex process, involving a broad array of actors and knowledge fields. They can therefore be seen as the material outcome of a multiplicity of factors: the artistic dynamics created by the MRAR; the rational support offered by Falcão and sociological inquiries in defining the pastoral programme; the role of the SNIP as the diocesan building agency; and the ambitious parish reform that was sanctioned by decree by Cardinal Cerejeira in 1959. As for the relationship between the two churches, Sagrado Coração de Jesus can be considered as both the culmination of a long investigation into the adequate pastoral response to rampant urbanisation and the starting point for new research and programmes more adapted to the real needs and possibilities of the situation at hand, which were then tested in Nossa Senhora da Conceição in Olivais Sul. For all these reasons, it is safe to say that both churches are not only representative of the pastoral challenges raised by the explosive urbanisation of Lisbon in the post-war era, but also central to the Portuguese — perhaps even European — debate about the position of the Church in an increasingly urbanising society and the place and role of religious infrastructure in the city.

By focusing on the MRAR and the SNIP, this chapter has shed light on the networks of people and knowledge, as well as the exchange of expertise, that are indispensable for making such innovation possible. By operationalising the MRAR's plea for a truly contemporary expression of religion and capitalising on the expertise it had gathered through its international contacts, the SNIP was able to set up a series of pioneering experiments in urban and rural areas that both supported and expressed the search for a genuinely contemporary expression of Catholic faith, in tune with the ideas promulgated by the Second Vatican Council. Through its dissemination tactics, such as the *Novas Igrejas* bulletin, the SNIP was able to occupy a unique pedagogical position in the field of religious architecture in Portugal and beyond. After the dissolution of the MRAR, the SNIP continued to address important challenges for architecture and for the architects involved in religious building, along with specifically liturgical themes related to the production of religious architecture and the debate surrounding it, though it was forced to change its strategies in the 1970s due to a significant drop in donations, combined with a changing social and political environment and the retirement of Cerejeira in 1971. The legacy of this influential office that existed for five decades has long been under-recognised and merits further study.

BIBLIOGRAPHY

Archives

Lisbon, Movimento de Renovação da Arte Religiosa (MRAR)
- 1953, April: Pereira, Nuno Teotónio et al. *Exposição de Arquitectura Religiosa Contemporânea*. Exhibition catalogue.

Lisbon, Secretariado das Novas Igrejas do Patriarcado (SNIP)
- 1959, April: Cardoso, Geraldes. *Terrenos para as igrejas das novas paróquias de Lisboa*, Lisbon, CML - Gabinete de estudos de urbanização.
- 1960, March: Pimentel, Diogo Lino. *Relatório referente ao 1º trimestre de estágio junto do Centro di Studio e Informazione per l'Architettura Sacra – Bolonha*.
- 1962: Pereira, Nuno Teotónio. *Ante-projecto da igreja do Sagrado Coração de Jesus – Memória Descritiva*.
- 1962: SNIP, ed. *Programa de construção da igreja paroquial do SS. Coração de Jesus e de seus anexos [1957]*. Competion brief.
- 1968: SNIP, ed. *Novas igrejas do patriarcado*. Campaign flyer.
- 1970: Almeida, Pedro Vieira de. *Nova igreja de Olivais Sul. Memória descritiva e justificativa do concurso de esbocetos*.
- 1970, 28 February: Pimentel, Diogo Lino; Santos, José Maya; Maurício, Luís; Murta, José Marques; Baptista, Paulo Loureiro; Cleto, Albino. *Relatório do júri - Concurso de esbocetos para a nova igreja de Olivais Sul*.
- 1978: *Projecto de divisão paroquial da cidade de Lisboa*, SNIP Archive, 16 August 1957.
- Ribeiro, D. António. "Apelo do Cardeal Patriarca de Lisboa ao Povo de Deus do Patriarcado". *Novas igrejas do patriarcado*. Campaign flyer.

Published sources

Almeida, João Miguel. "Progressive Catholicism in Portugal: Considerations on Political Activism (1958-1974)". *Histoire@Politique*, 3 (2016) 30, 60-74.

Almeida de Carvalho, Rita. "Ideology and Architecture in the Portuguese 'Estado Novo': Cultural Innovation within a Para-Fascist State (1932-1945)". *Fascism*, 7 (2018), 141-174.

Azevedo Maera, Luis de. "Lisboa No Tempo do Cardeal Cerejeira, Historia Religiosa". *Fontes e Subsidios*, 1997. (Online at <https://repositorio.ucp.pt/bitstream/10400.14/7217/1/HRFS_3_LisboaNoTempo.pdf> (accessed 10/07/2019).

Brandão, Pedro Ramos. *Salazar - Cerejeira a 'força' da Igreja*. Lisbon: Editorial Notícias, 2002.

Cerejeira, D. Manuel. "Ainda o problema do Clero. Resultados, necessidades, previsões [1.Nov.1948]". In: *Obras Pastorais, quarto volume 1948-1953*. Lisbon: União Gráfica, 1954, 49-77.

Cerejeira, D. Manuel. "As igrejas novas do Patriarcado [2.Oct.1955]". In: *Obras Pastorais, quinto volume 1954-1959*. Lisbon: União Gráfica, 1960, 217-227.

Cerejeira, D. Manuel. "Decreto de criação do Secretariado das Novas Igrejas do Patriarcado, [6.Jan.1961]". *Novidades*, 7 January 1961, 2.

Cerejeira, D. Manuel. "Decreto Patriarcal - Remodelação Paroquial da Cidade de Lisboa, [25.Mar.1959]. *Novidades*, 26 March 1959, 1.

Cerejeira, D. Manuel. "O grave problema das igrejas no Patriarcado [Carta Pastoral 15.Dec.1959]". In: *Obras Pastorais, quinto volume 1954-1959*. Lisbon: União Gráfica, 1960, 63-90.

Cerejeira, D. Manuel. "Pastoral sobre Arte Sacra [Mar.1953]". In: *Obras Pastorais, quarto volume 1948-1953*. Lisbon: União Gráfica, 1954, 121-132.

Cerejeira, D. Manuel. "Sua eminência o cardeal patriarca". *Revista Oficial do Sindicato dos Arquitectos*, 7 (November-December 1938), 186.

Cerqueira, Silas. "L'Église catholique et la dictature corporatiste portugaise". *Revue française de science politique*, 12 (1972), 3, 473-513.

Clemente, Manuel. "As paróquias de Lisboa em tempo de liberalismo". *Didaskalia*, 25 (1995), 1-2, 391-410.

Comissão Executiva da Exposição de Obras Públicas, ed. *15 Anos de Obras Públicas 1932-1947*. Vol. 1. Lisbon: Ministério das Obras Públicas e Comunicações, 1949.

Concordata entre a Santa Sé e a República Portuguesa, 7 May 1940.

"Concurso de anteprojectos para a Igreja Paroquial do Sagrado Coração de Jesus e seus anexos". *Arquitectura*, 76 (October 1962), 11-32.

Cunha, João Alves da. "A igreja de Nossa Senhora de Fátima, em Lisboa: novidade e tradição na arquitectura e liturgia de uma obra singular". In: *Igreja de Nossa Senhora de Fátima em Lisboa: 75 anos*. Lisbon: Paróquia de Nossa Senhora de Fátima, 2013, 67-87.

Cunha, João Alves da. "João de Almeida: da Europa Central ao MRAR". In: *João de Almeida: Arquitectura, Design, Pintura*. Lisbon: Fundação Medeiros e Almeida, 2012, 8-9.

Cunha, João Alves da. *MRAR – Movimento de Renovação da Arte Religiosa e os anos de ouro da arquitetura religiosa em Portugal no século XX*. Lisbon: Universidade Católica Editora, 2015.

Cunha, João Alves da. *O MRAR e os anos de ouro na arquitetura religiosa em Portugal no século XX. A ação do movimento de renovação da arte religiosa nas décadas de 1950 e 1960*. Thesis (D Ph. il). Lisbon: Faculdade de Arquitectura da Universidade de Lisboa, 2014.

Decreto-lei n°28:912, I série, n°186. Ministério das Obras Públicas e Comunicações, 12 August 1938.

"Église Notre-Dame de Fatima à Lisbonne". *L'Architecture d'Aujourd'hui*, 5 (May 1939), 34-35.

Falcão, Manuel Franco. "Assistência à missa dominical no Patriarcado de Lisboa". *Lumen*, XXI (June 1957), 431-449.

Falcão, Manuel Franco. "A prática dominical no Patriarcado de Lisboa em 1955". *Boletim Diocesano de Pastoral*, 29-30 (1970), 3-18.

Falcão, Manuel Franco. "A paróquia, sua crise, seu valor". *Lúmen*, 22 (1958), 379-380.

Falcão, Manuel Franco. "O Cardeal Cerejeira, Pastor da Igraeja Lisbonense". *Lusitania Sacra*, 2 (1990), 89-121.

Falcão, Manuel Franco. "O interesse pastoral da sociologia religiosa". *Novellae Olivarum - Revista do Seminário de Cristo Rei – Olivais*, October 1956, 132-142.

Falcão, Manuel Franco. "Sondagem à assistência à missa dominical no Patriarcado de Lisboa". *Novellae Olivarum - Revista do Seminário de Cristo Rei - Olivais*, June-July 1956, 68-79.

Ferreira, Nuno E. *A Sociologia em Portugal: da Igreja à Universidade*. Lisbon: Imprensa de Ciências Sociais, 2006.

Fulda's Bishops Conference, ed. "Directivas para a construção das igrejas segundo o espírito da liturgia romana". *Novellae Olivarum - Revista do Seminário de Cristo Rei – Olivais*, January 1955, 1-7.

Gresleri, Giuliano and Gresleri, Glauco. *Le Corbusier: Il programma litúrgico*. Bologna: Editrice Compositori, 2001.

Gresleri, Glauco; Bettazzi, Beatrice and Gresleri, Giuliano. *Chiesa et quartiere: storia di una revista e di un movimento per l'architettura a Bologna*. Bologna: Editrice Compositori, 2004.

"La cité religieuse". *L'Architecture d'Aujourd'hui*, 6 (July 1934), 89.

Lopes Días, Tiago. *Teoria e Desenho da Arquitectura em Portugal 1956-1974: Nuno Portas e Pedro Vieira de Almeida*. Doctoral thesis, Polytechnical University of Catalunya, 2017.

Marques, João Luís. "Entre lo provisional y lo definitivo. Experiencias de las capillas-salón del Secretariado das Novas Igrejas do Patriarcado de Lisboa". In: *Actas del Congreso Internacional de Arquitectura Religiosa Contemporanea 'Más allá del edificio sacro:arquitectura y evangelización'*. Seville, 2014, 204-213.

Marques, João Luís. *A igreja na cidade, service e acolhimento, arquitectura portuguesa 1950-1975*. Thesis (D Phil). Oporto: Faculdade de Arquitectura da Universidade do Porto, 2017.

"O cardeal construtor de igrejas". *Flama*, 195 (30 November 1951), 12-13.

Pereira, Nuno Teotónio. "A Arquitectura Cristã Contemporânea". *Ala*, 31 January 1947, 2.

Pereira, Nuno Teotónio. "Conversando com o arquitecto Teotónio Pereira (entrevista)". *O Século*, 28 June 1959, 4.

Pereira, Nuno Teotonio. "Die Architektur des Regimes 1938-1948". In: Annette Becker, Ana Tostoes and Wilfried Wanger, eds. *Portugal. Architektur im 20. Jahrhundert*. Munich: Prestl, 1997, 33-39.

Pereira Coutinho, José. "Sociologia e antropologia da religião em Portugal: agentes e publicações". *REVER*, 18 (2018), 1, 271-299.

Pimentel, Diogo Lino and Almeida, João de. "Condizioni di inserimento dell'edificio nello spazio sociale urbano". In: Pino Ciampani. *Architettura e Liturgia*. Assisi: Edizioni Pro Civitate Christiana, 1965, 21-22.

Pimentel, Diogo Lino and Almeida, João de. "Programmazione per la costruzione di nuove chiese". In Pino Ciampani. *Architettura e Liturgia*. Assisi: Edizioni Pro Civitate Christiana, 1965, 47.

Pinto, Antonio Costa and Rezola, Maria Inacia. "Political Catholicism, Crisis of Democracy and Salazar's New State in Portugal". *Totalitarian Movements and Political Religions*, 8 (2007) 2, 353-368.

Portas, Nuno. "Arquitectura Religiosa Moderna em Portugal". *Arquitectura*, 60 (October 1957), 20-23.

Ramos, Rui; Gonçalves, Eliseu and Silva, Sérgio. "From the Late 19th Century House Question to Social Housing Programs in the 30s: the Nationalist Regulation of the Picturesque in Portugal". *Docomomo Journal*, 51 (2014), 60-67.

Salazar, António Oliveira. "O meu depoimento - Palácio da Bolsa, 7 de Janeiro de 1949". In: *Discursos e notas políticas IV 1943-1950*. Coimbra: Coimbra Editora Lda, 1951, 372-373.

Santos Costa, Paulo Alexandre Dos. "A Igreja de N. Senhora de Fatima em Lisboa e a arte moderna em Portugal". *Lusitania Sacra*, 12 (2000), 413-430.

Silva, Sérgio and Ramos, Rui. "Housing, Nationalism and Social Control: The First Years of the Portuguese Estado Novo's Affordable Houses Programme". In: Joana Cunha Leal et al., eds. *Southern modernisms from A to Z and back again*. Porto: Centro de Estudos Arnaldo Araújo - CESAP/ESAP, Instituto de História da Arte - FCSH/UNL, 2015, 255-274.

SNIP, ed. "A igreja na cidade". *Novas Igrejas*, 1 (January-March 1961), 16-17.

SNIP, ed. "Novos conceitos de igrejas". *BIP – Boletim de Informação Pastoral*, 56-57 (January 1969), 28-32.

SNIP, ed. "Programa de construção de novas igrejas". *BIP – Boletim de Informação Pastoral*, 46-47 (April 1966), 25-38.

Winninger, Paul. *Construire des églises*. Coll. Rencontres. Paris: Editions du Cerf, 1957.

7
"A SILENT REVOLUTION"
JACINTO RODRÍGUEZ OSUNA, LUIS CUBILLO DE ARTEAGA AND THE 1965 *PLAN PASTORAL* FOR MADRID

JESÚS GARCÍA HERRERO

In the 1960s, Madrid faced the same problems as other European capitals, namely an exponential growth in its population and a building boom along the city's periphery. In response to the ensuing pastoral challenge, Archbishop Casimiro Morcillo (1904-1971) presented a *Plan Pastoral* (Pastoral Care Plan) for Madrid in 1965. Using the latest insights emanating from the sociology of religion and similar experiences abroad, it proposed tripling the number of parishes and readapting their boundaries to the city's administrative divisions. To force through this ambitious reform, a small but determined Oficina Técnica de Sociología Religiosa (Technical Office for Religious Sociology) was created, whose *Instrucciones para la Construcción de Complejos Parroquiales* (Instructions for the Construction of Parish Centres) became the blueprint for future church buildings in Madrid over the next decade.

With a view to assessing the motivating potential of that document and the obstacles faced upon its implementation, we discuss a series of churches built by Luis Cubillo de Arteaga (1921-2000) under the auspices of the *Plan Pastoral*.[1] As we argue, within the contours of an easily repeatable typology,

1   This article builds upon the doctoral research performed by the author for his dissertation, *La arquitectura religiosa de Luis Cubillo de Arteaga (1954-1974)*, Universidad Politécnica de Madrid, 2015. The research was carried out in the Archivo del Arzobispado de Madrid (AAM, Archive of the Archbishopric of Madrid) and the Archivo del Servicio Histórico del Colegio Oficial de Arquitectos de Madrid (ASHCOAM, Archive of the Historical Service of Madrid Architects Association, Cubillo de Arteaga papers, LCA). Morcillo's *Plan Pastoral* was also investigated by Pedro García for his thesis *Arquitectura religiosa en Madrid a partir de 1940*, Universidad Complutense of Madrid, 2005; another helpful source was

he managed to develop a simple, yet effective, architectural language that acquired both symbolic and social meaning. Thus, Cubillo's work embodies the shift from the church being seen as a "temple of God" towards it being a "house for God's people", as promoted by the Oficina Técnica — a change that was not without significance at a time of severe socio-political tension in Spain.

Casimiro Morcillo, Jacinto Rodríguez Osuna and the *Plan Pastoral* for Madrid

Morcillo was appointed as the first archbishop of the new Archdiocese of Madrid-Alcalá by Paul VI on 24 March 1964; he took office on 7 May 1964.[2] Prior to that, Morcillo had been the auxiliary bishop in the Diocese of Madrid between 1940 and 1950 under the mandate of Bishop Leopoldo Eijo Garay (1878-1963), before moving to Bilbao, a working class city that profoundly shaped his social consciousness.[3] This became apparent during his subsequent tenure as Bishop of Zaragoza, where he created parishes, schools and facilities for social assistance in the poorer areas of the city's periphery. After the death of Eijo Garay, he returned to Madrid as archbishop.

The swift pace of Morcillo's career can only be understood against the light of his close ties to the Franco regime, since the Concordat signed between the Holy See and the Spanish state in 1953 (the follow-up to a previous agreement in 1941) allowed the head of state considerable weight in the appointment of bishops — in essence muzzling any critical opposition in the higher ranks of the Church. If the traumatic experience of the Spanish Civil War helps explain Morcillo's endorsement of the regime (just like most of the Spanish Church hierarchy), it should also be understood that he was also an active part of it as a member of Parliament between 1964 and 1969, one direct-

---

Ramón Saiz's *Madrid-Alcalá, una diócesis en construcción*, 1982. The architecture emanating from the *Plan Pastoral* has not yet received the scholarly attention it deserves, although the outright negative criticism in earlier accounts (e.g. Isasi, 1998) is gradually making room for more balanced evaluations such as Delgado Orusco's *Arquitectura sacra española, 1939-1975: de la posguerra al posconcilio*, Universidad Politécnica de Madrid, 2000, or recent studies on the work of individual architects, including Luis Moya Blanco, Francisco Coello de Portugal, José Luis Fernández del Amo Moreno, Luis Laorga Guttiérez and Rodolfo García-Pablos. Silvia Blanco-Agüeira (Blanco Agüeira, *Rodolfo García-Pablos: La construcción del espacio sagrado*, 2009), in particular, offers an accurate approach to the period under study here and provides useful bibliographical references. The author wishes to express his gratitude to Sven Sterken for his insightful comments on previous versions of this article.

2 For Morcillo's biography, see the special issue of *Alfa y Omega*, 25 (May 1996).
3 Leopoldo Eijo Garay (1878-1963) headed the Bishopric of Madrid-Alcalá from 1923 to 1963.

ly appointed by Francisco Franco (1892-1975).[4] Moreover, Morcillo's influence expanded beyond the national borders: as an undersecretary at the Second Vatican Council, he participated in the preparatory phases and all four conciliar periods between 1962 and 1965. Most notably, he was part of the Coetus Internationalis Patrum, a conservative group that defended the denominational character of state policy and opposed the religious freedom promoted by the declaration *Dignitatis Humanae* (1965).

However, there was perhaps also a pragmatic side to his openly conservative attitude. Indeed, as his successor, Cardinal Vicente Enrique y Tarancón (1907-1994), pointed out:

> Morcillo was not an ultraconservative bishop and had provided proof of that. He admitted the regime constraints, but he was persuaded that this was the true embodiment of the homeland and the only one that could guarantee Catholic unity, which he considered the essential basis for the greatness and unity of Spain.[5]

Nonetheless, even for Morcillo it was difficult to balance his fidelity to the renewed post-conciliar Church with his support for the Franco regime. This became apparent in his social thinking, particularly where human rights and migration were concerned.[6] Although he manifested a great sensitivity for social rights, he was not so clear about political rights and fundamental freedoms. Migration was another of his major concerns, especially the relentless migration from rural areas to the capital, where the Franco regime was promoting the development of heavy industry that was making it the undisputed political and administrative centre of the state. As a result, Madrid witnessed the fastest growth ever experienced by a European city.[7] Although Morcillo was fully aware of the pastoral problems originating from this forced growth curve, he never criticised (at least openly) the territorial imbalance the government was causing. It must be said, though, that when he came to head the Arch-

[4] During the Spanish Civil War, more than 20,000 churches had been destroyed or looted, and 6,832 priests had been murdered in the Republican zone (see Casanova, *A Short History of the Spanish Civil War*, 44-80). The Spanish clergy, therefore, saw in Franco a protector rather than a dictator, as expressed in the "Collective letter of the Spanish bishops to bishops around the world on the occasion of the war in Spain" (1 July 1937), one of the authors of which was Eijo Garay. This openly professed support by the Spanish Catholic Church allowed the Franco regime to claim the identitary concept of "National Catholicism". Morcillo was appointed deputy for the 1964-1967 and 1967-1971 legislatures. He abandoned his seat in 1969, however, when he was appointed president of the Spanish Episcopal Conference.

[5] Delgado de la Rosa, "Una iglesia en cambio", 266. Unless otherwise noted, all translations are the author's own.

[6] Fernández de Torres, *El pensamiento social de los arzobispos de la Archidiócesis de Madrid después del Concilio Vaticano II*, 2-122.

[7] Terán, *Madrid*, 267.

7.1 Substandard housing on the periphery of Madrid and floor plan of public housing prototype developed by Luis Cubillo de Arteaga for the INV (National Housing Institute). Cover of *RNA magazine*, no 193 (1958).
[Colegio Oficial de Arquitectos de Madrid, Library]

diocese of Madrid-Alcalá in 1964, the situation was not as serious as it had been in the mid-1950s, when the most socially minded clergy were denouncing the proliferation of substandard housing along the periphery of Madrid.[8] [Ill. 7.1]

Although a man of strong principles, Morcillo's thinking also evolved over time. For example, his concept of the urban parish evolved from an ascetic–priestly one based on a preponderance of local clergy to a more co-operative structure in which the laity also had a role to play — which proves that he was not unaware of the latest insights from, for example, the emerging science of religious sociology at home and abroad.[9] A relevant event in this evolution

---

8   The case of the Jesuit José María Llanos is paradigmatic. He lived in the El Pozo del Tío Raimundo slum and denounced its poverty every Sunday in the *Arriba* newspaper in his "Christian Letters".

9   To appreciate this evolution, it suffices to compare the ideas in his *La Iglesia diocesana y sus parroquias* (1960) with his prologue to Rogelio Duocastella's *Cómo estudiar una parroquia* (1965). While in the former, Morcillo developed a theology of the parish (151-185) without any reference to religious sociology, in the latter, he lauded that new science: "Fortunately religious sociology is today descending from the intellectual level to the pastoral level, which has a more direct and familiar contact with human communities".

was the first National Week of the Parish he organised in April 1958, during his tenure in Zaragoza, which was accompanied by an exhibition of sacred art. During one of the sessions covering the current state of pastoral theology, various cases from abroad were presented, along with instances of their later assimilation by Spain.[10] At the closing, Morcillo affirmed that "this [problem] of the parish must be resolved if we want to pass from a drowsy Catholicism to a Catholicism of conquest; from traditional conformism to a militant attitude; from decadent mediocrity to missionary action".[11] During that same week, Morcillo also openly endorsed the more progressive artworks in the exhibition, notwithstanding the incomprehension of many of the conference attendants.[12] This open-minded (or was it pragmatic?) attitude towards the new trends explains why Morcillo, upon his appointment as Archbishop of Madrid, turned to two young priests specialised in religious sociology to address the reorganisation of the parish landscape in the Spanish capital: Ramón Echarren (1929-2014) and Jacinto Rodríguez Osuna (1929-2017). Each had earned a bachelor's degree in social science: Echarren at Université catholique de Louvain, with a study on the position of the clergy, and Rodríguez Osuna at the École Pratique des Hautes Études in Paris, with a study on the state of the parishes in Madrid.[13] They were thus ideally positioned to advise Morcillo in his endeavour to "renew the diocesan pastoral action according to the spirit and forms desired by the Council for the whole Church".[14]

10 *Comunidad cristiana parroquial. 1° semana nacional de la parroquia*, 7-45. According to Bishop Angel Morta Figuls's chronicle of the National Week, there were in fact too many topics to be discussed; yet, they were all felt necessary for obtaining an overall view of the issues at hand. Casiano Floristán from Universität Tübingen gave a paper on the current status of pastoral theology in France, Belgium, the Netherlands and Germany. In doing so, he underlined the role of the Belgian cleric Jozef Cardijn, who stressed the importance of lay apostolate, particularly in the working environment. According to Morta Figuls, despite the relevance of this topic, the audience at the National Week seemed to be mainly interested in the economic problems faced by parishes.
11 *Comunidad cristiana parroquial. 1° semana nacional de la parroquia*, 570.
12 A few months later, Morcillo provided a written record of his tolerance for the new, non-figurative artistic tendencies in his "Carta Magna del Arte Sacro en España".
13 Alongside Jesús Iribarren (*Introducción a la sociología religiosa*, 1955) and Rogelio Duocastella (*Mataró 1955: estudio de sociología religiosa sobre una ciudad industrial española*, 1961), Echarren and Rodríguez Osuna can safely be considered as the main protagonists in introducing religious sociology in Spain. Interestingly, the latter three were all linked to the Catholic charity Cáritas: Duocastella directed its social section; Echarren acted as a delegate for Cáritas at the diocese; and Rodríguez Osuna headed its studies department. Moreover, in 1965, Cáritas created FOESSA (Fomento de Estudios Sociales y Sociología Aplicada, which stood for the Promotion of Social Studies and Applied Sociology). Echarren and Rodríguez Osuna pursued quite different careers, however: Echarren became auxiliary bishop in Madrid in 1969 and Bishop of the Canary Islands in 1978; Rodríguez Osuna, by contrast, left the priesthood and developed an academic career as a professor in the political science and sociology department at Universidad Complutense in Madrid. His *Métodos de Muestreo* (1991) is still considered a basic text on survey research techniques.
14 Rodríguez Osuna, "La nueva estructuración parroquial de Madrid", 391.

This was no vain talk: in July 1964, only two months into his appointment, Morcillo took the bull by the horns and created various committees to tackle the problem. To start with, he formed the Comisión Central de Acción Pastoral (Central Commission of Pastoral Action), with Echarren and Rodríguez Osuna as technical consultants.[15] Three other working groups were also created: the aforementioned Oficina Técnica (in fact the "technical agency" of the Comisión Central), the Comisión de Aranceles (Fees Commission) and the Comisión de Arquitectos (Architects Commission). The magnitude of the task soon became apparent: a preliminary study by the Comisión Central and the Oficina Técnica showed that between 1900 and 1964, the population of Madrid had quintupled; moreover, more than half of its 2.6 million inhabitants lived on the city's periphery. This large population was served by only 107 churches in total, each of which, if they had been equally distributed across the territory, thus theoretically served 25,140 parishioners.[16] In reality, however, most of the existing parishes were located in the historic city centre and the nineteenth-century Ensanche (extension); consequently, the shortage of churches — as well as priests to staff them — was most pressing in the ever-expanding suburban areas. The same held true for schools, religious communities and institutions: almost all were located in the city centre. As Rodríguez Osuna pointed out, the situation in Madrid was perhaps even worse than in Paris or Buenos Aires, where "monster parishes" with over 34,000 inhabitants had been recorded.[17] Furthermore, the rapid, and relentless, urbanisation did not confine itself to the city of Madrid; smaller towns around the capital were also experiencing the consequences of internal migration (often forced) and rapid industrialisation, while the villages closer to the mountains became a preferred recreation place for city residents. Rodríguez Osuna and his team quickly understood that in light of this rapid evolution, a threefold strategy needed to be adopted: first, new parishes needed to be founded and churches built to serve them; second, the priests and religious communities needed to be proportionally distributed in relation to the number of inhabitants in each neighbourhood; and, finally, Catholic schools needed to be installed along the periphery. In the discussion that follows, we focus primarily on the first aspect, namely the establishment of new parishes and their religious infrastructure.

Rodríguez Osuna relied on three complementary sources of information in laying out the new parish divisions: an extensive preparatory study; a detailed report of each of the present parishes (drawn up by their vicars); and a field study. The preparatory study reviewed pastoral plans of other dioceses in the world and the current views on urban planning. Based on that, a deci-

15 *Guía de la Archidiócesis de Madrid-Alcalá*, 39.
16 Morcillo, "La archidiócesis de Madrid-Alcalá en esta hora", 29.
17 Rodríguez Osuna, "La nueva estructuración parroquial de Madrid", 393.

sion was quickly made to use Canon François Houtart's (1925-2017) study of Brussels and subsequent pastoral plan as a model for Madrid. Central to that approach was the idea that pastoral action needed to be taken on the scale of the agglomeration and no longer that of the individual parish. To this effect, the city was to be subdivided into spatially and socially coherent zones (*zones urbaines*), which were further subdivided into sectors (*secteurs*), each encompassing one or more parishes.[18] For Madrid, it was decided to rely on the existing concept of deaneries as an intermediate scale. As to the size of the parishes, Rodríguez Osuna and his team tried to match their delimitations with the urban units defined in the Plan Nacional de Vivienda (National Housing Plan) of 1961 (see further in this contribution).[19] This had been produced by the Spanish Ministry of Housing and stipulated that each neighbourhood of 20,000 inhabitants should be equipped with two parish centres, the number of 10,000 souls per parish thus being considered ideal. Consequently, deaneries would comprise 40,000 to 60,000 inhabitants and pastoral zones roughly 300,000. As to the distance from any point in the neighbourhood to its parish church, it was assumed that it should be no more than 400 metres (about a ten-minute walk). Whereas this was easily achieved in the city centre — where these radiuses sometimes even overlapped — this was by no means the case in the peripheral areas.

The reports by the local vicars were sent to the archdiocese in record time and provided Rodríguez Osuna and his team with an invaluable wealth of information, for they contained a detailed mapping of all existing churches and their provisions in terms of educational and health facilities, as well as a list of vacant lots and commercial buildings under construction.[20] The local clergy were also invited to reflect upon the physical, administrative and social aspects of their parish, with a view to subdividing them into units serving under 10,000 inhabitants. The final step in the preparation of the parish plan was the field study. Rodríguez Osuna spent six months in 1964 thoroughly exploring Madrid, verifying *in situ* the information provided and the viability of the reordering proposals. This brought to the fore that there did indeed exist relatively homogenous territorial areas according to "their economic level, de-

18 See the contribution on Houtart and the Centre de Recherches Socio-Religieuses by Weyns and Sterken in this volume.
19 The contribution of the architect García Pablos (1913-2001) could be relevant in this regard. He was Planning Manager in the Directorate General of Urbanism, a personal friend of Morcillo and, between 1939 and 1947, also the diocesan architect of Madrid. In July 1964, he participated in the National Week of Sacred Art II with a presentation on religious urbanism. It included a review of the parish planning abroad, with references to Houtart and Gaston Bardet, and cited examples from Milan, Paris and the Netherlands. He also spoke about the structure based on parishes, deaneries and zones. See García-Pablos, "Necesidad de establecer ordenaciones parroquiales integradas en los Planeamientos Urbanísticos", 118-121.
20 Rodríguez Osuna, "La nueva estructuración parroquial de Madrid", 402-403.

gree of citizen mentality and degree of social community". A reordering of the diocesan structure according to Houtart's principles thus seemed feasible and was effectively put through.[21] On 16 January 1965, Morcillo, flanked by Rodríguez Osuna and Echarren, gave a press conference at the Archbishop's Palace in Madrid during which he explained how he hoped to address the pressing pastoral problem in the capital.[22] The new parish subdivision, which took effect on 7 March 1965, divided the city of Madrid into twelve pastoral zones and the surrounding province into nine regions. Except for the historic centre and the Ensanche, the delimitation of the zones followed existing infrastructure and geological features, such as the various radial and ring roads that departed from the centre or the Manzanares River. [Ill. 7.2] These zones were then subdivided into deaneries (seventy-three instead of five), each with their own dean and pastoral commission, while the total number of parishes was supposed to grow from one hundred and seven to three hundred and sixty in the following years.[23]

Thus, a pastoral network was put into place that, it was hoped, would halt the ever accelerating process of "dechristianisation" in the new districts, where the rate of church attendance was found to be as low as fifteen or twenty per cent. In this respect, the situation in Madrid was no different than that of any other major city across Europe, however. As Rodríguez Osuna pointed out, the drop in religious adherence had perhaps less to do with the phenomenon of urbanisation per se as with the awkwardness of the traditional pastoral strategies deployed in these areas. Designed for a rural world, these models were no longer effective in the city, whose inhabitants no longer belonged to a single social group but to many and where an ever-increasing mobility made the establishment of stable social bonds increasingly difficult. Apropos of his enmeshment in the international network of religious sociology, Rodríguez Osuna had thus arrived at exactly the same conclusions in Madrid as Houtart had in Brussels. This confirmed the imperative that the pastoral problem of the capital needed to be addressed at the diocesan level, as Morcillo himself stipulated in a Pastoral Letter dated 2 February 1965:

> Let our diocesan church be a sign of salvation (...). (...) We open this period under the pressure of spiritual and distressing needs and subject to a communal or joint pastoral care plan, so called because it aims to cover

21 *Nuevas estructuras pastorales en la Archidiócesis de Madrid-Alcalá*, 29. Madrid's population was classified into "eleven different types, which respond to eleven types of territorial areas, eleven types of problems and specific circumstances". At the economic level, the areas were classified into high, high-medium, medium, medium-low, low or very low. Each one of these types (except "very low") was then split in two (old and new areas) to yield the eleven types.
22 "El 7 de marzo entrará en vigor en la Archidiócesis la unificación de todos los servicios religiosos", 74-75.
23 Ramón Saiz, *Madrid-Alcalá, una diócesis en construcción*, 25-37.

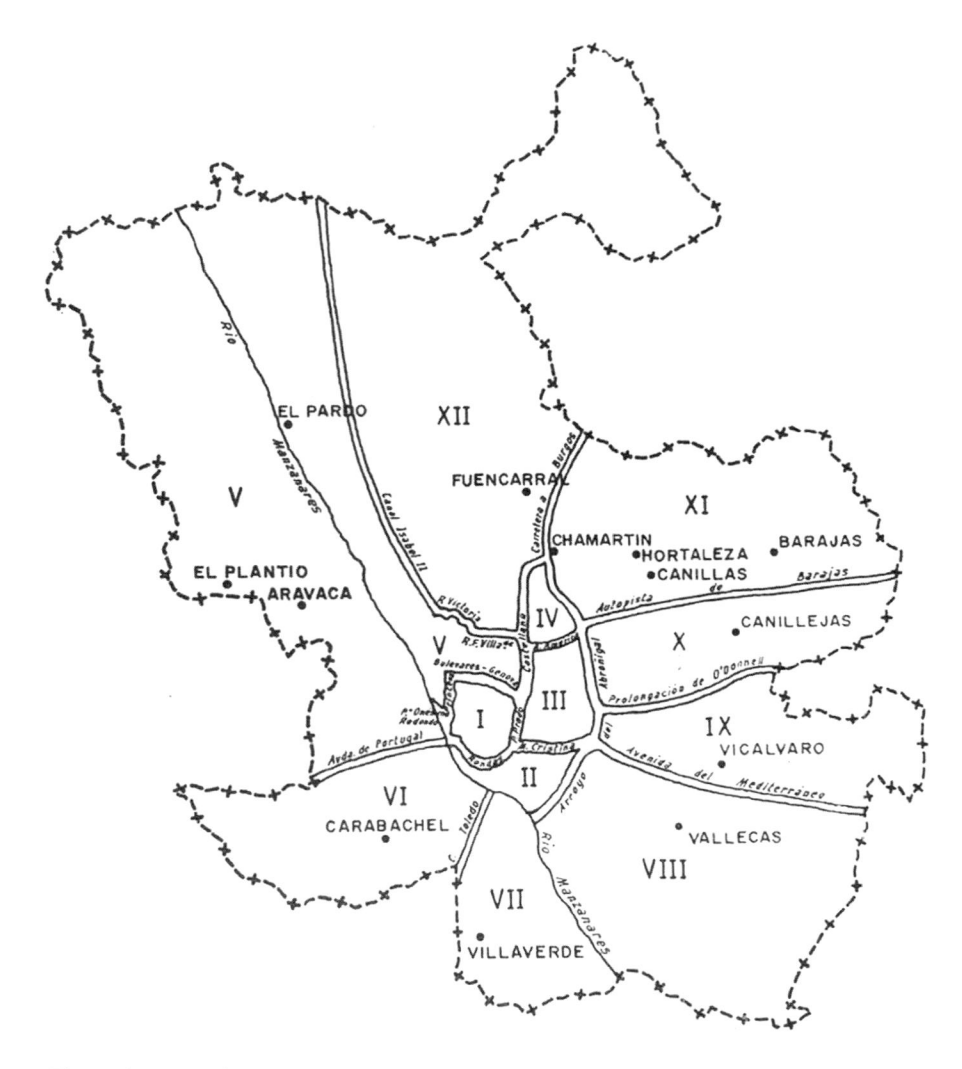

7.2 The twelve pastoral zones as defined in the 1965 *Plan Pastoral* for Madrid.
[Reproduced from *Nuevas estructuras pastorales en la Archidiócesis de Madrid-Alcalá*, 12. Courtesy of the Archdiocese of Madrid]

>all problems and all personal and real factors, to reach all the souls of the archdiocese and to respond to all situations of men.[24]

In this Pastoral Letter, Morcillo cautiously praised the instrumental value of religious sociology in the design of the *Plan Pastoral* as "satisfying a more

---

24   Morcillo, "La archidiócesis de Madrid-Alcalá en esta hora", 34-35.

or less scientific concern".[25] He was quick to point out, however, that such scientific tools should in no way interfere with the message they were intended to help spread: "Ours is the urgency that all of Spain and the whole world must receive Christian thought clean of any contaminations and armed against subtle infiltrations that are now more dangerous than ever."[26] This search for a doctrinal "purity" explains why he also proposed constructing a new seminary for 3,000 students, meant to not only provide the human resources required for the new parishes, but also reclaim Spain's historical role in the evangelisation of America.[27] However, it became quickly apparent that the proposed pastoral offensive would have to make do with the existing resources; the seminary was never built, and the shortage of personnel thus remained. As a result, various religious orders became entrusted with pastoral duties; their churches were claimed for public worship and their priors were appointed, by persuasion, as parish priests.

The Implementation of the *Plan Pastoral*, 1965-1972

The *Plan Pastoral* got off to a flying start: in six months' time, Morcillo signed no fewer than two hundred sixteen decrees of foundation for new parishes.[28] The accompanying pastoral infrastructure lagged behind, however; hundreds of thousands of Madrilenians still had to travel several kilometres on a Sunday to find the nearest church. In many cases, Mass was celebrated in basements, garages, commercial premises, private flats or hastily erected prefabricated structures.[29] [Ill. 7.3] The lack of religious infrastructure in the new urban areas derived from the urgent housing problem of the 1950s. Because the Franco regime would not tolerate having a state capital surrounded by substandard housing, it set up massive public housing schemes along the periphery, mainly through the Poblados Dirigidos (Programmed Settlements) programmes of the Instituto Nacional de la Vivienda (INV, National Housing Institute).[30] Top priority was given to the construction of dwelling units, meaning that the socio-cultural infrastructure for the new districts, including parish centres, was either delayed (sometimes for decades) or relegated to less desirable plots of land.

In 1961, the INV launched the Plan Nacional de Vivienda with the aim of actively promoting the principle of owner-occupied dwellings, to the detri-

25 Ibid., 32. See also Doucastella, *Cómo estudiar una parroquia*. In its prologue, Morcillo wrote: "Religious sociology finds justification for its existence only in pastoral work."
26 Morcillo, "La archidiócesis de Madrid-Alcalá en esta hora", 32.
27 García Herrero, *La arquitectura religiosa de Luis Cubillo de Arteaga (1954-1974)*, 46-80.
28 Rodríguez Osuna, *Informe sociológico sobre la situación social de Madrid*, 209.
29 Morcillo, "Carta Pastoral sobre el día del templo parroquial", 260-261.
30 Moya González, *Barrios de Promoción Oficial*, 93-94.

7.3 Images showing the evolution of the San Eduardo parish: Mass upon the parish's founding (1965); provisional church in a commercial premises (1965); a prefabricated church (1967-1978); and the parish complex by Luis Cubillo de Arteaga (inaugurated in 1979).
[Courtesy of the San Eduardo Parish Archive]

ment of rental units. To this effect, the public authorities encouraged private developers to invest in affordable housing. The underlying ideology was most clearly expressed by José Luis Arrese (1906-1985), Minister of Housing at the time, who stated in an interview in 1959: "We do not want a Spain of proletarians, but of owners."[31] The numbers speak for themselves: of the 217,613 residential units built in Madrid between 1961 and 1966, only 25,000 were built by the state, and over 180,000 were built by private companies.[32] Another goal of the Plan Nacional de Vivienda was to correct the severe want of social and cultural infrastructure in the new districts; although strictly speaking, the plan applied only to public housing, the fact that this constituted almost eighty-five per cent of the total new housing stock meant that its guidelines were

31 "No queremos una España de proletarios sino de propietarios", 41.
32 The numbers come from Rodríguez Osuna, *Informe sociológico sobre la situación social de Madrid*, 191-192.

very far reaching.[33] It stipulated, for example, that each new district should be equipped with amenities for religious practice, commerce, culture, health, administration and recreation. Interestingly though, in most cases, almost none of this was realised, except for churches and schools. That is hardly unsurprising, given that precisely those two types of infrastructure were the most appropriate, in the eyes of the authorities, for exercising social control.[34] Thus, even if the reasons both the Church (and Morcillo, in particular) and the state had for providing the new districts with churches rested upon diverging interests, they collaborated successfully towards the pursuit of that goal.

Despite this public support, the laws of economics still prevailed. This became apparent in the Plan General de Ordenación Urbana del Área Metropolitana de Madrid (Urban Development Plan for the Metropolitan Area of Madrid) of 1963 which covered the greater Madrid conurbation. It was based on the aforementioned Plan Nacional de Vivienda and echoed its prescriptions with regard to the sociocultural infrastructure for new areas, albeit with less ambition: it prescribed one parish centre per 10,000 to 20,000 inhabitants.[35] As Rodríguez Osuna has noted, this ambiguity meant that each partial plan for a new area became an open duel between the public authorities and the private developers trying to make a maximum profit on their investments. As a result, he stated, in some areas, it became totally impossible to build churches or schools because there was no more place for them.[36] This led to some remarkable, but inventive, solutions, such as the establishment of parishes in commercial premises, most of them on the ground floor of a housing block — although initially intended as a temporary solution, these became permanent in several instances.[37]

Despite the intimate relationship between the Catholic Church and the Franco regime, government support for the *Plan Pastoral* was, in fact, quite limited. Indeed, apart from the few churches built by the INV, the state did not contribute directly to the massive church-building campaign. The annual contribution it had committed to in the 1953 Concordat with the Holy See was intended to provide the clergy with a decent income and a good education — which explains why no fewer than sixty-six seminaries were built or restored between 1939 and 1959. The construction of new parish churches or conservation of older ones in Madrid was not an intrinsic part of that agreement. In order to acquire land to build on, the diocese, and later archdiocese, thus had to appeal to the INV or other semi-governmental bodies such as Renfe (National

33 *Plan Nacional de la Vivienda 1961-1976*, 47-51; Moya González, *Barrios de Promoción Oficial*, 45.
34 See Baldellou, "Neorrealismo y arquitectura", 48.
35 *Normas Urbanísticas para el término municipal de Madrid*, 34-37.
36 Rodríguez Osuna, *Informe sociológico sobre la situación social de Madrid*, 211.
37 For more information on this typology, see García Herrero, *La arquitectura religiosa de Luis Cubillo de Arteaga (1954-1974)*, 176-182.

Railway) or the Banco Central (Central Bank), as well as to private developers — one developer, URBIS, even offered ten plots and also constructed four church buildings for free. This generosity can partly be understood in light of the deep imbrication of the Catholic faith and the Spanish establishment under Franco; nevertheless, there was also a pragmatic side to it, for it was a way of socially legitimising the big, speculative real estate deals these actors were putting through. Their grandiose gestures somehow eclipsed the sincere piety of many private individuals with whom the archdiocese negotiated on the basis of barter, cession and donation.[38]

Apart from the difficulty involved in securing adequate sites, the sheer number of new churches being built also required vast resources and posed daunting technical challenges. Until 1972, such aspects were handled by the Secretariado de Templos Parroquiales (Secretariat for Parish Churches) and the Oficina Técnica, respectively. The former was heir to the Comisión de Aranceles created in 1964, which had had to develop new sources of income after Morcillo abolished the fees for administering the sacraments in 1958, a decision widely hailed in the press since it meant that "baptisms, weddings and funerals will be the same for the billionaire as for the most modest pawn. There will be no differences within the church, during these ceremonies, between any social class."[39] A new funding principle, based on monthly contributions and gifts from the parishioners, was tested in twenty parishes in 1966 and subsequently extended to the entire archdiocese. A semi-annual Diocesan Church Day was also established, with special collections for the church construction programme; under the motto *Madrid necesita templos* (Madrid Needs Churches), the faithful were called upon to donate according to their means, be it in the form of monetary contributions or in kind — for example, by donating land or even buildings. [Ill. 7.4]

Between 1964 and 1974, the Archdiocese of Madrid spent no less than 497 million pesetas (the equivalent of 3 million euros in today's currency) on purchasing land, building churches and converting existing commercial premises into places of worship. That was still not enough, however; in the early 1970s, faced with an expected growth of about 150,000 new residents per year, the diocesan services calculated that roughly that same amount was still needed to carry out the *Plan Pastoral*.[40] This prospect led to a revision of the financing

---

38 *Oficina Técnica. Dotación de equipo parroquial, solares, locales e iglesias. Realidades y proyectos* (Technical Office. Provision of parish equipment. Plots, premises and churches. Realities and projects). This document reviews the work of the Oficina Técnica between 1964 and 1974 and provides details about the acquisition of land for building on: thirty-eight plots were obtained for free; fifty-two were purchased; three were obtained by barter; and twenty-one were donated.
39 "El 7 de marzo entrará en vigor en la Archidiócesis la unificación de todos los servicios religiosos", 75; Morcillo, *La iglesia diocesana y sus parroquias*, 210.
40 Ramón Saiz, *Madrid-Alcalá, una diócesis en construcción*, 182-186.

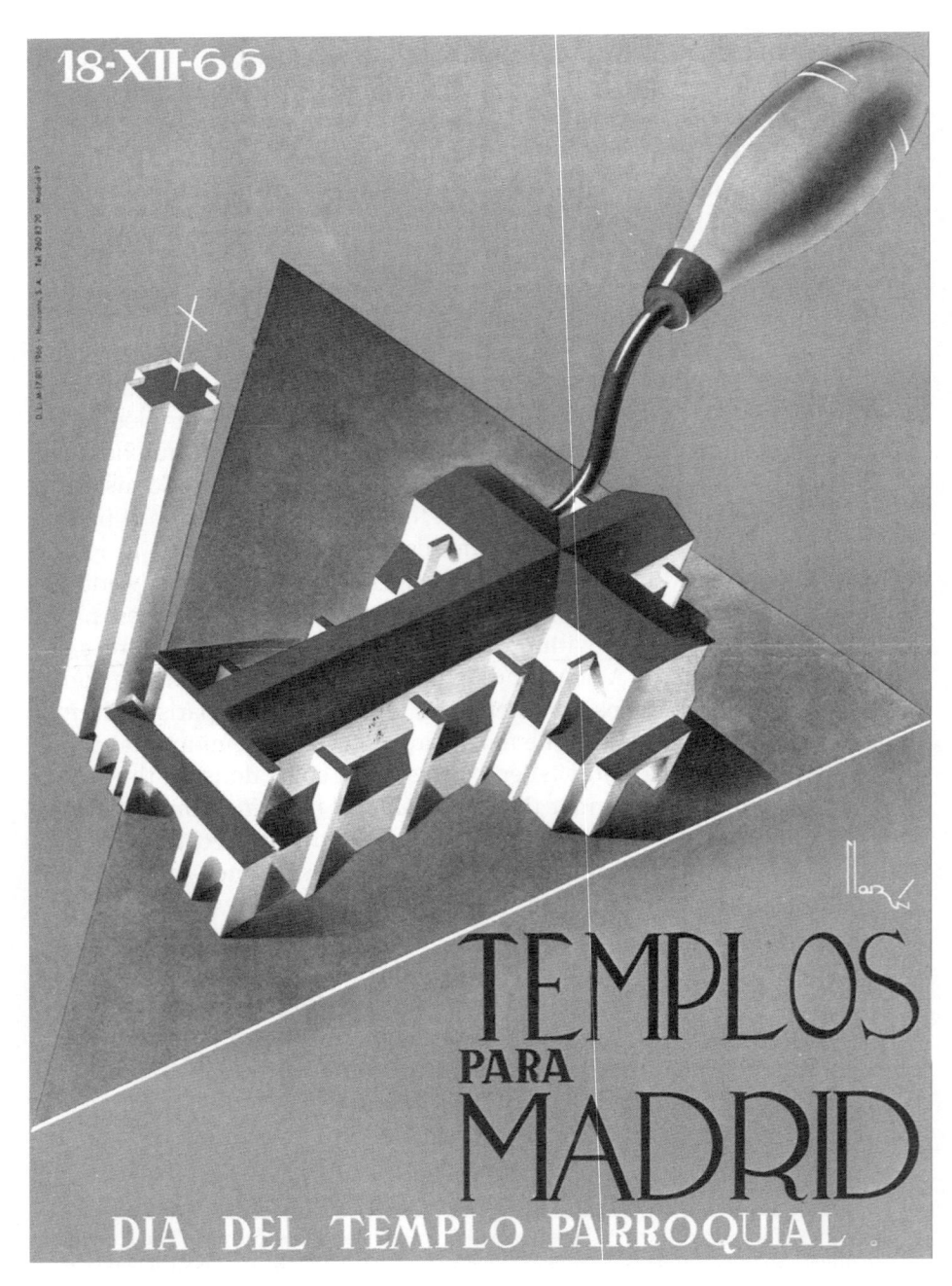

7.4 Poster from the Secretariado de Templos Parroquiales. The title reads "Day of the Parish Church: Churches for Madrid".
[Reproduced from Rafael Ramón Saiz, ed., *Madrid-Alcalá, una diócesis en construcción*]

system in 1972, coinciding with the appointment of Cardinal Tarancón after the death of Morcillo: individual parishes could still contract long-term loans with the archdiocese, but its initial contribution (usually twenty-five per cent) was eliminated. Similar to examples abroad, a system of godparent parishes was also installed, whereby existing parishes showed solidarity with newly established ones. At the same time, though, some local clergy demanded more independence from the archdiocese in consonance with the new self-financing system.

Despite the seemingly unsurmountable difficulties, the enormous effort paid off: by 1974, at the end of Rodríguez Osuna's management of the archdiocese's Oficina Técnica, eighty-one new churches had been completed in the city of Madrid and twenty more in the province; fourteen were still under construction and forty-one were on the drawing table. In addition, twenty commercial premises had been purchased with a view to converting them into places of worship. In an attempt to synthesise and assess this great effort, Rodríguez Osuna had reviewed all the new churches in 1972 for a publication that, sadly enough, was never finished.[41] One finding that can be derived from his preparatory documents is his own involvement in the appointment of the architects. Especially where the projects of the INV were concerned, he made sure that the design of the church was entrusted to architects he favoured, such as Cubillo (see further in this contribution); usually, though, the architects who were responsible for the residential units also designed the corresponding place of worship. Rodríguez Osuna made much of professionalising this process, establishing a close relationship with the various architects; for example, rather than having them work for free — as was often the case — he insisted on paying them properly. He did not interfere in the choice of the artists or the religious artwork, however; this he left to the architects or clients.[42] The same is true for the design of the churches: once a commission passed to a certain architect, the Oficina Técnica restricted itself to verifying its economic viability and compliance with the *Instrucciones para la Construcción de Complejos Parroquiales,* which the office had compiled in 1965.

---

41 The reason this project was halted may have to do with the administrative restructuring of the archdiocese in 1972-1973. Cubillo preserved the files, however, which consist of a heterogeneous collection of graphic documentation provided by the individual architects and include 61 of the 101 churches built up to 1972. See García Herrero, *La arquitectura religiosa de Luis Cubillo de Arteaga (1954-1974),* II.2.

42 This changed after the reform in 1972, which granted parish priests greater responsibility. As a result, they also weighed in more on artistic choices, to the detriment of the architects.

The Instructions for the Construction of Parish Complexes

Given that the Oficina Técnica did not have any architects on its staff, it drafted a set of guidelines to be used by the architects in charge of designing parish churches in the Archdiocese of Madrid. These *Instrucciones para la Construcción de Complejos Parroquiales* were drafted in collaboration with experts in theology and liturgy appointed by Morcillo and an architects commission composed of three experienced practitioners: Miguel Fisac (1913-2006), José Luis Fernández del Amo (1914-1995) and Fernando Terán (°1934).[43] Two teams were set up to develop the Instructions, each studying the typology of the parish complex from a different angle. While the first team was charged with defining the appropriate programme for each type of pastoral unit defined in the 1965 *Plan Pastoral* (parish, deanery and zone), the second team focused on guiding the architects in the "unknown demands of the new Liturgy" in light of the uncertainties brought about by the Second Vatican Council.[44] As stated in the Instructions, the role of the parish in the urban pastorate had to be considered from a threefold perspective: liturgical, charitable and missionary.[45] With regard to the first aspect, the orders from *Inter Oecumenici* were quoted at length. The charitable role of the parish was also to be reconsidered; active encouragement of social engagement was to replace the traditional, "passive" distribution of alms. A new type of collaborator, the social worker, was also introduced, whose task was to animate the parish and circulate relevant information amongst its members. The parish was not to remain a closed ecosystem, however, for as Rodríguez Osuna pointed out in an article in *ARA* (a magazine devoted to religious art), pastoral action in an urbanised society entailed reaching out:

> The urban parish must be eminently a missionary parish because it is located in the middle of a population that mainly ignores religion. This is how the most varied forms of informal missionary pastoral work start, which

43   Rodríguez Osuna had met these three architects during a seminar on the topic of religious infrastructure organised by the INV in 1964, at which Carlos Castro Cubells (expert in theology and liturgy), Rodríguez Osuna, García-Pablos and Fisac participated as speakers. It was probably also on that occasion that he invited them to collaborate on the guidelines, which the archdiocese had started to outline in August of that year. This can be deduced from the fact that an important part of the seminar's proceedings (including the ideas about "religious urbanism" from García-Pablos) were incorporated into the Instructions. Fisac became an authority in the field of religious architecture, designing remarkable churches such as San Pedro Mártir (Madrid, 1955), La Coronación (Vitoria, 1958) and Santa Ana (Madrid, 1965). Fernández del Amo was also fundamental in this period, not only for the quality of his architecture, but also for his outstanding role in the world of art as director of the National Museum of Contemporary Art. Terán started his professional career designing new colonisation towns and later became a master in urbanism.
44   *Instrucciones para la construcción de complejos parroquiales*, 5-6.
45   Ibid., 7.

have their headquarters in the parish complex and which must be reflected in every program of the parish complex: the club, for example, responds to this missionary pastoral care.[46]

As the Instructions stated in no uncertain terms, this vocation required that the architects and artists involved in the design of parish infrastructure efface themselves and subordinate their personal ideas to the functional and liturgical requirements imposed upon them; indeed, they were to look for "noble beauty, more than mere sumptuousness".[47] As a token of this humble attitude, parish centres were to blend in with the neighbouring buildings through the use of similar materials or appropriate formal expression, avoiding any extravagance; the use of bell towers or religious symbolism was neither prescribed nor encouraged. By contrast, particular attention was given to the design of the worship space, which had to be conceived from the inside out and devoid of any monumentality or abundance. Although primarily related to the cost of construction, an extremely important factor, this imperative of simplicity for the new churches also had a theological underpinning: a then common trope had it that contemporary worship practices did not require a temple for God, but rather a "house for God's people".[48] This also applied to the location of the parish complex: rather than occupying a triumphalist, preeminent position, it was to blend in with the city fabric and, preferably, be located in areas with many passers-by. To balance the busy city din with the desired interior atmosphere of piety and introspection, architects were advised to provide a small square in front of the new church building as a transitional element; a separate entrance to the parish hall and canteen was also required. Fisac's design for Santa Ana (1965) offers a salient example of this desired interaction between inner and outer spaces. [Ill. 7.5] Apart from its pragmatic underpinning and theological significance, this blending of the church with its surroundings may perhaps also be interpreted politically as a countermovement to the pomposity of most public buildings. Stating that "its [i.e. a church's] architectural expression should indicate the independence of church and state, even at the cost of breaking a secular tradition", the Instructions seemed to undermine Morcillo's resolute defence of the confessional state — even though his resolve to self-finance the *Plan Pastoral* had prefigured that separation.[49]

The programme for the parish complexes in Madrid depended on the type of pastoral unit they were to serve (parish, deanery or zone) and varied primarily in terms of the number of residential units and offices they comprised. Again, the Instructions were almost a carbon copy of the INV guide-

46   Rodríguez Osuna, "El complejo parroquial urbano", 7.
47   *Instrucciones para la construcción de complejos parroquiales*, 13.
48   Ibid., 33.
49   Ibid., 26.

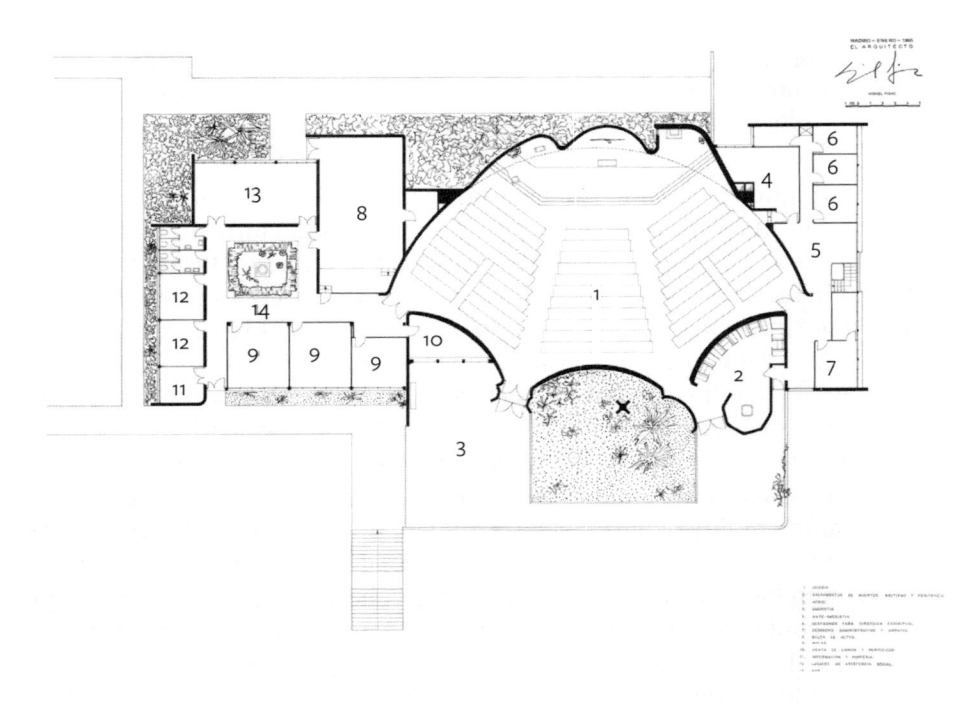

7.5 Floor plan for the Santa Ana parish complex (1965) (Miguel Fisac, architect). Top left: Independent entrance to the assembly hall (8) and canteen (13). Centre: Main entrance to the church (1), with former patio area (3) and garden.
[Courtesy of Fisac Legacy (MFS.P01), Madrid, ASHCOAM]

lines. For example, the total useful area of a parish centre was set at 1766 m^2 in the Instructions, compared to 1727 m^2 for the INV. Where the church proper was concerned, the latter estimated its average at about 850 m^2 (sacristy, storage, weekday chapel and baptistery included). Rodríguez Osuna proposed a smaller size: in his view, a parish of 10,000 inhabitants could manage with a church of between 400 and 600 m^2.[50] The right shape for the space of worship was — quite logically — a topic of much debate. Congregants' active participation in the liturgy — the core principle of the post-Vatican II liturgical reform — required optimal visibility and acoustics. Therefore, Rodríguez Osuna put forward the model of the Roman theatre, by which the faithful could easily be grouped around the altar.[51] This led to numerous fan-shaped churches in Madrid, such as Fisac's Santa Ana. Functionality was not everything, though; obtaining the right atmosphere was also key. Hence the importance accorded in the Instructions to the use of light in the church's interior, both natural and artificial. Beyond technical prescriptions, such as a minimum luminosity of 100 lux, the document also stated that the sanctuary was to be accentuated in

50 Rodríguez Osuna, "El complejo parroquial urbano", 10.
51 Interview with Jacinto Rodríguez Osuna by the author, 27 April 2011, Madrid.

order to guide the worshippers' attention to the altar, while lateral illumination was encouraged in order to prevent glare.[52] Although this often gave rise to highly poetic gestures, it also, paradoxically, frequently placed worshippers in semi-darkness due to the strong Spanish sunlight, as was the case in Fisac's Santa Ana, for example.

It should be clear by now that the Instructions provided a detailed, and at times rigid, framework for designing churches intended to be simple, yet dignified, and well made. Given the very limited financial margins, reconciling such seemingly contradictory expectations required great effort on the part of all parties involved, particularly the architect. Nonetheless, one man in particular, Luis Cubillo de Arteaga, seemed perfectly suited to the task, becoming the most prolific church architect in Madrid during the early 1970s.

Luis Cubillo de Arteaga's Contribution

By the time he started to work for the archdiocese's Oficina Técnica, Cubillo had already built a reputation for himself as a specialist in low-cost housing and was a professor in the architecture school of the prestigious Madrid Polytechnic. Amongst his most outstanding projects were the Poblado Dirigido of Canillas (1956), where he also designed the remarkable tent-like church (1961), and the Mater Dei seminary in Castellón (also 1961).[53] His sound knowledge of the latest liturgical trends, the radical simplicity of his plastic expression and his skilful integration of the arts earned him a position at the forefront of religious architecture in Spain. Interestingly, he applied the same basic principles in both his religious and non-religious work: constructive rationality, straightforward functionality and a formal language inspired by then fashionable Nordic examples. His predilection for repeating prototypical solutions, which he applied in his commissions for housing and schools, would also find fertile ground in the work he undertook for the Archdiocese of Madrid in the early 1970s.

The close cooperation between Cubillo and the archdiocese started after the former had been entrusted with the design of parish centres for San Federico (1968), Santas Perpetua y Felicidad (1969) and San Fernando (1969) upon the resignation of the architects initially chosen.[54] Once Cubillo took over, the

52 *Instrucciones para la construcción de complejos parroquiales*, 30.
53 See García Herrero, *La arquitectura religiosa de Luis Cubillo de Arteaga (1954-1974)*, I.2.
54 San Federico's parish priest originally chose Mario Gómez-Morán Cima as architect, but he never did the project, so the archdiocese called in Cubillo, who was well known for designing low-cost churches. Santas Perpetua y Felicidad's original architect was Terán (a fellow member of the Comisión de Arquitectos mentioned above), but he resigned six months after his appointment (that same year, 1969, he was launching *Ciudad y Territorio*, the first Spanish magazine about urbanism). San Fernando's original architect (Emilio Chinarro Matas) was sacked because of disagreements with Rodríguez Osuna. Madrid, AAM.

7.6 Exterior view of the San Fernando parish complex (1970) (Luis Cubillo de Arteaga, architect). [Courtesy of Cubillo de Arteaga Legacy (LCA.F007), Madrid, ASHCOAM]

projects quickly fell into place. According to Rodríguez Osuna, this had to do with the fact that "Cubillo was very consistent with the Instructions; austerity did not have to be imposed".[55] His purposiveness was a welcome quality given the frantic pace at the Oficina Técnica in those years: between 1968 and 1974, Cubillo designed no fewer than twenty-six projects for his new client (new churches, but also interventions in existing buildings and conversions of commercial premises), of which eighteen were eventually realised. Moreover, he also advised the archdiocese on the acquisition of plots or premises for future churches.

In the various parish centres Cubillo designed during this period, a typological evolution comes to the fore: whereas initially, he stuck to a simple rectangular geometry, he later also shaped the assembly space according to circular, pentagonal and square plans with the chancel at one end of the diagonal and the entrance at the other. Convinced that the final option (the square plan) worked best, Cubillo applied it in the church of San Fernando (1970) and then in thirteen other projects — albeit with certain variations. [Ill. 7.6] He was thus taking up the initiative of his colleague Terán, who had designed

55 Interview with Jacinto Rodríguez Osuna by the author, 27 April 2011, Madrid.

a prototype back in 1967 for a low-cost, easily repeatable parish centre that, for whatever reason, had not received a favourable response from the archdiocese. It should be noted, however, that despite the fact that the San Fernando project was touted in the local press and specialised magazines as a model, this "church with the beautiful roof" was not quite representative of this series of projects, since it was realised in a unique environment and the available resources were quite exceptional.[56] By contrast, the parish centres of San Bonifacio (1971) and Jesus de Nazaret (1972) more fully illustrated the adaptability of Cubillo's model. As he commented on the former:

> A suggestive volumetric solution, adapted to the significant slope of the plot, was suited to the resolution of the different uses (...). The church was designed with a square plan, a solution I had already proposed on other occasions due to its unquestionable economy, emphasising one of the vertices as a singular point and developing the assembly around it. The roof shows this singular point, in which the chancel is located. (...) The complex is integrated into a modest garden that contrasts with the feverish vitality of the city through its environmental tranquillity.[57]

In all the projects of this series, the church space is conceived as a square with each side measuring about 20 m long, resulting in a minimum surface area of 400 m², perfectly in accordance with the norms proposed in the Instructions. Cubillo also systematically included a weekday chapel, which acted as a link to the rest of the parish complex. By giving it independent access, he emancipated it somehow from the subsidiary character it generally possessed in pre-conciliar proposals. As to emphasise its new status as a separate space for devotion, it housed the tabernacle and the confessional. For covering these spaces, Cubillo relied on his experience in public housing, using a simple, exposed structural system without intermediate supports. [Ill. 7.7] Together with the facing brick walls and abstract stained-glass windows, the interior atmosphere was one of deliberate simplicity and austerity — certainly a worthy response to the guidelines set by the archdiocese, but not always understood and appreciated by the parishioners or the local clergy, who were more accustomed to opulence where religion was concerned.[58]

Whereas the church and the weekday chapel were systematically treated the same by Cubillo in all thirteen projects, he allowed himself more freedom in the rest of the parish complex, accommodating it to the shape of the

56 See "San Fernando. Complejo parroquial-Madrid", 48.
57 Madrid, ASHCOAM, Cubillo de Arteaga papers, LCA.D171.
58 In 1974, the parish priest of San Bonifacio wrote a letter to the director of the Secretariado with several complaints. In it, he asked, "Why is there, among many commissions, no review of the projects so that they do not make us industrial spaces or garages, very functional, as they say now, but no similar to churches and not inviting of retreat and devotion?" Madrid, AAM.

7.7 Interior view of the Santiago Apóstol parish complex in Alcalá de Henares (1970) (Luis Cubillo de Arteaga, architect).
[Courtesy of the author]

available plot or site; he either organised the rooms along an interior street, as in San Bonifacio, or clustered them around an inner courtyard, as in Jesus de Nazaret. [Ill. 7.8a & 7.8b] Regardless, Cubillo's systematic mind seeped through in the uniform functional organisation into three separate zones: one liturgical (including church and weekday chapel); one administrative (comprising offices for the clergy, Cáritas and social assistance, as well as lodgings for the clergy); and one social (with meeting rooms and a multi-purpose hall). In the case of Jesus de Nazaret, the three zones were juxtaposed on the ground floor, while in San Bonifacio, they were superimposed: the church on the ground floor; lodging on the upper floors; and the parish hall and meeting rooms in the semi-basement. Finally, Cubillo also attached great importance to the circulation areas tying together the various zones; more than simple corridors providing easy access, he conceived of these as interior "streets". In San Bonifacio, for example, the central gallery provided access to the parish complex from two different streets, connecting the parish complex with the surrounding urban fabric.

The examples discussed here exemplify Cubillo's ability to adhere strictly to the Instructions and yet give each church a dignified appearance by virtue of a particular roofscape that, in the imagination of the architect, seemed

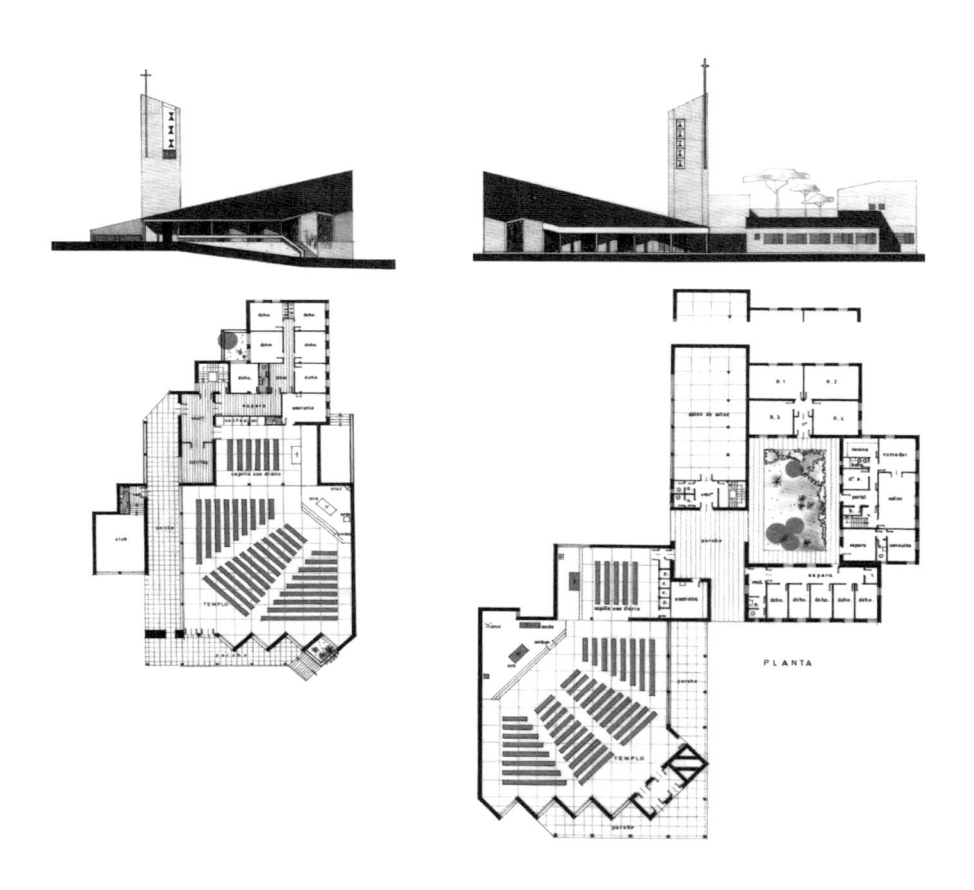

7.8a and 7.8b Floor plan and elevation drawings for the parish complexes of San Bonifacio (1971) and Jesús de Nazaret (1972) in Madrid (Luis Cubillo de Arteaga, architect).
[Courtesy of the Cubillo de Arteaga Legacy (LCA.P472), Madrid, ASHCOAM]

to rise up from the surrounding garden — the latter acting as a transitional space between the busy street and the quietness of the church space. This scenography — indispensable in the mind of Cubillo, for he defined in great detail the vegetation and trees that were to form a counterpoint to the exposed brickwork of the architecture — was, in fact, the Achilles heel of his prototypical scheme, for it lost its effectiveness in cases where the parish centre had to be built close to existing structures or a garden simply was no option. The same held true for the bell towers that Cubillo systematically integrated into his designs. Located next to the main entrance of the church and flanked by two porches that prolonged their roofs, their compositional effectiveness becomes immediately apparent when contemplating the few examples without a bell tower. Yet, in the post-conciliar climate, bell towers were called into question, for they were associated with the bygone rural parish church, expressed

7.9 Exterior view of San Bonifacio parish complex in Madrid (1971) (Luis Cubillo de Arteaga, architect). [Photograph by Agustín Rico. Courtesy of the Cubillo de Arteaga Legacy (LCA.F002), Madrid, ASH-COAM]

dominance in an era when the Church wanted to be humble and — last but not least — were very expensive to build and maintain. Yet, as Cubillo's designs illustrate, in the hands of a skilful master, a bell tower could still be a contemporary signifier of faith.[59] [Ill. 7.9]

Conclusion

Reflecting upon the restructuring of the parish landscape in Madrid, Rodríguez Osuna referred to it as a "silent revolution".[60] Allegedly, he meant to say that, in the first place, the pastoral policies of the archdiocese had indeed undergone a radical change, and at great cost, in terms of human and financial effort. As we have seen, from the start, the implementation of the *Plan Pastoral* was severely hampered by financial constraints, to the extent that in 1973, the archdiocese was forced to review some of its fundamental premises. It quickly became apparent that the neat distinction between a weekday chapel and a proper church space, as developed by Cubillo, was no longer tenable; instead, architects were now asked to design modular, polyvalent places of worship that could be expanded in the weekend. The optimum size of the parish centres was also systematically reduced from 1766 m² to 1200 m², and even 700 m² in some cases.[61] Although these draconic measures must have been a bitter pill to swallow for many pastors, architects and churchgoers, it was worth the effort: thanks to the new self-financing system installed with the appointment of Cardinal Vicente Enrique y Tarancón (1907-1994) in 1972, almost all the planned parish centres were effectively built. That said, soon a new problem arose that undermined the effectiveness of the parish plan, namely the increasing shortage of priests and the aging clergy. Consequently, in 1981 the optimum parish size had to be increased from 10,000 inhabitants to 15,000, or in some cases, even 20,000.[62]

Yet, beyond the statistical data, Rodríguez Osuna's concept of a silent revolution also had a deeper meaning. Perhaps he meant to hint at the impact of all this religious infrastructure on the mind of his fellow Spaniards. As to the real effect of the *Plan Pastoral*, we can only speculate. In 1975, the year of Franco's death, the FOESSA Foundation (a Catholic study centre linked to Cáritas) published a sociological analysis of Spanish society, pointing out that the economic growth, rapid industrialisation, rampant urbanisation and mass tourism were decisively altering the socio-religious behaviour of its citizens.

59 Busquets, "Un nuevo programa para las iglesias", 3.
60 Interview with Jacinto Rodríguez Osuna by the author, 27 April 2011, Madrid. According to Rodríguez Osuna, the word "revolution" was used by Morcillo during the initial stages of the Plan in a private conversation with him.
61 Ramón Saiz, *Madrid-Alcalá, una diócesis en construcción*, 192-194.
62 Letter from the Oficina Técnica to the deans. Madrid, AAM.

Nonetheless, eighty-five per cent of the population of Madrid at that time declared itself an adherent of the Catholic faith.[63] This seems to suggest that the *Plan Pastoral* was indeed effective — though these figures should obviously be interpreted with caution, given that in 1975, the denominational character of the Francoist state was still omnipresent.

As far as its architectural outcome is concerned, the parish plan can effectively be called a success, as apparent from the aforementioned compilation of churches that Rodríguez Osuna was not able to complete. Although his expectations for a prototype for a standardised parish centre adaptable to different situations (as proposed by Terán and resumed by Cubillo) were probably not entirely fulfilled, he must have felt that the Instructions proved a valuable blueprint for a new type of church — not only as a material artefact, but also as an institution. With hindsight, the Instructions can indeed be read as a sort of manifesto that encapsulates the urge for renewal that its authors shared with a large part of the Spanish clergy, who, in the unstable post-conciliar times, were gradually distancing themselves from Franco's regime.

So it was that Rodríguez Osuna's silent revolution became a reality only a few years later, albeit in a very different manner than he and Morcillo envisioned in 1965. When the latter's successor, Cardinal Tarancón, became president of the Spanish Episcopal Conference in 1972, he increasingly took a stance in favour of the "Democratic Transition" supported by Paul VI — a detachment from the regime that produced great tensions within the Spanish church. At the same time, Spanish society was in turmoil, as evidenced by the feverish activity of trade unions, opposition parties and all sorts of associations. Gradually, progressive forces within the Spanish church started to sympathise with this political counterculture that, to a large extent, had its roots in the newly erected parish centres in Madrid.[64] Thus, Rodríguez Osuna's silent revolution pertained as much to the archdiocese's new take on pastoral care as to the radical change of mind of the Spanish clergy during the swan song of the Franco regime — a rupture that he, albeit indirectly, had helped to push through.

---

63   Versus seventy per cent in Barcelona and sixty-three per cent in the Canary Islands; the Spanish average was eighty-four per cent. *Estudios sociológicos sobre la situación social de España 1975*, 559.
64   Montero, "Iglesia y política en la transición: Los católicos ante la transición política", 342. The case of Nuestra Señora de la Montaña parish in Moratalaz was a prime example. The first church was a prefabricated structure with the words "*Casa del Pueblo de Dios*" (House of God's people) written on its façade in big letters. The Comisiones Obreras (Workers Commisions) trade union started its activity there, and the parish priest, Mariano Gamo, was jailed several times for his political activity.

BIBLIOGRAPHY

Archives

Madrid, Archivo del Arzobispado de Madrid (AAM)
Madrid, Archivo del Servicio Histórico del Colegio Oficial de Arquitectos de Madrid (ASHCOAM), Cubillo de Arteaga papers, LCA D171

Published sources

Baldellou, Miguel Ángel. "Neorrealismo y arquitectura. El "problema de la vivienda" en Madrid, 1954-1966". *Arquitectura*, 301 (1995), 20-58
Blanco Agüeira, Silvia. *Rodolfo García-Pablos: La construcción del espacio sagrado*. Thesis. A Coruña, 2009.
Busquets, Juan Antonio. "Un nuevo programa para las iglesias". *Arquitectura*, 159 (1972), 1-4.
Casanova, Julián. *A Short History of the Spanish Civil War*. London: I.B. Tauris, 2012.
Comunidad cristiana parroquial. 1º semana nacional de la parroquia. Madrid: Eurámerica, 1959.
Delgado de la Rosa, Juan Antonio. "Una iglesia en cambio. 50 años del concilio Vaticano II: la recepción del concilio en España". *Las Torres de Lucca*, 7 (December 2015), 235-273.
Delgado Orusco, Eduardo. *Arquitectura sacra española, 1939-1975: de la posguerra al posconcilio*. Thesis. Madrid, 2000.
Duocastella, Rogelio. *Cómo estudiar una parroquia*. Barcelona: Instituto de Sociología y Pastoral Aplicadas, 1967.
"El 7 de marzo entrará en vigor en la Archidiócesis la unificación de todos los servicios religiosos". *ABC (Madrid)*, (17 January 1965), 73-76.
Estudios sociológicos sobre la situación social de España 1975. Madrid: Eurámerica, 1976, 529-692.
Fernández de Torres, Ignacio María. *El pensamiento social de los arzobispos de la Archidiócesis de Madrid después del Concilio Vaticano II, 1964-1994*. Thesis. Madrid, 2009.
García García, Pedro. *Arquitectura religiosa en Madrid, a partir de 1940*. Thesis. Madrid, 2005.
García Herrero, Jesús. *La arquitectura religiosa de Luis Cubillo de Arteaga (1954-1974)*. Thesis. Madrid, 2015.

García-Pablos, Rodolfo. "Necesidad de establecer ordenaciones parroquiales integradas en los Planeamientos Urbanísticos". In *Arte sacro y Concilio Vaticano II*. León: Junta Nacional Asesora de Arte Sacro, 1965, 115-122.
Guía de la Archidiócesis de Madrid-Alcalá. Madrid: Oficina Técnica de Sociología Religiosa del Arzobispado de Madrid, 1965.
Instrucciones para la construcción de complejos parroquiales. Madrid: Oficina Técnica de Sociología Religiosa del Arzobispado de Madrid, 1965.
Isasi, Justo. "Iglesia y vanguardia en la España de la posguerra". *Arquitectura Viva*, 58 (1998), 23-29.
Montero, Feliciano. "Iglesia y política en la transición: Los católicos ante la transición política". *Espacio, Tiempo y Forma. Serie V, Historia Contemporánea*, 12 (1999), 335-356.
Morcillo, Casimiro. "Carta Magna del Arte Sacro en España". *Revista Nacional de Arquitectura*, 200, (1958), 27.
Morcillo, Casimiro. "Carta Pastoral sobre el día del templo parroquial". *Official Bulletin of the Archdiocese of Madrid*, (15 May 1967), 260-264.
Morcillo, Casimiro. "La archidiócesis de Madrid-Alcalá en esta hora. Carta Pastoral al clero y fieles de la archidiócesis del arzobispo don Casimiro Morcillo". In: Rafael Ramón Saiz, ed. *Madrid-Alcalá, una diócesis en construcción. Exposición sobre las parroquias creadas en la diócesis de Madrid desde 1961 a 1982*. Madrid: Editorial service of the Diocese, 1982, 25-37.
Morcillo, Casimiro. *La iglesia diocesana y sus parroquias*. Barcelona: Juan Flors, 1960.
Morta, Angel. "Chronica: Universidad Pontificia de Salamanca. Semana Nacional de la Parroquia (Zaragoza, 13-20 abril 1958)". *Salmancitensis*, 6 (1959), 1, 269-271.
Moya González, Luis. *Barrios de Promoción Oficial. Madrid 1939-1976*. Madrid: COAM, 1983.
"No queremos una España de proletarios, sino de propietarios". *ABC (Madrid)*, (2 May 1959), 41-42.
Normas Urbanísticas para el término municipal de Madrid: Plan General de Ordenación Urbana del Área Metropolitana de Madrid. Ley 121/1963, del 2 de Diciembre. Madrid: COAM, 1967.
Nuevas estructuras pastorales en la Archidiócesis de Madrid-Alcalá. Madrid: Oficina Técnica de Sociología Religiosa del Arzobispado de Madrid, 1965.

Plan Nacional de la Vivienda 1961-1976. Madrid: I.N.V., 1962.

Ramón Saiz, Rafael, ed. *Madrid-Alcalá, una diócesis en construcción. Exposición sobre las parroquias creadas en la diócesis de Madrid desde 1961 a 1982*. Madrid: Editorial service of the Diocese, 1982.

Rodríguez Osuna, Jacinto. "Características religiosas de las concentraciones urbanas. Planificación pastoral". In: *Problemas de concentración urbana: semanas sociales de España, XXIV sesión*. Madrid: Junta Nacional, 1966, 217-234.

Rodríguez Osuna, Jacinto. "El complejo parroquial urbano". *ARA. Arte Religioso Actual*, 15 (1968), 4-18.

Rodríguez Osuna, Jacinto. *Informe sociológico sobre la situación social de Madrid*. Madrid: Euramérica, 1967.

Rodríguez Osuna, Jacinto. "La nueva estructuración parroquial de Madrid". *Anales del Instituto de Estudios Madrileños, T.1* (1966), 391-404.

"San Fernando. Complejo parroquial-Madrid". *ARA. Arte Religioso Actual*, 36 (1973), 44-49.

Seminarios del INV. Edificios religiosos. Madrid: I.N.V. editions. Ministerio de la Vivienda, 1965.

Terán, Fernando: *Madrid*. Madrid: Mapfre, 1992.

AUTHORITY

8
A LABORATORY OF PASTORAL MODERNITY
CHURCH BUILDING IN MILAN UNDER CARDINAL MONTINI AND ENRICO MATTEI FROM 1955 TO 1963

UMBERTO BORDONI, MARIA ANTONIETTA CRIPPA, DAVIDE FUSARI, AND FERDINANDO ZANZOTTERA

The pastoral strategies of Cardinal Giovanni Battista Montini (1897-1978, later Pope Paul VI) during the eight years of his tenure as Archbishop of Milan, from 1955 to 1963, had a profound impact on the city's infrastructure. In particular, during this short period, he succeeded in having no fewer than 123 churches built throughout the diocese. It is worth examining how this came to pass. Montini reaffirmed the ambition of his predecessor, Cardinal Alfredo Ildefonso Schuster (1880-1954), to establish a "capillary presence" for the Church in the city by establishing large parish centres catering to not only religious, but also cultural, social and educational needs. Yet he also realised that in the post-war context, this could only be achieved with stronger support from society as a whole and the industrial and financial establishment in particular. For this reason, he appointed Enrico Mattei (1906-1962), one of Italy's chief captains of industry and an emblematic figure of the Milanese Catholic establishment, as head of a body called the Comitato pro Templi Nuovi (Committee for New Temples), whose mission was to develop strategies for the implementation of parish centres.

The mechanisms behind the *"Miracle à Milan"* — as the French periodical *L'Art sacré* called it in a special issue on the diocese from 1959 — were manifold, stemming from the operations of various committees and offices created to enable the pastoral infrastructure to keep pace with the city's extraordinary growth in the 1950s and 1960s.[1] [Ill. 8.1] The roles of Montini and Mattei were particularly pivotal in this. As mentioned, Montini's tenure was

---

1   *Miracle à Milan*. The title refers to an Italian fantasy film directed by Vittorio De Sica (1951).

8.1 "Miracle à Milan". Cover of *L'Art sacré*, 1-2, 1959.

characterised by an experimental pastoral approach, which worked in deep harmony with Mattei's modernising impulse, itself supported by the diocesan curia's constantly updated analytical and planning framework. A close study of the diocesan archives, including material only recently made available to researchers and hitherto only discussed in studies in Italian (including by the present authors), reveals insights that contribute to the already substantial body of literature on post-war church building in Milan.[2] To start with, the role played by Mattei in this church-building campaign, both conceptually and operationally, has not been adequately explored before. Furthermore, closer examination of the specific modernity of Montini's pastoral policies shows how his Milanese experience may have helped pave the way for the reforms endorsed by the Second Vatican Council.

Schuster versus Montini: Continuity and Innovation

In the aftermath of the Second World War, the Ambrosian Diocese, and the city of Milan, in particular, witnessed an extraordinary growth in population as a result of industrial development and immigration from the south. In only twenty years, the population grew by over half a million inhabitants, or almost forty per cent.[3] The economic boom between 1955 and 1965 led to a surge in building activity, particularly in the new working-class areas outside the historic centre of Milan, as well as to a rapid growth of heavy industry across a vast expanse around the city. This expansion of the suburbs (to the detriment of the historic centre) presented a pastoral challenge without precedent, which was keenly felt on the outskirts of Milan and in the belt of villages and small towns to the north and north-east of the city. In his widespread account of diocesan policies to address the rampant urbanisation across Europe, the French cleric Paul Winninger described the situation tellingly: "One is rarely seized by the oppression of the sprawling city, of its insatiable expansion, and the hectic excitement like in Milan."[4] He observed that while old, and often dilapidated, churches abounded in the city centre, there were extensive tracts along its periphery without a bell tower in sight. Two local cardinals, in

2 The Archivio Storico Diocesano di Milano (ASDM) made 26,000 documents related to Montini's activities as Archbishop of Milan available for research in 2013. On church-building policies in Milan after the Second World War, see: Winninger, *Construire des Églises. Les dimensions des Paroisses et les contradictions de l'apostolat dans les villes*, 88-112; Crippa, "L'esperimento pastorale del card. Giovanni Battista Montini nella diocesi ambrosiana".
3 Milan had 268,000 inhabitants in 1861 (Italian unification); 1,100,000 in 1936; 1,274,000 in the 1950s; 1,582,474 in the 1960s; and 1,732,068 in the 1970s. Grandi and Pracchi, *Guida all'architettura moderna*.
4 Winninger, *Construire des Églises*, 98. Unless otherwise noted, all translations are the authors' own.

particular, decided to address this pastoral concern: Schuster and Montini.[5] Each prelate dealt with the challenge differently, but their approaches shared points of both continuity and innovation compared to previous practice.

In fact, the Diocese of Milan had a long tradition of supporting new and poor parishes in establishing pastoral infrastructure. Cardinal Federico Borromeo (1564-1631) had established the Opera Pia delle Chiese e Case Parrocchiali Povere (Charitable Organisation for Poor Churches and Parish Buildings) in 1617. A body with its own legal status, it broadly functioned as a bank, taking on obligations and receiving donations in the form of money, titles or buildings. It collected funds for the construction of churches and redistributed them amongst parishes in need. With the ever-increasing scale, speed and complexity of twentieth-century urbanisation, a more responsive body was deemed necessary, not only to collect funds, but also to coordinate church building across the diocese. Inspired (but only in ecclesiastical management terms) by Cardinal Jean Verdier's (1864-1940) interwar church-building campaign in Paris, Les Chantiers du Cardinal (The Cardinal's Construction Sites), Cardinal Schuster founded the Comitato pro Templi Nuovi in 1937, which immediately began construction on fourteen new "temples". The use of this term – "temples" rather than "churches" – is significant, as it indicates the prevalence, initially, of a "monumental" conception of the parish church in terms of both size and shape: a large building, with 3,000 seats, to be managed by a parish priest and four assistant priests and serve a parish of about 15,000 inhabitants on an area of 60 hectares. The notion of the temple also suggested a dominant visual presence in the city. Indeed, the Comitato collaborated closely with the municipal administration responsible for executing the city's Piano Regolatore Generale (General Regulatory Plan) from 1934 in order to secure centrally located sites in the newly planned areas that would provide sufficient open space for the churches to be freestanding.

This broad conception of the parish was part of the Ambrosian tradition, in which it was at the centre of almost all aspects of community life, regardless of the residents' differences in age, class and profession. Apart from worship and catechism, parish activity encompassed academic and professional education, sports, cultural activities and charity, aiming to play a central role in the community. Indeed, as pointed out by the Comitato:

> Worship remains the chief aspect of the parish complex, but the new parish must be a centre from which works of charitable assistance and religious and moral education for children, young people and adults will radiate. This will result in a network of connections and relationships between the

---

5   Alfredo Ildefonso Schuster, a Benedictine monk, was Archbishop of the Diocese of Milan from 1929 until 1954. Nobili, *Ildefonso Schuster e il rinnovamento Cattolico (1880-1929)*. Giovanni Battista Montini was appointed Archbishop of Milan on 1 November 1954, took office on 6 January 1955 and was elected pope on 21 June 1963.

Church and families and individuals, allowing that direct personal communication between priest and people which is now no longer merely a convenience, but an absolute necessity.[6]

These activities were housed in a centrally located group of buildings, including a church, a presbytery with flats for the parish priest and his assistants, one or two buildings with rooms for meetings, and an *oratorio*: usually a large area of playing fields and rooms for various activities, often with a theatre or cinema, open to all, though with segregated spaces for young men and women. The diocese paid for the land and the building shell (the *rustico*) and acted as the architect's client so that the priests would not be distracted from their pastoral duties. The parish only had to handle the finishing and equipment installation. Significant philanthropic donations were also sought from the industrial and financial establishment, and local newspapers supported the collections held throughout the diocese, culminating in an annual Church Day.

Despite these efforts, pastoral provision in Milan failed to keep pace with urban growth, becoming an especially daunting problem after 1945, since the war had caused developments to stall. The Comitato resumed its activities as before, but its organisation was modified to respond more proactively to the rapidly changing circumstances. Amongst other changes, the Comitato engaged actively with the municipal authority as the city prepared its new urban development plan (the 1953 Piano Regolatore Generale). It also established contact with the various social housing boards to discover where new residential developments — and thus pastoral needs — were to be expected. When Mattei was appointed president of the Comitato in 1953, he also gave it a new impetus. [Ill. 8.2] Prior to that, Mattei had been assigned the task of dismantling the Azienda Generale Italiana Petroli (AGIP), the national oil company established in 1926. Once it was enlarged and reorganised as the Ente Nazionale Idrocarburi (ENI), it soon became an important player in the international oil market. Mattei is recognised today as a cultured entrepreneur and progressive public executive who helped modernise Italy. He was a highly influential figure in the industrial and financial Catholic establishment in Milan and beyond, pragmatically forging alliances with political leaders in the pursuit of his goals.[7] For Mattei, the expansion of ENI was as much a cultural undertaking as an economic enterprise, for in his view, the company was an all-encompassing laboratory for a new, modern — yet still predominantly Christian — Italian identity. To support this endeavour, he hired Italy's fore-

---

6 "L'attività del Comitato per le nuove Chiese nell'Archidiocesi di Milano".
7 There exists an abundance of literature on Mattei. See, for example, Morini, *Enrico Mattei. Il partigiano che sfidò le sette sorelle*; Li Vigni, *Enrico Mattei: l'uomo del futuro che inventò la rinascita italiana*.

8.2: Giovani Battista Montini with Enrico Mattei at a public meeting, 1958.
[Reproduced from *Le nuove chiese di Milano 1950-1960*. Courtesy of the Archdiocese of Milan]

most intellectuals and created a newspaper (*Il Giorno*), a magazine (*Il Gatto Selvatico*) and even a cutting-edge company town, Metanopoli, on the edge of Milan. Mattei had a reputation as an efficient (and sometimes ruthless) business manager, but equally as a guardian of Christian values, qualities that led Cardinal Schuster to recommend him as head of the Comitato when its president, Beniamino Donzelli, passed away.

Within a couple of months of taking the helm, Mattei had proposed a structural reorganisation, persuading the *fine fleur* of the Milanese industrial and financial establishment to become members of the newly restructured committee (including Carlo Pesenti, president of Italcimenti; Alberto Pirelli, of the eponymous tire manufacturer; and Giordano Dell'Amore, of the Cassa di Risparmio delle Provincie Lombarde, a bank) with a view to setting up a new fund-raising campaign. The committee also changed its name to the Comitato per le Nuove Chiese (Committee for New Churches), implying that the context of post-war reconstruction required not ostentatious "temples", but rather buildings that accommodated the worshipping "churches" of their parishes. Its mission remained the same, however, namely the promotion and coordination of church building in the Diocese of Milan and fund-raising for this purpose. This different approach first emerged with the church of Santa

8.3 Aerial view from 1955 of the church of Santa Maria Nascente (1953-1955) in the QT8 district of Milan (Vico Magistretti and Mario Tedeschi, architects).
[Courtesy of ISAL (Istituto per la Storia dell'Arte Lombarda)]

Maria Nascente in the famous QT8 district, which was approved and started during the final years of Schuster's tenure: instead of being monumental, it was built to smaller dimensions to contain costs.[8] [Ill. 8.3]

A second event that significantly impacted church-building activity in Milan was Pope Pius XII's appointment of Montini as Archbishop of Milan on 1 November 1954 after Schuster's death.[9] The challenges he faced when he took office on 4 January 1955 were truly daunting. The Diocese of Milan was the most important in the Catholic world, at least in quantitative terms: it comprised over 3 million inhabitants, 3,700 priests and almost 1,000 parishes. As Montini wrote in his Pastoral Letter for Christmas 1955, the lack of decent pastoral infrastructure was not only a pastoral problem, but a matter of wider

8   Vico Magistretti and Mario Tedeschi, winners of the competition in 1946, proposed a building for about 800 seats with a modern central plan. Construction began in 1953 and ended in 1955. Bottoni, "Chiesa al quartiere QT8".
9   Originally from Lombardy, Montini possessed an unusual combination of skills developed through deep contacts with French and German culture; an exceptional awareness of the tensions between modernity and tradition within Catholicism and of the problems faced by the Church on a global scale, having been directly involved in Vatican affairs, particularly during the papacy of Pius XII; and a profound knowledge of the Italian socio-political situation, having been first a guide and then a friend to eminent politicians, business people and intellectuals. Cf. Adornato, "L'episcopato Milanese".

public interest.[10] He believed that, alongside the missionary work of Azione Cattolica (Catholic Action), the Church needed a stable and reliable basis from which to evangelise the increasingly secularised suburbs. Montini argued that the only durable way to keep city dwellers in the Church was by establishing a parish network on a smaller, more intimate scale, with 5,000 inhabitants per parish being his preferred ideal. Since according to canon law, every parish required a dedicated place of worship, church building thus naturally occupied a central place in Montini's pastoral project. Indeed, not a day passed without him checking on the activities of the Comitato per le Nuove Chiese. During an audience for its members, for example, he stated:

> (...) The new churches are a truly urgent problem (...). The committee's activity is one of the things I hold most dear and is foremost amongst the enormous responsibilities of our city's pastor, a role which Divine Providence has chosen to bestow upon me, its humble servant.[11]

This sense of urgency and mission may explain why his tenure was characterised by a constant desire to not only conceive new plans, but also execute them as rapidly as possible.

Although Montini had no pastoral experience before his appointment as archbishop, he understood that bringing city dwellers back into the Church required contact in their daily lives, not merely once a week in church. Thus, he launched the extraordinary *Missione di Milano*: from 4 to 24 November 1957, 1,288 preachers (including two cardinals, Giacomo Lercaro from Bologna and Giuseppe Siri from Genoa) toured the city, holding 15,000 sermons in over 400 venues, including secular sites such as factories, schools and banks.[12] Despite the general enthusiasm with which it was received, the participation of an impressive number of lay people and extensive media coverage, the Mission led to some uncomfortable conclusions, convincing Montini that a process of irredeemable secularisation was in progress. He interpreted this tendency as a signal that a change in attitude was needed. Well before the Second Vatican Council, therefore, Montini felt that he was witnessing a change from an era of Christianity to one of a secularised world. Faced with increasing numbers distancing themselves from the Church, he argued for a missionary approach, at the same time revitalising Catholic traditions and opening new paths to seek people out in their own spheres of life.[13]

The *Missione di Milano* reveals correspondences and differences between Schuster's and Montini's pastoral policies. Initially, the latter may seem to

10 Winninger, *Construire des Églises*, 106.
11 Montini, *Discorsi e scritti milanesi (1954-1963)*, vol. I, 8.
12 On the *Missione di Milano*, see, *La Missione di Milano 1957*.
13 Rumi, "La Missione di Milano: oltre i confini della tradizione".

have continued along the lines set out by his predecessor in both operational and conceptual terms. Indeed, the role of the Comitato and the various diocesan offices remained unchanged at first, as did the guiding principles on the role and nature of the parish complex: its broad social relevance; its physical and spiritual proximity to individuals and families; the direct and personal contact between clergy and faithful; and the role of worship as a cornerstone of daily life. The most evident difference was a definitive reduction in the size of building projects, as the diocese's financial situation necessitated the purchase of smaller plots of land.

The theological and pastoral intentions of the two prelates were different, however. Schuster aimed to restore the *civitas Christiana*. He conceived of art and architecture as "handmaidens" of the liturgy but kept his distance from contemporary art, only permitting the moderate expression of it proposed by Monsignor Giuseppe Polvara, founder of the Scuola Beato Angelico. Schuster asked the architects and engineers who planned churches to adhere to the Borromean *Instructiones fabricae* of 1577 (by Federico's cousin, Cardinal Carlo Borromeo, 1538-1584), retranslated and republished in 1952. Montini, by contrast, distanced himself from this text. In the context of fragile national democratic politics and the surging industrialisation that was rapidly altering the Italian people's way of life, he intended his reformism as a faithful renewal of tradition, characterised by the mottos "to deepen and to enlarge" and "continual Christian reform". This thinking led to his notion of dialogue between the Church and the secular world as a trusting relationship between "two societies with the same foundation" and his attention to the "two complementary but distinct levels, laity and clergy".[14] It was this pastoral line that guided the new evangelisation of the city's suburbs. He sought a general connection between the multiplication of parishes and the construction of new neighbourhoods in Milan. He also further pursued the experiments started by his predecessor in the final years of his administration. In short, Montini stabilised and strengthened a process already in place.

The resulting churches varied in terms of their success in pursuing these objectives. While the Madonna dei Poveri in Baggio by Luigi Figini and Gino Pollini embodied the new diocesan guidelines of material simplicity and spiritual richness particularly well [Ill. 8.4], the technological modernity of the church of Nostra Signora della Misericordia at Baranzate by Angelo Mangiarotti and Bruno Morassutti caused some controversy, not because of its shape but because it was built using experimental techniques and materials that were not always of the highest quality.[15] [Ill. 8.5] The building consists of four slender pillars supporting a large, prefabricated, flat roof, encased in a trans-

14   Adornato, "L'episcopato Milanese", 260.
15   This building has recently been the subject of a very important restoration. Cf. Barazzetta, ed., *La chiesa di vetro di Angelo Mangiarotti, Bruno Morassutti, Aldo Favini. La storia e il restauro*.

8.4 Interior view of the Church of Madonna dei Poveri (1952-1954) in Baggio (Milan) (Luigi Figini and Gino Pollini, architects).
[Photograph by Alessandro Nanni, 2018]

8.5 Interior view of the Church of Nostra Signora della Misericordia (1956) in Baranzate (Milan) (Bruno Morassutti and Angelo Mangiarotti, architects).
[Courtesy of ISAL (Istituto per la Storia dell'Arte Lombarda)]

lucent "skin" of glass and polystyrene. In his sermon at the consecration Mass of 1957, Montini asked rhetorically:

> Is it possible for your bishop to bless such a church? Yes, it is possible, because I see a deep symbolism in the new construction, one that recalls the essence of the house of the Lord, that is, a meeting place where people raise their minds to God and find themselves brothers. This church of glass has, in fact, its own language that can be derived from Revelation, where it is said: "*Vidi civitatem sanctam descendentem de coelo*"; "its walls", the Book of Revelation continues, "were of crystal".[16]

This statement was not unique; Montini would go on to entrust further church commissions to modern architects, out of his conviction that:

---

16   Montini, *Discorsi e scritti milanesi (1954-1963)*, II, 2418.

> The Church also presents a novelty and novelty comes within the category of things sacred: when religion is alive, not only does it permit novelty, but it desires it, demands it, seeks it out, knows how to draw it out of the soul. "*Cantate Domino canticum novum*," says the Scripture. And I am here to welcome with open arms everything new that art can bring. I have nothing against novelty, provided that the novelty is not mere whim.[17]

His attitude of openness gave great freedom of expression to architects and artists. He stated,

> We left behind the bridle, we opened all the roads, we admitted all the good experiences. (...) We can tell that we are satisfied with this first experience (...). I refrain from judging and judging myself (...).[18]

At the inauguration of the Sant'Ildefonso parish church [Ill. 8.6], Montini wondered if the building was a work of art, then affirmed that it was:

> Suffice it to consider that it is new and as such represents the search for new expression in art. Yes, a search (...). In this research, original and averse to convention, you can find a gift worthy (...).[19]

The church was designed by Carlo De Carli (1910-1999), not a traditionalist architect by any means. Montini was interested in focusing on the freedom of the artist, not on modern expression. As such, the churches built during his rule are all very different; some, such as San Giovanni Battista alla Creta by Giovanni Muzio (1893-1982), do not in fact abjure modern monumentality. [Ill. 8.7]

Although Montini kept the pastoral, procedural and financial aspects of church building firmly under his control to ensure rapid execution, he also combined a centralisation of decision-making with the widest possible involvement of lay people and lower clergy. He brought a vigorous, long-lasting dynamism to the church-building activities of the diocese, a project that went beyond the mere provision of pastoral infrastructure to have civic, as well as religious, implications. There was a new, trusting openness on the part of the diocese towards the urban modernity of Milan as an industrial city of manual labour. Under Montini, Milan thus became a laboratory of pastoral modernity before the advent of the Second Vatican Council, which Montini also managed and ultimately closed as Pope Paul VI.

---

17 Montini, *Discorsi e scritti milanesi (1954-1963)*, II, 2418.
18 Ibid., IV, 5569.
19 Ibid., I, 1003.

8.6 Interior view from 2000 of the Church of Sant'Ildelfonso (1954-1956), Milan (Carlo De Carli, architect).
[Courtesy of ISAL (Istituto per la Storia dell'Arte Lombarda)]

8.7 Exterior view from 1960 of the church and parish complex San Giovanni Battista alla Creta (1956–1958), Milan (Giovanni Muzio, architect).
[Courtesy of ISAL (Istituto per la Storia dell'Arte Lombarda)]

Enrico Mattei and the Church of Santa Barbara in Metanopoli

Despite Montini's deep personal involvement in the Comitato, he accepted Mattei's strong, pragmatic leadership and allowed him to assume growing authority over the organisation. First, Mattei established a small executive council, transferring to it the powers of the committee; then, he assumed more of its powers for himself. The minutes of the annual plenary sessions of the committee, which Mattei always carefully annotated and passed on to Montini with his recommendations, provide insight into not only the multifaceted nature of the church-building programme, but also Mattei's personal views on the topic and the decisive nature of his managerial style. There were many items to deal with simultaneously: fund-raising campaigns and their results; reviews of churches completed, under construction, awaiting agreement for building contracts or still in the planning stages; property acquisitions and costs (in Milan and elsewhere in the diocese); reports of publicity and promotional activities for new parish centres, including the organisation of New Churches Day; publications, television broadcasts and the setting up of committees to help new and existing parishes; and so on. His idea of Milan's development followed the principles laid out in the city's Piano Regolatore Generale of 1953: a theoretically unlimited growth in the city's geographical size, occurring in phases, through a series of "rings" around the historic centre. While he did not explicitly discuss different models for the parishes, he frequently did stress the need to reduce the size, scope and cost of building projects.

Mattei also showed great interest in the typology and aesthetic expression of the new churches. He argued for the development of a compact church type which he called the "*monoblocco*", consisting of one building containing communal parish facilities on the ground floor or below ground, surmounted by the worship space. As we shall see later, he entrusted a group of young, talented Milanese architects with the task of developing this idea. Only in cases where a sponsor, either private or public, agreed to bear the costs could more "monumental" creations be justified. It is clear, therefore, that Mattei's reflections were guided by efficiency and economy:

> We want to combine, with an industrial mindset, a healthy and appropriate rationalism with economic wisdom (...). We have got to spend the sums we receive well and extremely frugally. From that comes the need for a construction system that is both good value for money and worthy of the task.[20]

Mattei's preference for the "rational" German trend in architecture grew even stronger when he read *Dieci anni di architettura sacra in Italia*, the catalogue of the first international show of sacred art in Bologna in 1955; even though the buildings it described assimilated modern principles, he was critical of their high construction costs.[21] None of those projects, he asserted, adhered to "the healthy Galilean precept of keeping to the simplest and most obvious means of expression".[22] He demanded a method for planning and creating ecclesiastical buildings in a more holistic way instead, encompassing everything from the walls and furniture to the organs and bells, similar to the "holistic conception that Gropius has imposed for civic building works".[23] Following this principle, his vision of a contemporary church was of a high, well-lit, "large rectangular hall", a "modern church which is noble but not costly, which can be finished on the same day it is consecrated and will not quickly become dilapidated".[24] His intervention was not aimed at expressing evaluations of taste. This is demonstrated by the church of Metanopoli, for which he had commissioned the architect Mario Bacciocchi (1902-1974), who was his reference architect, as described further below. The pressure to raise sufficient funds for five churches a year was enormous, highlighting "the shameful disparity between the sacrifice made by poor, humble people every year and what the wealthy producers contribute".[25] [Ill. 8.8]

20 Mattei, "Milano ha bisogno di nuove chiese".
21 Gherardi, Giordani, Lullini, and Trebbi, *Dieci anni di architettura sacra in Italia 1945-1955*. The National Congress on Sacred Architecture was held in Bologna at the Università degli Studi from 23 to 25 September 1955.
22 *Attività del Comitato Nuove Chiese*, 21.
23 Ibid., 22.
24 Ibid., 26.
25 Ibid., 29. The number of letters sent in 1956 was 1,305, increasing steadily each year to reach 4,000 in 1959.

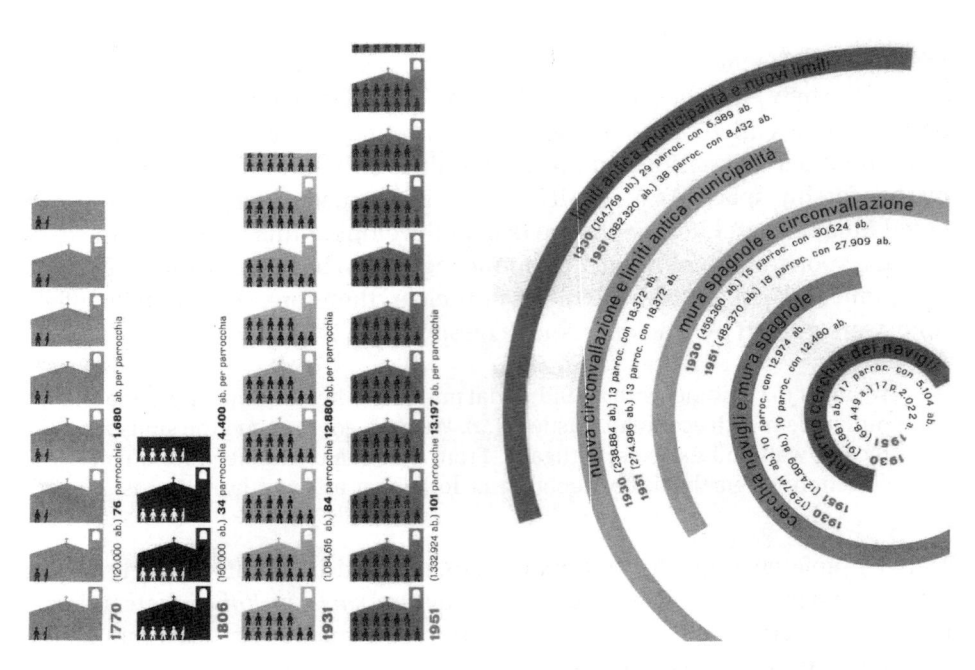

8.8 Graphic rendering of church-building activity throughout the centuries.
[Reproduced from *Attività del Comitato Nuove Chiese* (1958)]

It is perhaps surprising that someone as high-ranking and active as Mattei was able to devote so much time and energy to diocesan work in between his many travels and business meetings. This commitment was not just pragmatic, but also cultural, humanistic and political. As he argued in a committee meeting in 1956:

> It is not just churches we should be building, but buildings which can tell our contemporaries, and above all posterity, that this era (...) has been able to find its own form of language and expression, even in the difficult attempt to express the supernatural world.[26]

And reflecting on the political role of the Church, he said:

> It is on the outskirts of the big cities that the great struggle raging for fifteen years between democracy and totalitarianism will be decided — and we are convinced that the Church must bring all its reserves into play here, engaging its best men in a courageous and warlike vanguard.[27]

Here, Mattei was alluding to a commonly held belief in Catholic thought during the Cold War that the Church could act as the last bulwark against the

26   Ibid., 31.
27   Ibid., 31.

8.9 Church of Santa Barbara (1954) in Metanopoli (now San Donato Milanese, near Milan) (Mario Bacciocchi, architect).
[Courtesy of Archivio Storio ENI]

extreme ideology of communism (and its counter-image, fascism), which was seen as the principal contemporary enemy of the spiritual values and moral principles of the Catholic Church.

Perhaps Mattei's commitment to church building derived from his ambition to not only reshape religion in modern society, but also modernise society according to Christian morality. This became clear in his boldest project of all, the construction of Metanopoli, a company town on the outskirts of Milan built for 1,500 ENI employees and their families. Conceived of by Bacciocchi, a close acquaintance of Mattei's, as a symbol of order, rationality, progress and community, the new company town was distinguished by the high quality of its architecture and orderly city planning, corresponding to an idealistic vision of the relationship between its inhabitants and the company that employed them. Situated close to the main transport arteries around Linate airport — the historic Via Emilia and the new Autostrada del Sole — Metanopoli included not only offices, laboratories and workshops, but also a motel for the company's truck and car drivers, homes for the company's employees, sports facilities, a school and even one of the first large supermarkets in Italy.

Metanopoli catered to not only the material wellbeing of the employees and their families, but also their spiritual needs. To this effect, the new town had its own church, dedicated to Santa Barbara, dominating the only real square of the new settlement. [Ill. 8.9] In typological terms, it recast traditional compositional schemes in a modern architectural guise, with a gabled façade and polychromy recalling historic Tuscan churches. Montini performed the church's consecration ceremony on 3 December 1955 and granted it full status as a parish church shortly before his election as pope in 1963, though it had always been intended as the centre of a new parish.[28] The planning and design of the church remained under Mattei's direct control, as agreements he made with Montini specified. Mattei was thus the only layman to have such power over church architecture in the diocese.[29] He also took personal responsibility for acquiring artworks for both internal and external decoration. He chose high-quality works, mostly by Lombard artists, in agreement with the diocese, ignoring objections from the parish priest, whom he did not consult. It is telling for Mattei's relationship with Montini that even when the latter was away from Milan to attend the Second Vatican Council in Rome, Mattei called upon him for his opinions. Montini referred him back to the diocesan curia, which had oversight according to canon law.[30] Nevertheless, he did intervene personally to resolve other problems, such as the absence of a male *oratorio* next to the church and the need to establish a second parish church in Metanopoli. After some shuffling of property in 1963 between the Società Nazionale Metanodotti (a subsidiary of Mattei's company), the diocese and the parish of Santa Barbara, the district was split into two parishes, with the second accorded a site for a church at its centre dedicated to Sant'Enrico.[31] [Ill. 8.10]

The need to establish a second parish church had been prompted by Metanopoli's rapid population growth, as well as the religious fervour of its

28   Decree establishing the new parish of Santa Barbara, 15 June 1963 (Metanopoli, APSB, rac. I, cart. 4). In fact, the church had assumed that role ever since its consecration (when "quasi-parochial" powers had been conferred upon its priest) in the hopes that an independent parish with clearly defined boundaries would be established in the district.
29   For the sake of completeness, we should mention here that Mattei also commissioned the parish church of Sant'Angela Merici in the Villaggio dei giornalisti (Journalist Village) area of Milan; it was designed by the same architect (Mario Bacciocchi), and some of the same artists (such as the brothers Gio and Arnaldo Pomodoro) were involved. Mattei donated this building — of the *monoblocco* type he promoted — to the diocese as a private citizen in memory of his mother, Angela. Furthermore, churches were also a crucial component of the other company towns constructed by ENI in Ravenna, Gela and Borca di Cadore.
30   Decree establishing the new parish of Santa Barbara, 15 June 1963 (Metanopoli, APSB, rac. I, cart. 4).
31   Sources: deed of sale, 5 September 1963; deed of donation, 4 June 1963 (Metanopoli, APSB, rac. I, cart. Documenti più importanti). In 1963 the Metanopoli company sold the entire building complex, consisting of the church of Santa Barbara, the bell tower, the baptistery, the parsonage and an annexe on the site, to the Opera Pia delle Chiese e Case Parrocchiali Povere della Diocesi di Milano, respecting the provisions laid out in resolution no. 226 (9 October 1962) of the Opera Pia and decree no. 36243 of the Prefect of Milan (18 February 1963) and a resolution from the Board of Directors of SNAM S.p.A. (27 March 1963). The entire patrimony was subsequently donated by the Opera Pia to the expanding Santa Barbara Church in Metanopoli on 4 June 1963 (notary deed of donation drawn up by notary Alessandro Guasti on 4 June 1963; Metanopoli, APSB, rac. I, cart. Documenti più importanti).

8.10 Exterior view from 2015 of the Church of Sant'Enrico (1961-1966) in Bolgiano, Metanopoli (now San Donato Milanese, near Milan) (Ignazio Gardella, architect).
[Photograph by Ferdinando Zanzottera, 2021]

population. From 2,663 inhabitants in 1951, the population rose to 5,802 in 1958 and 10,456 in 1960, and the parish's annual reports reveal a vital community with a prolific social life and strong sense of collective identity.[32] Montini purposely left the faithful under the care of a single priest, as a way of unifying the quite divergent traditions and social backgrounds of the approximately 1,500 families living in Metanopoli. Mattei also invested in the social life of the company town as an overlap to its religious programme, promoting, for example, the establishment of charities, health facilities, a canteen within the *oratorio* and a parish cinema. There were also sewing courses and, in response to the young community's needs, as well as the international nature of ENI's activities, an English language course. Furthermore, there was a branch of the Associazione Cattolica Lavoratori Italiani (ACLI, Catholic Association of Italian Workers) and a number of co-operative associations providing professional training. Reading was also encouraged: Catholic newspapers were delivered to homes and a small public library was established. A civic committee concerned with aspects of social life and groups that discussed and monitored national politics and electoral results in Metanopoli and its surroundings were also set up.[33] Impressed with this combined civic and religious activity that closely corresponded to his conception of the ideal parish, Montini provided

32   Metanopoli, APSB, rac. I, cart. Inchiesta sulla catechesi, Statistica, Monitor. Devozioni, Consiglio pastorale, Consulta parrocchiale.
33   Metanopoli, APSB, rac. I, cart. Relazioni fine anno 1956-1959.

an extra assistant for the *oratorios* and, in agreement with ENI, entrusted a congregation of nuns with the task of running the school, the nursery and the female *oratorio*. Thanks to all this effort, a critical collective consciousness and religious zeal seems to have developed rapidly in Metanopoli; on their own initiative, for example, groups of inhabitants undertook to analyse and discuss the documents of the Second Vatican Council, posting them on walls for all to read. After his election as Pope Paul VI, Cardinal Montini remained fond of Metanopoli: he gave an audience to ENI employees on 29 March 1964, in which he referred to the town as a "quiet and picturesque corner of the Lombard countryside" and a modern Catholic settlement that suggested a model for the "new times to come".[34]

The Activities of the Milanese Clerical Offices

After the reconstruction phase that followed the Second World War, the Comitato Pro Templi Nuovi, the original curial entity presided over by Schuster himself, started meeting again in May 1950. It was headed by Monsignor Vittore Maini (1886-1959), who devised two new organisations that gradually took over the committee: the citizens' committee discussed above (the Comitato per le Nuove Chiese, which served as the Archbishop's council to study the complex issues related to new churches), as well as a new organism, the Ufficio per le Nuove Chiese (Office for New Churches), in 1952. The diocese thus now had two organisations founded in the final years of Schuster's administration that gained pre-eminence during Montini's reign: the *committee* for new churches, with engineer Mattei as president, which was composed primarily of laymen and acted independently, also from a civic point of view; and the *office* for new churches, comprising mainly priests and chaired originally by Monsignor Maini and then, after his death in 1959, Monsignor Aldo Milani (life dates unknown). The incredible flowering of new churches in the Montini period can be attributed to the power dynamics and operational agreements between these two committees. Whereas Montini and Mattei were the most visible actors in Milan's church-building campaign, the work carried out behind the scenes by Monsignor Maini, who until his death in 1959 assured continuity between Schuster's and Montini's tenures, and his successor, Monsignor Milani, should also be considered. Each headed the Ufficio per le Nuove Chiese, which assumed all the responsibilities of a building patron: acquisition of land, choice of designers, project financing, monitoring

---

34   Paul VI, quoted in Zani, ed., *Paolo VI e il mondo del lavoro*, 42-43.

of construction and so forth.[35] A significant indicator of the intense working relationship between first Maini and then Milani and Montini is perhaps the number of audiences the latter gave them: no fewer than 276 for Maini and 115 for Milani — numbers that also indicate the importance Montini accorded to the church-building programme.[36]

Two sources give us an insight into the procedural side of the campaign: first, a summary of the Comitato's work between 1937 and 1953 compiled by Maini for Mattei's appointment in 1953, entitled *Un problema urgente della più grande Milano*; and second, the logbook of the Milanese curia's activities from 1950 to 1960, edited by Milani.[37] In the former, Maini offers a short but effective survey that explains how the transformations of Milan in the immediate aftermath of the Second World War and the roles and objectives assumed by the Church in building new churches and parish structures relate to Italian urban planning law. He shows how the Church was able to take advantage of the existing legal framework by building public housing so as to acquire state subsidies for new churches. This approach, which Montini adopted, thus recognised parish churches as public buildings.[38] Maini further highlights the most important aspects of the city affecting church building, such as the significant reconstruction in central areas after the wartime destruction; the surge in post-war immigration, resulting in an uncontrolled population increase; the striking phenomenon of population exodus towards city outskirts as a result of the war damage; and the planned zoning of the centre. Finally, he explains how the Comitato had proved the value of its planning activities in three ways: by working closely with the Municipality of Milan and the various public housing bodies to acquire church sites; by formulating a plan for completely redefining parish boundaries; and by developing a new conception of the parish.

These policies were largely retained under Montini and Mattei and later further developed by Milani in collaboration with the architects Vittorio Gandolfi (1919-1999) and Antonello Vincenti (°1926) on the basis of emerging re-

---

35 Crippa and Santi, "G.B. Montini e le nuove chiese di Milano", 35. In Italy, the relationship between church and state is subject to specific legislation: although parishes are private subjects, there is a public use of churches, so churches are always open to everyone.
36 We should add that Montini sent quick notes to Maini and Milani on a daily basis, pointing out urgent problems and asking for information and clarification on the most wide-ranging subjects; these are included in the ASDM's files.
37 Maini, ed., *Un problema urgente della più grande Milano*; Milani, ed., *Le nuove chiese di Milano 1950-1960*. It is also worth mentioning the special issue of *Fede et Arte* edited by Milani ("Il cantiere dell'Arcivescovo di Milano").
38 The main laws pertaining to this were: 1150, 8-7-1942, for the Piano Regolatore Generale (in which parish churches were registered as public buildings); 240, 17-4-1948; 154, 1-3-1945; 43, 28-2-1949; 2522, 18-12-1952. On the relationship between the Church and the Italian state, we refer the reader to the recent *Codice dei Beni Culturali e del Paesaggio* (Code on Cultural Heritage and Landscape), 2004.

search in the fields of sociology (especially of religion), urban planning and architectural history.[39] Milani and his team also sought greater publicity; they presented their findings, for example, at the international conference on parish planning and church building at the World's Fair in Brussels on 8 May 1958 and in public meetings held in Milan and Rome.[40]

All this effort seems to have paid off: unlike the debate about the crisis of the parish going on at that time in Northern Europe (led by scholars such as François Houtart), Maini and his team were able to report encouraging results from 1955 onwards. The new churches immediately filled up with worshippers of all ages; social and associative life in the new parishes was thriving; and teenagers and young people found safe spaces for educational and recreational activities. The extension of parish area by 10,000 square metres proved ideal, though these larger parishes were served by increasingly modest, rapidly executed church buildings. The focus on the relationship between parish and district was also clearly having beneficial results. Montini, for his part, expressed his support by calling upon various Catholic associations (such as the Azione Cattolica) to make donations; stimulating the diocesan clergy to construct a church dedicated to Saint John Vianney, or the Curé d'Ars, patron saint of the apostolate; and encouraging the religious orders to take on pastoral duties. This was needed to solve one of the major negative factors threatening this positive momentum, namely a shortage of priests due to a decline in vocations.

The second source referred to above, namely the curia's logbook between 1950 and 1960, gives us an insight into the criteria that were applied for determining the establishment of new parishes and churches and how their distribution across the territory was decided. This was based on the *sestieri*, the six historic subdivisions arranged like rings around the city centre of Milan, and there are brief files presenting temporary chapels, domestic churches or *domus* (rooms bought or rented in civic buildings), prefabricated churches and thirty-four completely new churches. Summaries of the layouts of the *sestieri* show that the new parishes were more densely concentrated in areas that were expanding more rapidly. The diocese aimed for its churches to have an average capacity of 1,000 to 1,500 seats by the end of the 1950s, while each parish catered to the needs of roughly 15,000 inhabitants. It is also evident that a large number of engineers and architects were involved, some of them prominent figures in the architecture of that period.

Over the years, Mattei became increasingly involved in the practical aspects of church building, expanding his role as president of the Comitato. Whereas initially his main responsibility was fund-raising, he soon assumed

---

39 Milani, *Nuove chiese per nuovi quartieri*.
40 Milani, *La parrocchia nella realtà del quartiere*. Also: Bressan and Maffeis, eds., *Montini Arcivescovo di Milano*.

full authority over the entire operation. He endeavoured to obtain for the Comitato a legal status of its own, in order to be able to negotiate directly with public and private bodies (e.g. for the acquisition of land). Nevertheless, despite the new, efficient structure of the diocesan services and the positive outcome of their efforts, momentum seemed to wane in the mid-1960s. While this decline may be attributed to a complex set of social and cultural factors, the disappearance of the two personalities who only ten years earlier had given Milan's church-building campaign such a decisive impulse was significant. Not only did Cardinal Montini leave for the Vatican on his election as Pope Paul VI in 1963, but Mattei died suddenly on the night of 27 March 1962 when his private plane crashed near Linate Airport.

The Centro Studi per l'Architettura della Comunità Cristiana di Milano

In the scholarship on the church-building activities of the Milanese curia under Montini, the involvement of architects, engineers and artists has received scant attention to date. It was in large part thanks to Mattei's drive that the Comitato was able to appoint some of the best architects then working in Milan, people who were deeply invested — personally, as well as professionally — in sacred architecture and its relationship to modernity. The extent to which their typological, technological and aesthetic choices might have been informed by ecclesiological and liturgical trends has not yet been adequately established. Nevertheless, various parish files in the diocesan archives suggest at least two diocesan bodies that could be said to have mediated between clergy and architects, namely the Commissione Diocesana per l'Arte Sacra (Diocesan Commission for Sacred Art) and the Centro Studi per l'Architettura della Comunità Cristiana (Study Centre for the Architecture of the Christian Community). The role of the former body, founded in 1927 under Cardinal Eugenio Tosi (1864-1929), was to check the liturgical and aesthetic consistency of church designs and their iconographic programme. Little is known about its directives prior to the Second Vatican Council (when the commission was reformed), and the scant available sources suggest that its approach was rather pragmatic and "ad hoc", thus rather empirical.[41]

The Centro Studi per l'Architettura della Comunità Cristiana, meanwhile, was inspired by the Centro di Studio e d'Informazione per l'Architettura Sacra in Bologna (Study and Information Centre for Sacred Architecture in Bologna, established on Cardinal Lercaro's initiative) and its influential magazine, *Chiesa e Quartiere*. Mattei helped set up this new study centre in Milan

---

41 Santi, "Il Ruolo della committenza nella diocesi Ambrosiana", 34–35. So far, we do not know the names of its members, nor have the minutes of its meetings been found.

in 1957 and appointed Vittorio Gandolfi (his personal secretary's brother) as its head.[42] The principal aim was to develop typological solutions for planning parish infrastructure capable of accommodating a complex programme in limited space that was compact in volume and low in cost. The Milan study centre's goals went beyond the mere development of economical prototypes, however. The intention of its members was:

> to contribute towards defining modern thought on sacred architecture and the welfare structures connected to it and to formulate new ideas and concrete proposals for the Diocese of Milan, thereby creating a new consciousness of the problem using various cultural activities to spread awareness.[43]

These activities would include a series of monographs on specific architectural problems; a specialist library; a permanent but constantly evolving exhibition on recent work, open to all; participation in conferences, exhibitions, shows and competitions; educational courses at seminaries; and last but not least, an active relationship with artists and artisans working in the liturgical sphere.

Under the auspices of the newly formed study centre, an existing informal group of architects, who had already been working together to contribute to the development of the diocesan church-building programme, became formalised on more ambitious footing. In 1954, for example, after hearing an inspiring speech by Mattei, several of its future members had independently devised prototypes of a so-called *Domus Ecclesia* suitable for dense urban areas that combined the worship hall and rooms for community life in a single, compact volume. This was the *monoblocco* referred to above, which became the basis for a parish centre prototype in the diocese that was designed for a rectangular plot of 1,200 m² (compared to the 10,000 m² that had been considered standard by the curia until then) to serve a community of about 20,000. Luigi Caccia Dominioni (1913-2016), for example, stacked the entire programme in one rectangular building of three storeys. It had a male *oratorio* and gym on the ground floor; a church and sacristy on the first floor; and a small cinema, meeting rooms, the female *oratorio* and lodgings for the parish priest on the top floor. The vertical circulation was arranged around the bell tower.

The Castiglioni brothers, Livio (1911-1979), Pier Giacomo (1913-1968) and Achille (1918-2002), meanwhile, placed the worship hall between two linear structures accommodating the parish offices. This scheme was then adapted to provide four possible variations in volume, ingeniously presented in a tai-

---

42 Among its members: Lodovico Barbiano di Belgiojoso, Luigi Caccia Dominioni, Pier Giacomo Castiglioni, Carlo De Carli, Luigi Figini, Ignazio Gardella, Vico Magistretti, Mario Tedeschi and Enrico Villa.

43 De Carli, "Il tema architettonico della chiesa negli episcopati di Schuster e Montini", 55.

lor-made package which took account of the wide range of contexts for which the scheme could be used. It provided the basis for the church of San Gabriele Arcangelo in Mater Dei (1956-1960). The church was being built along Viale Monza in a heavily urbanised area of the city that the Comitato had decided badly needed one, and the scheme provided an intelligent response to the limited sizes of building plots available in the area.[44] Confronted with the impossibility of designing the church as a freestanding building, the architects harked back to the idea of the *chiesa domestica*, with the church occupying one portion of the quadrangular site, in the centre of which is a tree-lined courtyard. The architectural plan consists of two orthogonal wings: one, rectangular and aligned with the street, houses the parish offices; the other, the church, has a less regular shape and extends back into the site. A flight of stairs acts as a hinge between these two blocks, providing access to the elevated churchyard above and the basement below, with the latter including a conference room.

Gandolfi's model solution was designed with a similar concept, stacking the various parts of the programme above one another. He adopted his own scheme in designing the church of San Francesco di Sales ten years later. It provides yet another striking example of a refined integration into the dense urban fabric of Milan's historic centre. With an L-shaped plan sited on a rectangular plot, it manages to maintain the integrity of the street façade, while distinguishing itself from its surroundings with loggias on the upper part of the building and a portico on the ground floor, sheltering the entrance. The portion of the building that faces Via della Commenda has three floors with parish offices and residences. The other wing of the building contains a gym in the basement, a theatre and service areas. The church proper (with a tennis court on the roof) is on the ground floor and is connected to street level by a series of stairs and ramps, which also form a sort of protected churchyard.[45]

There was keen public and professional interest in these experiments: the *Domus Ecclesia* schemes and the design for San Gabriele Arcangelo in Mater Dei were published in *Dieci anni di architettura sacra in Italia* and formed the occasion for lively exchanges on the topic of modern church building between the Milanese architects and their Bolognese colleagues, which resulted in some of the former being invited to design new parish complexes in Bologna.[46] *Chiesa e Quartiere* devoted a themed issue to the topic of building churches in the dense urban fabric that featured designs from both Bologna and Milan, comments by Lercaro and Montini, and contributions by Italian and international artists, architects, art critics, liturgists and philosophers.

44 Milani, ed., *Le nuove chiese di Milano 1950-1960*, 35.
45 The building is discussed in *Parametro*, 122 (1983), 36-37.
46 The only one to be fully realised was Vittorio Gandolfi's design for the parish church of Sant'Andrea Apostolo. See also *Parametro* 122 (1983), 34-35.

For Montini, it must have felt as if his efforts were paying off when he asked rhetorically: "Is this the birth of a new 'golden century' of sacred architecture? Are the new construction techniques entering the sacred enclosure?"[47] That golden age was not to be, however: the study centre ceased its activities after only a few meetings, despite having grown organically out of the enthusiastic contributions of architects to the diocese's work.

Conclusion

In the eight years that he headed the Diocese of Milan, Montini inaugurated or consecrated no fewer than thirty-four churches of the over one hundred built during his tenure. After Montini was elected Pope Paul VI, both the Comitato and the Ufficio per le Nuove Chiese continued under his successor, Cardinal Giovanni Colombo (1902-1992), who consecrated another dozen churches left unfinished by his predecessor in the next few years. Soon after that, however, the Comitato stopped meeting. The social climate was changing, but more importantly, the adventurous, self-confident spirit of modernity propelled by Mattei, Maini and Montini seems to have disappeared: as in other dioceses across Europe, the new keywords became "simplicity", "modesty" and "prefabrication" – reflecting the protective fears of the clergy and the economic hesitancy of the laity. The Comitato published a small book on Montini the year he became pope, *G.B. Montini. Le sue chiese*, as an homage to his extraordinary commitment.[48] This was followed a couple of years later by *Ventidue chiese per ventidue concili*, a collection of essays related to Montini's initiative to build a crown of twenty-two churches around Milan, one for every council that had been held in the past — a Herculean undertaking meant "as a token of the secular and universal history of Catholicism and to reflect it experientially in a living religious event, as a synthesis of past history and foretelling of that to come".[49]

Yet although most of these churches were eventually built, and Montini's pastoral policy was celebrated by his successors, his work was not methodically followed or developed. There was no real implementation of his criteria, for which, in any case, he had only sketched out proposals. Montini's role in the Second Vatican Council, both as a cardinal and as pope, has inevitably dominated assessments of his innovations in the Church. Similarly the many dramatic events that shook Italian society in the 1960s (including the mysterious death of Mattei) have preoccupied histories of this period, to the neglect of Montini's attempts to test out, in terms adequate to the times, a renewed

47   *L'Art sacré*, 1-2 (1959), 4.
48   *G.B. Montini. Le sue Chiese*.
49   Gnech, *Ventidue Chiese per ventidue Concili*.

evangelism rooted in the old territorial principle of the diocese and the parish.[50] Meanwhile, Mattei's work for the diocese was later almost completely forgotten in a kind of *damnatio memoriae*, as opinions turned against his controversial personality and the historiography of that turbulent period lacked the detachment that is only now possible with our distance from events. Much has changed in Milan since the 1960s: the building and population density is now high even along the periphery, and the phenomenon of general secularisation, though perhaps not as pronounced as in Northern Europe, is increasingly evident. The parish landscape is changing accordingly. More and more of the old churches in the historic core of the city are becoming redundant, while a redistribution of parishes (through unification) is under way.

As far as Mattei's involvement in diocesan matters is concerned, our research suggests that he acted on his own entrepreneurial instinct and that Montini, pragmatically and also daringly, placed complete trust in him. The Cardinal appreciated the value of the businessman's expertise at an urgent moment of sudden transformation in social and economic conditions. Montini left an enduring ecclesiastical and cultural mark on his diocese, and his great pastoral project was astounding in its breadth and effectiveness — as testified to by the lively activity in the parishes he established in the suburbs, which are still characterised by a strong sense of community.

There are many aspects of this church-building campaign that await further investigation. Sufficient evidence has yet to come to light to explain the operational roles of members of the curia in organising its offices and its relationships with the sacred art commission, which included prominent architectural figures. The dynamics of the relationships between the curia and parishes and the local government administration also require further research: so far, we have found only inconsistencies, indicating that they were sometimes in agreement and sometimes distanced from each other. The relationships between religious and lay members of the parish centres and the curia at various points when the buildings were under construction, first taken into use and ultimately in regular use would benefit from detailed study. We wonder, too, what the sociological consequences of this experiment were on the religious ideas and practices of the Catholic population itself, since documentation tends only to reinforce an official view of developments in the Church. Finally, the Milanese story ought to be placed in a wider context, both by comparing it with what happened during the same period in larger, more dynamic Italian archdioceses (such as Bologna and Turin) and by connecting it with the directives issued by the Vatican in that period. So far, texts both in the main diocesan archive and in parish archives reveal controls on the building work through links between the diocese and the Pontificia Commissione per l'Arte

---

50 Routhier, Bressan, and Vaccaro, eds., *Da Montini a Martini: il Vaticano II a Milano*.

Sacra in Italia (Papal Commission for Sacred Art in Italy), highlighting the role played by the latter organisation.

While these processes require further study to fully understand their causes and effects, at least some insight has been provided here into the current state of research on modern church building in Milan under Montini. Montini's pastoral project can be considered a coherent whole, and the new churches are the concrete evidence of this project in the urban landscape. Though often architecturally exceptional, their historical value is as a contribution to an experiment the parish had to first implement and then manage, bringing a particular kind of critical self-awareness to the diocese. Furthermore, Montini devised this coherent project in positive relationship to the period in which he lived. His modernity emerges in the rationality and efficiency of his aims and in his use of language to motivate others to achieve them; in his awareness of the limited range of action of the Church; in his recognition of contemporary debates about social, cultural and economic problems; and in his realistic approach to urban, architectural and artistic themes. Montini's ability to co-opt bureaucratic structures and talented individuals, secular or otherwise, into the work of the diocese and involve them in his project was also fundamentally important to its achievement. This meant continuity with Schuster's administrative structures and the clergymen employed in them; the involvement of Mattei and the large field of operations he could open up; and the valuing of artists' and architects' research. This ability to involve others elicited strong, concrete, passionate responses from those he called upon in one-to-one correspondence. For this reason, a strong consonance developed between Montini and his colleagues, starting from a shared empathy for the problems of the city, parish communities and modern life in general. This consonance would soon find its expression, not just at a diocesan level, but at that of the Roman Catholic Church as a whole, in Paul VI's preface to *Gaudium et spes*, the Second Vatican Council's Pastoral Constitution on the Church in the Modern World.[51]

---

51 Vatican II, Pastoral Constitution *Gaudium et spes*, N. 1.

BIBLIOGRAPHY

Archives

Metanopoli, Archivio Parrocchiale Santa Barbara (APSB)
Milan, Archivio Storico Diocesano di Milano (ASDM)

Published sources

Adornato, Giselda. "L'episcopato milanese". In: Xenio Toscani, ed. *Paolo VI. Una biografia*. Rome: Studium, 2014, 289-304.
Attività del Comitato Nuove Chiese (1958). Milan: Arti grafiche Cisalpine, 1959.
"L'attività del Comitato per le nuove Chiese nell'Archidiocesi di Milano". *Rivista Diocesana Milanese*, 3 (1954).
Barazzetta, Giulio, ed. *La chiesa di vetro di Angelo Mangiarotti, Bruno Morassutti, Aldo Favini. La storia e il restauro*. Milan: Electa, 2015.
Bottoni, Piero. "Chiesa al Quartiere QT8". *Diocesi di Milano*, 8-9, 1961, 466-471.
Bressan, Angelo and Maffeis, Luca, eds. *Montini Arcivescovo di Milano*. Rome-Brescia: Studium-Istituto Paolo VI, 2017.
Cripp,a M.A., "L'esperimento pastorale del card. Giovanni Battista Montini nella diocesi ambrosiana". In: L. Lazzaroni, ed., *La diocesi di Milano e le nuove chiese 1964-2014*. Milan 2016,Centro Ambrosiano, 61-96.
Crippa, M.A. and Santi G. "G.B. Montini e le nuove chiese di Milano". In: G. Gresleri. *Parole e linguaggio dell'archittettura religiosa 1963-1983: venti anni di realizzazioni in Italia*. Monza: Faenza, 1983, 31-47.
De Carli, Cecilia, ed. *Le nuove chiese della diocesa di Milano 1945-1993*. Milan: Vita e Pensiero, 1994.
De Carli, Cecilia. "Il tema architettonico della chiesa negli episcopati di Schuster e Montini". In: Cecilia De Carli. *Le nuove chiese della diocesa di Milano 1945-1993*. Milan: Vita e Pensiero, 1994, 39-64.
G.B. Montini. Le sue Chiese. Milan: Comitato per le Nuove Chiese, 1964.
Gherardi, Luciano; Giordani, Pier Luigi; Lullini, Luciano; and Trebbi, Giorgio. *Dieci anni di architettura sacra in Italia 1945-1955*. Bologna: Edizione dell'Ufficio Tecnico Organizzativo Arcivescovile, 1956.
Gnech C., ed. *Ventidue chiese per ventidue concili*. Milan: Comitato per le nuove chiese, 1969.
Grandi, Maurizio and Pracchi, Attilio. *Guida all'architettura moderna*. Bologna: Zanichelli, 1980.
Li Vigni, Benito. *Enrico Mattei: l'uomo del futuro che inventò la rinascita italiana*. Rome: Editori Riuniti, 2014.
Maini, Vittore, ed. *Un problema urgente della più grande Milano*. Milan: Comitato per le Nuove Chiese, 1953.
Mattei, Enrico. "Milano ha bisogno di nuove chiese". In: *Attività del Comitato Nuove Chiese (1954-1955)*. Rome: IGAP, 1956, 25-26.
Milani, Aldo. "Il cantiere dell'Arcivescovo di Milano". *Fede e Arte*, 1962, 3, 216-223.
Milani, Aldo. *La parrocchia nella realtà del quartiere*. Milan: Comitato Nuove Chiese, 1961.
Milani, Aldo. *Nuove chiese per nuovi quartieri*. Milan: Arcivescovado di Milano, 1960.
Milani, Aldo, ed. *Le nuove chiese di Milano 1950-1960*. Milan: Comitato per le Nuove Chiese, 1962.
"Miracle à Milan". *L'Art sacré*, Sept.-Oct. 1959.
La Missione di Milano 1957. Atti e documenti, Arcivescovado di Milano. Milan: Ufficio Studi dell'Arcivescovado di Milano, 1959.
Montini, Giovanni Battista. *Discorsi e scritti milanesi (1954-1963)*. 4 volumes. Brescia: Istituto Paolo VI, 1997.
Morini Raffaele. *Enrico Mattei, Il partigiano che sfidò le sette sorelle*. Milan: Mursia, 2011.
Nobili, Elena. *Ildefonso Schuster e il rinnovamento Cattolico (1880-1929)*. Milan: Guerini, 2010.
Routhier, Gilles; Bressan, Luca and Vaccaro, Luciano, eds. *Da Montini a Martini: il Vaticano II a Milano*. 2 volumes. Brescia: Morcelliana, 2013.
Rumi, Giorgio. "La Missione di Milano: oltre i confini della tradizione". In: Luciano Vaccaro, ed. *Il cristiano laico. L'eredità dell'arcivescovo Montini*. Brescia: Morcelliana, 2004, 169-176.
Santi, G. "Il Ruolo della committenza nella diocesi Ambrosiana". In: Cecilia De Carli. *Le nuove chiese della diocesa di Milano 1945-1993*. Milan: Vita e Pensiero, 1994, 27-38.
Toscani, Xenio, ed. *Paolo VI. Una biografia*. Roma: Studium, 2014.
Winninger, Paul. *Construire des Églises. Les dimensions des Paroisses et les contradictions de l'apostolat dans les villes*. Paris: Cerf, 1957.
Zani, R., ed. *Paolo VI e il mondo del lavoro*. Brescia: Ufficio diocesano di Pastorale Sociale della Diocesi di Brescia, s.d.

9
RECONSTRUCTING THE DIOCESE OF BARCELONA
PARISH REFORM AND CHURCH BUILDING UNDER MONSIGNOR MODREGO CASAUS FROM 1943 TO 1967

ALBA ARBOIX-ALIÓ AND SVEN STERKEN

Similar to most cities in Europe, the historic core of Barcelona developed through the seventeenth century around parish churches that formed the spatial, religious and social centre of each area. That paradigm changed in modern times as new neighbourhoods were built around factories or planned on the drawing board. Yet, in Barcelona, we find that churches continued to serve an anchoring function, with over a third of the city's parish churches having been built in the twentieth century, mostly after the Spanish Civil War (1936-1939).[1] It is our theory that this pattern had perhaps less to do with the proverbial Spanish piety than with a specific interaction between politics, religion and urban development. In the context of post-war Spain, and Barcelona in particular, this comes down to studying the interplay between nationalism, Catholicism and architectural modernism, as embodied, respectively, by the figures of the dictator Francisco Franco (1892-1975), Archbishop Gregorio Modrego Casaus (1890-1972) and a group of Catalan modernist architects called Grup R.

The authoritarian climate of the post-war years and the close connections between church and state created a favourable context for church building. Indeed, Modrego managed to build no fewer than ninety-three new churches

1   Out of the 132 existing parish churches in Barcelona today, 56 have been built since 1952, excluding restorations, rebuilds and the like. For a quantitative survey, see Gomez Val, *La Construcción de templos parroquiales en Barcelona entre 1952 y 2000*, 35, 123. On the impact of the churches on the contemporary morphological structure of Barcelona, see: Arboix-Alió, *Església i ciutat. El paper dels temples parroquials en la construcció de Barcelona*, 2016.

throughout the Catalan diocese during his reign (1943-1967).[2] Perhaps surprisingly, quite a few of these were designed by modernist architects, which seems to suggest that despite the general conservative climate of the day, there was an opportunity for typological and liturgical renewal. We seek to unravel this alleged contradiction by looking at Modrego's take on modernising his diocese and focusing on two flagship developments that arose under his tenure, namely the El Congrés neighbourhood and the modernist estate of Montbau.

Modrego, the Housing Crisis and the 1953 Comarcal Plan

Although Spain remained neutral during the Second World War, it should not be forgotten that just prior to that, the country had suffered from the devastating Spanish Civil War, a military revolt against the Republican government of Spain supported by conservative elements in the country. When an initial military coup failed to win control of the entire country, a bloody civil war ensued, fought with great ferocity on both sides. The Nationalists, as the rebels were called, received aid from Fascist Italy and Nazi Germany. The Republicans, on the other hand, received aid from the Soviet Union, as well as from the International Brigades, composed of volunteers from Europe and the United States.[3] After the war, Franco seized power and installed a regime that can best be characterised as conservative, authoritarian, nationalist and, above all, based on Catholic faith and morals. One of the constants that defined the ideological coordinates of the new regime was, in fact, that of an "official religiosity". The bombast of the following statement by Franco at the instalment ceremony for the new papal nuncio in Spain, Federico Tedeschini (1873-1959), in 1938 leaves no doubt as to the relationship between church and state under the new regime:

> Most Reverend Eminence: You can assure His Holiness that it was neither Spain nor true Spaniards who, obeying foreign directives, burned the temples of the Lord, martyred His ministers and implacably destroyed, with

---

2   Muñoz et al., *Gregorio Modrego Casaus*, 216.
3   There is abundant literature on the Spanish Civil War and its manifold dimensions. See, for example, Preston, *A Concise History of the Spanish Civil War*; Forrest, *The Spanish Civil War*; Ealham and Richards, eds., *The splintering of Spain: cultural history and the Spanish Civil War, 1936-1939*. On the role of the Catholic Church in this conflict, see, amongst others, Callahan, "The Evangelization of Franco's 'New Spain'"; Raguer, *Gunpowder and Incense: The Catholic Church and the Spanish Civil War*. On the situation in Catalonia, see Dowling, "The Catholic Church in Catalonia. From Cataclysm in the Civil War to the "Euphoria" of the 1950s".

unprecedented viciousness, all that in our country represented the manifestation of culture and expression of the Catholic faith.[4]

In other words, Franco presented himself as the protector of Catholicism in Spain. To this aim, he claimed the so-called Privilege of Presentation that previously belonged to the Spanish Crown; in the event of an episcopal vacancy, the regime would propose six possible candidates to the Holy See. The pope, in turn, would chose three of them, of which Franco would pick his favourite.[5] Although the Holy See initially disavowed his demand, it did eventually recognise this principle in the Concordat of 1941; and with Franco now having the first and last word about who would be heading the Spanish dioceses, he was de facto steering the course of the Spanish Church.[6]

Modrego, who headed the Catalan diocese between 1943 and 1967, was the type of bishop Franco preferred: self-confident, vigorous, conservative and loyal. He can perhaps best be described as a moderate whose conciliatory posture helped rebuild the Diocese of Barcelona. Nevertheless, Modrego was a man full of contradictions. On the one hand, he is generally considered a champion of *nacionalcatolicismo* — a term evoking the myth that Spanish history and identity were essentially Catholic and intertwined, a connection which under Franco translated into the equation of faith with patriotism. Or, in other words, "an irreligious person could simply not call himself Spanish".[7] On the other hand, at times he seemed to distance himself from the regime. This may have had to do with the fact that Franco's Falangists had killed sixteen members of his family during the Civil War. Moreover, previous to his appointment in Barcelona, he had been the auxiliary bishop to a Catalan cardinal, Isidre Gomà i Tomàs (1869-1940) — which might explain why he never pressed charges against clergy who spoke Catalan instead of Spanish even though the regime prohibited it.

The challenges Modrego faced during his tenure were numerous and considerable. The years of the Franco dictatorship (1939-1975) were characterised by unbridled urban growth and the massive construction of cheap public housing to absorb the migration from surrounding rural areas to Barcelona, whose population rose from 1.3 million to 1.8 million between 1950 and 1970. Despite the fact that as early as 1945, a commission had been created to halt the territorial imbalance resulting from the massive interior migration, the uncontrolled expansion of the suburbs continued relentlessly. This consisted primarily of illegal, self-built housing settlements (a phenomenon referred

---

4   Franco's response to Pius XI's apostolic nuncio (1938, June the 24th), in: *Iglesia, Estado y Movimiento Nacional*, 32. Unless otherwise noted, all translations are the authors' own.
5   *Acta Apostolicae Sedis*, 33, in Muñoz et al., *Gregorio Modrego Casaus*, 157.
6   Ibid.; Martí, *Historia de las Diócesis Españolas. Vol 2*, 356.
7   Muñoz et al., *Gregorio Modrego Casaus*, 158; "National Catholicism".

to as *barraquisme* in Catalan). Thus arose the 1953 Plan Comarcal (Regional Plan), an attempt to integrate the city with the neighbouring municipalities and satisfy the strong demand for housing, while simultaneously curbing real estate speculation and improving the urban environment. Overseen by José Soteras Mauri (1907-1989), the influential municipal architect, it was the first general urban plan for Barcelona since that developed by Ildefons Cerdà in 1859 for Barcelona's urban expansion.[8] It quickly became apparent, however, that the plan was more of a visionary document than an effective planning tool — one of its major shortcomings residing in a consistent underestimation of the demographic changes the city was facing. Although the plan acquired legal status through the Urban Planning Act of 1956, its impact was de facto nullified by city administrators such as Mayor Josep Porcioles (1904-1993), who during his long tenure (1957-1973), bypassed any legal framework if it stood in his way and cut the budget for parks, culture, sports and education to a minimum. Whereas under Porcioles's tenure, a staggering 700,000 housing units were built (accounting for almost seventy per cent of the current housing stock in the city), the basic standards and regulations of the 1953 plan were systematically disregarded; much-needed amenities for recreation, sports and education were cut back on or abandoned altogether. A major actor in this field was the Patronat Municipal de l'Habitatge (PMH, Municipal Housing Board), which developed large-scale housing estates such as Montbau (1958-1961), Besós (1959-1960) and Canyelles (1974).

To counterbalance the excesses of the real estate sector and developers, the city council proposed an ambitious Pla general metropolità (Metropolitan Master Plan) in 1966 (encompassing no fewer than 163 municipalities, it would only be finalized in 1976). This sought to reconcile profitability with qualitative urban development and rebalance the distribution of industry and residences over the territory; again however, its guiding nature did not imply a practical realisation.[9] It can therefore safely be stated that much of Barcelona's explosive growth in the 1960s occurred without much effective planning. The city morphed into a disorderly urban agglomeration where social segregation and urban poverty became everyday realities. Its laissez-faire policy, which benefited unbridled speculation, led to and prolonged conditions of substantial material disadvantage and inequality that would eventually spawn an urban-based critique of the regime.[10]

---

8   The plan was published in *Cuadernos de Arquitectura*, (1953) 15-16. See also Soteras, "Barcelona y el Plan Cerdá". For a good introduction, see <https://historyofbarcelona.weebly.com/general-plan.html> (accessed 24/06/2019). Soteras is almost forgotten today, but he was a very prominent figure in the Barcelona of the Franco era. For biographic details, see Lopez Alonso, "José Soteras Mauri y Lorenzo Garcia-Barbon".
9   Parcerisa, *Barcelona: 20th Century Urbanism*.
10 Bollens, *Cities, Nationalism and Democratization*, 37 and following.

Although an ephemeral event, the Congress left an enduring mark on the city, for an entire new district was built and named after it: El Congrés. The project was allegedly initiated by Modrego himself, who had been publicly expressing his concerns since 1949 about the massive migration to the city and its dramatic impact on the social and spiritual well-being of the people of Barcelona. Calling upon their Christian duty of charity, he put pressure on the political classes, the industrial elite and the architectural profession to do something about the enormous housing problem, for, as he stated, the lack of decent housing formed not only a spiritual and moral threat, but also endangered Christianity in general:

> Inadequate housing for the normal development of a Christian family is a serious, if not insurmountable obstacle to the observance of morality. (...) Aggravating the problem contributes to undisciplined immigration (...). The excessive number of immigrants gives rise, in large part, to the immorality of our city. (...) The problem remains urgent, as does the remedy against the evils of every order that follow the lack of housing.[12]

With this message, he voiced the widespread idea that something had to be done to control the unbridled expansion of the city and that, for lack of any other sufficiently powerful organisation in society, it was the Church's responsibility to take action. Thus, Modrego planned to construct a new neighbourhood to house working class families as a tangible and lasting souvenir of the Congress. Addressing his flock in a pastoral letter, he wrote:

> I propose collecting a large sum through voluntary contributions of one hundred thousand pesetas [the Spanish currency at the time]. Ours, the first, would be used to build large groups of homes of various types that will preserve, as the best of monuments, the memory of the 35th International Eucharistic Congress, the largest event without a doubt to have ever taken place in Barcelona throughout its glorious history. Can Barcelona make this effort? Of course it can. Then it must.[13]

His goal of finding 1,000 families or organisations to contribute 100,000 pesetas each was quickly reached, and construction of the new district started swiftly. Designed by the inevitable Soteras together with Carles Marquès and Antoni Pineda, the El Congrés neighbourhood counts as one of the most important urban developments in Barcelona during the dictatorship, in terms of not only scale, but also quality. [Ill. 9.2] With its attention to typological varia-

---

12 Modrego, G. "Habitación, pan y trabajo", in *La Vanguardia Española*, Barcelona, 20-1-1950; quoted in Hereu, Rosselló, Paricio & Rodríguez, *Les vivendes del Congrés Eucarístic de Barcelona*, 11-12.
13 Modrego, quoted in Martí, *Historia de las Diócesis Españolas. Vol 2*, 389.

9.2 View of the square of the Eucharistic Congress in the heart of the El Congrés neighbourhood. In the background, the Sant Pius X church (1952-1963), designed by Josep Soteras.
[Reproduced from Hereu Payet et al., *Les vivendes del Congrés Eucarístic de Barcelona, 1952-1962*, 57. Courtesy of the Archdiocesan Archives, Barcelona]

tion and social composition (only middle-class Catholics), it was a pilot project that signalled the beginning of massive residential construction in the 1960s.[14] Quite fittingly, El Congrés boasted at its core a large (and relatively modern) church dedicated to Pius X (again, designed by Soteras), the monumentality of which was reinforced by the symmetrical layout of the area, which itself stood out from the surroundings through its height and uniformity.

14   Hereu, Rosselló, Paricio & Rodríguez. *Les Vivendes del Congrés Eucarístic de Barcelona, 1952-1962*. On the Patronato De las Viviendas del Congreso Eucarístico (Patronage Committee for the Eucharistic Congress Dwellings), the association that was set up for the occasion and acted as the project's promotor (and would go on to build cheap housing in other parts of the city, as well), see Andrade, *El planejament metropolità de la Barcelona predemocràtica: Plans, protagonistes i referents teòrics (1939-1976)*.

Reconstructing Catholicism in Barcelona

Beyond the 1952 congress and the El Congrés neighbourhood, Modrego's legacy lives on first and foremost in the impressive array of initiatives he undertook to reconstruct the Catholic Church in Barcelona after the devastations of the civil war. Not only had 160 churches been burned down, 74 partially destroyed and 35 left in ruins, the spiritually undernourished and ever more sprawling suburbs around Barcelona constituted an existential problem.[15] Unafraid, Modrego seized the opportunity to set up the biggest administrative reform of the diocese since the Cerdà plan, with a view to evangelising a city (and by extension, also a region) that had the reputation of being not quite as pious as the rest of Spain. Accordingly, on 9 October 1945, Modrego issued a decree that established a redistribution of the parish boundaries within the Diocese of Barcelona; to counterbalance the overpopulation and all-too-expansive surface area of most parishes, their number was increased from 61 to 154, grouped into 36 *arxiprestat* or "archpriesthoods".[16]

According to canon law, each parish has to be equipped with a proper church; this administrative reform thus entailed a massive church-building programme. To that effect, and with a view to requesting grants from the central government in Madrid, Modrego ordered an inventory of all the Catholic churches in his diocese, which provided him with details about the former and current use of each one: its condition, the damages it had suffered, the cost for its reconstruction and so forth. This resulted in a comprehensive picture of the pastoral equipment of Barcelona in the early 1950s and helped secure financial aid from the state, whose support was badly needed given the scale of the destruction, as outlined above.[17] Almost all of the parish churches within Barcelona's municipal limits had suffered profanation and been damaged.

Along the same lines, Modrego also understood that any successful policy relies first and foremost on adequate data. To this aim, he founded the Institut Catòlic d'Estudis Socials de Barcelona (Catholic Institute for Social Studies of Barcelona) in 1951, directed by Emili Boix i Selva. The institute studied social problems from a Christian point of view and also published a magazine called *Perspectiva Social*.[18] This initiative was typical for the rise of the sociology of religion in Spain and almost everywhere else in Europe, the most prominent representative of which in Catalonia was Rogelio Duocastella (1914-

---

15   Martí, *El martiri dels temples a la Diòcesi de Barcelona*, 82.
16   Checa Artasu, "La Dioceses de Barcelona en la Posguerra. Entre la reconstruccion de edificios religiosos y la produccion inmobiliara (1942-1962)".
17   Martí, *Historia de las Diócesis Españolas. Vol 2*, 360; Martí, *El martiri dels temples a la Diòcesi de Barcelona (1936-1939)*, 82. It should be noted here that at the time, the Diocese of Barcelona extended far beyond the municipal boundaries and included cities such as La Llagosta, Corbera de Llobregat, Badalona and many more.
18   Truscott and Garcia, *A Dictionary of Contemporary Spain*, 156.

9.3 Slums in the Riera Blanca area between the Carrer de Sants and the Travessera de Les Corts. In the background the football stadium of FC Barcelona.
[Photograph by Joan Jané Brugada, 1958. Courtesy of Arxiu Municipal del Districte de Sants-Montjuïc]

1984). A cleric and disciple of the French sociologists Fernand Boulard and Gabriel Le Bras, Duocastella set up the Instituto de Sociologia y Pastoral Aplicada (ISPA, Institute for Applied Sociology and Pastorate) in 1955, which supervised the first survey of church attendance in Spain. Apart from his seminal role in developing methods to chart the religious zeal (or lack thereof) of the faithful in the Diocese of Barcelona, Duocastella also organised the "Semana del Suburbio" (Week of the Suburbs) in Barcelona in February 1957, a series of manifestations, presentations and debates on the topic of massive suburban growth. As part of the effort to combat *barraquisme*, this initiative was actively supported by Modrego and brought together clergy, architects, medical specialists and pedagogues. Interestingly, all these actors seemed to agree that aside from the poor quality of the housing and the disorderly sprawl, one of the primary problems of the suburbs was, quite unsurprisingly, the poor quality of the social and spiritual life there.[19] [Ill. 9.3]

The construction of parish infrastructure (church, meeting hall, school) was seen as an effective tool in remediating this alleged increasing moral apathy. The situation at hand required a firm dose of pragmatism in acquiring land and obtaining funds, however. When requesting subsidies from the Fondo de Reparaciones de Guerra (War Compensation Fund) and the Junta Nacional de Reconstrucción de Templos Parroquiales (National Board for the Reconstruction of Parish Churches), Modrego also promoted barter and exchange between parishes. Some churches were built on land donated by the archbishopric; other building plots were donated by wealthy parishioners or charities. In some cases, private property developers gave up some of their land in the understanding that the erection of a new church would create added value and foster further development of the surrounding area.[20] Quite surprisingly perhaps, once the land and finances had been secured, Modrego left the responsibility for the actual building of the church to the local clergy. One building pastor recalled, for example, "I received the site for Mare de Déu de la Salut church thanks to Doctor Modrego, but after that, he told me, 'Espinosa, now you're on your own.'"[21]

In any event, the diocese's strategy appears to have been effective, given that 62 new parishes were canonically established throughout Barcelona and over 300 religious buildings were restored during Modrego's tenure. As has by now become clear, Modrego himself played no small part in this. In addition to serving as an instrument for advancing the diocese's pastoral ambitions, the church-building activity he promoted obviously also had an impact on the urban development of post-war Barcelona. Indeed, most of these new churches were conceived as free-standing buildings on a public square, significantly enhancing the surrounding urban space as a token of the solid position of

---

19 On the "Semana del Suburbio", see Duocastella, ed., *Los suburbios 1957: compendio de las ponencias y coloquios desarrollados durante la "Semana," seguido de gráficos y estadísticas*. See also the theme issue of *Cristiandad*, 14 (1957), 321/322 (online: <http://cristiandad.orlandis.org/1957/08/4905/>), with contributions by Modrego ("El Problema de los Suburbios esta en toda conciencia catolica barcelonesa", 220-221) and Duocastella ("La Iglesia y los suburbios", 222-223). On the battle against the slums in general, and the role played by the "Semana del Suburbio" in particular, see Camino et al., *Barraquisme. La Ciutat (im)possible. Els barris de Can Valero, el Carmel i la Perona a la Barcelona del segle XX*. On Duocastella and the ISPA, see Griera, "Politics, Religion and Sociology in Spain: The History of a Discipline". ISPA gained international recognition and hosted the VIII Congress of the International Society for the Sociology of Religion in Barcelona in 1965. On that occasion, *Social Compass* devoted a special issue to Spain (*Social Compass*, 12 [1965] 3).
20 Ap. III, no. 24, in Muñoz et al., *Gregorio Modrego Casaus*, 217.
21 Father Miquel Espinosa, in Muñoz et al., *Gregorio Modrego Casaus*, 219.

the Catholic Church in Spanish society under Franco. Similar to the Acción Católica (Catholic Action), which Modrego actively supported, he fostered the emergence of all sorts of professional and social Catholic associations, such as the Asociación Católica de Dirigentes (Catholic Association of Patrons, which united the most influential employers of the city), the new parish infrastructure created a densely knit network capable of reaching almost all members of society — and, indirectly, also controlling them.

Montbau, Grup R and Sant Jeroni

The alleged self-evident position of the Catholic Church in post-war Spain, and the Church's ambivalent relationship with the modernising forces in society, can be illustrated through one of Barcelona's flagship housing estates of the 1960s, namely the Montbau district in the north of the city. A unique experiment in the recent urban development of Barcelona, it is a manifesto of efficient circulation, distribution, orientation and architecture following the principles of the CIAM (Congrès Internationaux d'Architecture Moderne), although it later also became plagued with all the typical problems of this type of segregated development.[22] The master plan of what was to become one of the largest housing estates in Catalonia was entrusted to the group LIGS, composed of Pedro López Iñigo (1926-1997), Guillermo Giráldez Dávila (°1925) and Xavier Subias i Fages (1926-2014), whose surname initials formed the group's acronym.[23] Their much acclaimed project for the Law Faculty of the University of Barcelona had not only shown their ability to swiftly resolve complex building programmes (the building was designed and built in only nine months' time), but also illustrated the ambiguous moral position of the architectural profession in Franquista Spain — for the extremely tight timeframe imposed upon the architects had less to do with a sudden lack of academic infrastructure or need to demonstrate the rapidity of prefabricated construction than with the authorities' urge to remove the rebellious law students from the centre of the city as quickly as possible. Nevertheless, with its rational expression, functional diversity and expressive handling of the prefabricated parts, the building was a clear departure from the adjacent Faculty of Pharmacology,

---

22   On the origins and layout of Montbau, see Bohigas, "El Poligono de Montbau"; Arboix-Alió, *Església i Ciutat. El paper dels temples parroquials en la constucció de Barcelona*, 86-96; Sequeira, "De Interbau en Berlín a Montbau en Barcelona. Una contribución para el estudio de la influencia de las exposiciones internacionales en la arquitectura moderna española"; Rieradevall i Pons, *Rehabilitacion energetica de edificios. Los polígonos de vivienda de los años 70 en Barcelona La rehabilitación del polígono de Montbau*, 51-75.
23   On LIGS, see Tena, *Universalidad y adecuación en la obra de LIGS. Pedro López Iñigo, Guillermo Giráldez Dávila y Xavier Subías Fages (1956-1966)*.

which bore the unmistakable stamp of the rhetorical academism typical of public buildings under the Franco regime.

López Iñigo, Giráldez and Subias were all members of Grup R, a loose group of progressive architects founded in 1951 by, amongst others, Josep Antoni Coderch (1913-1984) and Oriol Bohigas (°1925). Proposing to "study the problems of contemporary art and especially of architecture", the group embraced the functional principles of the Modern Movement but interwove them with a complementary care for local and regional forms.[24] According to Bohigas, the group's most outspoken member, the "R" in the group's name referred to "reinstatement" and "restoration", as well as to "revolution", "refusal" and "reconsideration". Suffice it to say, the group's conceptual stance was ambivalent at the very least. Indeed, as one critic had it:

> Their goal was to restore the Modern Movement and its revolutionary principles, but this very act of restoration implied a distance from the past and a will to recuperate something that was no longer present.[25]

Thus, in the case of Grup R, the radical break with tradition as proclaimed by the Modern Movement turned into its opposite; instead of exhibiting strict loyalty to the "modern" past, the group showed allegiance to the tradition of modernity itself. Or, in other words, "by trying to remain faithful to the modernist principles, Grup R necessarily betrayed them."[26] In particular, the group attempted to re-establish the lost connection with the international avant-garde and restore the modernist impetus infused by the GATCPAC group before the war.[27] To this effect, its members organised exhibitions and seminars and skilfully used the media to position themselves in organs of opinion such as the *Cuadernos de Arquitectura*, the architectural journal of the Colegio de Arquitectos. Unlike GATCPAC, however, Grup R lacked a clear leadership and formal doctrine, making it perhaps more a collection of individuals acting against the prevailing academism than a real group endeavouring towards a common goal. Nonetheless, by the time of its dissolution in 1961, the group

---

24 Statutes of Grup R as quoted on <https://www.metalocus.es/en/news/motor-modernity-grup-r-architecture-art-and-design> (accessed 29/10/2019). On Grup R, see Rodríguez Pedret et al., *Grup R*; Illias, *Thinking Barcelona*, 142-145. On the religious work of Grup R's members, see Delgado Orusco, *¡Bendita vanguardia! Arquitectura religiosa en España 1950-1975*, 117-127.
25 Illias, *Thinking Barcelona*, 142.
26 Ibid.
27 GATCPAC (Grup d'Arquitectes i Tècnics Catalans per al Progrés de l'Arquitectura Contemporània) [Group of Catalan Architects and Technicians for the Progress of Contemporary Architecture] was an architectural movement that emerged in Catalonia in the 1930s, coinciding with the Second Spanish Republic. Its objective was to promote avant-garde architecture, mainly rationalism, in tune with the European currents of that time. The group

had proven very effective in fostering a modernist consciousness amongst private and public clients alike.

The development of the Montbau estate is a prime illustration of this. Conceived as a model solution for the rapid growth of the city, it was intended as a self-sufficient entity or satellite town. Typical of the speculative pragmatism under Porcioles, the beautiful site at the foot of the Collserola mountain range — which had initially been reserved in the 1953 urban development plan for a major hospital because of its natural fresh air climate — was seized by the PMH to test several concepts and ideas that could subsequently be applied in later projects. In an effort to avoid the monofunctional, sterile aspect of many contemporary dormitory neighbourhoods, much attention was given to social amenities in the form of a "civic centre" with shops, religious buildings and other such facilities. The allocation of the dwellings was also consciously regulated, with the aim of reproducing the social diversity of Barcelona in miniature according to a pre-planned social composition, which was to comprise twenty-five per cent *barraquistas* (unqualified workers); twenty-five per cent skilled workers and lower-ranked officials; forty-five per cent higher-ranked civil servants, liberal professionals, traders, members of the military and so forth; and five per cent senior civil servants and members of the high-class.[28] Further emphasising the showcase aspect of the project, and illustrative of its international scope, was the name given to the new development by the municipal authorities. Deriving from the name of a stream running close to the site, the river Mumbau, it resonated with "Interbau", the name of the international building exhibition in Berlin which López Iñigo and Subías had visited only a few months prior to receiving the commission, as part of a prospective trip organized by Porcioles, with the objective of acquiring knowledge on the new international urban models.[29] The name "Montbau" thus reflects the municipal authorities' ambition of anchoring the modern promises of the Berlin showcase in the local topology of the site.

All this had to be done in record time; just as with the Law Building, LIGS had to work under extreme time pressure. The central premises of the master plan were laid out in only a couple of weeks, by the end of 1957. In keeping with similar schemes abroad, the basic ideas behind Montbau were threefold: a "unitary nucleus" of dwellings with a distinct character based on the notion of free-standing blocks; landscaped spaces as centres for play and recreation; public buildings as focal points in the composition; and a clear distinction

---

28 Antich Garcia, *El Poligon del Sud Oest del Besos. Habitatge social dels anys 50*, 19.
29 Sequeira, "De Interbau en Berlín a Montbau en Barcelona", 621. As the author points out, the link with the Hansaviertel (the district where Interbau is located) can also be taken literally: LIGS later designed Block N (1966-1968), which had a system of duplex flats with access corridors that was directly inspired by the tower designed by Jaap Bakema and Jo van den Broek for Interbau. On Interbau and the experiment in the Hansaviertel, see the contribution by Marina Wesner in this volume.

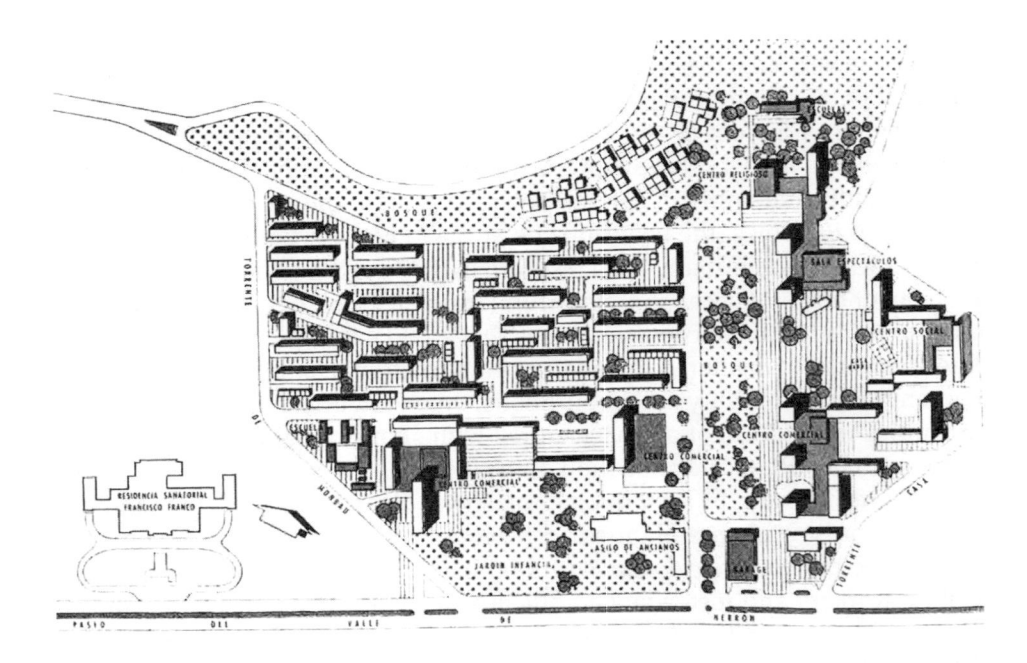

9.4 Initial master plan for Montbau by LIGS, 1957. The parish centre is located at the end of the main axis. [Courtesy of Arxiu Municipal de la Ciutat de Barcelona]

between pedestrian and vehicle circulation routes.[30] [Ill. 9.4] In total, Montbau was to contain 1,800 dwellings for 8,000 inhabitants. Whereas construction of the first (south-west) sector started swiftly, in 1958, the ever-increasing pressure on the housing market led to a revision of the initial scheme, the original density of which was now deemed largely insufficient in relation to the demographic prognoses. This explains why a new team, led by Soteras (including, apart from López Iñigo, also Manuel Baldrich (1911-1966) and Antoni Bonet Castellana (1913-1989)), was appointed in 1961 to revise the layout of the second (eastern) sector and double the number of dwellings. [Ill. 9.5] While the second sector was also completed swiftly, it would take another decade for the social amenities to be built — thus hypothesizing Montbau's position as an independent satellite from the very outset.

Interestingly for our discussion, these social amenities included plans from the beginning for a parish centre. Indeed, a church and ancillary facilities were originally positioned at the top of the site, with the foot of the mountain range as a backdrop. According to the planners, this solemn location close to nature referenced the monastery that had once stood on the site. Monsignor Narcís Jubany (1913-1996), Modrego's right hand with regard to all church construction (and his later successor), disagreed however, exclaiming,

30 "Planeamiento del núcleo satélite de Montbau". For a critical review of the master plan, see Bohigas, "El polígono de Montbau".

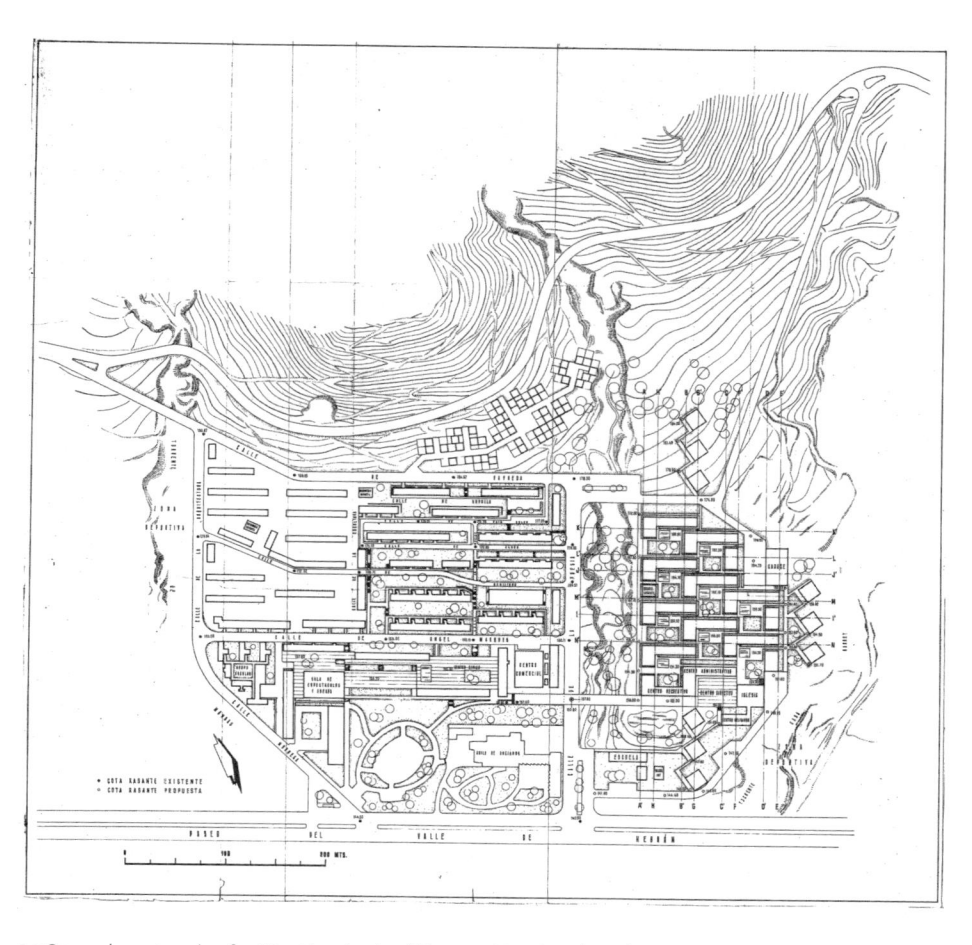

9.5 Second master plan for Montbau by José Soteras Mauri, Pedro López Iñigo, Manuel Baldrich and Antoni Bonet Castellana, 1962. The parish centre has now been moved to the bottom right of the plan, behind the three squares.
[Courtesy of Arxiu Municipal de la Ciutat de Barcelona]

"This can't be possible. Don't you understand that no one will come if you put the church up there?"[31] Consequently, in the second version of the plan, the parish centre was moved closer to the city, on the periphery of the neighbourhood, slightly hidden from sight. Ultimately, though, the complex was moved a little more to the left, along the neighbourhood's main axis.[32] The idea was that the new parish church — clearly conceived of by the planners as a monumental building with a tall bell tower — would act as a marker for the Montbau development at that spot.

31   Sagarra et al., *De les cases barates als grans polígons*, 119.
32   Arboix-Alió, *Església i Ciutat*, 88-89.

Given the symbolic function of the new church — marking the presence of a new district that in itself was to mark the city's newly acquired modernity — its architectural design was of prime importance. The expectations in this regard can be measured against the bold idea to invite no one less than Le Corbusier to design the parish church of Montbau. The old master politely refused, however, telling the team who came to speak to him in person that despite his great love for Barcelona, where he had often enjoyed a stroll down Las Ramblas, he was now in his seventies and his doctors had forbidden him to travel.[33] The PMH and the diocese therefore decided to join forces and organise a nationwide architectural competition. This gave the project even more importance: the Sant Jeroni church was not only to become an expression of modernity (architectural and otherwise), contestants were also supposed to incorporate into their submission the latest liturgical insights from the Second Vatican Council.[34] For example, the competition brief explicitly stated that the representatives of the diocese had the right to veto the project if it did not comply with the reforms agreed upon during the council and that the winners would also follow the diocese's directives in further executing the design. Thus, Montbau became a showcase for not only the municipal authorities, but also the diocese — a way to express the latter's recently acquired status as an archdiocese.

Presumably seduced by the publicity that would befall the winner's proposal, no fewer than sixty architects from all over Spain submitted a proposal. The jury awarded the first prize (and execution) to the proposal entitled "ROSA EA", designed by Francesc Vayreda Bofill (1927-2011) and Pau Monguió Abella (°1932), the last two members to join Grup R.[35] Their proposal consisted of two separate buildings (a dominant box-like volume for the church and a more modestly shaped parish hall with offices and a presbytery), placed perpendicularly along a rectangular square and linked by a covered passageway — which gave the plaza the allure of a cloister. The architectural expression of both buildings was clearly inspired by the then-popular brutalist aesthetic of

[33] Segarra et al., *De les cases barates als grans polígons*, 42 and 119. This is according to Subias, one of the partners in LIGS. We have not been able to find evidence of this exchange in the Le Corbusier archives in Paris.

[34] Barcelona, HADAB, folder no 103. See also Delgado, *Arquitectura sacra española, 1939-1975: de la posguerra al posconcilio*, 313-314.

[35] "Concurso de anteproyectos para un conjunto parroquial en la unidad residencial de Montbau". Amongst the participants were names that would later become famous, such as Rafael Moneo, Juan Daniel Fullaondo, Francisco J. Sáenz de Oiza and Jordi Bonet Armengol. The second prize was awarded to José Antonio Corrales from Madrid and the third prize to the architects Vicente Bonet, Luis Nadal and Pedro Puigdefábregas from Barcelona. The jury was composed of two delegates from the PMH, two clerics appointed by the diocese, two architects appointed by the housing board and one architect chosen by the contestants. Vayreda and Monguió subsequently became known for their Casa Vayreda in Prat de l'Eruga (Girona), amongst other works. See <https://www.udg.edu/ca/Portals/21/Tcomposicio/07.pdf> (accessed 05/02/2020).

Le Corbusier; the vaulted roofs of the presbytery, in particular, refer to the Catalan vaults the latter used for the roofs of the Maisons Jaoul and can be seen as a nod towards the old master. [Ill. 9.6] As far as the liturgical arrangement was concerned, the competition documents reveal that Vayreda and Monguió had made a very thorough study of the liturgical reforms; indeed, they submitted an extensive report together with their design justifying every gesture and every intention from the viewpoint of Christian worship, presenting their proposal as a "modern treatise on liturgy".

Thus, the Sant Jeroni competition not only led to a commission for a building, it also fostered a thorough reflection on contemporary religion and its architectural expression. Indeed, in the same year as the competition, the PMH organised a national congress called "Conversaciones de Arquitectura Religiosa" (Conversations on Religious Architecture), to which Le Corbusier was invited as a keynote speaker but again declined with apologies. Held at the headquarters of the Collegi d'Arquitectes de Catalunya, the aim of the colloquium was to promote a better understanding between clergy and lay people, experts and believers, technicians and administrators. As the proceedings reveal, the congress indeed seems to have instigated a real dialogue between architects and theologians centred around the question of what Barcelona's future places of worship should look like.[36] Amongst the participants from the field of architecture, the audience included Manuel de Solà-Morales, Joan Margarit and Bohigas, while the Catalan historian of religion Manuel Trens, the French cleric and scholar Paul Winninger and Monsignor Aldo Milani (Montini's right hand in Milan before he became Pope Paul VI) — to name only a few distinguished personalities — represented the ecclesiastical field. Winninger tackled his favourite topic, namely the need for adequate pastoral infrastructure in the form of more, but smaller, churches; Milani spoke about religious sociology and city planning.[37] Topics were discussed from a different viewpoint each day: whereas the first day was devoted to religious sociology and urban planning, dealing with the planning and construction of parish infrastructure, for example, the second focused more on the liturgical, symbolical and cultural dimensions of religious architecture. The third and final day was devoted to the iconography and symbolism of stained glass, murals, sculptures and so forth.

Although most of these discussions were theoretical in nature, the winners of the Sant Jeroni design contest — who also attended the colloquium, where their project was discussed — clearly benefited from these exchanges in further elaborating on their project. However, whereas the ground breaking ceremony for the church, led by Modrego, took place on 6 November 1966,

---

36 *Conversaciones de arquitectura religiosa.*
37 On Winninger, see the introduction to this volume; on Milani, see the contribution by Bordoni et al.

9.6 Rendering of the Montbau church for the competition proposal "ROSA EA" by Francesc Vayreda Bofill and Pau Monguió Abella (1963).
[Courtesy of Arxiu Històric de l'Arquebisbat de Barcelona]

9.7 Photograph of the ground breaking ceremony for the San Jeroni church on 6 November 1966. [Barcelona, Sant Jeroni Parish]

it would take another ten years before his successor, Monsignor Jubany, was able to consecrate it, on 26 April 1975.[38] [Ill. 9.7] The parish complex that was eventually built (in fact designed by Vayreda alone) differed quite substantially from the competition scheme, however. The size and height of the church were significantly reduced; and, now covered by a shallow, pitched roof, the pews were turned ninety degrees towards a non-axial disposition more in tune with the post-conciliar guidelines concerning the active involvement of the faithful. This shift in the interior arrangement also impacted the relationship between the church and the square, for the latter had originally been conceived as a natural extension of the liturgical space. Now, the church volume was set back, allowing for the creation of a small enclosed contemplative garden between the church and the square. Most important, though, was the decision to abandon the bell tower for fear that it would be dwarfed by the bulk of the apartment towers next to it and hence lose its significance. As a result, the Sant Jeroni church did not become a monumental marker as had been conceived of by Montbau's planners, but was rather a modest piece of functional infrastructure at the service of worshipping and the associative life in the new parish. Nevertheless, today, the church of Sant Jeroni — and Montbau as a whole — is recognised for its modernity and enjoys monument status.[39] [Ill. 9.8]

38 <http://www.santjeroni.es/historia.html> (accessed 29/10/2019).
39 As a token of its significance as part of the Catalan Modern Movement heritage, Sant Jeroni has been listed by DOCOMOMO Iberia in its register of modern buildings in Spain. See <http://www.docomomoiberico.com/index.php?option=com_k2&view=item&id=852:iglesia-parroquia-de-sant-jeroni&lang=es> (last accessed 05/02/2020). On Montbau as modern urban heritage, see Bargallo Sanchez, "Montbau, un poligono modelo. ¿Patrimonio Urbano Moderno?"

9.8 Courtyard view of the Montbau church today.
[Photograph taken by Alba Arboix-Alió, 2017]

Conclusion

During his long tenure as first bishop, then archbishop of Barcelona, Modrego undertook a substantial reform of his diocese; it is believed that he himself dedicated no fewer than 158 churches. Moreover, to staff all this new infrastructure, he ordained over 800 priests.[40] These numbers did not constitute a goal per se, but derived from the Bishop's strategy to provide pastoral support for *all* the citizens of Barcelona. Indeed, if one looks at the map of the city today, one finds that its parish churches constitute a surprisingly homogeneous, fine-grained and equidistant matrix of pastoral infrastructure — an achievement mainly attributable to Modrego himself, since only a handful of new churches were built after his retirement in 1967. [Ill. 9.9] It thus seems as if he left in place a valuable system by which both the Church and the regime could advance their ideological and political agenda. Yet, as illustrated by the cases discussed above (the Pius X church in El Congrés and Sant Jeroni in Montbau), a closer look at this network reveals an important shift. Whereas in

40 Muñoz et al., *Gregorio Modrego Casaus*, 216; Martí, *Historia de las Diócesis Españolas. Vol 2*, 365.

9.9: All parish churches existing today in Barcelona. The churches built during Modrego's tenure represent nearly 50% of the total. San Jeroni (to the North) is indicated with a circle.
[Reproduced from Arboix-Alió, *Església i Ciutat. El paper dels temples parroquials en la constucció de Barcelona*, 104-105]

both cases, the very idea of a parish church remained self-evident, it became materialised in totally different ways. Indeed, the dominant and self-confident appearance of the Pius X church, designed by an architect close to the regime as the focus of the El Congrés development, gave way to an off-centred, rather modest piece of religious infrastructure in Montbau, designed by young members of a critical group of architects (Grup R).

This typological transformation cannot be ascribed solely to the international trend in religious architecture towards simplicity and functionalism, for it reflects first and foremost the fact that in the interim between the consecrations of the two churches (1962 and 1975), the Spanish Church had changed dramatically. In the first place, the conclusions of the Second Vatican Council, with its emphasis on human rights and religious and political freedom, rocked the very foundations of both church and state in Spain, because they provided ammunition to clerics, intellectuals and even politicians in their criticism of Spanish National Catholicism. Second, with support from the lower clergy, associations of lay Catholics began assuming a role equivalent to trade unions (which were officially banned under Franco), thus placing the Church hierarchy in an increasingly difficult position. Parish churches such as Sant Jeroni played no small part in this change of mentality, for they offered a safe base for these critical movements. With pressure from the Vatican, and as older priests and conservative bishops died, it was only a matter of time before social awareness began to filter upwards. Indeed, in 1973, the Spanish Church issued a statement in which it recognised fundamental rights such as the right of expression and association and expressed its intention to cooperate with the state on new terms that excluded clerics from political institutions. Thus, the typological shift between the Pius X church in El Congrés and Sant Jeroni in Montbau can be seen as a metaphor for the fact that, over the course of Modrego's tenure, the Church inevitably lost its spatial and social structuring capacity, both as embodied in its church buildings and as an institution — a phenomenon that appears to have been only amplified by the extensive parish network laid out so vigorously during that tenure.

BIBLIOGRAPHY

Acknowledgements

The authors wish to acknowledge the help of Monsignor Martí i Bonet for his clarifications with regard to Archbishop Gregorio Modrego Casaus during an interview granted on 11 May 2018 at the offices of the Archdiocese of Barcelona.

Archives

Barcelona, Historical Archive of the Diocese of the Archbishopric of Barcelona (HADAB), Folder 103 (Sant Jeroni)
Barcelona, Municipal Archive (MA): Poligon Montbau, 4-12; Patronat Municipal de l'Habitatge, 1962, Q127, 621366 and 621365
Barcelona, Sant Jeroni parish

Published sources

XXXV Congreso Eucaristico Internacional, Barcelona 1952: la Eucaristia y la paz. Barcelona: Huecograbado Planas, 1952.
Andrade, Gustavo Pires de. *El planejament metropolità de la Barcelona predemocràtica: Plans, protagonistes i referents teòrics (1939-1976)*. Doctoral thesis, Universidad Politécnica de Catalunya, 2015. <https://upcommons.upc.edu/handle/2117/96031> (accessed 04/09/2019).
Antich Garcia, Bartomeu. *El Poligon del Sud Oest del Besos. Habitatge social dels anys 50*. Unpublished report. Universitat Politècnica de Catalunya, 2010. <https://core.ac.uk/download/pdf/41795818.pdf> (accessed 29/10/2019).

Arboix-Alió, Alba. *Església i Ciutat. El paper dels temples parroquials en la constucció de Barcelona*. PhD Thesis, UPC, Architectural Design Department, 2016. <https://www.tdx.cat/handle/10803/387815>.

Bada, Joan. *Guerra Civil i Església Catalana*. Barcelona: Abadia de Montserrat, 1987.

Bargallo Sanchez, Isabel. "Montbau, un poligono modelo. ¿Patrimonio Urbano Moderno?" In: M. Viladevall i Guash and M. A. Castrillo Romon, eds. *Espacio público en la ciudad contemporánea. Perspectivas críticas sobre su gestión, su patrimonialización y su proyecto*. Valladodid, Instituto de Urbanística de la Universidad de Valladolid, 2012, 201-213.

Bohigas, Oriol. "El polígono de Montbau". Cuadernos de Arquitectura, 1965, no 61, 22-34.

Bohigas, Oriol. *Modernidad en la Arquitectura de la España*. Barcelona: Tusquets Editores, 1998.

Bollens, Scott A. *Cities, Nationalism and Democratization*. London: Routledge, 2007.

Busquets, Joan, et al. *Cerdà i la Barcelona del futur. Realitat versus projecte*. Barcelona: CCCB, 2009.

Callahan, William J. "The Evangelization of Franco's 'New Spain'". *Church History*, 56 (1987) 4, 491-503.

Camino, Xavi et al. *Barraquisme. La Ciutat (im)possible. Els barris de Can Valero, el Carmel i la Perona a la Barcelona del segle XX*. Barcelona: Generalitat de Catalunya, 2016.

Checa Artasu, Martin. "La Dioceses de Barcelona en la Posguerra. Entre la reconstruccion de edificios religiosos y la produccion inmobiliara (1942-1962)". In: Horacio Capel Sáez and Paul-André Linteau, eds. *Barcelona-Montreal. Desarrollo urbano comparado = développement urbain comparé*. Barcelona: Universitat de Barcelona, 1998, 435-458.

"Concurso de anteproyectos para un conjunto parroquial en la unidad residencial de Montbau". *Cuadernos de Arquitectura y Urbanismo*, 54 (1963), 40-41.

Conversaciones de arquitectura religiosa: Barcelona del 8 al 11 de octubre 1963. Barcelona: Patronato Municipal de la Vivienda, 1965.

Delgado Orusco, Eduardo. *Arquitectura sacra española, 1939-1975: de la posguerra al posconcilio*. PhD Thesis, Universidad Politécnica de Madrid, Composition Department, 1999.

Delgado Orusco, Eduardo. *¡Bendita vanguardia! Arquitectura religiosa en España 1950-1975*. Madrid: Ediciones Asimétricas.

Dowling, Andrew. "The Catholic Church in Catalonia. From Cataclysm in the Civil War to the 'Euphoria' of the 1950s". *Catalan Review*, (2006), 83-100.

Duocastella, Rogelio, ed. *Los suburbios 1957: compendio de las ponencias y coloquios desarrollados durante la "Semana," seguido de gráficos y estadísticas*. Barcelona, 1957.

Ealham, Chris and Richards, Michael, eds. *The splintering of Spain: cultural history and the Spanish Civil War, 1936–1939*. Cambridge: Cambridge University Press, 2005.

Equipamientos: Lugares públicos y nuevos programas, 1925-1965. Registro DOCOMOMO Ibérico. Vol. 1. Barcelona: ArquiaTemas, Fundación Caja de Arquitectos, 2010.

Forrest, Andrew. *The Spanish Civil War*. London: Routledge, 2000.

Gil, Paloma. *El templo del siglo XX*. Barcelona: Ediciones del Serbal, 1999.

Gomez Val, Ricardo. *La Construcción de templos parroquiales en Barcelona entre 1952 y 2000*. Unpublished PhD thesis, Universitat Politècnica de Catalunya, 2012.

González, Maria. "Politics of the Void: Franquista Spain at Expo'58". In: Rika Devos, Alexander Ortenberg and Vladimir Paperny. *Architecture of Great Expositions 1937-1958: Messages of Peace, Images of War*. Farham: Ashgate, 2015.

Gregorio Modrego Casaus. Labor pastoral de un gran pontificado. Barcelona: S.A.D.A.G., 1962.

Griera, Mar. "Politics, Religion and Sociology in Spain: The History of a Discipline". In: Anthony Blasi and Giuseppe Giordan, eds. *Sociologies of Religion: National Traditions*. Leiden: Brill 2015, 268-293.

Hereu Payet, Pedro; Rosselló i Nicolau, Maribel; Paricio Casademunt, Antoni; Rodríguez Pedret, Carmen. *Les vivendes del Congrés Eucarístic de Barcelona, 1952-1962*. Barcelona: Edicions UPC, 2011. <https://upcommons.upc.edu/handle/2117/15121> (accessed 28/06/2019).

Illias, Edgar. *Thinking Barcelona*. Liverpool: Liverpool University Press, 2012.

Lopez Alonso, Ignacio. "José Soteras Mauri y Lorenzo Garcia-Barbon". *RA: revista de arquitectura*, 18 (2016), 61-70.

Mària, Magda. *Religión, sociedad y arquitectura: las iglesias parroquiales en Catalunya, 1545-1621*. PhD Thesis, Universitat Politècnica de Catalunya, Architectural Composition Department, 1994.

Martí, Josep M. *El martiri dels temples a la Diòcesi de Barcelona (1936-1939)*. Barcelona: Editorial Museu Diocesà, 2008.

Martí, Josep M and Marquès Planagumà, Josep M. *Historia de las Diócesis Españolas*. Vol 2: *Barcelona, Terrassa, Sant Feliu de Llobregat, Girona*. Madrid: Biblioteca de autores cristianos, 2006.

Muñoz, Francisco et al. *Gregorio Modrego Casaus: obispo del XXXV Congreso Eucarístico Internacional de Barcelona: documentos y notas históricas*. Barcelona: Claret, 2002.

"National Catholicism". In: *World Literature in Spanish: An Encyclopedia*. Vol. II. Santa Barbara: 1BC-CLIO, 2011.

Official Gazette of the Diocese of Barcelona, 1867-1868

Olivé, Félix. *Sant Jeroni de la Vall d'Hebron*. Barcelona: REPGRAF, 1993.

Parcerisa, Josep. *Barcelona: 20th Century Urbanism*. Barcelona: Marge, 2014.

"Planeamiento del núcleo satélite de Montbau". *Cuadernos de Arquitectura*, (1959) 37, 13-15.

Preston, Paul. *A Concise History of the Spanish Civil War*. London: Fontana Press, 1996.

Raguer, Hilari. *Gunpowder and Incense: The Catholic Church and the Spanish Civil War*. London: Routledge, 2011.

Rieradevall i Pons, Josep M. *Rehabilitacion energetica de edificios. Los polígonos de vivienda de los años 70 en Barcelona. La rehabilitación del polígono de Montbau*. Unpublished doctoral thesis, Universidad Politècnica de Catalunya, 2014.

Rodríguez Pedret, Carmen et al. *Grup R*. Barcelona: G. Gili, 1994.

Sagarra, Franscesc et al. *De les cases barates als grans polígons: el Patronat Municipal de l'Habitatge de Barcelona entre 1929 i 1979*. Barcelona: Ajuntament de Barcelona, 2003.

Sequeira, M. "De Interbau en Berlín a Montbau en Barcelona. Una contribución para el estudio de la influencia de las exposiciones internacionales en la arquitectura moderna española". In: *Actas del IX Congreso Internacional Historia de la Arquitectura Moderna Española*. Pamplona: Ediciones T6, 2014, 619-628.

Solà-Morales, Manuel de. *Les formes de creixement urbà*. Barcelona: Edicions UPC, 1993.

Soteras, José. "Barcelona y el Plan Cerdá". *Revista de Obras Publicas*, (1960), 108, 5-12.

Tena, Pablo. *Universalidad y adecuación en la obra de LIGS. Pedro López Iñigo, Guillermo Giráldez Dávila y Xavier Subías Fages (1956-1966)*. PhD Thesis, Universidad Politécnica de Catalunya, Architectural Design Department, 2010. <https://www.tdx.cat/handle/10803/6821> (accessed 29/10/2019).

Truscott, Sandra and Garcia, Maria. *A Dictionary of Contemporary Spain*. New York: Routledge, 1998.

Vilar, Paul. *La Catalogne dans l'Espagne moderne: recherches sur les fondements économiques des structures nationales*. Paris: Le Sycomore, Éditions de l'EHESS, 1982.

10
MASS HOUSING AND THE CATHOLIC HIERARCHY IN DUBLIN, 1930S-1970S
THE CASE OF BALLYMUN ESTATE

ELLEN ROWLEY

In 1970, Father Liam Breen (life dates unknown), the parish priest of the rapidly expanding parish of Saint Pappin's, Ballymun, on the northern edge of Dublin, issued a fundraising pamphlet. In outlining the limitations of the nineteenth-century chapel-at-ease for the new population of 14,000, the cover juxtaposed a concrete tower block ("Ballymun, 1970") with Saint Pappin's church, a small, pitched roof, masonry structure ("Ballymun, 1848") [Ill. 10.1]. The extreme contrast was expressed in the name of seeking funding for community amenities. The mutually beneficial arrangement between local government in Ireland and the Irish Catholic Church was hidden in plain view: it was fully expected that the Church would provide the schools and intrinsically parish or religious structures, and the local authority would facilitate the Church in terms of site acquisition and planning applications.

Ballymun Estate was extraordinary for Ireland. Under construction on Dublin's northern edge from 1965, it was Ireland's first wholly prefabricated housing estate, and crucially, it comprised Ireland's first tower block flats. With its seven towers, nineteen spine blocks and ten walk-up blocks, the estate was defined by flats. It was also defined by its large scale and comparative high-rise, the speed of its making in response to a municipal housing crisis and its separation away from the city. [Ill. 10.2] Ultimately, it was defined by its apparent (but always imperfect) wholeness: it was to be a "New Town". And as such, much has been written about Ballymun's social geography and its architectural genesis. For instance, the delay of the promised swimming

10.1 Pamphlet cover, Ballymun, 1970.
[Courtesy of the Dublin Diocesan Archive]

9.1 Simultaneous ordination of 657 priests in Montjuïc Stadium at the 35th International Eucharistic Congress on 31 May 1952.
[Photograph by Pérez de Rozas. Courtesy of Arxiu Fotogràfic de Barcelona]

Against this background of poverty and exclusion, the pomp and circumstance of the 35th International Eucharistic Congress held in Barcelona from 26 May to 1 June 1952 at the instigation of Modrego may seem somewhat out of place. It was attended by delegations from 77 countries and attracted over 300,000 participants, amongst whom 12 cardinals, 302 archbishops and bishops and 15,000 lower clergymen.[11] Hundreds of events were held in the span of one week, the most spectacular of which was the simultaneous ordination of 657 priests from all over Spain on 21 altars built in the Montjuïc Stadium. [Ill. 9.1] Although the event can be interpreted as a sublime example of self-promotion — afterwards, Modrego was promoted to the rank of cardinal by Pope Pius XII — the Congress also had a profound meaning for the people of Barcelona. Attended by Franco in person, it publicly consecrated the position of the Catalan Church — and by extension, the entire region — in the eyes of the world, and in its wake, the Diocese of Barcelona was reorganised into an archdiocese covering the entire agglomeration.

11   An International Eucharistic Congress is an assembly of the Catholic Church summoned by the pope that meets for a few days in a city determined by the Holy See to worship the Eucharist and guide the mission of the Catholic Church in the world. On the congress, see *XXXV Congreso Eucaristico Internacional, Barcelona 1952: la Eucaristia y la paz*.

10.2 Girls in front of tower blocks, Ballymun.
[Photograph by Elinor Wiltshire. Courtesy of the Elinor Wiltshire Collection, National Library of Ireland]

pool and other services have taken on metaphorical status in recent Irish urban studies.[1] With their concrete high-rise nature, the seven tower blocks of housing became *the* expression of a local late-twentieth-century dystopia; lest we forget, pop legend U2 references the estate in one of their songs, *Running to Stand Still* (1987): "I see seven towers but I only see one way out." However, the development of church-related infrastructure in Ballymun has not been explored, so the analysis below is an attempt to understand the Catholic Church's role in the making of such a supposedly exceptional 1960s environment for urban Ireland. Did Ballymun's exceptionalness come out of the Church's disengagement with the place? Or has Ballymun's said exceptionalness been overstated?

[1] Examples of Ballymun histories and commentaries are: McDonald, *The Construction of Dublin*; Montague, "The architecture of Ballymun"; Power, 'The Development of the Ballymun Housing Scheme, Dublin 1965-1969"; Prior, ed., *Hotel Ballymun. Seamus Nolan*; Rowley, "Ballymun, Case Study"; Somerville-Woodward, *Ballymun, A History*.

Looking at mass-housing development in the Dublin diocese, Ireland's largest archbishopric, this chapter opens up a discussion around the influence of the Catholic Church on Irish architecture and planning processes. As the chapter develops, it foregrounds the case of Ballymun (1965-1969), with its technocratic architecture, and looks at the Dublin prelate, Archbishop John Charles McQuaid's (1895-1973) correspondence and the provision of Catholic social infrastructure in this 1960s edge city. It further takes as its premise that independent Ireland was a Catholic corporatist state from the late 1930s: through the ongoing shared culture of clergy and statesmen, through the entrenchment of the Constitution as a Catholic mantel and through church-building and parish establishment campaigns across the state. But from 1958, there was a significant shift in Irish economic policy, whereby many social processes were ultimately modernised, coinciding with the reform of the transnational Catholic Church through the Second Vatican Council of the 1960s. Should Ballymun, then, be understood primarily within this latter context, with its development encouraged by the Church?

Because of its high-rise, prefabricated nature, Ballymun Estate is posited as an Irish heterotopia, at once "other" and indigenous, where the declining influence of the theocracy was made manifest. Or was it? The Irish hierarchy's position in terms of cultural censorship and resistance to ecumenism and architectural modernism, as well as to education reform, presented distinct dichotomous moments. As we argue here, and the case study of Ballymun Estate specifically evidences, these dichotomies seemed to dissolve in the realm of housing and planning, where church and state pragmatically collaborated. At first glance, the estate's late modernist image might be the architectural byword for the Irish secularisation of the late 1960s and 1970s. Yet upon closer examination, embedded beneath Ballymun's technological materiality was a network of Catholic pastoral infrastructure, being made and then enforced through the 1970s, which this contribution seeks to expose and understand. As a continuation of early research into the relationship between Irish architecture and the local Catholic Church through the 1940s and 1950s, we examine the 1960s Ballymun phenomenon, only to come to a zero hypothesis in terms of architectural, urban and Catholic pastoral modernism: this was a hybrid, tentatively radicalising, episode for urban Ireland, further enforced by the grey and inconclusive evidence presented by the Ballymun Estate and its relationship to the local Catholic hierarchy.[2]

---

2 See Rowley, "The Architect, the Planner and the Bishop: The shapers of Ordinary Dublin 1940-1970" and footnote 7.

Mid-Century Moral Monopoly: Church and State in 1930s-1960s Dublin

In 1937, the Irish Free State redrafted its Constitution. At its heart was the family:

> The State recognises the Family as the natural primary and fundamental unit group of Society, as a moral institution possessing inalienable and imprescriptible rights, antecedent and superior to all positive law. (Article 41.1.1, Irish Constitution, 1937)

The first government, in place since Irish independence in 1922, had been superseded by the more republican, and it would transpire, professional, parliamentary party, Fianna Fáil in 1932. Their charismatic leader, Eamon de Valera (1882-1975), remained in power as Taoiseach (prime minister/leader) until 1948, not retiring from Irish politics until 1973, thereby introducing the stability that the nascent state craved. Evidently, the Constitution inherited by De Valera was read as a hurried and harried script made in 1922, just as the War of Independence (which would be overtaken by the bitter Civil War) closed and the capital city, Dublin, was smouldering and shuddering in its desecration. By the 1930s, in a move to distance the Free State from the Civil War memory, the Constitution was to be reconstructed with Catholic social teaching and papal encyclicals as its basis.

Doubtlessly influenced by the heady celebrations of the Catholic Emancipation centenary of 1929 and, as we will see, the International Eucharistic Congress of 1932, the Taoiseach, De Valera, understood the psycho-emotional grip that the Catholic Church held on the newly independent Irish. Furthermore, his own education conformed with the Irish middle-class norm of Catholic and Jesuit, which, over the life of his term in office at least, contributed to the propagation of a homogenous Catholic society underpinned by the shared culture of its statesmen and churchmen. In the remaking of the Irish Constitution, explicitly from 1935, the Taoiseach consulted various Catholic intellectual sources, such as the writings of Dr Michael Browne (1895-1980), appointed Bishop of Galway in 1937, and the advice of Dr McQuaid, Archbishop of Dublin from 1940 until 1972 and the most powerful member of the Irish Catholic hierarchy.[3] With emphasis laid on family, the place of women in the home, the education of children and the right to property, the new Irish Constitution was a barely veiled translation of the 1931 papal encyclical, *Quadragesimo Anno*.

---

[3] Kennedy, "Two Priests, the Family and the Irish Constitution"; Keogh, "The Irish Constitutional Revolution: An Analysis of the Making of the Constitution", 11. The most recent analysis, Barr and O Corrain's "Catholic Ireland, 1740-2016" maintains that scholarship overstates the relationship between *Quadragesimo Anno* and the 1937 Irish Constitution.

10.3 View of 31st International Eucharistic Congress Main Mass, Phoenix Park, Dublin, 1932. [Courtesy of the Robinson Keefe and Devane Collection, Dublin]

In census terms, the strength of the Catholic Church was already reflected by the 1930s in the 93.5 per cent of the population who identified as Roman Catholic. This monocultural Catholic identity and religiosity was translated in spatial terms with the colonisation of Dublin for the 31st International Eucharistic Congress in 1932. [Ill. 10.3] For five days in June, swathes of the city, from tenement laneways to Dublin's huge Phoenix Park and the city's high street of O'Connell Street, were embellished with temporary altars and grottoes, shrines and flower arrangements. About one million people attended the High Mass, framed by the ephemeral architectural structures designed by John J. Robinson (1887-1965). The international visitors were accommodated in vast camps at the edge of the city, national schools and libraries or in the liners by which they had travelled to Ireland — "floating hotels" docked in the River Liffey's basins. This temporary transformation of a newly independent Dublin was about celebrating the presence of Christ in the Eucharist, a central tenet of Roman Catholicism. And the effects of this spiritual and material transformation were not forgotten for two generations.

Through the 1940s and Irish neutrality in the Second World War, and from the post-war years through the 1950s, the Catholic Church in Ireland flourished, deepened and expanded in adherence to the central state tenet — "For the Glory of God and the honour of Ireland". Dublin's Archbishop McQuaid had urged Ireland's leader De Valera to assert the Catholic Church as the only church, but as other Catholic priest advisors to De Valera pointed out, to install Catholicism as the state religion would be totalitarian, with the potential replacement of "Catholicism" with "Communism".[4]

Though the Constitution fell short of announcing a Christian State, the fledgling Irish state and the Church were wed. The customary image of mid-century Ireland is one of bucolic anti-materialism and religiosity. Certainly, the census continued to reflect that image, with over ninety-five per cent of its dwindling population counting itself Catholic and actively church-going; parish priests were the social and cultural leaders; ever-increasing parish boundaries circumscribed the landscape; and the Irish Catholic Church was the most heavily staffed in the world, so its nuns and priests became the providers of health care, schooling and almost all charity in the state.

Ireland's bishops and archbishops, particularly the figures of Bishop Browne in Galway, Archbishop McQuaid in Dublin and Bishop Cornelius Lucey (1902-1982) in Cork, enjoyed immense power during the middle of the twentieth century, to the extent that they dominated their communities. In 1955, Lucey stated that the bishops:

> were the final arbiters of right and wrong even in political matters. In other spheres the state might for its own good reasons ignore the advice of the experts, but in faith and morals it might not.[5]

Extreme censorship was a fact of Irish life, with over 600 books banned in the period 1950-1955, including international classics by Graham Greene, Ernest Hemingway and Jean-Paul Sartre. Galway's Bishop Browne upheld excruciatingly tight control of the public libraries, their shelves and their librarians in his Diocese of Galway and Kilmacduagh. Browne was also renowned for his stance against mixed bathing off the Galway coast in the seaside suburb of Salthill.[6] Into the 1950s, the spatialisation of this Catholic hegemony was manifest in the growing amount of Corpus Christi processions, for instance, of children each May processing through the cities' streets [Ill. 10.4]; in the vast revivalist churches from the 1950s, particularly; and in the abundance of Marian grottoes dotted across the countryside and in the suburban housing colonies and crumbling historic city streets.[7]

---

4 Kennedy, "Two Priests, the Family and the Irish Constitution"; see also Cullen and O hOgartaigh, *His Grace is displeased*, 16-27.
5 Bishop Cornelius Lucey of Cork, speech at a religious congress in Kerry, cited in Whyte, *Church and State*, 312.
6 Donnelly, "Bishop Michael Browne of Galway and the Regulation of Public Morality".
7 For overviews of Irish Catholic mid-century hegemony and its architectural consequences for suburban Dublin, see Rowley, "The Architect, the Planner and the Bishop" and Id., "Transitional Modernism: Post-war Dublin Churches and the Example of the Clonskeagh Church Competition, 1954".

10.4 Communion procession, 1969.
[Photograph by Elinor Wiltshire. Courtesy of the Elinor Wiltshire Collection, National Library of Ireland]

Tentative Modernism: Vatican II and Irish church design

Archbishop McQuaid was hesitant to engage in the liturgical and physical reforms promoted under Pope John XXIII during the mid-1960s, whose great contribution was, of course, the Second Vatican Council (1962-1965), during which international committees and councils met to liturgically and devotionally reform the Catholic Church.[8] The consequences of Vatican II's redirection were most keenly felt in the experience of the Mass in Ireland — formerly in

8   For an example of McQuaid forbidding two liberal theologians — Father John Courtney Murray (US) and Father Gregory Baum (Canada) — to speak in 1964, see Whyte, "Economic Progress and Political Pragmatism, 1957-63", 299, and Cooney, *John Charles McQuaid*, 365. As the collection of letters to the Archbishop displays, there was still resistance to ecumenism by 1965; see Cullen and O hOgartaigh, eds., *His Grace is displeased*, 169.

Latin, then in English or Irish — and in apparently greater ecumenism and freedom of expression. But through the 1950s, arguably the zenith of his social power, McQuaid appeared to control the direction of Catholic artistic representation. Among the many anecdotal and recorded instances of this control are his overturning of the assessment for an architectural competition for a suburban church in Clonskeagh, south Dublin (1954), and his expulsion of a painting by George Roualt from a visiting exhibition of French contemporary sacred art in 1957.[9] Both instances become metaphorical, pointing to the Irish hierarchy's deep-set reluctance towards architectural and liturgical reform at this mid-century juncture. Having appointed a committee of three trusted clergy advisors to assist him in the development of new churches, McQuaid promoted revivalist architecture externally, replete with factory-made statutory internally.

To the frustration of Ireland's younger architects, the Irish Catholic hierarchy maintained this conservative revivalist stance for church architecture in the face of a not insignificant Catholic building boom from the 1940s through to the 1960s. Then, in response to Vatican II's nudge towards architectural reform, Ireland's Committee on Sacred Art and Architecture — which was a mixture of increasingly (since the mid-1950s) activist architects and reformist clergy — advised the Episcopal Liturgical Commission of Ireland at Maynooth (the academic heart of Catholic Ireland) issuing the "Pastoral Directory on the Building and Reorganisation of Churches" in 1966.[10] This directory echoed the Second Vatican Council's *Sacrosanctum Concilium* and other documents calling for reform of churches to prioritise congregation participation. However, as some of McQuaid's 1960s correspondence around tabernacle placement in certain new Dublin churches highlights, any design changes which were contemporaneous or subsequent to this 1966 Pastoral Directory were hard-won. One younger architect, Andy Devane (1917-2000) of Robinson Keefe Devane (who was himself deeply religious, while a confirmed modernist and co-author of the Pastoral Directory), had gained commissions for several Jesuit chapels and parish churches at this time.[11] Devane's impulse to place the tabernacle off-centre within the potentially radicalised sanctuary spaces worried his patron priests. And their anxiety when faced with this modernist Catholic architect and the possibility for a barrier-free dialogue mass emanated from their archbishop's conservativism.

9   See Rowley, "Transitional Modernism".
10 "Pastoral Directory on the Building and Reorganisation of Churches". In the directory's opening, the co-authors state that the document is in adherence to the *Constitution on the Liturgy*, the *Instruction on the Proper Implementation of the Constitution on the Sacred Liturgy*, the *Ordo Missae et Ritus Servandus* in *Celebratione Missae* and the *Ritus Servandus* in *Concelebratione Missae*.
11 Rowley, "Chapels and Churches of Andrew Devane 1960-75".

10.5 Queen of Heaven, Airport Church, Dublin, by Andy Devane of Robinson Keefe Devane Architects, completed in 1964.
[Courtesy of Robinson Keefe and Devane Archive, Dublin]

While one Jesuit (Father White) privately urged the architect onwards, towards reform of churches — "I still hope and pray that your work for Maynooth may help us to get nearer to our ideal here,"[12] — another, the parish priest for the Dublin airport church, pulled Devane right back, forcing him to redesign his altar area. [Ill. 10.5] And yet another, the principal of the national teacher training college in Drumcondra, Dublin, was so frustrated by the architect's insistence on reform, that he wrote to Devane in 1965:

> What am I to do? You asked me to send three alternative sketches to the Archbishop with the request that he choose between them. He wrote back asking that the Tabernacle be placed on the altar and the altar so arranged that the priest can say Mass facing or with his back to the people. It may be that in time the post-conciliar Liturgical Commission will give a definite ruling that the Tabernacle must not be placed on the altar.[13]

---

12   Correspondence from Father White to the architect Andy Devane, 1 April 1966, Box 313, Gonzaga file, Robinson Keefe Devane (RKD) Archives.
13   Letter from Father Donal Cregan to Devane, 20 December 1965, Father Cregan's Papers, Correspondence with Robinson Keefe Devane (RKD) A/19/3.2, Saint Patrick's Drumcondra archive, DCU Library.

10.6 Galway Cathedral, view across Salmon Weir bridge, by John. J. Robinson of Robinson Keefe Devane Architects, completed in 1965.
[Courtesy of Robinson Keefe and Devane Archive, Dublin]

This was a tentative period. As late as September 1964, one national newspaper, the *Irish Independent*, ran a headline that read "Priest faces people in new Irish church" at the same time as the most radical of Irish building study tours — to Stockholm, Paris and Copenhagen — was unfolding.[14] The latter was the official government search for new housing methods in response to the Dublin housing crisis of 1963, which ultimately lead to Ballymun Estate. Meanwhile, as Ballymun was being imagined in continental Europe, Archbishop McQuaid was instructing the sculptor Imogen Stuart to remake her figure of Our Lady Queen of Heaven for the airport church because it was too abstract, resembling "a Greek or Roman matron".[15] Also, at this mid-1960s juncture, the new cathedral for Galway, in the west of Ireland and the Republic's third city, was complete and being consecrated.[16] [Ill. 10.6] A huge neo-baroque/Hiberno-Romanesque hybrid of limestone and copper dome, this was Bishop Browne's career-long project (1949-1965), which he funded by means of the Irish dias-

14 The article refers to a church in Ballinahown, in the Galway Diocese; see "Priest Faces People in New Irish Church", *Irish Independent*, 4 September 1964, 1.
15 Letter from Archbishop McQuaid to Andy Devane, 9 June 1967, in job 374 (Airport Church) in Box 313, RKD archives.
16 Rowley, "Hidden Histories Galway Cathedral: The Bishop as Architect".

pora in America and, to a lesser extent, in Australia. In his critique of 1966 for *The Observer*, Ian Nairn commented:

> The Roman Catholic Church in every other country of Western Europe has accepted modern architecture. In West Germany and France it is probably the most intelligent and adventurous single client (...). Even England, after years of wavering, now seems committed, and Liverpool, that most Irish of British cities, is to dedicate its own Roman Catholic cathedral next month. Only Ireland lags behind; the country which first brought Christianity to the West has become the last outpost of reaction.[17]

All of these instances of clerical control and formal conservativism through the 1960s provide a greyer and more nuanced backcloth to the received narrative of 1960s Ireland as a radicalising place. Inarguably, this was a period of broad cultural change with educational and economic modernisation, which coincided with transnational reform in the Catholic Church. By the mid-1960s, almost thirty years after the Irish Constitution was redrafted, public commentators signalled "the end of an era", pointing to massive contemporary shifts in Ireland's socio-economic, political and religious cultures. Politically, key protagonists from the Civil War era were retiring, while economically, according to cultural commentator David Thornley, and in response to the First Programme of Economic Expansion of 1959-1963, there was an "acceptance of the principle that the maintenance of economic growth is the first charge upon political administration".[18] Following from this, and moving Ireland ever closer to membership in the European Economic Community (the later European Union), was a reassessment of attitudes to social services, including, markedly, to housing:

> It is now being slowly recognized that niggardliness towards health, mental illness, housing, old age, and above all education, is ultimately inefficient and wasteful of natural resources in competitive terms.[19]

Ireland's rural economy was weakening, with industrial employment growing, and urban populations, despite mass emigration, were on the rise. In fact, while the population of Ireland fell from just under 5.5 million to 2.8 million between 1874 and 1961, the population of Dublin City rose from 265,000 to 600,000. Moreover, standards of living were improving with wages climbing in industry by 63.3 per cent and in agriculture by 50.3 per cent, while car own-

---

17   Ian Nairn, "Ecclesiastical All-Sorts", *The Observer*, 24 April 1966, 30.
18   Thornley, "End of an Era", 10.
19   Ibid.

10.7 Liberty Hall, Dublin Quays, by Des Rea O'Kelly, built 1958-1963.
[Courtesy of Hugh Doran Collection, Irish Architectural Archive]

ership doubled between 1954 and 1964.[20] Ireland's annual economic growth rate was only one per cent until 1958, but thereafter it shot up to four per cent. In the space of five years, from about 1960, and with the ascendancy of a generation of technocratic civil servants as architectural patrons, rectilinear and tall structures with glazed façades appeared on Dublin's skyline. New buildings for the tourism board, the national theatre, the trade union and various corporations disrupted the city's grain of Georgian house plots and brought a strain of Americanised modernism to Dublin's streets.[21] [Ill. 10.7]

Such material changes lent physical weight to Thornley's 1964 written exposition, and for us, they substantiate the revisionist thesis of 1960s Ireland as a radically changing place. And yet, meanwhile, as the Dublin diocesan correspondence attests, the Irish Catholic hierarchy maintained an anti-reform position, seemingly exercising considerable social and official control. From 1954, the Archbishop established the Committee of Vigilance, which was actively investigating groups such as the Irish Housewives Association, Dublin Teddy Boys, UCD's International Student Union, trade unions and more.[22] This need to maintain oversight of mainstream and fringe social activities alike within his diocese and beyond extended through the 1960s, with often remarkable daily consequences. One example from 1969, highlighting the reticence of the hierarchy to embrace post-Vatican II calls for ecumenism, was when the Lord Mayor of Dublin's wife wrote to McQuaid seeking permission to officially open and attend the (Protestant) Salvation Army sale of work![23]

Perhaps this can be explained away as a case of ever-growing polarisation in Ireland between church and state through and by the end of the 1960s, particularly in urban areas, with the state pushing forward and the Church pushing back. Certainly, as observed with cultural censorship, ecumenism, architectural modernism and church design, and as we will see around education reform, the Catholic hierarchy's position presented distinct dichotomous moments. But interestingly, these dichotomies evaporated in the realms of housing provision and the related urban planning at the time, with church and state (local government) pragmatically collaborating.

---

20 Ibid., 12: "In 1970 there will be one passenger car to every eight to ten people — the same figure as obtained in Britain in 1960."
21 Rowley, "From Dublin to Chicago and Back Again: The Influence of Americanised Modernism on Dublin Architecture 1960-1980".
22 Cullen and O hOgartaigh, *His Grace is Displeased*, 169.
23 Dublin, DA, McQuaid Papers, Memo, 2 August 1967, File 1: XVIII/56/95 – 104, Dublin Corporation 1960-1965.

Housing Estates in Green Fields: Dublin's Housing Trends, 1930s-1960s

As Catholic congregations in Dublin swelled through the 1940s, 1950s and 1960s, the establishment responded with *new* parishes in *new* suburban neighbourhoods. The local authority — and to a lesser extent, private housing co-operatives — provided the roadways and the dwellings; the Church provided the spaces for congregation and education. Moreover, there was consensus (amongst housing officials, government economists and planning professionals) in terms of the suburban locations of Dublin's new housing during the mid-century and a shared antipathy towards flat blocks; both trends coming out of slum-clearance legislation of 1931 and 1932, which set the standard for how working-class Dubliners were to live and be housed for the rest of the twentieth century.

Unsurprisingly, given the influence of Raymond Unwin and Patrick Geddes in Dublin as judges of the 1914 Civic Competition for a new plan for the city and later as advisors to the Dublin Corporation (the local authority), Dublin's new 1930s housing had followed British Garden Suburb ideals. Ultimately motivated by the high densities and insanitary conditions blighting Dublin's slum tenements — in 1911, 87,000 people lived in unfit tenement housing, and this only decreased to 81,000 by 1936, despite a major slum-clearance project through the 1930s — the new housing colonies at the city's edge were made up of single-family, two-storey houses with front and back gardens set into terraces and topped off by pitched tiled roofs. Expectations for significantly lower densities were met with between thirty-seven and forty-five houses per hectare. And given the large amount of rural depopulation in Ireland through migration to Dublin at this time, rural conditions were partly emulated in the provision of individual allotment-type gardens and public green spaces.

This type of development dominated from the 1930s at the two key sites of Cabra and Crumlin Estates, to the west of Dublin, arguably colouring Dublin's housing development and policy through the rest of the twentieth century. Dublin Corporation would first make the roadways and water/waste infrastructure, and thereafter, the new housing architect (Herbert Simms, 1898-1948) and his team designed terrace after terrace of mass-concrete parlour or kitchen house types. Importantly, there was an explicit relationship between the houses and the supporting public structures of the Catholic Church in the form of large revivalist church buildings and low-lying modernist schools. At Cabra, two huge Catholic churches served the growing community: the 1931-1933 Italian Romanesque Christ the King church (Robinson and Keefe) and the 1953 Church of the Most Precious Blood (architect unknown). [Ill. 10.8] The making of the older church of Christ the King with funds raised from the nascent community describes the common process through the twentieth cen-

10.8 Christ the King Church, Cabra, Dublin, built 1931-1933
[Courtesy of Paul Tierney for C20th Architecture in Dublin City project, Dublin City Council]

tury in Ireland of collective donation for pastoral social infrastructure. Parish records cite how 7,000 people each contributed a shilling to the cost of "seven thousand bricks which comprised the outer walls of the church".[24] At the opening ceremony, the parish priest and Dublin's Lord Mayor, among others, asserted the community's funding responsibility, inadvertently describing the reciprocity between housing and the Catholic Church in mid-twentieth-century Dublin:

> This debt is a painful necessity. The presence of so many new houses and such a teeming population demanded fresh facilities for worship and for Christian education, and also additional priests. However as faithful and loyal subjects, we shall endeavour to assist you to bear and liquidate this heavy liability.[25]

The later Church of the Most Precious Blood was most fully embedded into a symmetrically designed suburban scape; placed on an axis between terraces of shops but on a slope overlooking the housing, it was a physical reflection of the Church's dominant pastoral position. This Garden Suburb model of low-density, low-rise, single-family dwellings with public structures of

24 "New Cabra Church", *Irish Times*, 30 October 1933, 5. See also Merlo Kelly, "Christ the King" case study, in Rowley, ed., *More Than Concrete Blocks*, Vol 1, 258-265.
25 "New Cabra Church", *Irish Times*, 30 October 1933, 5.

Catholic authority at the estates' hearts was favoured across Irish officialdom, while urban flats and tenements were regarded with distrust and met, from their earliest iterations, with accusations of "Red Vienna in Dublin", which by the early 1940s, had grown into outward opposition to new flat block development from Dublin officials and housing professionals.[26] From the late 1930s, with the first consolidated state-sponsored slum clearance programme in Dublin, there was a significant flat-building campaign. Simms and his team turned to Liverpool, London, Rotterdam and Amsterdam for inspiration, thus bringing a blend of British Victoriana and Dutch Expressionism to 1930s Dublin. Despite this extensive development, the housing crisis worsened, thereby instigating the Department of Local Government tribunal and investigation of 1938, published in 1943 as *The Report of Inquiry into the Housing of the Working Classes of Dublin*. Markedly, the tribunal revealed that a four-roomed flat unit in a new urban block cost almost twice as much as a four-roomed cottage in a new suburban housing colony.[27] Compounding this economic perspective, flats were deemed less healthy for family formation and development, with the same enquiry citing their "cramped conditions" and the "drudgery" associated with "stair climbing".

By the mid-1940s, the state's flat-building programme had lapsed, while its house-building programme had accelerated. Enabling a de-intensification of the city centre, the housing of Dublin's "working classes" at its primarily eastern and northern edges was most efficient, as well as morally preferable. For many, the suburb's inchoate nature represented a liminality, or a compromise between urban and rural lifestyles. Dublin Corporation's joint Town Planning and Housing Committees' report of 1947 stated that lower densities improved the "spiritual as well as physical health" of working-class citizens.[28] At the same time, a Catholic spokesman, Reverend John Kelleher, stated that rural migrants to Dublin were innately pious and brought "a fresh accession of strength to the Church in the cities".[29]

---

26 Cited by Rothery, *Ireland and the New Architecture 1900-1940*; see also O'Gorman, *Looking to Vienna: A Reflection on the Discourse Surrounding Viennese Housing in 1930s Dublin*.
27 "Altered Policy Regarding the Classes of Accommodation to be Provided: Flats or Cottages", quotation is from point 333 and the statistic is from point 338 in *The Report of Inquiry into the Housing of the Working Classes of the City of Dublin*, 118 and 120.
28 Report No. 8, Housing and Town Planning Committees joint report (signed off by Norman Chance and Michael O'Brien), *Reports and Printed Documents of the Corporation of Dublin*, January-December 1947, 70.
29 Kelleher, "Catholic Rural Action", 421.

Enter Ballymun: Dublin's Edge City Described

This was an era of extreme expansion for the Dublin Diocese, at least, and the pastoral potential of the newfound parish was not lost on McQuaid and his army of vicars general. Enter Ballymun Estate: at once a radically different housing colony, developed from 1965 and occupied by 1969, but crucially, it was carved out of former rural demesne territory, thus signalling continuity in terms of its virgin greenfield setting. Should Ballymun then be understood primarily within this context, so that its development was encouraged by the Church? Certainly, there were no contrary public statements issued by the Archbishop or evidence of his private opposition to the scheme in his personal papers or in parish archive files.[30] McQuaid was not disinterested, though. He held extensive Dublin Corporation documents in his private collection and commented directly on many technical and public matters, from the suitability of street lighting to the vandalism of tenement properties.[31] But what of Ballymun's high-rise architecture, its massive scale and its sought-after autonomy, associated as these situations were with foreign precedents — either Communist Russian prototypes or secular Swedish New Towns?

For the government of early 1960s Ireland, Ballymun Estate was a housing manifestation of an industrialising urban nation.[32] It was to be massive in scale and in aspiration. The vision, as realised, was for 3,000 families to live on the 192-acre site (circa 78 hectares), broken down into 400 five-roomed, two-storeyed houses, 52 one-roomed flats in two-storeyed buildings, 1354 four-roomed flats, 490 three-roomed flats and 725 two-roomed flats.[33] The vast estate was organised into five neighbourhoods — Sillogue, Balbutcher, Balcurris, Coultry and Shangan — which were to be clustered around a town centre, with emphasis laid on motor access. [Ill. 10.9] Contemporary discourse, coming from the local government debates as well as the building industry's polemic, concentrated on the housing type of flat, high-rise and otherwise, and the housing technology, as well as the many playgrounds, the swimming pool, the skating rink, the golf course and the good transport links (includ-

---

30   The contentious McQuaid biography by John Cooney claims that McQuaid made representations to the Minister of Local Government, Neil Blaney, about Ballymun; however, Blaney denies that he had meetings with the Archbishop; see Cooney, *John Charles McQuaid*, 385 and 501.
31   Such documents in the Archbishop's collection include folders on public lighting (1941); the *Report of Inquiry 1939-1943*; a file on vandalism of tenement properties (1943); an extensive housing report (1947); a file on a new power station in Dublin's dockland area (1949); and a file on the proposed lighting of key Dublin churches for a national festival, *An Tostal* (1953). Dublin, DA, McQuaid Papers, Dublin Corporation/Government Box, AB8/B (also numbered on its lid, 555).
32   Waters, "The National Memory Town", 264.
33   Cubitt Haden Sisks, *Ballymun Housing Project* (NBA, Dublin, 1966).

10.9 Master-planning of Ballymun Estate by Arthur Swift & Partners and Cubitts Haden Sisk, built 1965-1969.
[Reproduced from a Sisk construction booklet. Courtesy of the Irish Architectural Archive]

ing the location's proximity to Dublin Airport) that were to be provided.[34] The three marked conditions of Ballymun, differentiating it from its local precedents, were its scale, its system-built technology and its high-rise elements. The seven fifteen-storey towers, nineteen eight-storey spine blocks and ten four-storey walk-up blocks made up the majority of Ballymun's 3021 units, and as such, the estate was an assertion of the viability of the multi-storey flat block for Irish working-class housing. At this time, and until Ballymun started to be occupied in 1969, there was little or no official discussion on schools and churches. One rare mention of schools in an early planning overview — "Houses are served by pedestrian walkways strong enough to take milk floats or an ambulance (...). The walkways serving the flats are covered and lead directly to the schools and town centre," — was only in relation to the architectonics of the flats and the orientation of the roadways.[35]

Certainly, at first glance, Ballymun presented the communality of stacked living as an appropriate residential solution. And its architectonics of concrete and rectilinear massing set on to a Radburn-like network of roads and pathways were clearly in celebration of architectural modernism. [Ill. 10.10] Even the estate's incorporation of single-family houses, as a nod to more traditional housing practices, was underpinned by modernist leanings because of the houses' prefabricated nature. Taken from an English industrial system, Lowton-Cubitt, these Ballymun houses were still only the second or third time that

---

34 The sophisticated facilities promised Ballymun were listed in the local newspapers; see, for instance, "Model New Town", *Irish Press*, 31 July 1969.
35 "Ballymun: Ireland's Greatest Housing Scheme", *Irish Builder*, 10 April 1965, 255.

10.10 Aerial view of Ballymun Estate, 1971.
[Courtesy of Dublin City Library and Archive]

the Irish state engaged with system-built housing.[36] While they always kept an eye on the prefabricated methods being used in post-war Britain, the Irish had conservative tendencies, maintaining, for instance, the Dublin bye-laws of nine-inch-thick walls and favouring traditional load-bearing wall technologies, as well as traditional typologies of single-family houses. Importantly, at 90 m², these Ballymun Estate houses were considerably roomier than their Dublin Corporation counterparts, and after just eighteen months from the signing of contracts between government and builders, the first 112 houses were complete and ready for occupation.[37] This process was all about speed: the on-site factory was capable of fabricating eight houses in a normal five-day working week. With the flats, the system adopted came from France, from Balency et Shul, and comprised concrete flooring slabs, replete with built-in heating coils. The heating and water were controlled mechanistically and generated by Ballymun's own district central boiler plant. Each tower was serviced by two lifts, with seventy-three lifts in total on the estate; all flats had balconies and were centrally heated by a district heating system. With a

36 For a discussion of other prefabricated housing experiments, see Rowley, *Housing, Architecture and the Edge Condition: Dublin is Building 1930s-1970s*.
37 See <http://www.sisk150.com/wp-content/uploads/2008/10/ballymun.pdf>, accessed May 2017. For an architectural history of Ballymun, see Montague, "The Architecture of Ballymun".

breakdown of six flats per floor, either two- or four-roomed units, each tower contained ninety flats.

All such amenities were stressed from the outset; the technical sophistication was unique in Irish housing, bringing unprecedented domestic comfort. With its high-rise structures and central heating for all, arranged in almost 500 acres of green open space, Ballymun Estate stood in contrast to the urban tenements and rural cottages from which its first residents came. The tenements of Dublin and the cottages in the Irish countryside were known for their naïve sanitation: by the mid-1960s, most still had neither internal bathrooms nor reliable electricity. Ballymun thus represented something foreign externally and exotic internally. It was an indiscriminate utopia, and in its inclusivity, it brought relative luxury for all the people. In scale and intention, the estate surely signalled communality and social equality. When it was fully occupied, it housed thousands of children and about 15,000 people overall.

Notwithstanding, by the time Ballymun was completed at the dawn of the 1970s, high-rise architecture (and by extension, mass housing generally) had different significations representing relative accents in its varying settings and iterations; the estate chimed with socialist ideals. Indeed, it might comfortably be read as a singular socialist modernising programme for mid-century Ireland in its attempt to serve those unable to serve themselves with flat and tower block accommodation. Ballymun's patrons and commissioners, the Department of Local Government, handed over its management to an overburdened Dublin Corporation, upon naming the seven towers after the seven revolutionaries of the first battle for independence, the 1916 Easter Rising.[38] After all, the place was mid-construction when the young state, Ireland, celebrated the 1916 jubilee in 1966, and rather than emphasise the failures of Irish freedom — slums — the state sought to celebrate the achievements of independence. By naming the towers after these seven nationalist figures, the authorities tried to move the housing crisis project away from its socialist aesthetic and ally it rather to 1960s nationalist rhetoric. As such, while being made, Ballymun's socialist undertones were traced over, blocked out even, by triumphant nationalist overtones.

The official stance on, or di/stance from, socialism was unsurprising given its association with the subversive elements of communism and liberalism in Ireland's hegemonic Catholic culture. But seemingly, three aspects of the new scheme made it palatable for Dublin Corporation and the local hierarchy: that it would present a density of just sixty habitable rooms per acre on average (148/ha); that it would contain a certain portion of single-family homes;

[38] Ballymun's seven towers were named after the seven signatories of the iconic nationalist document, *The Proclamation of Independence*, which was read at the temple front of the General Post Office on Dublin's O'Connell Street during the Rising of Easter 1916. They were: Eamonn Ceannt, Tom Clarke, James Connolly, Sean MacDiarmada, Thomas MacDonagh, Patrick Pearse and Joseph Mary Plunkett.

and that it would contain large family-sized (three-roomed) flats.[39] Though the low-rise elements were prefabricated and in the minority, they mocked traditional buildings with their pitched roofs and brick faced elevations. Beyond these pragmatics, though, some of the more "emotional" aspects of the housing estate might be read as both feeding into and emanating out of contemporary Catholic social teaching. First, Ballymun's communality was in tune with Irish Catholicism's translation of the "common good": that is, the creation of a housing colony and certain living conditions from which to realise the potential of all individuals and groups. According to *Quadragesimo Anno*, as echoed in the Irish Constitution, the living environment must facilitate "the first relationships to arise (...), including the family, associations and local communities".[40] Also, central to Irish Catholic social teaching was the principle of "subsidiarity", which resisted state intervention in matters best handled at a community or individual level.[41] As such, McQuaid's 1950s Committee of Vigilance investigated organisations or groups which were deemed "interventionist" and might therefore confound the common good and subsidiary. On the other hand, vocationalism and the extensive interventions by the Catholic Social Service Conference (CSSC), for instance, were to be supported.

The CSSC was a consortium of Catholic charities which McQuaid brought together when he first became archbishop; he had been alarmed both at the great need and poverty in 1940s mid-war Dublin and at the dispersed organisation of support agencies. On a personal level, informing his professional approach to public morality, McQuaid was deeply rooted in the practice of charity, which brings us to a second teaching: the principle of "solidarity". As well as recognising the intrinsic social nature of people, solidarity prioritises equality and dignity and emphasises the individual's responsibility to others, spilling into the act of giving to the needy. In the example of the CSSC, we encounter McQuaid's charity and consciousness of the poor.[42] In the mid-war context, and in response to the appalling slum conditions in which Dublin's poor were existing, the CSSC established housing and fuel committees. It procured milk through donations from creameries, tonnes of turf from the Turf Board and children's clothes fabricated by guilds. Interestingly for our discussion, the Conference reconditioned a number of dilapidated buildings, creating some forty three-roomed flats for newly married couples, later taking on a building society role as it converted houses into the more economical and higher density flats.[43] Evidently, in the face of crisis and extreme poverty, Catholic charity found that flats were an appropriate housing solution.

39 Brady, *Dublin, 1950-1970. Houses, Flats and High Rise*, 205-228.
40 *Quadragesimo Anno*, paraphrased by Gray, "The Politics of Migration, Church and State: The case of the Catholic Church in Ireland".
41 Ibid.
42 See Earner-Byrne, *Letters of the Catholic Poor*.
43 Corish, *The Irish Catholic Experience*, 248.

In a similar vein, as a crisis reaction, Ballymun Estate was the explicit response to Ireland's housing crisis of 1963. In June 1963, the fragility of Dublin's eighteenth- and nineteenth-century housing stock, which had been barely maintained and always overused as tenements, was exposed. Three houses in central Dublin collapsed, killing four people.[44] In the space of one week, following the tragedy and as a knee-jerk reaction by officialdom, 156 old houses were demolished and 520 families evacuated. The demolition rally and de-tenanting of Dublin that ensued displaced 900 families and 326 single people.[45] The Minister of Local Government, Neil Blaney (1922-1995), was under pressure, and in April 1964, he and a team undertook a study tour of European system-built mass housing. By 1965, the contract was signed, the government (in the guise of the newly shaped National Building Agency, NBA, established since 1960) having chosen a consortium of Cubitt Haden Sisks (the British Lowton-Cubbit, Sisks contractors and the French Balency et Shul), following the master plan by the architects Arthur Swift and Partners and the landscape design by James Fehily Associates.

Despite its ambivalent nature — as we have seen, the Ballymun development could be interpreted both as a socialist manifesto (a threat) and a contemporary showcase of universal Catholic values (an opportunity) — McQuaid seems not to have capitalised upon it. Quite the contrary, he seems to have remained silent about Ballymun. So, are we to interpret the Archbishop's silence around the evolution of Ballymun Estate as benign acceptance of a unique solution? During the early 1960s, was McQuaid simply too perturbed by ecumenical questions such as maintaining the ban on Catholics attending Trinity College Dublin to be overly preoccupied with housing matters?

Developing into the 1970s: Pastoral Infrastructure at Ballymun

By the end of the 1960s, the first residents moved in to the Ballymun Estate, and from 1967 onwards, we find a stream of private, regular and concerned correspondence between the Archbishop and the parish priest of Saint Pappin's Parish, Ballymun, Father Breen. Evidently, McQuaid's silence was lifted in the face of operational need. In a general sense, the Archbishop had continued to be in direct correspondence with Dublin Corporation Town Planning Officer Michael O'Brien, who counselled him on development plans around

---

44 The shift in economic policy from 1958 outlined above, which moved the government away from protectionist programmes of house building and sought to boost employment instead through foreign direct investment schemes, had inadvertently neglected housing development.

45 Erica Hanna's excellent study presents the most coherent overview of this crisis: *Modern Dublin. Urban Change and the Irish Past, 1957-1973.*

new satellite towns in Dublin's western fringes.[46] For Ballymun, Archbishop McQuaid held site plans (1972) and copies of the Dublin Corporation housing committee minutes of 1966.[47] After all, such empire expansion demanded heavy management, and by the start of the 1970s, McQuaid and the prelates in Ireland's other major urban centres of Cork and Galway, at least, were in correspondence with the highest levels of local government. The close relationship, a bureaucratic and cultural reciprocity, had not dissipated during the radicalising 1960s. For instance, Galway's Bishop Browne was friendlier than ever with the Galway County Manager, A.A. Sharkey, and received notifications of plans around road-widening schemes, road safety campaigns and housing conditions from the Department of Local Government.[48]

As Dublin continued to expand, McQuaid had formalised his team of advisors into the Dublin Diocesan Development Commission. Seemingly, an area would not be developed without the Archbishop's involvement, who appeared to be primarily concerned not with church building, as one would expect, but with the provision of Catholic schools. As this chapter set out at its opening, in twentieth-century Ireland, the burden of church-building costs and about one-third of school costs fell upon the Catholic parishioner. School building was a priority for this mid-century Catholic Church. According to Jean Blanchard's 1963 study, *The Church in Contemporary Ireland*, "since primary education is integrated in the framework of the ecclesiastical parish" in Ireland, this was not unusual; all primary schools were denominational.[49] He explains:

> The Catholic Church considers it her mission to watch over the child in order to develop the seed of supernatural life which has been implanted in him. She therefore attaches the greatest importance to the educational problem.[50]

The emphasis on providing the spaces and structures for education in newly formed parishes was apparent at the Ballymun Estate. In early 1969, a newspaper article with the headline "Little Cash for Schools in Ballymun" irritated the Archbishop to the extent that he scolded the parish priest, Father Breen: "I regret very much the press report (...). If you had consulted me you could not have so spoken."[51] For McQuaid, the somewhat begging article outlining the

---

46 Dublin, DA, McQuaid Papers, Plans for Blanchardstown, demographic projections, XVIII/61/6-12, Dublin Corporation: Town Planning 1971.
47 Dublin, DA, McQuaid papers, Ballymun Parish files, Town Planning file, Government Box.
48 See, for instance, correspondence in folders 300-307, Box 12, Bishop Browne Papers, Galway Cathedral, Diocesan Archives, Diocese of Galway, Kilmacduagh and Kilfenora.
49 Blanchard, *The Church in Contemporary Ireland*, 35.
50 Ibid.
51 "Little Cash for Schools", *Evening Press*, 10 January 1969; scolding letter from McQuaid to Breen, 14 January 1969. Dublin, DA, McQuaid papers, Ballymun Parish files LIV/16/6/5.

lack of social infrastructure in the new massive housing estate revealed the diocese's vulnerabilities, and at the wrong time. In 1969, the archbishop was this defensive precisely because of contemporary developments in national education policy. Following a damning report on Irish education by the OECD in 1962 (entitled *Investment in Education*), which uncovered, for instance, that fewer than half of Ireland's 4880 national schools had modern sanitation and drinking water, legislation was introduced from 1967 to overhaul the system. This largely brought about free secondary and vocational education. And two secular school typologies emerged, the comprehensive and the community schools, upsetting the status quo of Catholic (or to a lesser extent, Protestant) secondary-level schools. By 1968, Ireland's post-primary population rose to 133,591, which would put pressure on the architectural infrastructure, then managed by a new Post-Primary Building Unit within the Department of Education.

In the context of Vatican II's decrees and the damning evaluation of contemporary Irish education, McQuaid must have felt under siege. Though Dublin's archbishop asserted to his congregation that "no change will worry the tranquillity of your Christian lives", the changes from within and without Irish society were doubtlessly affecting his ministry.[52] And arguably, given his own profession as a teacher, the battle to control Irish education was not something that he was willing to lose. Correspondence from the early 1960s shows that he remained adamant about preserving single gender denominational schools, despite the educational reform that was all about.[53] Interestingly, it is at Ballymun that we see how the Catholic primary schools arrived years before the new Catholic churches. Such development is perhaps illustrative of a barely discernible shift in McQuaid's policy, whereby church form and other aspects became wholly secondary to school production and governance.

As Blanchard reminds us, the responsibility for primary schools in Ireland was first and last placed with the parish priest:

> He buys the site, engages an architect and, having consulted the Department, he selects a Contractor (...). When the school is built, the parish priest, who is the manager, appoints the teacher or teachers (...). He is directly responsible for the upkeep, running and management of the school. The cost of the teachers' salaries is borne by the state.[54]

---

52 Cited in Ó Corrain, *Rendering to God and Cesar: The Irish churches and the two states in Ireland, 1949-73*, 206.
53 Correspondence between Monsignor Fitzpatrick and Archbishop McQuaid, 10 May 1961, in Cullen and Ó hOgartaigh, eds., *His Grace is Displeased*, 73.
54 Blanchard, *The Church in Contemporary Ireland*, 36.

Arguably then, one of the Archbishop's key roles was to ensure that his priests were supported in setting up these crucial pieces of pastoral infrastructure. Clearly, and unlike the situation in many equivalent new exurban communities across Catholic Europe and Britain, Archbishop McQuaid had no anxiety about the direction of the Ballymun Estate-as-parish and its congregation. In an almost desperate letter to the Archbishop in November 1969, Father Breen described the zealous and ever-growing appetite for mass. Having converted Ballymun's first primary school hall into a temporary church for Sunday masses, Breen needed to convert the recently completed second school hall as well:

> The second hall would cater for the people on the eastern side of the estate and would relieve the unhappy situation at St Pappin's where a third of the congregation at the later masses is outside the church in all weathers (...). The opening of this new hall would give us three centres for mass in the parish, with thirteen masses on Sundays, and will enable us to provide fairly adequately for the needs of the people until we can build the churches, which I hope to undertake as quickly as possible.[55]

The reality was that McQuaid's church was bursting at the seams, so most of his anxiety was financial. The financial burden of the pastoral infrastructure at Ballymun appeared particularly acute. In 1968, as a reporting letter from one of the Archbishop's vicars general, Monsignor Charlie Hurley, illustrates, the older surrounding parishes sought to differentiate themselves from this unfinished, yet seemingly ever-growing, neighbourhood. Hurley had undertaken a reconnaissance to Ballymun accompanied by the local priest of the nearby Our Lady of Victories/Ballymun Road neighbourhood, Father Bernard Brady (life dates unknown). Calling the new housing estate the "project area", Brady was "most anxious to cut off the 'project area'".[56] According to Hurley, "[Brady] suggests that the Project Area needs separate pastoral care. It has a temporary school hall, used as Church of the Holy Spirit, in addition to St. Pappin's. New schools are near completion."[57] Arising out of this report from the Archbishop's advisor, the so-called project area comprising Ballymun Estate's five housing neighbourhoods was constituted as three parishes by 1970. Nevertheless, enforcing the hypothesis that priorities had shifted, no church building was constructed here under Archbishop McQuaid's reign. Instead, as the parish accounts of June 1970 show, the school building expenses amounted to £167,851, while church building and furnishing amounted to

---

55 From Breen to McQuaid, 11 November 1969. Dublin, DA, McQuaid papers, Ballymun Parish files, LIV/16/6/6.
56 From Monsignor Charles Hurley to Archbishop McQuaid, 2 June 1968. Dublin, DA, McQuaid papers, Ballymun Parish files, LIV/17/6/1.
57 Ibid., Hurley to McQuaid.

10.11 Our Lady of Victories, Ballymun Road, by Guy Moloney, 1969.
[Reproduced from the parish pamphlet. Courtesy of the Irish Architectural Archive]

just £1,634. The three churches of Ballymun Estate opened in the decade after McQuaid's retirement: the Church of the Holy Spirit (Sillogue Road) and the Church of the Virgin Mary (Shangan), shed-like identikit structures, were both consecrated in 1975, and the finer Saint Joseph's (Balcurris) opened in 1981 but was consecrated on the occasion of Pope John Paul II's visit to Ireland in 1979. Judging from the delay in the churches' construction and consecration, it would seem that their sites were allocated in proximity to the neighbourhood schools; that is, church allocation was after the fact. From the first published planning brief for Ballymun (Summer 1966), with emphasis laid on motor car access, the technology of the various housing types and such "shiny" community buildings as a cinema and bowling alley that never arrived, schools and churches were hardly mentioned. At first, a single large octagonal church was proposed for the town centre, at the "heart of the community", while schools were discussed in vague terms, as a general entity, to be placed loosely to the west of the main Ballymun Road.[58]

Seeking to demarcate new parish boundaries while apportioning land most appropriately, Father Brady had wanted to dissociate his parish from the "project area", while maintaining connection with the established, and therefore richer, original Larkhill parish. As it turned out, he was all about building a new church and making a new parish — which he did, on the edge of the project area, but not for its population. Brady's Our Lady of Victories church (architect, Guy Moloney) was the only church at Ballymun that Archbishop McQuaid oversaw and consecrated. [Ill. 10.11] And its grandeur — albeit fol-

[58] "The Planning Brief. The Planning Concept" in Cubitt Haden Sisks, *Ballymun Housing Project* (Sisk and CHS, 1966), 1.2-1.3.

lowing a robust mid-century modernist aesthetic of coloured concrete and expanses of *dalle de verre* windows that might loosely be termed "post-Vatican II" in sentiment — was a cause of anxiety for the Archbishop; to the extent that in May 1970, he forbade Brady from building himself a house alongside it:

> I am hearing much about the dissatisfaction of the people about your building a house, while your debt is so great. Renting a house would not cause such a murmuring. I would not like, for your sake, that a deputation should wait on you, as has been suggested.[59]

Though the finances of Our Lady of Victories church were guaranteed by the Larkhill parish, diocesan indebtedness was a growing concern as McQuaid neared retirement. A 1971 memo outlining recent correspondence with the Bank of Nova Scotia pointed out that this new parish was defaulting on its repayments. As such, "it will affect the Bank's policy towards any religious group borrowing from the Bank, in particular the Diocese."[60] Meanwhile, up the road in Saint Pappin's, the parish heartland of the so-called project area with no sign of a new church building, Father Breen was struggling. We recall Breen's 1970 fundraising brochure from our introduction, which sought to raise 800 pounds per week and laid bare the pedantic financial workings of a new parish:

> In order to obtain from the Bank the future loans to build the churches and the third school, we must be able to tell the Bank Manager that the people of Ballymun have considered their needs, estimated how much they can afford to give each week and indicated their willingness to give that amount. (...) [This can only happen] if each Parishioner recognises his responsibility to Almighty God and to his neighbour.[61]

Behind the scenes, Father Breen was enacting a new fundraising programme, soon to be adopted across the diocese. Entitled "planned giving", and motivated by his 1969 evidence that "there is rather something more than a hardcore of parishioners opposed to contributing to anything which they conceive as 'for the priests'", Breen designed this programme so that eighty per cent

---

59 Letter from Archbishop McQuaid to Father Brady (underlining is part of the original document), 2 May 1970 (LIV/17/3/4). A few months later, McQuaid wrote: "The whole situation is being very closely watched and commented on by priests and people"; letter to Father Brady, 31 July 1970, LIV/17/3/9. Dublin, DA, McQuaid papers, Ballymun Parish files.
60 Memo to Archbishop McQuaid, 21 May 1971, LIV/17/1/20. Dublin, DA, McQuaid papers, Ballymun Parish files.
61 Breen, *Ballymun brochure 1970*, unpaginated.

of the parishioners' weekly contribution would feed the parish infrastructure itself, while ten per cent would go to the Archbishop and ten per cent would go to an international campaign (famine relief or other).[62] Was this then another informal shift in diocesan practices, coinciding with the early 1970s and McQuaid's impending retirement; coinciding, too, with the digestion of Vatican II decrees?

Ultimately underpinned by perceptions of need and priestly greed or power, the "planned giving" campaign and the provision of schools before churches may be read as some of the Archbishop's earliest concessions to Vatican II; that is, if Vatican II's effects might be read as humanising, softening and perhaps democratising the processes of the Catholic Church. Interestingly, another such concession also came out of the Ballymun Estate: Father Breen's "meetings in the homes", which he described as:

> a real attempt to put into practice the desire of the Vatican Council for dialogue between Priest and people. We would welcome open discussion on all parish topics, but at this moment in our development the question of money is of first importance.[63]

Notwithstanding its almost humorous financial bleakness, this activity was a solid pastoral move away from McQuaid's tendencies in a new urban Irish parish, in the aftermath of Vatican II.

In Conclusion: Ballymun as Dublin's heterotopia

From the outset, Ballymun was exceptional. It was a compromise, albeit a small one, because it was an extreme response to an extreme situation. The estate was conceived with a highly specialised function in mind — to accommodate a well-defined minority who were unable to support themselves — and for the government, and one imagines the church authorities too, this signalled an idiosyncratic departure from traditional housing policy.

The Ballymun estate, then, because it arose out of pragmatic concerns around a housing crisis, was never a utopia; it was never a radically different, "ideal" space. Rather, it might be understood as a heterotopia. Heterotopia is a term coined by Michel Foucault in his 1967 lecture "On Other Spaces" — coinciding, in fact, with the construction of Ballymun — to describe spaces which are never perfect or opposite to reality, but somehow different. These act as alternative or parallel spaces where deviant behaviour is tolerated; Fou-

---

62 Letter from Breen to McQuaid, 23 July 1969, LIV/16/1/1-33. Dublin, DA, McQuaid papers, Ballymun Parish files.
63 Ibid.

cault draws on the typologies of the prison or the asylum, for instance. This otherness or difference of the heterotopia is evidenced at Ballymun: Ireland's first high-rise architecture, in the context of what was still by the 1960s an obstinately low-rise landscape. While relating to the existing housing culture (low-density and greenfield), it was subject to a different technocratic "collectivistic" regime and was made manifest in high-rise form. This differentiation becomes even more explicit in public discourses, where on the one hand, the Ballymun Estate was presented as a crisis solution, and on the other, tall office and private buildings were presented as deviant and excessive. Blaney, the Minister of Local Government and midwife to Ballymun Estate, persistently discussed the estate in problem-solving terms, as a unique alternative:

> The Corporation's programme, while geared to produce the maximum number of dwellings by conventional means as fast as practicable, still leaves a serious gap which is now being filled by the scheme at Ballymun.[64]

Ballymun's towers and spine blocks were the preferable alternative to the housing shortage. But it is clear from the Dáil (Irish parliament) discourses and the ongoing reports from the local authority housing committee that high-rise dwellings were not the ideal space for family life. As a member of the government stated in 1964:

> It may be said that some people do not like six-storey or ten-storey buildings to live in. Some people regard living in such buildings as more or less equivalent to living in a pigeon hole. Maybe we would all love to house people on an acre of ground and to spread out all over the county, but all these matters bring their own problems. One would have to meet every individual case to get some comment on their requirements.[65]

Even Minister Blaney acknowledged, in a sense presaging the shift that Ballymun would take from housing *solution* to housing *failure* through the 1970s, that the estate was designed for those who could not help themselves and that the provision of low-rise housing would continue to underpin state housing policy.[66] Further enforcing the pragmatic justification of Ballymun for the Catholic prelate at the time was the undeniable fact that the estate was a low-density place. During 1964, as the officials tried to plan a varied environment which would accommodate as many people as possible, they consis-

---

64 Dáil debates, April 1965, Neil Blaney - Vol. 205, 12-11-63, C1340, and Neil Blaney - Vol. 215, 27-4-65, C66.
65 Dáil debates, James Gallagher - Vol. 207, 13-02-1964, C1029.
66 "While concentrating on their primary responsibility of providing houses for families who cannot help themselves, housing authorities should not overlook the need to encourage as many people as possible to provide their own homes." Dáil Debates, Neil Blaney, Minister for Local Government, Vol. 343, 16-12-1964, C62.

tently pushed for lower-rise solutions. In fact, the only perceived advantage to high-rise was that the system-built superstructure was quick to erect. Otherwise, tower architecture was expensive and necessitated the incorporation of lifts, which still by the 1960s in Ireland were a luxurious and precarious technology and had never before been used in Irish housing.

After a decade of occupation with broken-down lifts and incomplete community amenities, Ballymun had become notorious, cut-off and a socio-economic cautionary tale. At this point, McQuaid had retired, but it is worth wondering whether he was not dogged in the late 1960s, at the dawn of a new decade, by the question of modernism and its attendant structures (the heroism of the child) and idioms (abstract representation)? Certainly, he stayed largely outside of the Ballymun experiment, choosing not to conceive of new types of liturgy or urban pastoral. Other than such concessions as his endorsement of priests visiting homes and the "planned giving" campaign, McQuaid operated business-as-normal; probably calculating that Ballymun was a one-off experiment and drastic shifts were not ultimately necessary. His final word on Ballymun-in-development was pointedly about education, when he supported Father Breen's request for a crèche that would be managed by a nun.[67] McQuaid responded, "I agree: very useful. A Sister will have great influence on the families." He then sanctioned the proposal for a "crèche in Ballymun (...) to be run by a Little Sister of the Assumption from Finglas for small children of widows and deserted wives who have to go out to work."[68] Of course, such a reflection by the Archbishop corresponded to the thinking that a working mother was a shameful thing. As a key tenet of the 1937 Irish Constitution, the Irish woman should stay at home to nurture the family:

> 1. In particular, the State recognises that by her life within the home, woman gives to the State a support without which the common good cannot be achieved. 2. The State shall, therefore, endeavour to ensure that mothers shall not be obliged by economic necessity to engage in labour to the neglect of their duties in the home. (Article 41, 2)

Feminism, ecumenism and 1960s brutalist expressionism: the case study of Ballymun Estate shows us that the Irish Catholic hierarchy abided by none of these and as such, while hidden in plain view, worked counter-zeitgeist in 1967, thirty years after they had so endemically influenced the Irish Constitution. Despite the estate's potentially subversive form, Archbishop McQuaid remained steadfast in his role as provider of Catholic infrastructure.

[67] Breen to McQuaid, 6 October 1970. It is interesting to note that the Health Board was pushing Father Breen to begin the crèche project. Dublin, DA, McQuaid papers, Ballymun Parish files, LIV/16/10/1.
[68] Memo from Archbishop McQuaid, 9 December 1970. Dublin, DA, McQuaid papers, Ballymun Parish files, LIV/16/10/2.

BIBLIOGRAPHY

Archives

Dublin, Diocesan Archive (DA)
McQuaid Papers: Dublin Corporation Box, AB8/B
Government correspondence Box 6, AB8/b/XVIII
Apostolic Nuncio Correspondence AB8/b/XVII
Auxiliary Bishops Correspondence AB8/b/XV/D
Primary Education, school building, 1944-1967, AB8/B/XX1V/ Box 1 (1-6)
McQuaid Correspondence 1949-1971, Killiney collection 6 (uncatalogued letters to McQuaid's house in Killiney, South Co. Dublin)
Ballymun Parish Files (Archbishop's Palace, Clonliffe, Drumcondra, Dublin 9)
Dublin, Robinson Keefe Devane (RKD) Archive
Andy Devane job file correspondence, Box 313, 1 April 1966, Gonzaga file
Dublin, Saint Patrick's Drumcondra Archive
Father Cregan Papers, Correspondence with Robinson Keefe Devane (RKD) A/19/3.2
Galway, Diocesan Archive
Bishop Browne Papers, Folders 300-307, Box 12, Diocese of Galway, Kilmacduagh and Kilfenora, Galway Cathedral

Published sources

Bannon, Michael. *Planning: The Irish Experience, 1920-1988*. Dublin: Turoe Press, 1989.
Barr, Collin and Ó Corrain, Daithi. "Catholic Ireland, 1740-2016". In: Eugenio Biagini and Mary Daly, eds. *The Cambridge Social History of Modern Ireland*. Cambridge: Cambridge University Press, 2017, 68-87.
Becker, Annette; Olley, John and Wang, Wilfred. *Twentieth Century Architecture: Ireland*. Munich: Prestel, 1997.
Blanchard, Jean. *The Church in Contemporary Ireland*. Dublin: Clonmore & Reynolds, 1963.
Brady, Joseph. *Dublin, 1950-1970. Houses, Flats and High Rises*. Dublin: Four Courts Press, 2016.
Burke Savage, Roland. "The Church in Dublin: 1940-1965". *Studies*, 216 (1965), 297-341.
Cooney, John. *John Charles McQuaid. Ruler of Catholic Ireland*. Syracuse: Syracuse University Press, 1999.
Copcutt, Geoffrey. "Physical Planning in Ireland". *Build*, 3 Feb. 1967, 17-21.
Corish, Patrick. *The Irish Catholic experience: a historical survey*. Dublin: Gill & McMillan, 1985.
Craft, Maurice. "The Development of Dublin: Background to the Housing Problem". *Studies*, 59 (1970), 301-313.
Cubitt Haden Sisks. *Ballymun Housing Project*. Dublin: Sisk and CHS, 1966.
Cullen, Clara and O hOgartaigh, Margaret. *His Grace is Displeased*. Dublin: Irish Academic Press, 2013.
Daly, Mary E. *Sixties Ireland. Reshaping the Economy, State and Society, 1957-1973*. Cambridge: Cambridge University Press, 2017.
Department of Local Government. *Housing in Ireland*. Dublin: Stationery Office, 1962 and 1969.
Department of Local Government. *Housing in the Seventies*. Dublin: Stationery Office, 1969.
Department of Local Government. *White Paper. Housing Progress and Prospects*. Dublin: Stationery Office, 1964.
Department of Local Government and Public Health. *Report of Inquiry into the Housing of the Working Classes of the City of Dublin 1939-1943*. Dublin: Stationery Office, 1944.
Donnelly, James S. "Bishop Michael Browne of Galway and the Regulation of Public Morality". *New Hibernia Review*, 17 (2013), 1, 16-39.
Earner-Byrne, Lindsey. *Letters of the Catholic Poor*. Cambridge: Cambridge University Press, 2019.
Government of Ireland. *First and Second Programmes for Economic Expansion*. Dublin: Government Publications, 1958 and 1963.
Gray, Breda. "The Politics of Migration, Church and State: The case of the Catholic Church in Ireland". *International Migration Review*, 50 (2016), 2, 315-351.
Hanna, Erica. *Modern Dublin. Urban Change and the Irish Past, 1957-1973*. Oxford: Oxford University Press, 2013.
Horgan, Mervyn. "Anti-Urbanism as a Way of Life: Disdain for Dublin in the Nationalist Imaginary". *The Canadian Journal of Irish Studies*, 30 (2004), 2, 38-47.
Kelleher, John. "Catholic Rural Action". *Studies*, 4 (1974), 421-436.
Kennedy, Finola. "Two Priests, the Family and the Irish Constitution". *Studies*, 1998, 353-364.
Keogh, Dermot. "The Irish Constitutional Revolution: An Analysis of the Making of the Constitution". In: Frank Litton, ed. *The Constitution of Ireland, 1937-1987*. Dublin: Institute of Public Administration, 1987.

McDonald, Frank. *The Construction of Dublin*. Cork: Gandon Press, 2000.

Montague, John. "The architecture of Ballymun". In: Aibhlin McCrann, ed. *Memories, milestones and new horizons: reflections on the regeneration of Ballymun*. Newtownards: Blackstaff Press, 2008, 45-76.

Ó Corrain, Daithi. *Rendering to God and Cesar: The Irish churches and the two states in Ireland, 1949-1973*. Manchester: Manchester University Press, 2006.

O'Gorman, Ronan. *Looking to Vienna: a Reflection on the Discourse Surrounding Viennese Housing in 1930s Dublin*. Unpublished M. Arch Dissertation, University College Dublin, 2019.

O hUiginn, P. "Some Social and Economic Aspects of Housing - an International Comparison". *Administration*, 8 (1960), 1, 43-71.

Parish of St Pappins. *Ballymun Fundraising Brochure*. Dublin: Dublin Diocese, 1970.

"Pastoral Directory on the Building and Reorganisation of Churches". *The Furrow*, 17 (1966), 7, 471-477.

Power, Sinead. "The Development of the Ballymun Housing Scheme, Dublin 1965-1969". *Irish Geography*, 33 (2000), 199-122.

Prior, Aisling, ed. *Hotel Ballymun. Seamus Nolan*. Breaking Ground, Ballymun Regeneration Ltd. Dublin, 2008.

Report No 8, Housing and Town Planning Committees joint report. *Reports and Printed Documents of the Corporation of Dublin*. January-December 1947.

The Report of Inquiry into the Housing of the Working Classes of the City of Dublin. Dublin: Stationery Office, 1943.

Rothery, Sean. *Ireland and the New Architecture 1900-1940*. Dublin: The Lilliput Press, 1991.

Rowley, Ellen. "The Architect, the Planner and the Bishop: the shapers of ordinary Dublin 1940-1970. *Footprint*, 9 (2015), 2, 69-88.

Rowley, Ellen. "Ballymun, Case Study". In: Rolf Loeber et al., eds. *Architecture 1600-2000*. Vol IV. *Art + Architecture of Ireland*. New Haven-London: Yale University Press, 2014, 415-416.

Rowley, Ellen. "Chapels and Churches of Andrew Devane 1960-75". In: Lisa Godson and Kathleen James Chakraborty, eds. *Modern Sacred Architecture in Germany and Ireland*. London: Bloomsbury, 2019), 62-86.

Rowley, Ellen. "From Dublin to Chicago and Back Again: the Influence of Americanised Modernism on Dublin Architecture 1960-1980". In: Linda King and Elain Sisson, eds. *Ireland, Design and Visual Culture: Negotiating Modernity 1922-1992*. Cork: Cork University Press, 2010, 211-231.

Rowley, Ellen. "Hidden Histories Galway Cathedral: The Bishop as Architect". *Architecture Ireland*, 298 (2018), 37-39.

Rowley, Ellen. *Housing, Architecture and the Edge Condition: Dublin is Building 1930s-1970s*. London: Routledge, Taylor & Francis, 2019.

Rowley, Ellen. "Transitional Modernism: Postwar Dublin Churches and the Example of the Clonskeagh Church Competition, 1954". In: Carole Taaffe and Edwina Keown, eds. *Irish Modernism: Origins, Contexts, Publics*. Reimagining Ireland, 14. Bern-New York: Peter Lang, 2009, 69-88.

Rowley, Ellen, ed. *More than Concrete Blocks: Dublin's buildings and their stories*. 2 vols. Dublin: 2016 and 2018.

Somerville-Woodward, Robert. *Ballymun: A History*. 2 vol. Ballymun Regeneration Ltd. Dublin, 2002.

Thornley, David. "End of an Era". *Studies*, 53 (1964), 209, 10.

Waters, John. "The National Memory Town". In: Aibhlin McCrann, ed. *Memories, milestones and new horizons: reflections on the regeneration of Ballymun*. Newtownards: Blackstaff Press, 2008, 264.

Wheeler, Sheila. "Can Ireland Avoid England's Planning Mistakes?". *The Architects' Journal*, 1 September 1966, 595-610.

Whyte, J. H. *Church and State in Modern Ireland 1923-1979*. Dublin: Gill & Macmillan, 1980².

Whyte, J.H. "Economic Progress and Political Pragmatism, 1957-63". In: Jacqueline Rhoda Hill, ed. *A New History of Ireland*. Vol VII. Oxford: Oxford University Press, 2010.

Wright, Lance; Browne, Kenneth and Jones, Peter. "A Future for Dublin". *Architectural Review*, 156 (1974), 933, 267-330.

Wright, Myles. *The Dublin Region: Advisory Plan and Final Report*. Dublin: Government Publications, 1967.

11
EPILOGUE
A DIVINE DWELLING CRISIS?
NOTES FOR A PARADIGM OF EMPTINESS

KEES DOEVENDANS*

In 1972, in his book on the spatiality of God, the Dutch theologian Gerrit C. van Niftrik (1904-1972) wrote that theology has paid considerable attention to time, but relatively little to space.[1] He goes on to argue that spatiality also has a time dimension. A process of anthropologisation whereby God was positioned *within* the soul of man began during the twelfth century under the influence of theologians like Abélard (Petrus Abaelardus) and Bernard of Clairvaux. However, the human soul did not suffice as a home for God:

> He wants the whole of the cosmos as his own. (...) That is why people in the Middle Ages constructed massive, awe-inspiring, albeit impractical, churches. Space was claimed for the Lord, who selects not only people, but souls (however true and important that may be!); who is space, who bestows space and who calls the entire universe home (....).[2]

Between man and the cosmos, the individual soul and the universe, there are several levels of scale: humans take shelter in a dwelling and are part of a national or local faith community and church buildings are part of a parish, neighbourhood or district. This book is about the spatiality of God and how the faith community attempts to engage with it. The focus is primarily

---

* Translated from Dutch by Lilian Chamberlain.
1 Van Niftrik, *De hemel, over de ruimtelijkheid van God.*
2 Ibid., 39. Unless otherwise noted, all translations are by the translator from either the original Dutch or quotations given in Dutch.

on the twentieth century — the era of the modern, industrial city. The modern city, having transformed into its post-industrial variant, is characterised by its "need for abundance", which also seems true of church buildings: they are too large and too profuse — at least, so it is said.[3] There is thus a need for critical reflection or even a rethinking of the spatiality of God in modern times. This epilogue, therefore, contains several notes that employ the spatial dimension of church and faith as a point of departure and the phenomena of secularisation as a historical line.

Secularisation and the Divine Household

The concept of man described by Van Niftrik, one in whose soul God lived, originated in the Middle Ages, when the feudal world, with the parish as the obvious spatial entity, was being undermined by the emergence of cities. According to the theologian Conrad W. Mönnich (1915-1994), the people then being born anticipated the Protestant Reformation and "grew up in the stench, bustle and disorder of the medieval cities from the twelfth century".[4] The Reformation would, of course, have a profound impact on society as a whole. The sociologist Max Weber (1864-1920) contends it was at the root of commercial capitalism in the sixteenth and seventeenth centuries.[5] He also points out how, during the nineteenth century, the modern, industrial city broke with the traditional forms of belief. The world was *conquered* by the growing developments of science, industry and technology. This understanding laid the foundation for the traditional interpretation of the secularisation phenomenon. Because different, separate spheres of life, such as economics, education and art, had been created — each with their own laws — religious norms lost their meaning. The ensuing general rationalisation meant that appealing for supernatural intervention was no longer necessary. And this evolution had a clear spatial dimension: old village communities faded away, and supra-local connections led to more impersonal contacts, governed by bureaucracy. This is also part of the orthodox interpretation of the secularisation phenomenon according to the British church historian Hugh McLeod. People abandoned their faith and ecclesiastical life once they arrived in the big city.[6] The so-called "revisionist" view places this in perspective, though. Were the religious communities in non-urban settlements not being portrayed in too rosy a light?

---

[3] Term borrowed from Wolfgang Koeck, *De nood van de overvloed, het leven in een technisch-industriële wereld*.

[4] Mönnich, *Vreemdelingen en bijwoners, hoofdlijnen uit de geschiedenis van het protestantisme*, 30.

[5] Weber, *The Protestant Ethic and the Spirit of Capitalism*.

[6] McLeod, "Religion in an Urbanizing World, c. 1840-1939"; McLeod, ed., *European Religion in the Age of Great Cities, 1830-1930*.

Was the Church not also highly active in the city? For example, Bettina Hitzer describes how the Protestant Church in Berlin welcomed and protected migrants from the countryside from 1849 to 1914 by, amongst other things, establishing special youth associations.[7]

Might the emergence of the modern city be too superficial an explanation, then, for the changing role of faith, church and religion? Following the Second World War, French theologian Joseph Folliet (1907- 1972) pointed to the role of wars as another possible explanation for secularisation. According to Folliet, the Franco-German War (1870-1871) gave rise to an initial shock:

> Once people had rubbed their eyes, they discovered just how much social and political life had been secularised. Bit by bit, the former "Christian order" appeared to be deteriorating.[8]

The First World War was once again shocking, writes Folliet: Not only had the societal order been secularised, the process had penetrated into every last social structure. The aftermath of the Second World War was worse yet: man *himself* had become secularised. Man was discovered and recognised as a "heathen". Alfred Weber (1868-1958), a geographer and the younger brother of Max Weber, typified this "heathen" as a new kind of man, following in the sequence of the Neanderthals, primitive man and the so-called "third (or European) man", who was born in Greece and discovered the meaning of freedom and individuality. This "fourth man" was the man of the industrial age, who preferred to function as a mass man and felt free of transcendental values.[9]

The question that concerns us here is: How were the "third man" and the "fourth man" housed? What was their place in the world? Just as every religion has something to say about this, the Christian faith has also influenced how people build and live. No faith is limited to the confines of its religious buildings; it carries over into the home, the neighbourhood and the city. The way religious principles and concepts have influenced architecture and urbanism in the twentieth century remains a lacuna in the historiography of the modern city. However, as this book demonstrates, the examples are numerous. As stated in the introduction, the influence of the parish concept has been fundamental for the Dutch conceptualisation of urbanism, for example. Living in well-ordered districts and neighbourhoods was considered a prerequisite for the formation of communities and a buffer against the dangers and sheer sinfulness of the "big city". Parish and district or neighbourhood unit became

---

7   Hitzer, *Im Netz der Liebe. Die protestantische Kirche und ihre Zuwanderer in der Metropole Berlin (1819-1914)*.
8   Folliet, *Les Chrétiens au Carrefour II*. The quote is from J.C. Hoekendijk, "Orde, milieu, mens", *Wending*, 5 (1950), 5/6, 284.
9   Weber, *Der Dritte oder der Vierte Mensch. Vom Sinn des geschichtlichen Daseins*.

nearly interchangeable, widely supported concepts that were adopted by the Protestant Church after the Second World War as part of the idea of the "district congregation": each district was to have its own pastor and church building.

There are also other, less obvious, examples. As the urban sociologist and historian Graeme Davison has shown, the concept of the garden city introduced by Ebenezer Howard (1850-1928) was also strongly influenced by puritanical theological insights and beliefs.[10] Davison refers, amongst others, to William Cowper (1731-1800), a Protestant poet and defender of suburban living in London, who believed these were environments where man could be delivered from his fight between God and Satan, light and dark, heaven and hell, justice and sin, spirit and body and Christianity and the world. As Davison writes:

> In this spiritual battle, "home" was the safest earthly anchor for the Christian. (...) In his imagination, the family served as both the cradle of virtue and the foretaste of Heaven.[11]

The divine household was thus based on a God-imposed division of roles between husband and wife: the men, as spiritual heads of the family, were positioned under God, while women were entrusted with the day-to-day supervision of the household. For women, the Home was a business; for men, it was a place of refuge. The single-family house, complete with its own garden, became a stronghold of private domesticity. This "divine household", the nuclear family, has been a principal building block of Christian culture in Europe well beyond the Second World War. The avant-garde architects of the Modern Movement also took the family as their starting point, but in a rational, functional home where the housework was mechanised and electricity was the new servant.[12] Family faith was, in any event, safely stowed behind the front door.

However, the idea of the district did not hold up. People did not want to be locked away in neighbourhoods and districts; they did not find the spatiality of God there. The 1960s even saw a massive break with ecclesiastical life. These were the years of the real secularisation. People discovered that they were not quite as religious as they had always thought. Faith and church turned out to be, above all, the expression of a desire to socially connect. Social life had become secularised, and so the theological landscape evolved. The question of man became more important than the question of God. Or as theologian and philosopher Jan Sperna Weiland asserts: man was looking

---

10   Davison, "The Suburban Idea and its Enemies".
11   Ibid., 831.
12   Doevendans, "Wonen en religie, het moderne geloof in eengezinswoning en echtelijk bed".

for a "humanisation" of faith.[13] This also inevitably raised the question of a theology of the modern city, such as in the notorious *The Secular City* (1965) by American theologian Harvey Cox.[14] According to his vision, the secular city was the only city of God — a pragmatic, provocative attitude which had far-reaching consequences: Cox accepted displacement and anonymity as essential characteristics of the city, implicitly admitting that the idea of community might have been too ambitious. Indeed, Cox was not the only one to revive this discussion. The relationship between the sacred and the profane remained a central theme amongst philosophers and theologians for a long time in the Low Countries, as well. For example, Dutch philosophical theologian Arnold Ewout Loen (1896-1996) pointed out that one of the typical aspects of secularisation is the distinction made between two sectors of human life, namely the religious, sacred and spiritual, on the one hand, and the non-religious, profane and secular on the other. Secularisation involves the transfer of matters from the first sector to the second.[15] Flemish philosopher Jacques De Visscher (°1943) similarly states that "secularisation within the practice of everyday life leads to the sacralisation of the secular".[16]

Such ideas, perhaps more surprisingly, also crop up in modern thinking about architecture and urbanism. Initially, for example, the Congrès Internationaux d'Achitecture Moderne (CIAM) considered the efficient organisation of living, working, recreation and traffic in the city to be their main objective. After the Second World War, however, there was a growing understanding that human life could not be understood in a purely functional and rational way. At the Bridgwater Congress (1947), it was therefore stated that CIAM's objective from then on was "to work for the creation of a physical environment that will satisfy man's emotional and material needs (...) and stimulate man's spiritual growth."[17] This attention to the emotional and spiritual was new and quickly became intertwined with a discourse about citizenship and community spirit. For example, during the proceedings of the congress in Hoddesdon (1951), Le Corbusier wrote, "CIAM will help you to be a citizen and an individual. It will put you in touch with the infinite cosmos and with the common forms of nature — with God and with the spirits of the earth."[18] Here, Le Corbusier mixed a belief in God and heathenism, apparently making an appeal to a religious and spiritual awareness that was still generally present at the time.

13 Sperna Weiland, *Oriëntatie, nieuwe wegen in de theologie*, 10.
14 Cox, *The Secular City: Secularization and Urbanization in Theological Perspective*.
15 Loen, *Secularization: Science without God?*
16 De Visscher, *De zorg voor het Avondland*, 53.
17 Van der Woud, *Het Nieuwe Bouwen Internationaal: CIAM, Volkshuisvesting, Stedenbouw*, 84. Cited in English.
18 Ibid., 90. Cited in English.

The Dutch architect Jaap Bakema (1914-1981) also expressed these lofty ambitions in his well-known book *Van stoel tot stad*:

> The development of architecture and urbanism (....) is about constructing space that can assist man in his search for a healthy relationship with the miracle of his existence.[19]

Urbanism, which Bakema referred to as "space art", should place itself at the service of the declaration of life, because this could no longer be expected of a party, group or religion: the people, in effect, were left to their own devices. Urbanism could lend a helping hand in this and was assigned an "educational function". According to Bakema, space art could help man become part of the cosmos again:

> Human life is about learning to live consciously, and the function of space art is certainly also to promote, through architectural space, a human relationship with the universal (total) space. [20]

Might we say, then, that in talking about "openness and seclusion" and "corners, building rooms in the cosmos" or saying that "the one must be included in the all", Bakema was concerned with the spatiality of God as Van Niftrik formulated it?

(De)secularisation Today: Emptiness as the New Paradigm?

The book's introduction points out the importance of sociology in the thinking on urbanism and pastoral theology after the Second World War, but what significance can sociology still hold today? As early as 1924, religious phenomenologist Gerardus van der Leeuw (1890-1950) asked himself this very question. Despite its merits, Van der Leeuw argued, modern sociology lacked any awareness of the religious. Sociology could talk about human community as a social phenomenon, but it could not gauge the depth of the religious community.[21] Even now, we see that sociology is only able to establish the *fact* of secularisation. The status of *religiosity* remains an open question. The figures do not say otherwise. Based on a census from 2018, the Netherlands Institute for Social Research indicates that for the first time, the faithful are in the minority. In other words, the country can no longer call itself a Christian nation."[22]

19 Bakema, *Van stoel tot stad, een verhaal over mensen en ruimte*, 2.
20 Bakema, "Mens of monotype".
21 Van der Leeuw, *Inleiding tot de godsdienstgeschiedenis*, 150.
22 Sociaal en Cultureel Planbureau, *Christenen in Nederland, kerkelijke deelname en christelijke gelovigheid*.

This is, for that matter, a general phenomenon: Europe has long ceased to be a Christian continent.[23] Nevertheless, these findings seem to contradict the renewed — albeit individual — interest in religion and spirituality outside of denominations or parishes. Does this mean that in the wake of Alfred Weber's "fourth man", a "fifth man" has emerged who confuses religion (from *religare* or "connecting") with completely individual spirituality? And does this new spirituality have anything to do with the Christian faith? Does it mark the dawn of a new phase: a post-secular era, a period of desecularisation?[24] Or are we dealing with a "post-secular turn", based on the premise that contemporary thinking has been entirely stripped of Christian beliefs and that it is precisely for this reason that a return to and rethinking of these presuppositions is called for?

No matter the case, there is growing criticism of the accepted secularisation thesis, even within sociology: it is perceived as being too one-dimensional. That is why Monika Wohlrab-Sahr and Marian Burchardt introduced the "multiple secularities paradigm", which allows for a more nuanced perspective on religion and secularity.[25] The classical duality of the sacred and the profane, originally introduced by Émile Durkheim (1858-1917), is also increasingly contested. For example, the cultural anthropologist Talal Asad problematises the relationship between secularism, religion and modernity when he states that "the secular (…) is neither continuous with the religious that supposedly preceded it (that is, not the latest phase of a sacred origin) nor a simple break from it (that is, it is not the opposite, an essence that excludes the sacred)"; according to Asad, "the secular is a concept that brings together certain behaviors, knowledge and sensibilities in modern life."[26] In other words, the religious is inherent to the secular. For this reason, it is vital that churches involve themselves in this discussion, rather than viewing secularisation as a "hostile" phenomenon taking place in spite of them. Secularisation is not necessarily a negative phenomenon for the Church. As early as the 1930s and 1940s, modern theologians like Karl Barth (1886-1968) and Dietrich Bonhoeffer (1906-1945) advocated for *de*-confessionalisation, believing that Christianity should be part of the general culture. This means, amongst other things, that not every church building refers to the practice of Christianity by definition. The latter has a broader cultural, historical and social significance, and Christians are not supposed to exploit God for their own purposes. In other words, secularisation cannot be reduced to a sociological phenomenon. It is not a fact in itself, but a *concept* that aids in the understanding of the his-

---

23 Roy, *L'Europe est-elle chrètienne?*
24 Berger, *The Desecularization of the World: Resurgent Religion and World Politics.*
25 Wohlrab-Sahr and Burchardt, "Multiple Secularities: Toward a Cultural Sociology of Secular Modernities", 875. Cited in English.
26 Asad, *Formations of the Secular: Christianity, Islam, Modernity*, 23. Cited in English.

torical transformations in the relationship between the Church, society, faith, culture and science and gives them meaning.

In this context, the material culture and spatial paradigm of the Church are also at stake. As evidenced by the essays in this book, the mass construction of churches was not the right remedy for secularisation. On the contrary, the apostasy continued, and today there is a surplus of church buildings. What should be done with that? Are church buildings still the heart of a territory of faith (parish, district), or has the territorial dimension of the faith community completely faded in the meantime? Has liberalism triumphed over communitarianism, and do people exist primarily as individuals rather than as members of a community? Or is this a false dichotomy? Is man, to the contrary, an individual as a member of that community — the divine religious community, which is admittedly difficult to map out spatially? We cautiously draw the conclusion that the building blocks of the "old" paradigm — the nuclear family, parish or district and nation — have been lost. Has only the individual soul survived as a territory of faith? Or will secularisation — too few souls — lead to a divine housing crisis here? After all, churches increasingly stand empty.

Is it time to outline a new spatial paradigm for the material culture of the church? As regards a paradigm, we do not mean a new theory, but rather a way of working that takes shape in practice, in which expertise is gradually built up through a practice that combines the customary theoretical reflection of theology, religious studies and religious sciences, social sciences, and architecture, urban development and spatial planning.[27] This is a genuinely serious matter. Sociologists may indicate that the Church is dying, but theologically, according to John P. Bradbury, after that death, the Church will rise again in a new form, like the body of Christ.[28] That is to say, the spatial paradigm we seek is one of *resurrection*. We can find a point of departure for this in the account of the spatiality of God by theologian Van Niftrik at the beginning of this text. He, in turn, refers to the religious scholar Van der Leeuw, who believed that only a small portion of the church building should be occupied. The predominate portion of a real church should remain empty, due not to a lack of churchgoers, but rather to an abundance of space:

> There should be a very substantial amount of unused space, and not just below, in the aisles and the choir, but above all, upstairs, in the vaults. (...) If one were to measure the cubic metres of a church, it should be, at

[27] See, for example, Sandercock, "Spirituality and the Urban Professions: The Paradox at the Heart of Planning"; Yorgason and della Dora, "Geography, Religion and Emerging Paradigms: Problematizing the Dialogue"; Dewsbury and Cloke, "Spiritual Landscapes: Existence, Performance and Immanence". For a theological perspective, see Gorringe, *A Theology of the Built Environment*; Sheldrake, *Spaces for the Sacred*; Ward, *Cities of God*.
[28] Bradbury, "Towards a Theology of the Death of the Church".

most, one fifth for the people, with four fifths remaining empty, meaning: for God.[29]

Besides this sizable emptiness in the church building itself as a form, the overall number of empty church buildings continues to grow, as we have pointed out. Flemish architectural theorists Sylvain De Bleeckere and Roel De Ridder developed methods for tackling this problem in a "convivial" manner in their outstanding study, *Het open kerkgebouw*. The term convivial is derived from the work of the former priest and philosopher Ivan Illich (1926-2002), who believed that social decisions could not be left to the experts, bureaucrats, managers and institutes, but needed to be taken by "individuals who are politically interrelated".[30] De Bleeckere and De Ridder base their approach on the well-known actor–network theory of the French philosopher Bruno Latour (°1947); they do not restrict themselves to the "technical rationality" (to use a term from the book's introduction) of repurposing. The concrete, material vacancy of church buildings translates into the "current emptiness of the church building" as an underlying problem that requires a common-sense perspective. What is the significance of the church building in a self-modernising world?[31] This is where the phenomenon of secularisation resounds! The Church must entirely rethink its identity in this day and age.

Emptiness — or void — is an important concept in this context, one that also plays an important role in both theology and architectural theory. Barth, for example, spoke of faith as *Hohlraum*; his seventeenth-century predecessor Blaise Pascal referred to faith as the "God-shaped vacuum".[32] Geert Bekaert (1928-2016), the Flemish architectural critic and former Jesuit, stated that architecture is there to "create emptiness, an emptiness in which everything becomes possible, a silence in which everything becomes audible."[33] However, from the perspective of faith, what form does this emptiness or void take? Bekaert points out that Christianity has never had its own formal language. The first Christians gathered "in some house or other" to break bread; church buildings and cathedrals were built later, but these too were not an unequivocal materialisation of a specific belief in God, but rather "an expression of a lofty conception of existence whose centre fell outside the human person".[34]

---

29 Van der Leeuw, *Dogmatische Brieven*.
30 De Bleeckere and De Ridder, *Het open kerkgebouw*, 84.
31 Ibid., 40.
32 As a physicist, Pascal discovered the *vacuum* and the principle of *amor vacui* as a counterpart to nature's *horror vacui*, which tends to let everything grow together densely and overrun space. We recognise the *amor vacui* in the "plain" church buildings of Protestantism and the *horror vacui* in the style of Counter Reformation and neo-Gothic buildings.
33 Bekaert, *Architectuur zonder schaduw*.
34 Bekaert, *In een of ander huis. Kerkbouw op een keerpunt*; id., *Het einde van de architectuur*.

The age of constructing churches and cathedrals has now passed. The Church can no longer identify itself with the church building as object; it appears to be a bygone glory as a symbol of the Christian faith. Perhaps we should put the significance of the church building into perspective. What is the essence behind it? In 1933, Van der Leeuw argued that the church building was only there to protect the worshiping congregation against wind and cold. Nowadays, De Bleeckere and De Ridder remind us that the French word *église* comes from the Latin *ecclesia*, which refers to the Greek word for "the assembly or gathering of the people" (or, in the Christian interpretation, the ecclesial congregation). The German *Kirche* and the Dutch *kerk*, however, originate from the popular Greek *kurikon*, or "house of the Lord".[35] Barth has his doubts about the latter. According to him, the word goes back to a root that includes words like *circa*, *circum*, *circare* and *circulus*: "It therefore indicates a particular, finite and, to the extent thus characterised, special space."[36] At any rate, "*ecclesia*" and "church" are related to one another. Church is where one goes for a certain kind of meeting, a place one returns to time and again. Or, as Barth proposes, "Church is *congregation* — it is an assembly or a space where all who belong to it share a common cause that binds them in unity."[37] Spatially, the church is that piece of "holy ground" (Exodus 3.5) that ultimately encompasses the entire earth.[38] The congregation demarcates this piece of earth by spatially organising the items required for the liturgy and sacraments: baptism, communion and the sermon. But these are just furnishings, according to Barth, and there is nothing sacred about them.

Today, however, the spatial emptiness of church buildings manifests in another way: many church buildings are redundant and lie empty. There are too few churchgoers, and people are looking to repurpose these buildings or put them to multifunctional use. In and of itself, repurposing a church building is not a problem. It is a possibility allied with secularisation in its material sense, as standardised by abbé Antoine Furetière in his *Dictionnaire Universel* of 1690: the transfer of church goods and possessions to the secular world, assigning a public function to church buildings and monasteries.[39] But can some of the emptiness, the characteristic spaciousness of a church building, be maintained when it is reused for non-religious purposes? What about the essence of the church building — the liturgical space of Holy Communion, Eucharist, baptism and the sermon? Or is the repurposing of vacant church buildings just a temporary problem that is in fact immaterial for the Church and allows us to look ahead in anticipation of a future situation? That will

---

35 De Bleeckere and De Ridder, *Het open kerkgebouw*, 88.
36 Barth, *De Apostolische geloofsbelijdenis*, 164.
37 Ibid.
38 Jagersma, "De heilige aardbodem".
39 Latré, "De erfenis van het Löwith-Blumenberg debat".

11.1 Street view of the multifunctional centre De Veste, resembling a church building, in the Brandevoort neighbourhood of Helmond, the Netherlands, by KOW Architecten, completed in 2007.
[Photograph by Bart van Hoeck. Used with permission]

require imagination, however: what would a new design look like for our participation as a community of faith in the spatiality of God?

In the case of repurposing or reuse, the significance of a church building as a landmark by virtue of scale and form seems obvious; the relative historical permanence of the church building as a "primary object", as Aldo Rossi (1931-1997) calls it in his urban morphology, is also an important starting point.[40] Achievements from the architectural–phenomenological strategy used (light, spatial composition, materiality and atmosphere) also contribute to a theological aesthetics.[41] Vigilance is required, however, if the church building is too easily transferred to the world of post-secular spirituality and religiosity, whose relationship to the Christian faith is vague. Designers can have a tendency to take advantage of this spirituality. Have we not already seen this with Le Corbusier and Bakema? Transferring the formal language of the church building to the world of kitsch geography is to be avoided, as well, such as the transformation of an altar into a bar when a church is converted into a catering establishment. An even worse example of this is the mul-

---

40 Rossi, *The Architecture of the City*; Doevendans, "Metaphysical Reconstruction of the City".
41 The concept of "atmosphere" is important in this context. See, for example, Böhme, *Architektur und Atmosphäre*; Doevendans and Linskens, eds., "Theologisch esthetiek: over architecture en symboliek, leegte en licht".

tifunctional community centre in the neo-traditionalist new-build district of Brandevoort (Helmond, the Netherlands), the entrance architecture of which is meant to conjure up the image of a church. It turns out the medieval model on which the district is based called for a church along with a moat, a market hall and a square! [Ill. 11.1] Such a church building is nothing more than a hollow representation. Architect Rob Krier (°1938), the designer of Brandevoort, still regrets that the neighbourhood does not have a church, temple or house of prayer. Brandevoort, Krier says, was the most beautiful project of his life, but "a church would make it absolutely perfect."[42]

Conclusion: Moving to a Virtual, Post-parochial Time

Based on the above, it is clear that the familiar spatial units such as parish, district and housing need to be re-evaluated. The nuclear family in a single-family home with a garden is no longer the sole depiction of the divine household. The parish, long the obvious spatial concept, has had to pivot back to the old notion of the "foreigner" and the "stranger". After all, was not the parish and district concept as described above an anachronism in retrospect? Sociologists Samuel Nelson and Philip Gorski indicate that the medieval concept of the parish was undermined by modernity in the eighteenth and nineteenth centuries, and "de-parochialised forms of religious belonging" arose.[43] We can extend this line of reasoning further and say that we are currently living in a "post-parochial" era: the district is no longer a social community of people who come together every Sunday in the church as a territorial centre.

This time of COVID-19, when physical attendance at church has been impeded and churches have had to stream their services via the internet, is a period of drastic transformation. Will the traditional church hall ever return to its old shape and appearance? Or has this "habit" also become timeworn? One can regret that access to church services is limited, that the empty spaces of the church building no longer resound with congregational singing and that the social dimension has become lost, since we can no longer sip coffee together after the service (and not just because of the quality of the coffee!). More important, however, is the question posed by Andrew McGowan: Can we observe the sacraments virtually? Bread and wine are material items and this is a ceremony for which we want to gather as a community in a physical church. However, we are largely denied access to the church building; and the churches are becoming even emptier...

42 Krier, "Architect Rob Krier vindt 'zijn' Brandevoort bijna perfect: 'Het mist alleen nog een tempel'" (Architect Rob Krier finds 'his' Brandevoort almost perfect: 'All it's missing is a temple'), *Eindhoven Dagblad*, 10/04/2020.
43 Nelson and Gorski, "Conditions of religious belonging: Confessialization, de-Parochialization, and the Euro-American divergence".

In contrast to its original, unifying significance, religion is once more being pushed behind closed doors as an individual matter, while many believers still want to stay connected to the place and space that holds so much meaning to them. On the other hand, the internet makes many church services and celebrations of faith accessible and offers a wide variety of worship formats, with considerable attention for liturgy. As McGowan writes, it even provides hope: "Many clergy and lay people have been able to deepen their sense of the sacred in daily life, finding different understandings of space and place outside of churches."[44] Like society as a whole, the Church will likely never be the same as it was before the coronavirus epidemic of 2020. Perhaps we will look back on this time as another fundamental step in the secularisation process. In any case, a new reflection on God's spatiality, and our participation therein, is imperative. A virtual layer has definitively inserted itself. However, McGowan warns, worship "will not cease to be primarily a physical and communal activity if it remains typically Christian."[45]

BIBLIOGRAPHY

Asad, Talal. *Formations of the Secular: Christianity, Islam, Modernity*. Stanford: Stanford University Press, 2003.

Bakema, Jacob B. "Mens of monotype". *Forum*, 15 (1960-1961) 3, 140-142.

Bakema, Jacob B. *Van stoel tot stad, een verhaal over mensen en ruimte*. Zeist-Antwerp: De Haan-Standaard, 1964.

Barth, Karl. *De Apostolische geloofsbelijdenis*. Nijkerk: Callenbach, 1935.

Bekaert, Geert. *Architectuur zonder schaduw*. Rotterdam: Uitgeverij 010 Publishers, 1988.

Bekaert, Geert. *Het einde van de architectuur*. Hasselt: Limburgse Akademische Bibliotheek, 1967.

Bekaert, Geert. *In een of ander huis. Kerkbouw op een keerpunt*. Tielt: Lannoo, 1967.

Berger, Peter. *The Desecularization of the World: Resurgent Religion and World Politics*. Washington: Eerdmans, 1999.

Böhme, Gernot. *Architektur und Atmosphäre*. Munich: Fink, 2006.

Bradbury, John P. "Towards a Theology of the Death of the Church". *Theology*, 117 (2014), 4, 249-255.

Cox, Harvey. *The Secular City: Secularization and Urbanization in Theological Perspective*. New York: Macmillan, 1966.

Davison, Graeme. "The Suburban Idea and its Enemies". *Journal of Urban History*, 39 (5) 2013, 829-847.

De Bleeckere, Sylvain and De Ridder, Roel. *Het open kerkgebouw*. Kalmthout: Pelckmans, 2014.

De Visscher, Jacques. *De zorg voor het Avondland*. Kampen-Kapellen: Kok Agora-DNB, 1991.

Dewsbury, J.D. and Cloke, Paul. "Spiritual Landscapes: Existence, Performance and Immanence". *Social & Cultural Geography*, 10 (2009) 6, 695-711.

Doevendans, Kees. "Metaphysical Reconstruction of the City". *Archiprint*, 8 (2019) 14, 6-13.

Doevendans, Kees. "Wonen en religie, het moderne geloof in eengezinswoning en echtelijk bed". In: J. Smeets et al., eds. *Wonen: discoursen, praktijken, perspectieven*. Eindhoven: TU Eindhoven, 2016, 23-32.

Doevendans, Kees and Linskens, Brigitte, eds. "Theologisch esthetiek: over architectuur en symboliek, leegte en licht". Special issue. *NOVUS*, (2019) 2.

Folliet, Joseph. *Les Chrétiens au Carrefour II*. Lyon: La Chronique sociale, 1949.

Gorringe, Tim. *A Theology of the Built Environment*. Cambridge: Cambridge University Press, 2002.

---

44 McGowan, "Communion and Pandemic", 2-8. Cited in English.
45 Ibid., 8. Cited in English.

Hitzer, Bettina. *Im Netz der Liebe. Die protestantische Kirche und ihre Zuwanderer in der Metropole Berlin (1819-1914)*. Cologne: Böhlau, 2006.

Jagersma, Henk. "De heilige aardbodem". In: Y. Bekker et al., ed. *In de ruimte van de openbaring. Opstellen voor Nico T. Bakker*. Kampen: Kok, 1999, 172-176.

Koeck, Wolfgang. *De nood van de overvloed, het leven in een technisch-industriële wereld*. Utrecht/Antwerp: Aula/Het Spectrum, 1966.

Krier, Rob. "Architect Rob Krier vindt 'zijn' Brandevoort bijna perfect: 'Het mist alleen nog een tempel'". *Eindhoven Dagblad*, 10/04/2020.

Latré, Stijn. "De erfenis van het Löwith-Blumenberg debat". In: Stijn Latré and Guido Vanheeschwijk. *Radicale Secularisatie*. Kalmthout: Pelckmans, 2013, 9-27.

Leeuw, Gerardus van der. *Dogmatische Brieven*. Amsterdam: H.J. Paris, 1933.

Leeuw, Gerardus van der. *Inleiding tot de godsdienstgeschiedenis*. Haarlem: De Erven Bohn, 1924.

Loen, Arnold E. *Secularization: Science without God?* London: SCM Press, 1967.

McGowan, A. "Communion and Pandemic". *Journal of Anglican Studies*, 18 (2020) 1, 2-8.

McLeod, Hugh, ed. *European Religion in the Age of Great Cities, 1830-1930*. London/New York: Routledge, 1995.

McLeod, Hugh. "Religion in an Urbanizing World, c. 1840-1939". *Journal of Urban History*, 39 (2013), 6, 1175-1180.

Mönnich, Conrad W. *Vreemdelingen en bijwoners. Hoofdlijnen uit de geschiedenis van het protestantisme*. Baarn: Ten Have, 1980.

Nelson, Sam and Gorski, Philip. "Conditions of religious belonging: Confessialization, de-Parochialization, and the Euro-American divergence". *International Sociology*, 29 (2014), 1, 3-21.

Niftrik, Gerrit Cornelis van. *De hemel, over de ruimtelijkheid van God*. Nijkerk: G.F. Callenbach N.V., 1972.

Rossi, Aldo. *The Architecture of the City*. Cambridge (Mass.): The MIT Press, 1984.

Roy, Olivier. *L'Europe est-elle chrètienne?* Paris: Seuil, 2019.

Sandercock, Leonie. "Spirituality and the Urban Professions: The Paradox at the Heart of Planning". *Planning Theory and Practice*, 7 (2006), 1, 65-97.

Sheldrake, Philip. *Spaces for the Sacred*. Baltimore: Johns Hopkins University Press, 2001.

Sociaal en Cultureel Planbureau. *Christenen in Nederland, kerkelijke deelname en christelijke gelovigheid*. The Hague, 2018.

Sperna Weiland, Jan. *Oriëntatie, nieuwe wegen in de theologie*. Baarn: Het Wereldvenster, 1966.

Ward, Graham. *Cities of God*. London: Routledge, 2000.

Weber, Alfred. *Der Dritte oder der Vierte Mensch. Vom Sinn des geschichtlichen Daseins*. Munich: Piper Verlag, 1953.

Weber, Max. *The Protestant Ethic and the Spirit of Capitalism*. Oxford: Oxford University Press, 2010.

Wohlrab-Sahr, Monika and Burchardt, Marian. "Multiple Secularities: Toward a Cultural Sociology of Secular Modernities". *Comparative Sociology*, 11 (2012), 875-909.

Woud, Auke van der. *Het Nieuwe Bouwen Internationaal: CIAM, Volkshuisvesting, Stedenbouw*. Delft: Delft University Press, 1983.

Yorgason, Ethan and della Dora, Veronica. "Geography, Religion and Emerging Paradigms: Problematizing the Dialogue". *Social & Cultural Geography*, 10 (2009), 6, 629-663.

AUTHORS

João Alves da Cunha is an architect and lecturer at the Centre for Studies in Religious History of the Portuguese Catholic University (CEHR-UCP), Lisbon, Portugal. His research interests lie in religious architecture and the modern city. His PhD *MRAR. The Religious Art Renovation Movement and the Golden Years of Religious Architecture in Portugal in the 20th century* was awarded with the Professor Manuel Taínha Award for the best PhD in Architecture (2013-2014) and published by Universidade Católica Editora in 2015.

Alba Arboix-Alió is an architect and a researcher. She teaches Theory of Architecture and supervises Final Degree Projects at the Polytechnic University of Catalonia (UPC) and at the University of Barcelona (UB). Her research focuses on how churches play a role in the urban form of Barcelona and how these buildings can be adaptively reused. Her doctoral thesis (UPC, 2016) was published under the title *Barcelona: Esglésies i Construcció de la Ciutat* (2018).

Umberto Bordoni is a priest, responsible for the Church Patronage of the Arts in the Ambrosian Archdiocese, director of Scuola Beato Angelico in Milan and director of the *Arte Cristiana* magazine. He has been general coordinator and manager of the Evangeliario Ambrosiano Project (the new Book of the Gospel for the Ambrosian Rite) and curator of various exhibitions on religious art.

Angela Connelly (PhD) is a senior lecturer at the Manchester School of Architecture. Her research interests lie in tracing adaptation in the built environment over time. She worked on the project Sacred Suburbs with the Manchester Modernist Society which led to an eponymous publication and exhibition in 2015.

Maria Antonietta Crippa is an architect, Full Professor of History of Architecture at the Politecnico in Milan. She is also a member of the Academia de Bellas Artes S. Jordi (Barcelona), and the Pontifical Academy of Virtuosi del Pantheon (Rome). She specializes in the history of modern architecture, also related to conservation and restoration problems, and has done many investigations on Italian and European Churches in the second half of the 20th century. She directs also the magazine *Rivista dell'Istituto per la storia dell'Arte lombarda*.

Kees Doevendans is Professor Emeritus from Eindhoven University of Technology and KU Leuven, where he taught urban design. He has published numerous books and articles on the theory and history of urbanism. Professionally and personally engaged in various working parties of the Dutch Protestant Church concerning the future of its parish churches, he has widely published on the background and the meaning of church buildings, including the issue of their redevelopment.

Davide Fusari is an architect and an assistant lecturer at Politecnico di Milano where he formerly collaborated in the research field. He is currently working on places of worship and he is leading participatory processes for the construction of new parish complexes.

Jesús García Herrero is an Associate Professor at the Polytechnic University of Madrid (E.T.S.A.M.) since 2009. He defended his PhD in 2015 at the E.T.S. of Architecture of Madrid (UPM) on the post-war religious architecture of Luis Cubillo de Arteaga. In 2018, his research on the collaboration between Cubillo and the artist Arcadio Blasco resulted in the exhibition "Cubillo-Blasco: Spirals of Light (1956-1974)".

Judi Loach is Emerita Professor and held posts at Oxford Brookes and Cardiff Universities, with chairs in architectural history and then cultural history at the latter, as well as director of the Research and Graduate School in Humanities there; she is currently a member of the Laboratoire de Recherche Historique Rhône-Alpes (LARHRA). She has worked on 17th-century Jesuit commissions in France, on late Le Corbusier, and on the Art sacré movement. She has been editor or co-editor of Architectural History for over 15 years. She has also been a member of the Llandaff Diocesan Advisory Committee for 20 years and Chair of DOCOMOMO UK.

João Luís Marques is an architect and a research associate at the CEAU-FAUP, the centre for Studies in Architecture and Urbanism at the Faculty of Architecture of the University of Porto, where he also teaches history of Portuguese architecture. He obtained his PhD in Architecture in 2017 with the thesis *The church in the city, service and welcome, Portuguese architecture 1950-1975*. João also collaborates in research projects of the Centre for Studies in Religious History of the Portuguese Catholic University (CEHR-UCP).

Mélanie Meynier-Philip trained as an architect and obtained a PhD in architecture in 2018, with a thesis on the future of parish churches in the Lyons-Saint-Etienne region. She is currently a lecturer at the School of Architecture of Clermont-Ferrand, where she teaches in the field of history and architectural culture. She has a special interest in the reconversion of religious heritage and is one of DOCOMOMO representatives for the Auvergne Rhône-Alpes region for the Regional Directorate of Culture (DRAC).

Ellen Rowley is Assistant Professor in Modern Irish Architecture in the School of Architecture (APEP) at University College Dublin. She writes on Irish architectural modernism including most recently *More than Concrete Blocks, 1900-40* (2016) and *1940-72* (2019) and her history of Dublin housing *Housing, Architecture and the Edge Condition* (2019). As well as teaching and researching, she is committed to public engagement, curating Dublin's tenement museum (14 Henrietta Street, 2016-18), UCD's 50 year architectural history "Belfield 50" (2020) and a national radio series on housing and home (Davis Now lectures, Radio Teilifís Eireann, 2019-2020).

Sofia Anja Singler is a Junior Research Fellow in Architecture at Homerton College, Cambridge. She trained as an architect at the University of Cambridge and the Yale School of Architecture, and practiced architecture in the United States before returning to Cambridge for a PhD in Architectural History. Her doctoral research interrogated the relationship between religion and modern architecture with reference to the ecclesiastical portfolio of Finnish modernist Alvar Aalto. She currently sits as an elected member on the Alvar Aalto World Heritage Nomination Committee.

Sven Sterken is a Professor at the Faculty of Architecture of KU Leuven where he teaches courses in the history of architecture and urban planning. A founding member of the research group Architectural Cultures of the Recent Past (ARP), his research focuses on how religious, commercial and political bodies rely on architecture as part of their territorial and organizational strategies. A former vice-chair of DOCOMOMO Belgium, he is actively involved in the debate about the future of modern architectural heritage.

Marina Wesner is a freelance architect and a PhD researcher at the TU Berlin's Institute for Art History and Historical Urban Studies. Her doctoral research deals with the sacred topography of Berlin. She works in the field of architecture mediation, mainly for religious clients.

Eva Weyns is a PhD researcher at the KU Leuven Faculty of Architecture and works as a consultant for the Flanders Architecture Institute. She obtained a masters in architectural engineering (2012) and in heritage conservation (2015) from KU Leuven. As part of the research project "Catholic Territories in a Suburban landscape: Religion and Urbanization in Belgium, 1945-1975" , she investigates the role of architecture and urban planning in the pastoral strategies of the Roman Catholic Church in post-war Belgium.

Ferdinando Zanzottera graduated from the Politecnico di Milano and obtained a PhD in Building Engineering, option Architecture (Alma Mater Studiorum - University of Bologna). He is currently an associate professor of History of Architecture at the Politecnico di Milano. His research interests lie in architectural history, modern construction techniques, and monastic and religious architecture from the Middle Ages to the 20th century.

INDEX OF PERSONS

Aalto, Alvar 24-25, 95, 97-98, 101-103, 105-119
Abercrombie, Patrick 51
Adenauer, Konrad 150
Ala-Kulju, Reino 100
Almeida, João de 205, 207
Anderson, W. J. 44
Ansell, William Henry 42
Arrese, José Luis 231
Asher, Alice 101
Asplund, Gunnar 115

Bacciocchi, Mario 265, 267-268
Bakema, Jaap 294, 344, 349
Baldrich, Manuel 294-295
Banasch, Georg 146
Bardet, Gaston 20, 22, 160, 165, 167, 227
Barlow, Sir Montague 41, 49
Bärlund, Christer 101
Barth, Karl 345, 347-348
Bartning, Otto 104, 131, 135, 141, 146, 150
Bastin, Roger 9
Bauer, Hermann 205, 210
Baum, Gregory 312
Bazaine, Jean 75
Bekaert, Geert 9, 347
Belgiojoso, Lodovico Barbiano di 274
Bengsch, Alfred 127
Benjamin, Walter 133
Berliet, Paul 83
Bersarin, Nikolai Erastowich 124
Bissuel, Jean-Prosper 65
Bissuel, Joseph 65
Bissuel, Marc 65
Bissuel, Prosper-Edouard 65
Bissuel, Vincent 65
Blanchard, Jean 328-329
Blanco, Luis Moya 222
Blaney, Neil 322, 327, 334
Blomstedt, Pauli 101
Bohigas, Oriol 292, 297
Böhm, Dominikus 135
Boix i Selva, Emili 288
Boldt, Jean 109

Bolz, Lothar 128
Bonatz, Paul 134
Bonet, Vicente 296
Bonet Armengol, Jordi 296
Bonet Castellana, Antoni 294-295
Bonhoeffer, Dietrich 345
Bornard, Pierre 75
Borromeo, Carlo 259
Borromeo, Federico 254, 259
Boulard, Fernand 17, 161, 289
Brady, Bernard, 330-331
Braque, Georges 75
Breen, Liam 305, 327-328, 330, 332-333, 335
Brel, Jacques 83
Browne, Michael 309, 311, 315, 328

Cachemaille-Day, Nugent Francis 42, 47
Capellades, Jean 22, 76
Cardijn, Jozef 225
Castiglioni, Achille 274
Castiglioni, Livio 274
Castiglioni, Pier Giacomo 274
Castro Cubells, Carlos 236
Cerdà, Ildefons 284, 288
Cerejeira, D. Manuel Gonçalves 191-200, 203-205, 207, 217
Chagall, Marc 75
Chatelan, Olivier 64
Chevrier, Antoine 64
Chinarro Matas, Emilio 239
Chomel, Alain 74
Claudius-Petit, Eugène 22
Coderch, Josep Antoni 292
Coello de Portugal, Francisco 222
Collès, Émar 176-177
Colombo, Giovanni 276
Comblin, Joseph 28
Corrales, José Antonio 296
Cottin, François-Régis 71-72, 75, 79, 89
Couturier, Marie-Alain 64-65, 75, 205
Cowper, William 342
Cox, Harvey 28, 343
Craze, Romilly B. 42

Cruz, Lucínio 198
Cubillo de Arteaga, Luis 26, 221-222, 224, 231, 235, 239-246
Cupers, Kenny 19-20
Curtelin, Charles 65, 69
Curtelin, Georges 65
Curtelin, Paul 65
Cushing, Richard 18

Daniel, Yves 14
Debuyst, Frédéric 9
De Carli, Carlo 262-263, 274
de Chalendar, Jacques 11
de Galard, Louis 74-75, 83, 88
De Groër, Étienne 199, 202
De Keyser, Léon 180, 185-186
Dell'Amore, Giordano 256
Delouvrier, Paul 22
Denis, Henry 66
Denis, Maurice 65
Dessauvage, Marc 9
Desvignes, Louis 69
de Valera, Eamon 309-310
Devane, Andy 313-314
Deveraux, Jean 69
Devers, Paul 81, 83
Dibelius, Otto 126-127, 144
Dols, Chris 16-17
Dominioni, Luigi Caccia 274
Donzelli, Beniamino 256
Döpfner, Julius 127, 148, 150
Dubuisson, Jean 72
Duocastella, Rogelio 225, 288-289
Durkheim, Émile 345
Düttmann, Werner 131-132, 137

Echarren, Ramón 225-226, 228
Eerikäinen, Eero 101
Eiermann, Egon 131, 151
Eijo Garay Leopoldo 222
Ekelund, Hilding 101

Fairhurst, Harry S. 52
Falcão, Manuel 191-192, 197-198, 200, 207, 217
Fehily, James 327
Fehling, Hermann 132
Felix, Paul 9
Fernandes, Inácio Peres 198
Fernández del Amo, José Luis 222, 236
Fichter, Joseph 159
Figini, Luigi 259-260, 274
Fisac, Miguel 236-237-239
Fisher, Geoffrey 43
Fleury (General) 71
Focillon, Henri 65
Folliet, Joseph 340

Foucault, Michel 333
Franco, Francisco 26, 223, 230, 232-233, 245-246, 281-283, 285, 291, 301-302
Francz, Anatole 841
Friedrick III 139
Fries, Willy 144
Fullaondo, Juan Daniel 296
Furetière, Antoine 348

Gagès, René 68
Gamo, Mariano 246
Gandolfi, Vittorio 271, 274-275
Garay, Eijo 223
García-Pablos, Rodolfo 22, 222, 236
Gardella, Ignazio 269, 274
Garnier, Tony 74
Geddes, Patrick 19, 111, 319
Genevois, Daniel 67
Genton, Pierre 24, 63-64, 67, 69, 72, 74-91
Gerlier, Pierre 68
Gilson, Jean 174
Giráldez Dávila, Guillermo 291-292
Gisel, Ernst 205
Godin, Henry 14
Gogel, Daniel 132
Gomà i Tomàs, Isidre 283
Gómez-Morán Cima, Mario 239
Granpré Molière, Marinus 21
Greely, Andrew 159
Greene, Graham 311
Greer, William 40
Gresleri, Glauco 206-207
Grimal, Franck 67-68
Grimmek, Bruno 137
Gropius 265
Guimarães, Fernando Peres 195

Hébert-Stevens, Jean 75
Hemingway, Ernest 311
Heuss, Theodor 144, 150
Hofbauer, Reinhard 132, 152
Honecker, Erich 128
Houtart, François 11-12, 18, 21-22, 25, 157-166, 174, 176, 179, 182, 186, 188, 227-228, 272
Howard, Ebenezer 111, 342
Hurley, Charlie 330

Illich, Ivan 347
Iribarren, Jesús 225

Jaatinen, Martti 101
Jáchym, Franz 23
Jobst, Gerhardt 134-136
John XXIII 312
John Paul II 331
Jourdain, Joseph 180-181

Jubany, Narcís 294, 299
Jünemann, Hermann 132

Kaakinen, Veli 109
Kaikkonen, Jaakko 101
Karvinen, Erkki 101
Keefe, Richard Cyril 319
Kehoe, Martin 56, 58
Kelleher, John 321
Kempeneers, Joseph 178
Kira (Princess of Prussia) 144
Kowalski, Ludwig Peter 144, 147
Kreuer, Willy 134-135, 137, 146-150
Krier, Rob 350
Kropotkin, Pjotr 109
Kühn, Erich 138-139
Kuusela, Armi 96

Labbens, Jean 11, 15, 18, 21, 159
Laine, Yrjö 101
Langmaack, Gerhard 150
Lanotte, André 9
Laorga Guttiérez, Luis 222
Latour, Bruno 347
Le Bras, Gabriel 17, 161, 289
Lebret, Louis-Joseph 159
Leclercq, Jacques 159
Le Corbusier 20, 22, 64, 85, 115, 296-297, 343, 349
Léger, Fernand 75
Lemmer, Ludwig 134, 137, 141-142, 144-146, 150-151
Le Play, Frédéric 17
Lercaro, Giacomo 15, 22-23, 90, 199, 258, 273, 275
Lhande, Pierre 14, 162
Lindberg, Carolus 101, 110
Lipchitz, Jacques 75
Llanos, José María 224
Loach, Judi 23
Loen, Arnold Ewout 343
López Iñigo, Pedro 291-292, 294-295
Louis Ferdinand (Prince) 144
Lucey, Cornelius 311
Lurçat, Jean 75
Luxemburg, Rosa 133

Magistretti, Vico 257, 274
Maini, Vittore 270-272, 276
Mäkiniemi, Elsa 101
Mangiarotti, Angelo 259, 261
March, Werner 135
Margarit, Joan 297
Markelius, Sven 114
Marquès, Carles 286
Martin, Etienne 80
Marx, Karl 127, 134
Matisse, Henri 75

Mattei, Enrico 26, 251, 253, 255-256, 264-274, 276-278
Matteotti, Giacomo 255
Maufe, Edward 42
Mazioux, Joannès 66
McKeefrey, P.T.B. 13
McQuaid, John Charles 308-313, 315, 318, 322, 326-331, 333, 335
Meistermann, Georg 144-145
Mermet, Roger 67
Metzger, Fritz 205
Meurman, Otto-Iivari 110-111, 114
Mies van der Rohe, Ludwig 137
Milani, Aldo 22, 270-272, 297
Milis, André 180-182
Miller, Bernard 42
Modrego Casaus, Gregorio 26, 281-283, 285-286, 288-291, 294, 297, 300
Moloney, Guy 331-332
Moneo, Rafael 296
Monguió Abella, Pau 296-298
Mönnich, Conrad W. 340
Montini, Giovanni Battista 22, 26, 199, 251, 253-254, 256-259, 261-262, 264, 268-273, 275-278, 297
Morassutti, Bruno 259, 261
Morcillo, Casimiro 221-230, 232-233, 235-237, 245-246
Morta Figuls, Angel 225
Mortamet, Gabriel 65
Mortamet, Jean-Gabriel 65, 67
Mortamet, Louis 65, 69
Moser, Lorenz 101
Mumford, Lewis 111, 115
Murphy, John A. 56
Murray, John Courtney 312
Muzio, Giovanni 262, 264

Nadal, Luis 296
Nairn, Ian 316
Neuenschwander, Eduard 101
Nicholas, Rowland 48, 51
Novarina, Maurice 75-76, 79, 87, 89, 91

O'Brien, Michael 327
O'Kelly, Des Rea 317
Osbourne, F.J. 51
Otto, Karl 137-138

Paatela, Veli 109
Pablos, García 227
Pace, George Gaze 54
Pacheco, Duarte 194
Pardal Monteiro, Porfírio 194
Park, Robert Ezra 160
Parker, Barry 47, 53
Pascal, Blaise 347

Paul VI (Giovanni Battista Enrico Antonio Maria Montini) 26, 222, 246, 251, 262, 270, 273, 276, 278, 297
Pereira, Nuno Teotónio 25, 205, 210-211
Perkins, E. Benson 44
Perret, Auguste 64
Perry, Clarence 19
Pesenti, Carlo 256
Pfankuch, Peter 132
Pimentel, Diogo Lino 206-207, 216
Pineda, Antoni 286
Pirelli, Alberto 256
Pitkänen Pekka 101
Pius X (Giuseppe Melchiorre Sarto) 207, 287, 300-302
Pius XII (Eugenio Maria Giuseppe Giovanni Pacelli) 199, 257, 285
Ploton (Father) 81
Poelzig, Hans 137
Poëte, Marcel 160
Pollini, Gino 259-260
Polvara, Giuseppe 259
Pomodoro, Arnaldo 268
Pomodoro, Gio 268
Porcioles, Josep 284, 293
Portas, Nuno 25, 206, 210-211
Pradel, Louis 71
Puigdefábregas, Pedro 296

Raphael, Lutz 16
Régamey, Pie-Raymond 65, 75, 203, 205
Reis, Eduardo Alberto Henriques dos 198
Remillieux (Abbé) 64
Reyns, Willy 178
Richier, Germaine 75
Robinson, John J. 310, 315, 319
Rodríguez Osuna, Jacinto 26, 222, 225-228, 232, 235-236, 238-240, 245-246
Rossi, Aldo 349
Rouault, Georges 75, 313
Rufnick, Ralf 131

Saarinen, Eliel 115
Sabattier, Marcel 67
Sáenz de Oíza, Francisco J. 296
Sage, Konrad 132
Salazar, António de Oliveira 192-193, 196
Sartre, Jean-Paul 311
Schädel, Hans 132
Schließer, Wilhelm 134-135
Schmidt-Clausing, Fritz 141-142, 144, 146, 150
Schoenmaeckers, Paul 158, 180
Schrieber, Gabriel 134, 147
Schuster, Alfredo Ildefonso 251, 253-254, 256-259, 270, 278
Schwarz, Rudolf 104, 205

Schwerdtfeger, Bernhard 145-146
Scott, Adrian Gilbert 38, 54-58
Sert, Josep Lluis 19-20, 115
Sharkey, A.A. 328
Silkin, Lewis 44-46
Simms, Herbert 319, 321
Sirén, J. S. 105
Siri, Giuseppe 258
Söhngen, Oskar 105
Sokolski, Alexandre 166-167
Solà-Morales, Manuel de 297
Soteras Mauri, José 284, 286-287, 294-295
Sperna Weiland, Jan 342
Stocker, Hans 145
Stuart, Imogen 315
Stucky, Ulrich 101
Sturzo, Luigi 255
Subias i Fages, Xavier 291-292
Suenens, Leo 187
Swift, Arthur 323, 327
Swoboda Heinrich 14

Tarancón, Vicente Enrique y 223, 235, 245-246
Tedeschi, Mario 257 274
Tedeschini, Federico 282
Terán, Fernando 236, 239-240, 246
Theeuws, Paul 158
Thornley, David 316, 318
Tosi, Eugenio 273
Trebbi, Giorgio 206-207
Trens, Manuel 297
Trindade, João 207
Tuomisto, Olavi 101

Ulbricht, Walter 129
Unwin, Raymond 19, 319
Uthwatt Augustus 43

Vahtera, Olli 101
Van den Broek, Jo 294
van der Leeuw, Gerardus 344, 346, 348
Vandermeeren, Jacques 185-186
van Niftrik, Gerrit C. 339-340, 344, 346
Van Roey, Joseph-Ernest 158, 178, 199
Vayreda Bofill, Francesc 296-299
Verdier, Jean 199, 254
Vieira de Almeida, Pedro 26, 214-216
Villa, Enrico 274
Vincenti, Antonello 271
Vollmer, Johannes 139-140

Wasastjerna (family) 99
Weber Alfred 341, 345
Weber, Max 340-341
Weskamm, Wilhelm 127
White (Father) 314

Wickham, Edward Ralph (Ted) 14
William II 139
Williams-Ellis, Clough 42
Winninger, Paul 11, 22-23, 29, 166, 199, 253, 297
Wirth, Louis 16, 160
Wood, Sir Kingsley 43

Ziemann, Benjamin 16

INDEX OF ORGANISATIONS

Azienda Generale Italiana Petroli (AGIP) 255

Bauamt der Erzdiözese Wien, Vienna 23
Berliner Stadtsynodalausschuss, Berlin 144
Bonifatiusverein, Paderborn 23
Bund der Evangelischen Kirchen in der DDR, Berlin 126

Catholic Social Service Conference (CSSC), Manchester 326
Center for Applied Research in the Apostolate (CARA), Washington 18
Centre Belge de Sociologie Religieuse, Louvain 159
Centre de Pastorale Liturgique, Paris 65
Centre de Recherches Socio-religieuses de Bruxelles (CRSR), Brussels 18, 25, 157-158, 160-163, 166-167, 169, 172, 174-176, 178-179, 181-184, 186-188, 227
Centre Régional d'Etudes Socio-religieuses de Lille, Lille 18
Centro di Studio e Informazione per l'Architettura Sacra, Bologna 206, 273
Centro Studi per l'Architettura della Comunità Cristiana, Milan 273
CIAM (Congrès Internationaux d'Architecture Moderne) 19-20, 68, 114-115, 128, 135, 138, 160, 291, 343
Comisión Central de Acción Pastoral, Madrid 226
Comissão de Arte Sacra, Lisbon 209
Comitato per le Nuove Chiese, Milan 255-256, 258-259, 264, 270-273, 275-276
Comitato pro Templi Nuovi, Milan 199, 251, 254-256, 270-271
Comité national de construction d'églises, Paris 22, 29, 74
Conférence Internationale de Sociologie Religieuse (CISR), Louvain 197-198
Conversaciones de Arquitectura Religiosa, Barcelona (1963) 22, 297

Domus Dei, Malines 23, 158, 199

Ente Nazionale Idrocarburi (ENI) 255, 267-270
Evangelische Kirchenbautagung 22, 149

FOESSA Foundation, Madrid 225, 245

GATCPAC, Barcelona 292
Gereformeerd Sociologisch Instituut, Amsterdam 22
Groupe Alpha, Brussels 174
Groupe Structures, Brussels 185
Grup R, Barcelona 281, 291-292, 296, 301

Institut Catòlic d'Estudis Socials de Barcelona, Barcelona 288
Institut de Sociologie, Lyons 18
Institut Supérieur d'Urbanisme Appliqué (ISUA), Brussels 160-161, 174, 180
Institute for the Study of Worship and Religious Architecture, Birmingham 23
Instituto de Sociología y Pastoral Aplicada (ISPA), Barcelona 289-290
Instituto Nacional de la Vivienda (INV), Madrid 224, 230, 232, 235-238

Jeunesse Ouvrière Chrétienne 159
Juventude Universitária Católica, Lisbon 205

Katholiek Sociaal-Kerkelijk Instituut (KASKI), The Hague 18, 22, 160-161

Les Chantiers du Cardinal, Paris 14, 63, 199, 254
LIGS, Barcelona 291, 293-295
L'Œuvre du Christ dans la banlieue, Lyons 63-64, 81

Movimento de Renovação da Arte Religiosa (MRAR), Lisbon 25, 191, 203, 205-207, 209, 216-217

National Church Extension Committee of the Scottish Kirk, Edinburgh 23

Office Diocésain des Paroisses Nouvelles (OPDN), Lyons 24, 63
Oficina Técnica de Sociología Religiosa, Madrid 221-222, 226, 233, 235-236, 239-240
Opera Pia delle Chiese e Case Parrocchiali Povere, Milan 254, 268

Patronat Municipal de l'Habitatge (PMH), Barcelona 284, 293, 296-297
Pontificia Commissione per l'Arte Sacra in Italia, Rome 199, 277-278

Referat für Kirchenfragen, Berlin 127

Secretariado das Novas Igrejas do Patriarcado (SNIP), Lisbon 25-26, 191-162, 203-204, 207, 209, 211-212, 214, 217
Secretariado de Templos Parroquiales, Madrid 233-234
Sociologisch Instituut van de Nederlandse Hervormde Kerk, Utrecht 22
Sozialistische Einheitspartei Deutschlands (SED), Berlin 127, 129

Team X (Team 10) 115

Ufficio diocesano nuove chiese di periferia, Bologna 23
Ufficio per le Nuove Chiese, Milan 270, 276

World Council of Churches 151

COLOPHON

FINAL EDITING
Luc Vints

COPY EDITING
Lieve Claes

LAY-OUT
Alexis Vermeylen

KADOC-KU Leuven
Documentation and Research Centre on Religion, Culture and Society
Vlamingenstraat 39
B - 3000 Leuven
www.kadoc.kuleuven.be

Leuven University Press
Minderbroedersstraat 4
B - 3000 Leuven
www.lup.be